NEGOTIATING THE CONSTITUTION

The Earliest Debates over Original Intent

Joseph M. Lynch

Cornell University Press
Ithaca and London

First published 1999 by Cornell University Press.

Printed in the United States of America.

Library of Congress Cataloging-in-Publication Data

Lynch, Joseph M. (Joseph Martin), 1924–
    Negotiationg the Constitution : the earliest debates over original intent / Joseph M. Lynch.
      p.   cm.
    Includes index.
    ISBN 0-8014-3558-7 (cloth alk. paper)
    1. United States.   Constitutional convention (1787)
    2. Constitutional history—United States.   I. Title.
KF4510.L96   1999
342.73'029—dc21   98-43447

Cornell University Press strives to use environmentally responsible suppliers and materials to the fullest extent possible in the publishing of its books. Such materials include vegetable-based, low-VOC inks and acid-free papers that are recycled, totally chlorine-free, or partly composed of nonwood fibers.

Cloth printing   10 9 8 7 6 5 4 3 2 1

To Irene

The *threatening contest,* in the Convention of 1787, did not, as you supposed, turn on the degree of power to be granted to the Federal Govt: but
on the rule by which the States should be represented and vote in the Govt: . . .
The contests & compromises, turning on the grants of power, tho' very important in some instances, were Knots of a less "Gordian" character.

James Madison to Martin Van Buren, May 13, 1828

Contents

Acknowledgments

Constitutional law is part law, part politics, and part history, a history comprising legal precedents and the causes and effects of past political controversies. The pursuit of American constitutional history, for a person who is curious and has the time to pursue it, leads back to the initial debates in the Congress of the United States regarding the meaning of the constitutional text, and beyond, to the proceedings in the Constitutional Convention and to an investigation of the widespread controversies that arose during the campaign to secure ratification. The trail of this history goes back still further: to the Continental Congress under the Articles of Confederation and the attitudes and politics that animated the debates of that body.

A proper understanding of the origins of constitutional law requires more than a few years of patient research, and it helps to be a lawyer. It helps even more to be a law professor who teaches courses in constitutional law and constitutional legal history.

Most important, it helps to have a dean who will encourage the legal scholar and allow him or her the time to develop conclusions before committing them to premature publication. I was fortunate to have Ronald Riccio as my dean in my final years at the Seton Hall University School of Law. He supported me in my seemingly never-ending studies, even to the extent of relieving me of my more arduous teaching duties in my last year. That boon enabled me to finish my work sooner than I would have done otherwise.

I thank Associate Dean Patrick Hobbs of the Seton Hall University School of Law for his cooperation in arranging for assistance in this work after my retirement. I also thank William Clark, Kevin Walsh, and James Sheil for their help in preparing the manuscript for publication, as well as Henry Wilson for his help with an earlier version. My gratitude also to the courteous help extended to me on many occasions by the staff of the Firestone Library of Princeton University.

I am also grateful to those who have given me permission to quote from their works: to the State Historical Society of Wisconsin, publishers of *The Documentary History of the Ratification of the Constitution;* to the Johns Hopkins University Press, publishers of *Documentary History of the First Federal Congress of the United States of*

America; to the University Press of New England, publishers of *The Federalist;* to Columbia University Press, publishers of *The Papers of Alexander Hamilton;* and to the University Press of Virginia, publishers of the pertinent volumes of *The Papers of James Madison.* I also thank Princeton University Press, publishers of *The Papers of Thomas Jefferson* for permission to quote from vol. 11, Copyright © 1955; vol. 16, Copyright © 1961; vol. 19, Copyright © 1974; vol. 20, Copyright © 1982; vol. 23, Copyright © 1990; vol. 26, Copyright © 1995; and vol. 27, Copyright © 1997.

Finally, I extend my deepest thanks to three persons without whom I could not have finished this book. I should first mention Deborah Herrera, Director of the Peter W. Rodino Jr. Library at the Seton Hall University School of Law, for her full support in the prompt acquisition of the materials necessary for this book; and Eileen Denner, Director of Research at the Rodino Library, for the great amounts of material she produced for me from the long-ago beginnings to the very end of this project. I especially thank them for their unfailing willingness to help me and for the good cheer that made a monumental task less burdensome.

The last of this trinity is my wife, Irene, who encouraged me through the long years of study and composition, and who read and reread every line of each of my many versions until she was satisfied I had it right. When, straight from an early debate, I would write sentences resonant of eighteenth-century English, she would insist that I translate them into understandable American usage. When, after reading the overprecise and complicated prose of the legal opinions of any century, I would reproduce the sprawling statements of fact and complex summaries of judicial rationales, she would insist on simplicity. Many of her suggestions, emendations, and rearrangements have been absorbed into my text. She truly has been my collaborator.

JOSEPH M. LYNCH

Princeton, New Jersey

NEGOTIATING THE CONSTITUTION

Introduction

The problems of federalism are still with us: Under the Constitution of the United States, what are the limits to the powers of Congress? What are the powers reserved to the states? It was the basic thesis of James Madison in the *Federalist* that "the powers delegated by the proposed Constitution to the Federal Government, are few and defined. Those which are to remain in the State Governments are numerous and indefinite."[1]

This was the thesis that served as the cornerstone of the 1995 decision of the United States Supreme Court in *United States v. Lopez,* where it held that the mere act of possessing a firearm in a local school zone was not subject to federal regulation.[2] In response to the argument of the United States that a federal statute criminalizing such conduct was a valid exercise of congressional power to regulate commerce among the states, the Court held that possession in itself did not constitute "commerce" or an economic enterprise; in consequence, the statute was unconstitutional. "Areas, such as criminal law enforcement or education," added Chief Justice Rehnquist writing for the Court, "[are subjects] where States historically have been sovereign."[3] Four justices in dissent concluded the legislation was valid.[4]

Two years later, the Court once again invalidated federal legislation affecting the regulation of firearms. The statute at issue had imposed on state and local law enforcement officers the duty of conducting background checks on prospective handgun purchasers. Although such an imposition was deemed a valid exercise of federal power under the Commerce Clause, nevertheless, in *Printz v. United States,* it was held to be an invalid intrusion on state sovereignty.[5]

Again, as in *Lopez,* four justices dissented. They considered that coupling the power of Congress under the Commerce Clause with its power under the Necessary and Proper Clause made the imposition a valid one.[6] In reply, Justice Scalia for the Court derisively characterized reliance on the latter clause as "the last, best hope of those who defend *ultra vires* congressional action," and dismissed the argument out of hand. The justice, quoting Alexander Hamilton in the *Federalist,* regarded the regulation as "merely [an] ac[t] of usurpation [that] deserve[s] to be treated as such."[7]

The testimonials of respect in *Lopez* and *Printz* for statements made in the *Federalist* are part of an ongoing judicial endeavor to interpret the constitutional text in accordance with what is considered the original intent of those who framed the Constitution and those who ratified it.[8] This endeavor has provoked an extrajudicial inquiry, equally ongoing, concerning its relevance.[9]

Thus far, efforts to resolve the controversy have not been satisfying. One influential view, based on the position of Madison and Albert Gallatin in a Fourth Congress debate, is that from the beginning reliance on the framers' supposed intention or on statements made during the ratification process was considered improper.[10] That view, however, overlooks the arguments of those who opposed Madison and Gallatin in that debate and of President George Washington, who in a later message to the House rejected their position. The view also overlooks the fact that in the Fourth Congress Madison repudiated statements he made in the First Congress, when during the course of his opposition to the bill establishing the Bank of the United States he relied on his recollection of the proceedings of the Constitutional Convention and on statements made during ratification. It is not clear why we should prefer the position of the later Madison to that of the earlier Madison or of Washington.[11]

The existing literature on initial attitudes concerning the proper weight to be given original intent is minimal and scattered. In view of this circumstance, I undertook a systematic study of the constitutional debates in and out of Congress during the administrations of George Washington and John Adams to ascertain the respect then accorded to framers' intention and statements made during ratification, including those in the *Federalist,* concerning the meaning of the Constitution.[12]

The congressional debates in the first years of the new government centered repeatedly on opposing views of federal power and, in particular, on views of the enigmatically worded Necessary and Proper Clause. In the very first session of the First Congress, the clause played a crucial part in the discussions concerning Congress's power to require a uniform oath for state officials to support the Constitution and in the controversy over the president's power to remove incompetent executive officers.

The decisive role the Necessary and Proper Clause played in the third session of the First Congress regarding the establishment of a national bank is well known; its role in the passage of the bitterly contested Alien and Sedition Acts in the Fifth Congress is less so. Party positions, the same in both disputes, largely reflected regional differences: The Federalists, whose representation was clustered mainly in the mercantile North, argued that pursuant to the clause, Congress could legislate in the national interest; Republicans, the core of whose strength lay in the agricultural South, contended that thereby Congress was limited to providing for the incidental execution of the enumerated powers. Indeed, beginning with the debate over the bank bill, Republicans, led by Madison, steadfastly maintained that their construction of the Necessary and Proper Clause accorded with the assurances given during ratification.

The same regional differences governed the constitutional divisions regarding the extent of federal power to spend for the "general welfare" under Article I, Section 8, Clause 1 of the Constitution: Hamilton and northern congressmen, with Washington's support, recommended spending, in the general interest, for the promotion of manufactures, science, agriculture, and education. Madison and the South opposed such spending as beyond the purposes enumerated in Article I, Section 8, and therefore contrary to the assurances given during ratification.

These wide discrepancies of position led me to question why, during ratification, proponents of the Constitution should have considered it important to give assurances as to the narrow meaning of the Necessary and Proper Clause, and why, after the Constitution was approved, so many disregarded those assurances. The answer appeared to lie in the ratification debates.

A study of the ratification campaign, however, quickly led me back to the records of the Constitutional Convention. So intense was the antagonism of George Mason, one of the framers from Virginia, to ratification that immediately after the convention he organized a systematic opposition throughout the states, charging, among other things, that under the Necessary and Proper Clause, Congress would have an unrestricted power of legislation. Other framers, Governor Edmund Randolph of Virginia and Elbridge Gerry of Massachusetts, repeated the charge. The opposing views regarding the extent of federal power appeared to have their origin in the Constitutional Convention itself.

At the very beginning of the convention it was Randolph who on behalf of Virginia brought forth a proposal, prepared by Madison, by which Congress would be invested with broad powers to legislate "in all cases to which the separate States are incompetent, or in which the harmony of the United States may be interrupted by the exercise of individual Legislation." That part of the Virginia Plan, however, was conditioned on the convention's acceptance of a second proposal, that state representation in both branches of Congress be based on population. Since Virginia at that time included present-day Kentucky and West Virginia, and since its population was swollen by the large number of slaves who would be counted in the apportionment of representation, the state would be the largest in the Union, and as such could, with the other large states, dominate the national legislature. For that very reason, the small states, located principally in the North, objected to granting Congress broad powers.

After achieving equal representation in the Senate, however, the small states reversed themselves and pressed for an amended version of the proposal concerning congressional power. Virginia, which had voted against equal representation, also reversed itself and opposed granting broad powers to Congress. On behalf of their state and the South in general, Randolph and Madison strenuously objected. Their region's agricultural economy, dependent on the recruitment and maintenance of an adequate supply of slave labor, was especially vulnerable to the consequences of federal regulation which a northern-dominated and mercantile-oriented Congress might impose. Nevertheless, despite their objections, the proposal was narrowly approved and referred, along with all other resolutions that the convention had preliminarily approved, to the Committee of Detail. (Randolph was chosen as one of its five members.)

In committee, the language modeled on the Virginia proposal, enabling Congress to legislate in the general interests of the country, was deleted, and the Necessary and Proper Clause, one of the Constitution's key provisions, substituted in its stead. Both sides to the dispute accepted it. With little debate, the convention approved it. Virginia, it seemed, had won.

Mason, Randolph, and Gerry, however, did not think so. During the convention, Mason privately referred to the Necessary and Proper Clause as "the sweeping clause." As the convention neared its end, Randolph, refusing to approve the Constitution, complained specifically about the clause his own Committee of Detail had drafted, and invoked the need for a more definite boundary between federal and state legislatures. Mason, joining with Randolph, stated as one of his reasons for disapproving the constitutional text the framers had adopted the new government's dangerous power and structure. Gerry, following along, referred to the power of Congress to pass any laws it might decide to call necessary and proper.

If those objections were chimerical, it would have been simple for the framers to allay them, and to adopt, in place of the Necessary and Proper Clause, some other language to address their concern, such as that "Congress shall also have the incidental power to pass laws carrying into execution one of the enumerated powers." They didn't do so.

Because those and other objections were not addressed, Mason, immediately after the convention, organized his campaign against the Constitution and, in particular, against "the sweeping clause." Significantly, in the Virginia ratifying convention he made the charge that many framers had a plan to bring about "one great, national consolidated Government . . . [but] slowly and imperceptibly, rather than all at once." Madison did not deny it, but said he wasn't one of them.

All the evidence points to the conclusion that in composing the Necessary and Proper Clause, the Committee of Detail crafted a compromise, a masterpiece of enigmatic formulation, so artfully phrased that after the convention each side could argue its version of the clause: either, as Virginia and the South would have it, that Congress could merely approve measures incidental to the execution of the enumerated powers or, as those in the North would say, that Congress could enact laws in the general interests of the country. There were, in fact, no victors in the dispute over the extent of congressional power; the dispute was merely deferred.

Although Mason's subsequent campaign threatened the work of the Committee of Detail, his complaints did not hurt Virginia and the South. Indeed, he strengthened their hand. During ratification, Madison labored both in the *Federalist* and in the Virginia convention to assure everyone that the Necessary and Proper Clause was not a "sweeping clause" but one conferring merely incidental powers. It was the interpretation he favored in any case, and one he would assiduously advance after the government was formed.

On the other hand, Mason's charges adversely affected those who after the organization of the new government would want to propound a broad meaning of the clause. An admission of this view would have led to ratification's rejection in Virginia and elsewhere. Thus, Mason's tactics forced Hamilton to give assurances in the *Federalist* similar to those of Madison. He and others like him had no choice. Honoring those assurances after ratification, however, would mean undoing the convention compromise and handing Madison, his state, and his region a major triumph.

In the First Congress the seams of the compromise became visible. Some men, like Hamilton, who were committed to a government with power to legislate in the general interests of the nation, chose to ignore what was stated in the *Federalist* and in the state conventions concerning the limited meaning of the Necessary and Proper Clause. When this position was used for the advancement of northern commercial, banking, and manufacturing interests, Virginians, committed to the defense of their region's agricultural economy, protested. As in the Constitutional Convention, they realized the vulnerability of that economy to the adverse consequences of federal regulation.

In a few Virginians, however, commitment to the national interest, arising out of service in the Continental Army, prevailed over loyalty to state and region. Chief among them was Washington. While his views were not broadcast, dedication to the Union and the cause of nation building affected his interpretation of the Constitution. Against the opinions of Madison, Randolph, and Thomas Jefferson—his fellow Virginians—he signed the bank bill into law even though its provisions, while serving the general interests of the country, would in practice largely benefit the North. And in disregard of Madison and Jefferson, he supported the organization of a professional army and advocated federal spending for the funding of a national university and for the promotion of science and agriculture.

Thus, during the first six congresses of the United States, the Federalists, under Washington's quiet—and Hamilton's outspoken—leadership, disregarded the *Federalist* thesis that the Article I legislative powers of the federal government were few and defined, and opted instead for a broad formulation of the enigmatically phrased Necessary and Proper Clause and the spending power, so as to authorize Congress to legislate in the general interests of the country.

During this period Madison and his allies consistently argued in and out of Congress that, based on the assurances given during ratification and, sometimes, on a framer's recollection of the proceedings of the Constitutional Convention, the powers of Congress were strictly limited. In one striking instance, however, they departed from their usual mode of argumentation and rejected recourse to ratification assurances or to a framer's recollections: during the debates in the Fourth Congress.

There were two reasons for the departure. First, in the Fourth Congress, Madison and his allies were not concerned with the advancement of states' prerogatives at the expense of the Article I powers of the federal government. On this occasion, they were championing the prerogatives of the House against the Article II powers of the president and the Senate governing the negotiation and ratification of treaties. (From the Second Congress forward, indeed, Madison—breaking from the position he had espoused during the Constitutional Convention and in the First Congress favoring the extension of presidential power—usually argued in support of Congress's power at the expense of the president's, out of a desire to constrain Hamilton and his initiatives.) Second, and again contrary to the usual situation, in the Fourth Congress it was the Federalists who, in arguing on behalf of the president and the Senate under Article II, relied on the proceedings of the Constitutional Convention and the reports of the state ratifying conventions.

So striking was Madison's departure from his usual method of interpreting the Constitution that in the Fourth Congress the Federalists taunted him for his failure to rely on the proceedings of the Constitutional Convention and the Virginia convention. Their own interest in those proceedings lay in the fact that this time history supported their stance in the issue before the House, that is, that the House did not have the power to withhold legislative implementation of a ratified treaty.

Indeed, it was these taunts that prompted first Gallatin and then Madison to say that a framer's personal recollections and the reports of the state conventions were unreliable and that therefore their use was improper. The responses were necessary both to protect Madison from the charge of personal inconsistency and to advance the Republican cause in the House debate.

A close reading of the debates of the first six congresses makes clear that policy goals, not fidelity to past position, most often influenced the construction placed on the Constitution in discussions of the scope of federal power or, within the federal government, the scope of executive power. Those goals also determined the use— or deprecation of the use—made of a framer's recollections, of essays in the *Federalist,* or of the reports of proceedings of the state conventions. Politics, the desire to attain or maintain control of the government and to set its policies, personal rivalry, and the rivalries of state and region all played an integral part in the construction of the Constitution.

Nevertheless, politics and rivalries aside, for many in Congress and the administration one very important factor influencing the adoption of legislation and the construction of the Constitution was the aspiration to make the new government of the United States work. Thus, in some cases, where there was simply no original intent to find—where, for instance, the Constitution failed to provide for the removal of incompetent executive officers—Congress, with Washington's approval, acted to supply the deficiency. In others, where following the constitutional text and original intent would have led to results that were impractical, indeed potentially disastrous, Congress ignored them.

In one striking case, again in the Fourth Congress, Washington followed the framers' intent and deliberately invoked the proceedings of the Constitutional Convention: In his message to the House he rejected the Gallatin-Madison position concerning the power of the House to withhold legislative implementation of Jay's Treaty. The president would not permit the opposition to wreck the treaty and endanger peaceful relations with Great Britain. Washington's immense prestige and his resort to history, it should be added, overwhelmed Madison and humiliated him.

In summary, the factors governing constitutional construction were varied. For this reason, a simple reliance on statements of Hamilton or Madison in the *Federalist* or on statements of Madison or others in Congress as to the meaning of the Constitution, without regard to the context in which they were made, is misguided. Contrary to the opinion of the Court in *Lopez,* whether or not the powers of the federal government were "few and defined," as Madison would have had it, was very much a debated question. And contrary to the view expressed in *Printz,* Hamilton's declaration in the *Federalist* regarding the narrow meaning of the Necessary and Proper Clause was completely belied by his post-ratification position on the validity of the bank bill.

Despite this denigration of Madison's status as the preeminent authority in the construction of the Constitution, his participation in the early years of the government of the United States was certainly of great importance. Indeed, because the Constitutional Convention opened with a consideration of his Virginia Plan for granting Congress broad powers of legislation, and because he played a major role in the convention, the ratification campaign, and Congress, in attempting to narrow the meaning of the enigmatically phrased Necessary and Proper Clause and the spending power, this book begins with him and devotes much attention to his changing views on constitutional interpretation. As befits a late-twentieth-century study, Madison is the protagonist of this history, not its hero.

CHAPTER ONE

The Constitutional Convention: Virginians and Power

In the beginning, George Washington and James Madison were committed nationalists. Washington's service as commander in chief of the Continental Army and Madison's term in the Continental Congress had convinced them of the inadequacies of the powers and performance of that body under the Articles of Confederation. They were both convinced of the need for a strong national government with wide legislative powers, an executive able to check imprudent legislation and administer the laws energetically, and a judiciary to interpret those laws and give them effect. The Virginia Plan Madison prepared for the Constitutional Convention set forth a program which would achieve those goals. For this act of statesmanship, as well as for his later work in introducing the Bill of Rights in the First Congress, he has been frequently honored with the title "Father of the Constitution." [1]

But if Madison was a statesman, he was also a politician. Thus he structured his proposed constitution so as to make his state's influence in the new government predominant. The key to that influence lay in the legislature. Although his plan replaced the all-powerful unicameral Continental Congress under the Articles of Confederation with a government separated into legislative, executive, and judicial branches, it provided that Congress would elect the executive and appoint the judges. And while his Congress was to be bicameral, the plan proposed that state representation in both branches be based on population.[2] Since Virginia, whose boundaries then included the present states of Virginia, West Virginia, and Kentucky, had the largest number of both free persons and slaves, the plan would serve the state well.[3]

It was within that context that the Virginia Plan, contemplating a truly national government, boldly provided that the legislature, in addition to the powers granted to the Continental Congress under the Articles, would be authorized to pass laws "in all cases to which the separate States are incompetent, or in which the harmony of the United States may be interrupted by the exercise of individual Legislation." This proposal reflected Washington's judgment that the new legislature must have the power to act in matters of "general concern."[4]

Even more boldly, the plan, in emulation of the practice of the British crown respecting laws passed by colonial assemblies, empowered the new Congress to review state legislation for inconsistencies with national law and the national constitution. In a case of inconsistency, Congress could invalidate the offending state law and, if necessary, use force to exact state compliance.[5] Finally, the national judiciary was to have jurisdiction, inter alia, in cases involving "the national peace and harmony."[6]

Madison expected the plan's ready acceptance. A month before the convention began, he had told Washington that the northern states would vote for the proposed system of representation "by their present populousness; . . . the Southern by their expected advantage in this respect. The lesser States must in every event yield to the predominant will."[7] But much to Virginia's dismay, Madison had miscalculated. The "lesser States" did not yield to the proposal, and the convention did not approve it. Instead the delegates decided on the much-celebrated Great Compromise, whereby representation in the House would be based on population, but in the Senate would be divided equally among the states.

After the compromise, the Virginia delegation abandoned the proposal for broad legislative powers and fought instead for the specific enumeration of congressional powers, a fight which resulted in the adoption of the enigmatic Necessary and Proper Clause. Madison in committee and on the convention floor labored to affix to that clause a narrow and definite meaning: Congress would have merely the authority to enact measures which carried into execution its specifically enumerated powers. During the campaign to ratify the Constitution and later in Congress, he consistently espoused that meaning. Washington, however, made no such commitment. The consequence of that divergence was to have a permanent influence on the political and constitutional history of the United States.

The convention's decision to grant the states equal representation in the Senate, besides changing the constitutional formula regarding the scope of congressional power, led to a second result. With Washington's approval, Madison abandoned his original idea of having Congress choose the chief executive and joined with the delegates from the other large states in a campaign to have him elected by the people, and to strengthen his powers at the expense of the small-state-dominated Senate.

Thus Madison, who had entered the convention an earnest advocate of a strong Congress in a strong national government, left it an equally earnest advocate of a strong chief executive presiding over an only somewhat strengthened federal legislature. How strong Madison wanted that executive to be he would show in the First Congress when, even in the absence of a specifically enumerated power, he argued on behalf of the right of the president to remove executive officers.[8]

The convention had opened with Virginia Governor Edmund Randolph's presentation of his state's plan. The length to which Randolph pursued the cause of broad national power in his accompanying remarks is uncertain. In this instance, Madison did not follow his later course of summarizing a delegate's speech in his notes on the convention's proceedings. Instead, he inserted a copy of the speech Randolph had given him.[9]

But other reports indicate that the governor, in his call for powers to pass laws "in all cases to which the separate States are incompetent, or in which the harmony of the United States may be interrupted by the exercise of individual Legislation," went far enough to raise an alarm. Robert Yates of New York stated that Randolph "candidly confessed that they [the set of resolutions embodying the substance of the Virginia Plan] were not intended for a federal government—he meant a strong *consolidated* union, in which the idea of states should be nearly annihilated."[10] Among states' rights advocates, "consolidated" was a dirty word. For that reason, it was a word Randolph, with his usual circumspection, was likely to avoid in characterizing his state's plan. Most probably, "a strong consolidated union" was what Yates concluded from what Randolph said.

That the Yates version was not made out of whole cloth can be inferred from another summary of Randolph's remarks, one made by James C. McHenry of Maryland, and from the reaction to those remarks by the South Carolina delegation. As McHenry had it, Randolph said that among the blessings the plan would secure were "the establishment of great national works—the improvement of inland navigation—agriculture—manufactures—a freer intercourse among the citizens." (The construction of an interstate canal system was high on Washington's national agenda.)[11] And as Madison did report, Randolph's explanation was sufficiently alarming to elicit from Charles Pinckney of South Carolina the question "whether he [Randolph] meant to abolish the State Governts. altogether," a meaning which the latter denied.[12]

But the denial did not satisfy either Pinckney or John Rutledge, his fellow delegate from South Carolina, who the next day objected to "the vagueness of the term *incompetent*" in the proposal to give Congress power in all cases where the state legislatures were individually incompetent. They demanded "an exact enumeration of the powers comprehended by this definition." Pierce Butler, another South Carolina delegate who called on Randolph for an explanation, was of the opinion that the convention was "running into an extreme in taking away the powers of the States."[13]

The alarm of some delegates at the prospect of giving to the United States the power both to make laws in instances where the states were incompetent and to invalidate certain state laws is understandable in the light of the then recent history of the United States. The incompetency proposal, while not entirely novel, had not been one lately discussed in or out of the Continental Congress. Madison, including it in the Virginia Plan, had followed language Benjamin Franklin had used in a draft of the Articles of Confederation submitted to the Continental Congress twelve years earlier.

Franklin's draft had provided that while each colony should "retain as much as it may think fit of its own present Laws, Customs, Rights, Privileges, and peculiar jurisdictions within its own Limits," Congress should, in addition to the powers to decide on war and peace and foreign alliances, resolve disputes between the colonies, found new colonies, and have the power to pass "such General Ordinances . . . as particular assemblies cannot be competent to." Such ordinances would include the power to make laws governing commerce, finance, the post office, and the military.[14] But Congress had not acted on Franklin's proposal, and subsequent plans for the Articles omitted any such provision and limited congressional powers to specifically enumerated subjects. By the time Madison included the incompetency recommendation in the Virginia Plan, it appears to have been largely forgotten.

Moreover, after 1777 such a measure had become unthinkable. In that year Thomas Burke took up the cause of state sovereignty and independence and successfully secured the adoption of an amendment to the Articles, declaring that each state would retain "its sovereignty, freedom, and independence, and every power, jurisdiction, and right, which is not by this confederation expressly delegated" to the United States, in Congress assembled.[15] After that, the states were on the alert for any sign that Congress might attempt to aggrandize its power at their expense.[16]

The convention, however, had been convoked to break with this pattern. Therefore, Madison and Washington did not wish to miss the opportunity, as Franklin had, of winning approval of Congress's authority to pass laws whenever several states were incompetent and, going beyond Franklin, its authority to invalidate state laws it deemed inconsistent with national law.[17] These proposals, nonetheless, alarmed those delegates who were expecting only limited changes to the Articles.

First Randolph, then Madison, attempted to soothe their fears. In response to the charge that the incompetency clause would eliminate state powers, Randolph disclaimed any intent to give indefinite powers to Congress, assuring the convention that he was, as Madison reported, "entirely opposed to such an inroad on the State jurisdictions."[18] As though in answer to the Pinckney-Rutledge demand for "an exact enumeration of the powers comprehended by this definition [i.e., of incompetency]," Madison said that he himself "had brought . . . into the Convention a strong bias in favor of an enemeration [sic] and definition of the powers necessary to be exercised by the national Legislature; but [he] had also brought doubts concerning its practicability. His wishes remained unaltered; but his doubts had become stronger, . . . [in view of the necessity of providing] for the safety, liberty and happiness of the Community."[19] Indeed, in his original manuscript, Madison had characterized his doubts as "grave." While others adopted a more reassuring posture—George Wythe of Virginia and Rufus King of Massachusetts stated that the convention should establish general principles before it went into details—Roger Sherman of Connecticut agreed with Madison that "it would be hard to define all the powers by detail." And James Wilson of Pennsylvania said flatly that "it would be impossible to enumerate the powers which the federal Legislature ought to have."[20]

In view of these remarks it seems most unlikely that the Virginia resolution was not to be taken literally. But many years later, after the publication of the Journals of the Constitutional Convention and of the Yates reports of the debates, Madison in a private letter denied a literal intent: "The general terms or phrases used in the introductory propositions . . . were never meant to be inserted in their loose form in the text of the Constitution. . . . [I]t was understood by all, that they were to be reduced by proper limitations and specifications, into the form in which they were to be final and operative; as was actually done in the progress of the session."[21]

If Madison at the convention had intended to reduce the generalities of the Virginia Plan to specifics, he only had to say so. He did not. It is not surprising therefore that when the delegates sitting as a Committee of the Whole approved the resolution and moved on, doubts concerning Virginia's intentions had not been eased. Three weeks later, John Dickinson of Delaware, after listing as his first principal objection to the Virginia Plan its proposal for representation in both branches of Congress based on population, set forth as his second principal objection its "[d]oubtful Indefinite Expressions which give a power to legislate in *all Cases*."[22]

The Delaware delegation became more uneasy when, following early approval of the Virginia resolution that Congress negative inconsistent state laws,[23] Charles Pinckney moved that Congress be further empowered "to negative all [State] laws which to them shall appear improper."[24] In support of Pinckney, Madison argued for the additional power as necessary to combat "a constant tendency in the States to encroach on the federal authority."[25] If necessary, he added later, the United States could appoint an agent in each of the states to give "a temporary assent" to local legislation until Congress had the opportunity to review it.[26]

When Wilson also supported Pinckney,[27] Gunning Bedford of Delaware erupted, charging a plot on the part of the large states, such as Pennsylvania and Virginia, to injure the small states at their pleasure, and "to provide a system in which they would have an enormous & monstrous influence."[28] Pinckney's motion was easily defeated. Only Virginia, Pennsylvania, and Massachusetts—which, including within its territory at that time the present state of Maine, constituted the second largest state—voted in its favor.[29]

The bad feelings pervading the delegations from small states led William Paterson and David Brearley from New Jersey to challenge the heart of the Madison plan, the provision for representation in Congress. Brearley, charging Virginia with a power play, said that representation on the basis of a state's population would lead to a situation in which Massachusetts, Pennsylvania, and Virginia would "carry every thing before them" in the new government.[30]

Paterson, supporting Brearley, attacked the Virginia Plan on fundamental grounds. If, he reasoned, the assembly was to be true to the concept of a confederacy, which supposed sovereignty in the participating members, and if sovereignty supposed equality, representation in Congress would have to be equal, as under the Articles of Confederation.[31] If, however, they were to depart from such a concept and were "to be considered as a nation, all State distinctions must be abolished, the whole must be thrown into hotchpot, and when an equal division is made, then there may be fairly an equality of representation."[32]

After Wilson dismissed the last idea as impractical, albeit not without merit,[33] the delegates, sitting as a Committee of the Whole, approved both the proposals for broad-based powers in Congress and for fixing the representation in both branches of Congress on some equitable ratio. A ratio based on the number of free inhabitants and slaves in each state was suggested but not immediately considered.[34]

Nevertheless, the Virginia Plan was in trouble. The proposal for a population-based Senate had carried by only one vote. Five states had been against it. And earlier, over Madison's vigorous objection, the delegates had overwhelmingly decided that state legislatures, and not the first branch of Congress, should select the members of the second branch.[35] It was clear that there was a substantial sentiment for a direct participation by the state governments in the composition of the new Congress.

This being so, within the week Paterson was encouraged to introduce his own state-oriented plan. Instead of providing for powers to pass laws in all cases in which the states were incompetent, his New Jersey Plan would limit Congress to the powers enumerated in the Articles of Confederation and, in addition, to the following specifically enumerated powers: the adoption of certain revenue laws, the regulation of foreign and interstate commerce, the establishment of federal courts, and the provision for a uniform rule of naturalization. Most important, the plan would retain the provisions in the Articles regarding the equality of congressional representation for each state.[36]

In support of his plan, Paterson repeated his earlier argument: Since the states were governed by the Articles and the Articles constituted an agreement, indeed a treaty, among the states, they could not be changed without unanimous consent. And, he added, to obtain the consent of the smaller states to any change, the convention must arrange a fair disposition of the lands beyond the Alleghenies that the British had ceded to the United States under the Treaty of Peace, and to which Pennsylvania, Virginia, North Carolina, and Georgia each had asserted claims. Otherwise, Paterson said, repeating his earlier threat, they must "throw . . . the States into Hotchpot." That is to say, they must eliminate the existing state boundary lines and redivide the consolidated mass into thirteen geographically equal districts. Try it, he concluded with sarcasm, and "see whether the Citizens of Massts.[,] Pena. & Va. accede to it."[37]

This was of course unacceptable to the larger states, and, appropriately, Virginia's representatives led the counterattack on the New Jersey Plan. Randolph characterized the issue before the delegates in federal versus national terms: "whether we shall adhere to the federal plan [meaning the Articles of Confederation], or introduce the national plan [meaning the Virginia Plan]."[38] Against Paterson, he argued that a constitutional "provision for harmony among the States, as in trade, naturalization &c.—for crushing rebellion whenever it may rear its crest—and for certain other general benefits, must be made."[39]

Having said this, Randolph then made explicit Virginia's condition for supporting such a plan: "The powers for these purposes [i.e., for harmony among the states], can never be given to a body, inadequate as Congress are in point of representation, elected in the mode in which they are, and possessing no more confidence than they do: for notwithstanding what has been said to the contrary . . . [my] own experience satisfied . . . [me] that a rooted distrust of Congress pretty generally prevailed. A Natl. Govt. alone, properly constituted, will answer the purpose."[40] In other words, Virginia's interest in a truly national legislature turned on Virginia's ability to control it. A few days later, Madison furnished a lengthy and more detailed theoretical attack on the New Jersey Plan. Only at the end did he dismiss as impractical Paterson's idea, to throw all the states into one large mass out of which a new partition of equal congressional districts could be made: "The dissimelarities [*sic*] existing in the rules of property [referring to slave ownership], as well as in the manners, habits and prejudices of the different States, amounted to a prohibition of the attempt."[41]

Soon afterwards, the Committee of the Whole decisively rejected Paterson's plan—only New Jersey, Delaware, and New York supported it—and submitted its report. The delegates in the convention turned to a consideration of the Virginia Plan.[42] But in view of the close vote in the Committee of the Whole on the question of fixing state representation in both branches of Congress on the basis of population, the New York, New Jersey, and Connecticut delegations moved to reopen the question.[43]

A long and increasingly acrimonious debate ensued, during which Madison spoke at length on the virtues of a republic in which membership of the legislature was based on the population of the districts represented: "[In such a government, there would be] a perfect incorporation, of the 13 States . . . [in which the States] would be mere counties of one entire republic, subject to one common law. [From this, it followed that t]he true policy of the small States therefore lies in promoting those principles & that form of Govt. which will most approximate the States to the condition of Counties."

In conclusion, and in response to the earlier demands from the New Jersey delegation for an equal partition of the combined territories of the existing states, Madison envisioned a utopian future: "Give to the Genl. Govt. sufficient energy & permanency, & you remove the objection [of the large States to a partition]. Gradual partitions of the large, & junctions of the small [States] will be facilitated, and time [may] effect that equalization, which is wished for by the small States, now, but that can never be accomplished at once."[44]

Madison had stated his position with the utmost clarity. He was for a strong consolidated national government with broad powers of legislation. Equally, he was for treating the several states as so many counties, presumably with home rule powers of legislation in matters so local and diverse as not to admit of national regulation. Alexander Hamilton could not have put it better.

But the delegates from the smaller states dismissed the Madison vision out of hand. After the convention reaffirmed the position of the Committee of the Whole that representation in the House should be based on population, Oliver Ellsworth of Connecticut proposed his state's compromise: Representation in the House would be based on population, thus giving a national dimension to the new government and protecting the larger states against the actions of the smaller, while representation in the Senate would be based on state equality, thus preserving a federal dimension and protecting the smaller states against the larger.[45]

In a political response to Randolph's earlier warnings, Ellsworth backed his theoretical comments with his own threat: "[East of the Delaware River, only Massachusetts] would listen to a proposition for excluding the States as equal political Societies, from an equal voice in both branches. The others would risk every consequence rather than part with so dear a right. An attempt to deprive them of it, was at once cutting the body [of America] in two."[46]

Attempting to overcome the force of Ellsworth's argument, Madison replied that the states were not divided by size but by climate and slave ownership.[47] After a heated debate, the Ellsworth motion failed on a tie vote. Massachusetts, Pennsylvania, and Virginia, the three largest states, along with the slave states of North Carolina and South Carolina, opposed it.[48] The original Madison plan had again survived.

Its survival, however, was illusory. Ellsworth had been correct. Connecticut, New York, and New Jersey, all of the states present which were east of the Delaware River—with the exception of Massachusetts—had supported him. In addition, New Hampshire, whose delegation had not yet arrived at the convention, and Rhode Island, which did not send a delegation, would have supported the motion had they been present; Maryland and Delaware, even though west of the river, had done so as well.[49]

Charles Cotesworth Pinckney of South Carolina, a cousin of Charles Pinckney, determining that without some arrangement along the lines Ellsworth had suggested the proposed Constitution would not be ratified by the New England or Middle Atlantic states—save for Massachusetts and Pennsylvania—moved the formation of a special committee, composed of one member from each of the eleven states present, for the purpose of devising and reporting a compromise. Over Madison's objection, his suggestion carried.[50]

The committee adopted, with some refinements, the compromise Ellsworth had proposed.[51] After a lengthy consideration of the committee's first recommendation (that concerning the composition of the House), the convention decided on a complicated formula of representation based on a state's population, which in the main proved satisfactory to all sections and states.[52] The convention's decision to approve the committee's second recommendation (for equality of state representation in the Senate), proved to be deeply divisive, however, and set off a movement to restrict the scope of congressional powers.

Following the approval of a motion to let stand the committee's report on representation in the Senate, Madison served notice of the relationship, in Virginia's view, between that question and that of the extent of the powers with which the new legislature could be entrusted. Echoing Randolph's earlier warning that unless both branches of Congress were based on population the powers of the new government would have to be limited, Madison stated: "It wd. be impossible to say what powers could be safely & properly vested in the Govt. before it was known, in what manner the States were to be represented in it. [I am] apprehensive that if a just representation were not the basis of the Govt. it would happen, as it did when the articles of Confederation were depending, that every effectual prerogative would be withdrawn or withheld, and the New Govt. wd. be rendered as impotent and as short lived as the old."[53]

A week later, Madison vigorously supported a motion to substitute a new proposal providing for a specific allocation of senators for each state and fixing the total membership at thirty-six. The northern states' majority would be reduced thereby to four.[54] In words prophetic of Virginia's actions under his and Jefferson's leadership following the conclusion of the First Congress, he warned that if the motion were not adopted: "The people of the large States would in some way or other secure to themselves a weight proportioned to the importance accruing from their superior numbers. If they could not effect it by a proportional representation in the Govt.[,] they would probably accede to no Govt. which did not in great measure depend for its efficacy on their voluntary cooperation; in which case they would indirectly secure their object."[55] Thus if Virginia could not get its way, it would see to it that the new government—whatever its powers on paper—would in reality operate with powers not so different from those possessed by the government under the Articles of Confederation. He detailed the reasons for his position: Under a Senate as constituted by the committee report, a minority of the people could refuse to adopt legislation approved by the House, whose membership represented a majority of the people. It could withhold its approval until the majority acceded to its desires on other matters or, by virtue of the special powers of the Senate, affect measures the House might wish to adopt. Further, with the admission of new states, the situation would become worse.[56]

With all these reasons, any delegate from a large state could agree. But Madison had a final reason for objecting to equality of votes in the Senate, one peculiar to Virginia's interest and that of the South:

THE PERPETUITY IT WOULD GIVE to the [preponderance of the] Northn. agst. the Southn. Scale was a serious consideration. It seemed now to be pretty well understood that the real difference of interests lay, not between the large & small but between the N. & Southn. States. The institution of slavery & its consequences formed the line of discrimination. There were 5 States on the South, 8 on the Northn. side of this line. Should a proportl. representation take place it was true, the N. side would still outnumber the other: but not in the same degree, at this time; and every day would tend towards an equilibrium.[57]

Despite this rather veiled forecast of future developments (it proved correct in the formulation and adoption of the Kentucky and Virginia Resolutions eleven years later), the motion was defeated.[58] The Virginia delegation soon showed its displeasure with the outcome and its intention to give substance to Madison's warning that at least one large state, if it could not control or influence the government, would see to it that the scope of that government would be considerably limited.

The next item of business before the convention was the language the Committee of the Whole had approved, enabling Congress "to legislate in all cases to which the separate States are incompetent; or in which the harmony of the U.S. may be interrupted by the exercise of individual Legislation."[59] This was the language Madison had inserted in the Virginia Plan and Randolph had introduced as one of its integral features.

Butler, as he had at the start of the convention, called again "for some explanation of the extent of this power." In particular, he objected to the word "incompetent." Nathaniel Gorham of Massachusetts, defending the word, gave the explanation some had offered when Pinckney and Rutledge had earlier objected to it. The convention, he said, was only establishing general principles.[60] Precise and explicit details would follow.

But the opponents were not satisfied. Rutledge moved that the clause "be committed to the end that a specification of the powers comprised in the general terms, might be reported." The Virginia delegation, instead of defending its own language and the Gorham explanation, supported Rutledge. On a tie vote, however, the motion failed.[61]

The following day, Delaware's Bedford, who earlier had charged Pennsylvania and Virginia with plotting to harm the smaller states with their proposal empowering Congress to negative laws it deemed improper, espoused the cause of national strength by moving that the resolution encompassing the powers of Congress be clarified to state: "[and moreover] to legislate in all cases for the general interests of the Union, and also in those to which the States are separately incompetent, [or in which the harmony of the U. States may be interrupted by the exercise of individual Legislation.]"[62] Now that Delaware, at least in the Senate, was an equal partner in the management of national affairs, Bedford was apparently an enthusiastic convert to the Virginia Plan and the cause of national power.

On the other hand, for the same reason, Virginia made it clear that its enthusiasm for the plan had waned. Randolph objected to Bedford's change, characterizing it as "a formidable idea indeed." Echoing language that delegates from South Carolina had originally employed in commenting on his proposal when set forth as part of the Virginia Plan, Randolph said that the Bedford "idea" involved "the power of violating all the laws and constitutions of the States, and of intermeddling with their police." Then, apparently oblivious of the fact that he himself had introduced the notion of protecting the harmony of the United States against interruption from state legislation, he stated that its inclusion was "[also] superfluous, being included in the first."[63]

Randolph's *volte-face* on the meaning to be attributed to the language of the Bedford amendment, which closely tracked the language of his own earlier proposal, is the clearest proof that Bedford intended, as all the delegates understood, that the general language he proposed be inserted in the text of the Constitution in just that form. (It may be added that Randolph's change of position appears to be the earliest example of how the interests of a politician's constituency—in his case the protection of slavery—can determine the construction he places on the constitutional text at issue.)

To Randolph, Bedford answered reasonably that his amendment was no "more extensive or formidable than the clause as it stands: *no State* being *separately* competent to legislate for the *general interest* of the Union." With that explanation, his amendment carried, six states to four.[64]

One week later, the convention constituted the Committee of Detail and charged it with reporting "a Constitution conformable to the Resolutions passed by the Convention." Such a charge required the talents of persons skilled in the art of preparing legal instruments. Accordingly, four of the members chosen to constitute the committee, Rutledge, Randolph, Wilson, and Ellsworth, were lawyers.

But as a sign that more was expected from the committee than the routine refinement of language and the artful arrangement of provisions, the composition of the committee reflected the state and regional diversity of the delegates: Rutledge of South Carolina representing the slave-holding interests of the deep South; Randolph of Virginia, the largest of the United States, representing the slave-holding interests of the upper South; Wilson of Pennsylvania, the third largest of the United States, representing the commercial interests of the middle states; Ellsworth of Connecticut representing the interests of the small states and of New England; and Nathaniel

Gorham of Massachusetts, the nation's second largest state, representing the ship-ping interests of New England.[65]

The geographical diversity made possible wide-ranging interregional negotia-tions. Compromises were reached. As expected, the committee, going beyond a lawyerlike arrangement of the resolutions the convention had already adopted, rec-ommended measures that had not previously been discussed and important changes in those that had. Placating the entire South, the committee's report would prohibit taxes on exports, require a two-thirds congressional majority for commercial regu-lations, and mandate the delivery of fugitive slaves. Gratifying the wishes of South Carolina and Georgia, the committee would also prohibit interference with the im-portation of slaves.[66] To satisfy Connecticut, engaged in a land dispute with Penn-sylvania, the committee would lodge the settlement of such controversies in the Senate.[67]

But more was needed to satisfy the North, particularly the smaller states of the region, whose chief concern was the adoption of an acceptable statement concern-ing the scope of congressional power. As Madison said many years later, once the small states had secured the right to an equal vote in the Senate, their delegates "ex-ceeded all others in zeal for granting powers to the general government. Ellsworth [who served on the Committee of Detail] became one of its strongest pillars. Pater-son of New Jersey was for the rest of his life a federalist of federalists."[68]

In place of the Bedford formula, which was unacceptable to the South, the com-mittee proposed a compromise: a series of specific congressional powers, followed by a provision of indeterminate authority, whose scope, in practice, would be for Congress to determine. Since initially the northern states would control both branches of Congress, they would determine the extent of the authorization.[69]

The stages by which this part of the compromise was achieved can be ascertained from the fragmentary evidence of the committee's deliberations. Randolph took the initiative in the committee by submitting his draft of a proposed constitution. In keeping with the position he had advocated on the convention floor, his version confined the powers of Congress to a series of specific authorizations, and omitted any reference to a power of adopting laws "in the general interests" of the United States, in cases in which the states were "incompetent" or in which their "harmony" might be interrupted.

The powers that Randolph enumerated included those the Continental Congress had possessed under the Articles of Confederation; those detailed in the New Jersey Plan—affecting taxation, foreign and interstate commerce, naturalization, and the creation of inferior federal courts; and those authorizing suppression of state and national rebellions, repulsion of foreign invasions, and punishment for counterfeit-ing the country's coinage and for offenses against the law of nations.[70]

Someone evidently suggested an amendment, whereby Congress would have the incidental "right to make all Laws necessary to carry the foregoing Powers into

Execu—." [71] In a later version, Wilson, who at the convention had strongly favored the Bedford resolution, expanded the wording of the amendment so as to empower Congress "to make all Laws that shall be necessary *and proper* for carrying into (full and complete) Execution (the foregoing Powers, and) all other powers vested, by this Constitution, in the Government of the United States, or in any Department or Officer thereof." [72] In the end, the committee adopted the substance of Wilson's suggestion and recommended it to the convention. [73]

Did "necessary and proper" mean the same as "necessary"? Did either phrase mean that Congress was authorized to approve only such incidental measures as would aid in the execution of laws passed pursuant to the specifically enumerated powers? If this was as far as "necessary and proper" went, then the Committee of Detail had reduced the generalities of both the Virginia Plan and Bedford's later resolution to specifics, and rendered harmless the language to which Butler and Randolph had so strongly objected. But if the committee had meant to disregard the proposal to confer on Congress the power to legislate in the general interests of the United States or to preserve harmony among the states, we should expect to read of a discontented Bedford protesting the committee's betrayal of his handiwork, and of a happy Butler supporting the report. That, however, was not the case.

Just prior to the convention's deliberations on the section regarding congressional powers, Butler prepared a motion to eliminate the words "and proper" from the Necessary and Proper Clause and to substitute instead the phraseology of Randolph's version as amended in committee: "And to make all Laws, not repugnant to this Constitution that may be necessary for carrying into execution the foregoing powers and such other powers as may be vested by this Constitution in the Legislature of the United States." [74]

Evidently Butler considered "necessary and proper" capable of a construction much broader than merely "necessary." Nevertheless, he did not offer his motion. If he had, he would have challenged the committee's principal accommodation of northern interest and jeopardized its many accommodations of southern interest. More to the point, insofar as Butler was concerned, such a motion would have jeopardized South Carolina's interest in the prohibition of federal restrictions on the slave trade, and in the delivery of fugitive slaves.

No one from Virginia offered such a motion either, although, as we shall see, the scope of congressional power implicit in the Necessary and Proper Clause bothered both Mason and Randolph. [75] But because their chief concern was the protection of their state's export trade against federal legislation designed to benefit northern shipping, they regarded the retention of the requirement of a two-thirds majority for the enactment of commercial regulations as vital. [76] While that provision was pending, they too would not challenge the Necessary and Proper Clause. [77]

Although Madison did not regard the retention of the two-thirds requirement as vital to Virginia's interests, [78] he was committed to keeping the Necessary and Proper

Clause. Once it had been decided that the smaller states would have an equal vote in the Senate, his main priority had lain in the confinement of congressional powers to those specified in the Constitution. Yet he would have understood that for Virginia and the South the deliberate ambiguity of the Necessary and Proper Clause represented a substantial improvement over the Bedford resolution. Rather than risk reversion to the language of that resolution or a breakup of the convention, he would have found it better to accept the ambiguity and work to make it appear—once the Constitution was ratified—that the clause meant merely that Congress had the incidental power to adopt measures in execution of an enumerated power.

In accordance with that assessment, Madison, shortly before the convention was to consider the clause, moved that the Committee of Detail consider the addition of a host of other congressional powers he proposed: the disposal of the unappropriated lands of the United States, the institution of temporary governments for new states, the regulation of Indian affairs, the provision for a district within which the United States could center its seat of government, the protection of copyrights and patents, the establishment of a university, the procurement of lands for forts and other necessary federal buildings within the states, and, most significant, the "grant [of] charters of incorporation in cases where the Public good may require them, and the authority of a single State may be incompetent."[79]

Undoubtedly Madison believed that it would be desirable, if not essential, that the new Congress possess those powers. Without them, the new government in many instances would not function properly, with the result that proponents of particular measures would be induced to claim the necessity and propriety of federal legislation. The inclusion of specific powers would forestall such claims. But, equally important, the larger the number of enumerated powers, the harder it would be to argue later that "necessary and proper" was anything but an add-on incidental power to carry into execution the foregoing enumerated powers. And adoption of the clause authorizing the grant of corporate charters, with its expressed limitation to cases of public good and state incompetency, would imply that generally Congress was not empowered to act in such cases.

Charles Pinckney joined with Madison, offering an additional list of powers for the Committee of Detail's consideration. While some of his suggestions duplicated those of Madison, he did advocate on his own the establishment of institutions for the promotion of agriculture, commerce, trade, and manufacturing; the regulation of stages on the post roads; the grant of letters of marque and reprisal; and the adoption of a series of resolutions concerning the payment of the public debt. A few days later, he recommended that Congress be empowered to pass uniform laws of bankruptcy.[80]

Shortly after the Madison and the first Pinckney proposals were made, but before the Committee of Detail could consider them, the convention approved the Necessary and Proper Clause without significant debate.[81] That part of the committee's attempt at regional accommodation was successful.

Responding to the Madison-Pinckney proposals, the committee next recommended a pair of additional congressional powers: the regulation of commerce with the Indians and the payment of the debts. Then, as if in response to Madison's gambit of including an allusion to the public good and state incompetency in the authorization of granting corporate charters, and as if to show where its sentiments really lay, the committee added a recommendation for a general power, which must have delighted Bedford and his supporters: "And to provide, as may become necessary, from time to time, for the well managing and securing the common property and general interests and welfare of the United States in such manner as shall not interfere with the Governments of individual States in matters which respect only their internal Police, or for which their individual authorities may be competent."[82]

At that point, however, the authority of the Committee of Detail waned. On the day its report was received, the convention rejected its previous proposals for the uninhibited importation of slaves and a two-thirds majority for the enactment of commercial regulations, and recommitted them to a second committee comprised of one member from each of the eleven participating states. To that committee were also referred all matters on which Detail had not reported—including most of the Madison and Pinckney suggestions for the addition of specific powers—and all matters it had reported but not acted on, including Detail's controversial recommendation for the managing and securing of the general interests and welfare of the United States in cases not involving the internal police of the states and in which they were not competent.[83]

In the end, the second committee, the Committee of Eleven, fashioned another compromise: The states would be allowed to permit the importation of slaves until the year 1800 (later extended to 1808), and the requirement for a two-thirds majority for the enactment of commercial regulations would be deleted. The South Carolina and Connecticut delegations strongly supported both measures, and the convention adopted them.[84] Without debate the convention also adopted the recommendation of the Committee of Detail regarding the delivery of fugitive slaves.[85] The South Carolina delegation had what it wanted.

In the opinion of Mason and Randolph, however, Virginia did not. Unlike Madison, they regarded the retention of a two-thirds majority for commercial regulations as essential to the needs of Virginia's planters. At the same time, they opposed the continued importation of slaves. As a result, they felt that Virginia had received nothing from the compromise, and they were so exercised over the elimination of the two-thirds requirement for commercial legislation that they talked of withholding their approval of the Constitution.[86]

Having secured the convention's approval of its most controversial recommendations, the Committee of Eleven pushed on to fashion the remaining compromises. Probably in response to the efforts of Madison, who represented Virginia on the committee, it now reported out, and the convention adopted, resolutions providing for some of the specific congressional powers that he and Charles Pinckney had previously offered: the disposition of lands owned by the United States, the institution of government in the territories, the establishment of the territory in which the seat of the government was to be located, the purchase of lands in the states for forts and the like, the provision for copyright and patent protection, the issuance of letters of marque and reprisal, and the provision for uniform laws of bankruptcy.[87]

The Committee of Eleven also scrapped the recommendation of the Committee of Detail that would have authorized Congress to provide for the "general interests and welfare of the United States in such manner as shall not interfere with the Governments of individual States in matters which respect only their internal Police, or for which their individual authorities may be competent." Instead, borrowing from the Articles of Confederation, the Committee of Eleven proposed a clause whereby Congress could lay and collect taxes, pay the debts of the United States, and provide for the common defense and general welfare of the United States.[88]

These changes furthered Madison's strategy. The Constitution would be stripped of any Bedford-type provision whereby Congress could legislate in the general interests of the country or in matters where the states might not be competent to act or could not act without disturbing the harmony of the United States. And although all the new powers recommended by the Committee of Eleven would enable Congress to further the general interests of the country and to legislate in matters where the states were not competent, their inclusion advanced the premise that only in the instances in which the powers of Congress had been specifically enumerated had the mandate of the Bedford resolution been implemented. In that view, the misgivings of the Virginia and South Carolina delegations had been accommodated. Neither the general welfare language nor the Necessary and Proper Clause would be a threat.

On the other hand, the Committee of Eleven did not recommend the authorization of specific powers to grant corporate charters or establish a university. In rejecting the former, they also rejected the inclusion of Madison's accompanying language, which would have suggested that only in such an instance was Congress able to legislate in cases of state incompetency. In sum, the committee had decided on the addition of specific powers and the retention of the Necessary and Proper Clause. They stood by the Committee of Detail's original compromise.

Madison wanted the last word. In the concluding week of deliberations, with Randolph's concurrence, he renewed his proposal regarding corporate charters when, to a Franklin motion for a congressional power "for cutting canals where deemed necessary,"[89] he offered an amendment adding a power "to grant charters of incorporation where the interest of the U. S. might require & the legislative provisions of individual States may be incompetent."[90]

If it was Madison's strategy to buttress the position that the powers of Congress were indeed only those specifically enumerated, Rufus King countered it. The motion, he said, was not needed. Presumably, this was because the Necessary and

Proper Clause was really intended to confer general powers, and the power to charter a bank was already provided in that clause. And as if in confirmation of the conclusion that the clause had been broadly, if enigmatically, worded for tactical reasons, he also opposed the motion as imprudent: If it were stated in specific terms, it would be likely to create opposition to the Constitution in Pennsylvania and New York banking circles and among people opposed "to mercantile monopolies" in other states. Madison's and Franklin's motions were defeated.[91]

For a reason similar to King's on the Madison motion, Gouverneur Morris of Pennsylvania then successfully opposed the motion advanced by Madison and Pinckney enabling Congress to establish a university. (Along with canals, a national university was one of Washington's favorite projects.) Morris called the proposal unnecessary, because Congress's authority over the territory in which the seat of government was to be located implied the power to establish a university there.[92]

No further motion or comment was made on the subject of congressional power. The struggle concerning that subject had ended in compromise. As Madison later wrote to Martin Van Buren, the disputes concerning congressional power, unlike the contest over the rule by which the states were to be represented in the federal government, had not threatened to break up the convention: "The contests & compromises, turning on the grants of power, tho' very important in some instances, were Knots of a less 'Gordian' character."[93]

The compromises may be summarized as follows: The convention would delete the reference to a broad empowerment in all cases of state incompetence, the general interest and national harmony and, rejecting the empowerment to grant corporate charters, would also delete Madison's specific reference to the interests of the United States and state incompetence. While Madison obtained the enumeration of additional specific powers, both he and Butler would have to live with the unexpressed implications of "necessary and proper."

In the second great compromise of the convention, the delegates voted to permit the importation of slaves until 1808, to provide for the delivery of fugitive slaves, and to eliminate the requirement for a two-thirds majority for commercial regulations. A few days later the first evidence of objection to the Constitution based on the Necessary and Proper Clause appeared. Butler copied a list of eleven objections to the Constitution from a document probably prepared by Mason. The fifth objection, referring to the Necessary and Proper Clause as "the sweeping clause"—the derogatory label it would commonly receive during the ratification campaign—protested that it "absorbs everything almost by Construction."[94]

As the convention neared its end, Randolph refused his signature to the Constitution the delegates had approved. Among the reasons for his objection he listed—besides the lack of a two-thirds requirement for the enactment of commercial regulations—"the general clause concerning necessary and proper laws" and "the want of a more definite boundary between the General and State legislatures."[95] A few days later, repeating his protest, he decried "the indefinite and dangerous power given by the Constitution to Congress."[96] Coming from Randolph, a member of the Committee of Detail, this reading of the Necessary and Proper Clause takes on a special meaning: The clause was intended as a compromise by which Congress, under northern influence, could find the authority for the exercise of more than incidental powers.

Mason and Elbridge Gerry of Massachusetts followed Randolph's example and refused their approval of the Constitution. Mason gave as one of his reasons the dangerous power and structure of the new government. After the convention, he would become more explicit and specifically name the Necessary and Proper Clause.[97] In the convention, Gerry listed among his objections "the general power of the Legislature to make what laws they may please to call necessary and proper."[98]

As if in agreement, no one took issue with their perception of the clause. No one moved for clarifying language, whereby the clause would be construed as simply allowing Congress the incidental power of enacting legislation to carry into effect the enumerated powers. No one even made such a suggestion on the convention floor.

In the light of this cumulative evidence, it would seem that the Necessary and Proper Clause constituted the language of an essential compromise. The Committee of Detail, and later the convention, could not have adopted language embodying the sense of the Bedford resolution without driving the Virginia and South Carolina delegations into open opposition and endangering the adoption of the Constitution. But, equally, if they had gutted the Bedford resolution, they would have driven Pennsylvania, Massachusetts, Delaware, New Jersey, Connecticut, and other states into opposition and similarly endangered the adoption of the Constitution. The ambiguity of the language that the committee proposed and that the convention approved enabled both sides not only to approve its inclusion in the Constitution but also to argue afterwards that their construction was in accord with the framers' intent. Only Randolph, Mason, and Gerry objected.

As we have seen, Madison did not. Despite the ominous warnings he had uttered earlier over the consequences of giving equal representation to the states in the Senate, he was unwilling to support the threats of Randolph, Mason, and Gerry to work for a second constitutional convention.[99] As much as the Constitution fell short of his vision for the kind of national government he had outlined in the Virginia Plan, he preferred the Constitution as finally written to none at all. He was prepared to live with his failure to obtain a dominant role for his state in both chambers of Congress.

Madison's course is understandable in the light of his record. He was committed to reform, to the curtailment of the excesses of unbridled state legislative power, and to the creation of national institutions that would control those excesses. In this sense at least, he was a nationalist.[100] Before the convention, he had fought against Patrick Henry in the Virginia state legislature for measures to aid the collection of British debts and to suppress the issuance of paper money unsupported by taxation.[101]

The Constitution would insure the achievement of those goals. With its provision in Article III for the institution in federal courts of cases involving diversity of citizenship,[102] it would allow British creditors to sue Virginia debtors for the collection of their debts. Further, the Constitution would expressly prohibit the issuance of state paper money or the adoption of state laws impairing contractual obligations, including the obligation to pay one's debts.[103]

On the other hand, the Randolph-Mason-Gerry idea of a second convention would play into the hands of state legislatures, whose irresponsibility in the issuance of paper money and in the impairment of contractual obligations, Madison thought, had brought the United States to the brink of decline or ruin. Moreover, the resulting disunion would, in case of war, deprive Virginia and the entire South of the protection of northern arms, and leave them and their vast western lands open to the depredations of foreign invasion. The second convention strategy, if successful, might mean the failure to accept any constitution and entail a danger to state and region. In personal terms, it would represent a defeat for himself and a victory for the state-house politicians in Richmond. Finally, and most decisively for Madison, Washington, a confirmed nationalist, disapproved of any recourse to a second convention. Madison's only alternative was to fight for and stand by the best constitution possible.[104]

Where Washington stood at that time on the subject of the Necessary and Proper Clause and the question of implied powers is difficult to determine. He certainly disagreed with the Randolph-Mason-Gerry call for a second convention, and he approved the use of the Necessary and Proper Clause despite its ambiguity. He probably appreciated the efforts of Franklin, Madison, and Charles Pinckney to elicit authority for Congress to advance his own favorite projects: funding for interstate canal construction and the establishment of a national university.

But when King, arguing against Madison's motion to enable Congress to charter corporations, called the motion both unnecessary and imprudent, with whom did Washington agree? With King, who was saying in effect that the Necessary and Proper Clause embodied such a power? Or with Madison, who by making his motion was saying that the chartering of a corporation was more than the merely incidental power of executing an enumerated power? In 1787, Washington did not have to decide that question. It was still possible to be a Virginian and a nationalist.

The strategy concerning the construction to be given the Necessary and Proper Cause was the first of two that Madison conceived during the convention, following its repudiation of his plan for representation in both branches of Congress based on population. The second involved the restatement of the provisions concerning the selection and powers of the president of the United States. Since both strategies were calculated to advance the interests of his state and region, they emanated from the same spirit that had inspired the original Virginia Plan. Although the goal was the same—the furtherance of Virginian and, hopefully, southern power—the constitutional arrangements by which that goal would be achieved were different.

Before the convention, Madison, secure in the belief that Virginia with its large population would dominate Congress and that therefore Congress should dominate the new government, had not given much thought to "the manner in which [a national executive] ought to be constituted or of the authorities with which it ought to be cloathed."[105] His main concern had been to insure the independence of the executive from the legislature. To that end he had proposed, and the Committee of the Whole had approved, that while Congress would choose the executive, the president would not be eligible for a second term.[106]

But once the convention had decided upon equality of representation in the Senate, it was not in the interest of Virginia, the country's most populous state, to have the Senate, dominated as it was by small northern states, participate in the selection of a president or—as the Committee of the Whole had decided, in alteration of Madison's original plan—make judicial and ambassadorial appointments. Madison therefore now favored the suggestion that presidential electors, chosen by the people in state districts, elect the executive. And, since Washington was likely to be the first president, Madison also strove to secure for him, at the expense of the Senate, an appreciably enhanced role in the new government.[107]

While Washington and Madison quickly saw the wisdom of these changes, others in the Virginia delegation did not. Mason, a firm antimonarchist, disliked the idea of an enhanced presidency. Accordingly, when the convention took up the resolutions of the Committee of the Whole on the organization and powers of the executive branch, he vehemently opposed a motion advanced by his fellow Virginians, Madison and Dr. James McClurg, that the president should, as in the case of a federal judge, hold office "during good behaviour."[108] In addition, Mason spoke out against a second Madison motion, that the president, rather than the Senate, appoint federal judges, albeit with the Senate's consent.[109] Against Madison, he opposed a proposal to take from Congress the power of selecting the president and place it in popularly elected presidential electors.[110] Finally, against both Madison and Washington, he and Randolph voted for a two-thirds legislative override of a presidential veto instead of three-fourths.[111]

To make matters more difficult for Madison, John Blair supported Mason, and McClurg was suddenly called home for personal reasons in the middle of the debate on the presidency—never to return. Since Wythe had left the convention earlier, and Washington sided with Madison, Randolph became the person whose vote would swing the Virginia delegation. Randolph, however, was his usual unreliable self: One day he favored a senatorial appointment of federal judges; a few days later, a presidential appointment. And on the key vote of the debate, whether the convention should sustain the decision of the Committee of the Whole and have Congress elect the president, with Mason and Blair in favor and Washington and Madison against, Randolph, to use the words of Madison's report, just "happened to be out of the House." In consequence, Virginia was divided; its vote did not count. Since on that question, as on an earlier one concerning the appointment of federal judges, most states followed Mason, Madison's defeat was seemingly complete: Congress would elect the president, and the Senate would appoint the judges.[112]

But one of Madison's great strengths was his tenacity. Once he had taken a position, he devoted his considerable skills in argumentation and in committee to its practical realization. And on the matters of enhancing presidential power and reducing senatorial and congressional power, Madison had taken strong positions. For example, when Mason characterized the McClurg-Madison motion—that the president, if elected by Congress, should hold office during good behavior—"as a softer name only for an Executive for life . . . [and] an easy step to hereditary Monarchy," Madison had responded in defense that the past record of state governments indicated it was the legislatures who represented the greater threat of tyranny, not the governors whom they elected: "Experience had proved a tendency in our governments to throw all power into the Legislative vortex. The Executives of the States are in general little more than Cyphers; the legislatures omnipotent."[113] Was he thinking of Randolph's dependence on the Virginia legislature?

In the same manner, Madison had bluntly ascribed the reason for changing the appointing power of federal judges (from the Senate to the president) to the alteration in the Senate's composition. Since a state's representation in the Senate would no longer be determined by population, a continuation of the original arrangement would mean that "the Judges might be appointed by a minority of the people, tho' by a majority, of the States. . . . [It] would moreover throw the appointments entirely into the hands of ye Nthern States, a perpetual ground of jealousy & discontent . . . to the Southern States."[114]

Nevertheless, despite his oratory, Madison did not initially prevail. Thus when the Committee of Detail, reflecting the mandate of the convention, reported its version of the Constitution on the organization of the executive branch, it provided for the election of the president "by ballot of the legislature," and for the appointment of judges and ambassadors and the making of treaties by the Senate.[115]

But on the convention floor Madison, with the aid of the delegations from the other large states, strove to change the report. He suggested a change in the clause regarding senatorial power: Since "the Senate represented the States alone . . . it was proper that the President should be an agent in Treaties." Eventually, the entire clause was recommitted.[116]

When the convention determined that both houses of Congress would choose the president by a joint ballot with the vote of each congressman counting the same as that of each senator, the probability of the smaller states controlling the elections was foreclosed. Sentiment began to shift toward the use of presidential electors. Eventually the provision for presidential elections was also recommitted.[117]

In the end, the Committee of Eleven recommended a compromise which the convention approved: that the president be elected by persons appointed in such manner as the state legislatures should determine; and that the president make treaties and nominate and, with the advice and consent of the Senate, appoint ambassadors, judges, and other officers.[118]

Madison, however, was dissatisfied with one aspect of the committee's recommendations concerning the executive's role in treaty making. Fearful that a president "would necessarily derive so much power and importance from a state of war that he might be tempted, if authorized, to impede a treaty of peace," he moved that the process for concluding peace treaties should be made simpler than for other treaties. And when the proposal passed, he moved that peace treaties should require only the approval of two-thirds of the Senate. Thereby the president's concurrence would not be necessary.[119]

Madison's strategy seems curious, for if the president was to be precluded from approving peace treaties, it would seem he should also be excluded from their negotiation. If this were the case, the Senate would have to appoint their own agent for this purpose, an agent who would necessarily reflect the various state and regional interests represented in the Senate. But this was the very consideration which had led Madison earlier to argue for a presidential agency in treaty making.

In recognition of the difficulties that Madison's second motion would raise, Gouverneur Morris argued that no peace treaty should be made without the concurrence of the president, who, he said, was "the general Guardian of the National interests." Gerry also pointed out that "in treaties of peace the dearest interests will be at stake, as the fisheries, territory &c." Whereupon the convention decisively defeated the idea of excluding the president from concurring in peace treaties. Even Virginia voted against it. (Washington, we may assume, did not like the idea.) And the following day the delegates reconsidered the proposition for having a simpler process for peace treaties and rejected it.[120]

Yet, despite this defeat, Madison, and presumably Washington, had reason overall to be satisfied. Since the president would be elected on the basis of a state's population, Virginia, with its large population of both whites and slaves, along with the rest of the South, would have a good chance of influencing his selection. Their satisfaction in this regard was somewhat tempered by the fact that the Constitution did not directly provide for the popular election of presidential electors, but instead left it to the state legislatures, whom Madison and Washington distrusted, to determine how the electors would be appointed.

But the Virginians had other satisfactions. Madison had helped secure for the president the power to appoint ambassadors, subject to senatorial consent, and generally to make treaties, subject to approval by two-thirds of the Senate, thus rendering unlikely the conclusion of agreements unfavorable to his state and region. (In this respect, Madison's views concerning the process for concluding peace treaties constituted a marked exception to his usual positions.) He had also helped secure for the president the power to veto legislation, subject again to an overriding two-thirds veto of Congress. Thus it was also unlikely that Congress would be able to pass legislation inimical to southern interest, even if it chose to rely on powers supposedly implicit in the Necessary and Proper Clause.[121] He had further secured for the president the power to appoint the justices of the Supreme Court, thus seeing to it that the laws, when reviewed for meaning, and the Constitution, when the validity of the laws was challenged, would be subject to interpretation by a court composed of persons not unfriendly to southern interest.

In the end then, Madison had achieved a governmental system with which Virginia could live and be happy, subject to one important condition: that it be able to control or significantly influence the selection of the president of the United States and, after that selection, the content of executive policy. Since Washington was in all likelihood to be the first president, that happiness seemed initially assured. And since during the convention Madison had in effect been the future president's prime minister on behalf of presidential powers and prerogatives, he could look forward to continued service in that role in the First Congress.

All of this afforded additional reasons for Madison and Washington, in opposition to Randolph and Mason, to sign their approval of the Constitution and get on with the new government. But before such an auspicious state of affairs could commence, the Constitution had to be ratified. Its status hung in the balance until the following July—the convention ended in September 1787—by which time eleven states, including the crucial states of Virginia and New York, had ratified it.

The Politics and Promises of Ratification

If the Necessary and Proper Clause, despite the protestations of Randolph, Mason, and Gerry and the misgivings of Butler, passed the convention as it emanated from the Committee of Detail, its passage through the ratification process was stormy. As Hamilton remarked with rhetorical flourish in the *Federalist,* the Necessary and Proper Clause and the Supremacy Clause had become "the sources of much virulent invective and petulant declamation against the proposed constitution." He went on: "They have been held up to the people, in all the exaggerated colours of misrepresentation, as the pernicious engines by which their local governments were to be destroyed and their liberties exterminated—as the hideous monster whose devouring jaws would spare neither sex nor age, nor high nor low, nor sacred nor profane."[1]

The campaign against the Constitution generally and against the Necessary and Proper Clause in particular began early when George Mason, before leaving Philadelphia for Virginia after the adjournment of the convention in September 1787, disseminated his objections among the leaders of those members of the Pennsylvania legislature opposed to ratification.[2] On his return to Virginia, he wrote to Washington, informing him of his objections,[3] and followed that with a series of similar letters to others. Within the month, his stand was well known throughout Virginia.[4]

Mason did not stop there. By the middle of November, he had circulated manuscript copies of his reasons for opposing the Constitution in Pennsylvania, New York, and New Hampshire. In the next two months, copies would circulate in Massachusetts, Rhode Island, Connecticut, New Jersey, Maryland, and South Carolina as well.[5]

Among his objections, Mason included the Necessary and Proper Clause. Pointing to the understanding at the convention, implicit in the colloquy following Franklin's motion for a specific power to cut canals, and in the silent acquiescence to Randolph's repeated construction of the clause, he wrote: "Under their own Construction [i.e., that of the delegates to the Constitutional Convention] of the general Clause at the End of the enumerated Powers, the Congress may grant Monopolies in Trade & Commerce, constitute new Crimes, inflict unusual & severe Punishments, and extend their Power as far as they shall think proper; so that the State Legislatures have no Security for the Powers now presumed to remain to them; or the People for their Rights."[6]

Mason's dissemination bore quick fruit. In mid-October, "Old Whig," a Philadelphia pamphleteer, was referring to "that *undefined, unbounded, and immense power*" in the Necessary and Proper Clause and saying that, read together with the Supremacy Clause, it gave the power to "make all such laws which *the Congress shall think necessary and proper.*"[7] The next day "Brutus," a New York pamphleteer, was charging that the Necessary and Proper Clause, when combined with the Supremacy Clause, would lead to the annihilation of state governments and to the "complete consolidation of the several parts of the union into one complete government."[8]

The campaign against ratification in general, and against the Necessary and Proper Clause in particular, picked up when two weeks later Gerry's letter to the Massachusetts General Court, stating his reasons for not signing the Constitution, was published. Among the reasons he included the objection "that some of the powers of the Legislature are ambiguous, and others indefinite and dangerous." The letter received widespread circulation throughout the state, and in Pennsylvania and Virginia.[9]

Early in November the campaign came to a climax with the publication of the most celebrated—because the ablest—of all the pamphlets opposing ratification, the series of "Letters to the Republican," authored by the "Federal Farmer." Many have surmised him to have been Mason's Virginia neighbor and close political ally, Richard Henry Lee.[10]

In one of his letters, the Farmer, addressing the scope of the Necessary and Proper Clause, summarized the arguments pro and con the proposition that the clause contained a grant of broad and indefinite powers. With keen insight into the political process, he concluded that in practice politicians would construe the clause to suit their own desires. Thus he concluded that whenever a question arose in the government as to whether it had a particular power, those in charge would tend to give themselves the benefit of the doubt. Since his commentary anticipated the pattern of arguments in the first twelve years of the new government—with the Federalists under Hamilton giving themselves the benefit of the doubt and the Republicans under Madison denying them the benefit—it is worth quoting the Farmer in full:

I T IS SAID, THAT WHEN THE people make a constitution, and delegate powers, that all power not delegated by them to those who govern, is reserved in the people; and that the people, in the present case, have reserved in themselves, and in there state governments, every right and power not expressly given by the federal constitution to those who shall administer the national government. It is said, on the other hand, that the people, when they make a constitution, yield all power not expressly reserved to themselves. The truth is, in either case, it is mere matter of opinion, and men usually take either side of the argument, as will best answer their purposes: But the general presumption being, that men who govern, will, in doubtful cases, construe laws and constitutions most favourably for encreasing their own powers; all wise and prudent people, in forming constitutions, have drawn the line, and carefully described the powers parted with and the powers reserved.[11]

Against the background of this anti-ratification barrage, the Pennsylvania convention opened in late November 1787. Opponents within the convention repeated the already well-publicized charge that the Necessary and Proper Clause would be used as a pretext for the enactment of any laws Congress saw fit to adopt.[12] Appropriately, it was left to James Wilson, a member of the Constitutional Convention's Committee of Detail which had authored the enigmatic phrase, to explain its handiwork to the Pennsylvania convention.

On behalf of the proponents of ratification, Wilson, without referring to the Mason-Gerry thesis, in effect dismissed it. The Necessary and Proper Clause, he said, meant "no more than that the powers . . . already particularly given [in Article I, Section 8] shall be effectually carried into execution."[13] Later in the convention he maintained "that the powers [of the United States] are as minutely enumerated and defined as was possible, and . . . the general clause, against which so much exception is taken, is nothing more than what was necessary to render effectual the particular powers that are granted."[14]

Wilson, then, espoused a narrow construction of the clause. But his adversaries did not believe him. After the convention ratified the Constitution, the dissenters proposed a series of constitutional amendments, the last of which, probably inspired by Mason, was patterned on the provision in the Articles of Confederation governing the powers of Congress. It read: "That the sovereignty, freedom and independency of the several states shall be retained, and every power, jurisdiction and right which is not by this Constitution expressly delegated to the United States in Congress assembled."[15]

When their proposal was rejected, they took their case to the public, incorporating their amendments in a formal Dissent to ratification, which they published on December 18, 1788.[16] It was in response to their "virulent invective and petulant declamation" against the Necessary and Proper Clause that Hamilton, writing as Publius in the *Federalist,* restated the construction Wilson had given it in the Pennsylvania convention: Congress thereby had only the power to pass laws to carry into effect the specifically enumerated powers given earlier in the section in which it appeared.[17] The clause, Hamilton wrote, was "only declaratory of a truth, which would have resulted by necessary and unavoidable implication from the very act of constituting a Fœderal Government, and vesting it with certain specified powers."[18]

In other words, while without the words "necessary and proper" the provision for expressed powers would have implied a provision for their enforcement, the framers had, in adding the Necessary and Proper Clause, made explicit what was implicit. Hamilton conceded that in this reading the clause might "be chargeable with tautology or redundancy," but he concluded, somewhat ruefully, it was "at least perfectly harmless."[19]

His explanation did not reassure the opponents of ratification. Their suspicions about the purpose underlying the clause must have been confirmed when on the same day that the Hamilton explanation appeared, Randolph's letter setting forth his reasons for not signing the Constitution was finally published in Virginia. In that letter, belatedly released to the Virginia House of Delegates, Randolph as much as confirmed Mason's and Gerry's statements and the observations of the Federal Farmer.

Without specifically referring to the Necessary and Proper Clause, Randolph complained of the document's "ambiguities of expression" and expressed his hope that they be "precisely explained." He added a hope that "in drawing a line between the powers of Congress and individual states; and in defining the former; [care be taken] so as to leave no clashing of jurisdictions nor dangerous disputes: and to prevent the one from being swallowed up by the other, under the cover of general words, and implication."[20]

Randolph's belated attack drew forth a second defense of the Necessary and Proper Clause from Publius, this time Madison, in the *Federalist*. He reaffirmed what Hamilton had written. By adding the clause, the framers had merely expressed that which in its absence would have been implied: Congress would have the power to adopt measures in execution of the enumerated powers. Madison began his defense by referring to the practice of the Continental Congress. Even that body, he wrote, had recourse to the doctrine of implied powers, despite the strictures in the Articles of Confederation against the use of powers not expressly delegated. Because under the Constitution the new Congress was to have greater powers, the Constitutional Convention, he reassured his readers, had considered it advisable to make express provision for the exercise of incidental powers through the addition of the Necessary and Proper Clause.

The powers implied in the clause, he wrote, were the particular powers that "in every new application of a general power . . . are the means of obtaining the *object* of the general power." These, he added, "must always necessarily vary with that object; and be often properly varied whilst the object remains the same."[21] He continued in this vein:

HAD THE CONSTITUTION BEEN SILENT on this head, there can be no doubt that all the particular powers, requisite as means of executing the general powers, would have resulted to the government, by unavoidable implication. No axiom is more clearly established in law, or in reason, than that wherever the end is required, the means are authorised; wherever a general power to do a thing is given, every particular power necessary for doing it, is included.[22]

In several other papers in the *Federalist,* Madison assured his readers that the powers of the new government were limited. He denied that the proposed government was a national one, "since its jurisdiction extends to certain enumerated objects only, and leaves to the several States a residuary and inviolable sovereignty over all other objects."[23]

In the same vein, he argued that since the powers of the new government were to be less than those of the British Parliament, there was less necessity for frequent elections: "The smaller the power, the more safely may its duration be protracted."[24] For the same reason—the limited powers of the new Congress—he concluded that its members "need be less numerous than if they possessed the whole power of legislation, and were under no other than the ordinary restraints of other legislative bodies."[25]

But if by these repeated assurances Hamilton/Madison alias Publius seemingly closed the door to the assertion of more than incidental powers resident in the Necessary and Proper Clause, in other essays in the *Federalist* they suggested the possibility of such powers resident elsewhere in the Constitution. More than once they implied that in time of great need every basic legal document, such as the Constitution, was subject to the unwritten rule that the people expect public officials to do whatever the exigencies of the times require. Of necessity, they seemed to say, government must have implied powers that are more than incidental.

Hamilton first made the point in a paper defending the Constitution for its failure to prohibit a peacetime standing army. In time of emergency, he wrote, governments usually act without regard to legal restrictions. Without a standing army, he maintained, it would be impossible to protect the nation's vast interior against a sudden attack by Great Britain, the Indians, or Spain, or to suppress domestic insurrections. He referred to the experiences of Pennsylvania and Massachusetts, which, despite the prohibitions against a standing army in their constitutions, had found it necessary to raise troops to suppress rebellions within their borders. Their experience, he observed, had taught "how unequal parchment provisions are to a struggle with public necessity."[26] History, he continued, confirmed the truth

THAT NATIONS PAY LITTLE REGARD TO RULES and maxims calculated in their very nature to run counter to the necessities of society. Wise politicians will be cautious about fettering the government with restrictions, that cannot be observed; because they know that every breach of the fundamental laws, though dictated by necessity, impairs that sacred reverence, which ought to be maintained in the breasts of rulers towards the constitution of a country, and forms a precedent for other breaches, where the same plea of necessity does not exist at all, or is less urgent and palpable.[27]

Madison echoed these thoughts in a later paper in the *Federalist.* During the course of a long discussion concerning the deficiencies of the Articles of Confederation,

Madison adverted to one of its requirements: proposed legislation, before it can take effect, must, receive the consent of all thirteen states. He recalled that in providing for the administration of the western lands—a matter of the greatest importance to the country—Congress had in fact acted without consulting the states. Exercising what he termed "an excrescent power," Congress, he wrote, had "proceeded to form new States; to erect temporary Governments; to appoint officers for them; and to prescribe the conditions on which such States shall be admitted into the confederacy."[28]

Since Congress had done all these things "without the least colour of constitutional authority," Madison concluded, its actions constituted a usurpation. But following Hamilton's reflections on the inequality of "parchment provisions" in the face of public necessity, he held that Congress could not have done otherwise: "The public interest, the necessity of the case, imposed upon them the task of overleaping their constitutional limits. But is not the fact an alarming proof of the danger resulting from a government which does not possess regular powers commensurate to its objects? A dissolution or usurpation is the dreadful dilemma to which it is constantly exposed."[29]

Later in the *Federalist* Madison returned to this subject in recalling "the inconvenience of this omission [in the Articles of Confederation for admitting states], and the assumption of power into which [the Continental] Congress have been led by it." Commenting on Article IV, Section 3, of the Constitution, which empowered Congress to admit states, he stated: "With great propriety therefore has the new system supplied the defect."[30]

Skeptical readers might have noticed that Publius had pointedly suggested and left unanswered a difficulty of the greatest significance. Granted that under the Constitution the number of specific powers had been increased to supply the omissions of the Articles—such as the powers to admit new states and to make rules and regulations for the governance of the territories. But inevitably, although Publius did not expressly say so, the Constitution itself would in time be found to have omitted to provide for some case, even an important one, within the national interest. The question would then arise whether in such an instance the new Congress, like the old, should supply the defect. Not having expressly raised the question, Publius did not furnish an answer.

Some readers of the *Federalist* may well have expected that, in such a case, Publius would not hesitate to invoke again the law of necessity and urge the government to do what had to be done in the public interest. If he did so, would he then argue that the power to act, though not expressed in the Necessary and Proper Clause or anywhere else in the Constitution, was nevertheless implied? If so, that would be a different kind of implied power. Unlike the supposed power implicit in the Necessary and Proper Clause, this newly found implied power would not be incidental to the effective operation of another enumerated power. It would be a power in its own right.

Or would Publius, disregarding what had been written in the *Federalist*, argue that the power to do what was in the public interest was implicit in the Necessary and Proper Clause? If so, that would be a different reading of "necessary and proper," whereby the language included more than a meaning of merely incidental powers. Far from reassuring a nervous opposition, then, the comments of Publius were more likely to have increased their concern.

The main charge advanced by opponents to ratification was that the Constitution would lead to the annihilation of state governments and the consolidation of power in the United States through an expansive construction of the Necessary and Proper Clause and the employment of the Supremacy Clause. A second charge held that by conferring excessive powers upon the president, the Constitution had enhanced his ability to corrupt Congress. The subsequent breakdown of the separation of powers, it was claimed, would lead to a monarchical system of government and endanger the liberties of the people.

In leveling the latter charge, those against ratification invoked a tradition of political opposition familiar to Americans through their reading of the writings of Viscount Bolingbroke, an English opposition leader in the eighteenth century, and his followers, writings that had strongly influenced American political thought and action during the Revolution.[31] Since Jefferson and Madison would make effective use of the tradition in their decade-long campaign against Federalist rule, and since the tradition itself would have a profound effect on their views as to the proper mode of constitutional construction and the early development of constitutional law, a brief review of its lineaments is warranted.

It was Bolingbroke's position that the crown through its ministers had formed an alliance with British monied interests whereby, through monopoly grants and taxation, the wealth of the country had been redistributed from those who made a living by honest work, especially from the land, in favor of "stock-jobbers," that is, those who lived off speculation in public debt.

To carry this out, Bolingbroke claimed, the crown systematically employed patronage to "corrupt" the legislative branch, and thereby induced it to adopt its schemes. Members were bought off with provisions enabling them to benefit directly from the legislation enacted, or with the offer of subsequent places or positions in the military or in the civil administration. In thus gaining control over Parliament, the crown mixed the powers of government rather than maintaining their strict separation. By these practices the crown maintained an aristocratic-monarchical control over the government. The creation of a standing army, interposed between an aroused citizenry and government, consolidated its power. According to Bolingbroke, those who fashioned this system constituted "the Court," their followers, "courtiers." Those in opposition, whose leadership lived off the land, were the "Country" party.[32]

At the Constitutional Convention, many of the delegates, especially Mason, Gerry, and Randolph, had sounded "Country" themes. Moved by fears of aristocratic-monarchical rule, Randolph had spoken against the idea of a single executive,[33]

Mason against a motion to award the president tenure;[34] both had been concerned over the aristocratic complexion of the Senate.[35] The fear of monopolies had troubled Gerry and Mason.[36] And the speculation of stock-jobbers in public debt had brought forth a fulmination from Mason.[37]

What bothered them most was the possibility of the executive's corrupting the legislature and eroding the separation of the powers of government. The small number of representatives in the initial composition of the House worried Gerry: It might afford the executive an easy opportunity for corruption. To prevent such conduct he favored annual elections.[38] Mason, Gerry, and Randolph all warned against the practice of creating "placemen": congressmen appointed by the executive to positions in the military or the administration.[39]

The corruption of Congress through foreign influence also concerned Gerry and Mason. They feared that the Senate, which Gerry regarded as too small, might utilize its treaty-making power to sell out the country.[40] And Mason wanted a sufficiently extended period of citizenship for membership in the House to prevent its infiltration with recent immigrants who might vote for policies favored by British merchants.[41]

During ratification, each of the three, in addition to his opposition to the Constitution on the basis of the Necessary and Proper Clause and the want of a bill of rights, assigned reasons grounded in the "Court versus Country" ideology. Mason was the most outspoken. The president, he contended, would become the tool of the Senate; the office of the vice-president violated the principle of the separation of powers; Congress had the power to create monopolies; and the government would in fact constitute an aristocracy and might produce a monarchy.[42]

Randolph's and Gerry's opposition was more moderate. Randolph noted, rather mildly, that, among other things, the president's powers were too broad and that the tenure of his office should be limited to a specified term.[43] Gerry, in opposition to Mason, thought the executive branch would have an undue influence over Congress.[44]

Others charged that the Constitution, in granting the president the status of commander in chief of the armed forces and the duty of receiving foreign ministers, had clothed him with royal prerogatives. Hamilton deprecated these charges. Writing in the *Federalist,* he stated that unlike a king the president could not raise or regulate an army but only command it. His reception of foreign ministers was "more a matter of dignity than of authority, . . . which will be without consequence in the administration of the government." The president, Hamilton assured his readers, was no king.[45]

Against this background of fears of consolidating tendencies in the federal government and of aristocratic-monarchical tendencies in the president and Senate, the delegates to the various state conventions assembled and conducted their deliberations.

The proposed Constitution had provided that ratification by a total of nine states would constitute its establishment among the states so ratifying.[46] Proponents of the

Constitution pushed to obtain the requisite number as quickly as possible, using Washington's support to secure speedy approval.[47] Within three months of the referral to Congress, Delaware and New Jersey, besides Pennsylvania, ratified. In another month Georgia and Connecticut followed.[48]

In all these states, various factors besides Washington's prestige overcame oppositional fears of consolidation and monarchy and secured rapid ratification. In Delaware, the decisive factor was the state's enhanced political status that would follow from the constitutional provision for equality of state representation in the Senate, irrespective of the size of a state's territory or population. In New Jersey, the same consideration along with relief from the payment of port duties to New York, from whose benefits the state was excluded, were the determining factors. Connecticut also ratified quickly because of relief from the payment of port duties to New York and because the Constitution was in many key respects the handiwork of its delegates, who had pressed for compromises over congressional representation and over the necessity for a two-thirds congressional majority for navigation acts. Georgia ratified quickly because, beset to the south by Spanish troops in the Floridas and to the west by hostile Indians, it needed the protection of a continental army. Pennsylvania ratified because of the superior organization of friends of the Constitution, large numbers of whom, holders of continental debt, looked to the new government for its redemption at par value.[49]

The first serious opposition appeared in Massachusetts, where the group of farmers who had supported Shays' Rebellion organized against ratification, assisted by other proponents of state paper money and by Maine settlers apprehensive about the chance for separate statehood under a changed government. But, as in Pennsylvania, the state's mercantile classes worked for the Constitution, and were ultimately successful, albeit only after agreeing to the submission to the new Congress of a list of recommended constitutional amendments. Maryland and South Carolina followed shortly, with similar influences at work in both states, and again with the supporters of the Constitution being far better organized than its opponents.[50]

Eight states had ratified. When the ninth, New Hampshire, followed, the new government would be established.[51] But ratification in the remaining states would not be quick and easy. As long as Virginia, the most populous state in the country and the leader of the South, did not ratify, North Carolina would not. If they held out, South Carolina and Georgia would probably reconsider. And since New York and Rhode Island, with their strategic harbors of New York City and Newport, were also holding out, the new government could not effectively operate.

In both Virginia and North Carolina, unlike South Carolina, many feared the subjection of their economies, almost entirely agricultural, to northern commercial influence and a subsequent decline in their political influence. In New York, the prospective loss of substantial import and export duties had led the state's administration into opposition. In Rhode Island, paper money enthusiasts controlled.[52]

Virginia held back for other reasons: the presence of a charismatic and resourceful leader, Patrick Henry, who was opposed to ratification, and fears peculiar to that state, which he successfully exploited. Contrary to the Treaty of Peace of 1783 with Great Britain, Virginia alone among the states had by legislation systematically blocked in state courts the collection of prewar debt its citizens owed to British creditors. Those Virginia debtors naturally opposed ratification of a constitution providing for federal jurisdiction in cases involving the application of treaties, and no one did so more fervently than the influential Henry.[53]

In addition, Kentucky settlers who had denied the legitimacy of claims by out-of-staters to lands in their part of what was still Virginia were against the constitutional grant of federal jurisdiction in cases involving persons of diverse or foreign citizenship. And both Kentuckians and Virginians who had speculated in western lands feared that the new government, under the control of New England and New York shipping and mercantile interests, would sacrifice to Spain their interest in an unimpeded use of the Mississippi down to and through New Orleans, in exchange for liberal trading rights with that country. Such a decision, besides its adverse effect upon the economy of Kentucky, would depreciate the value of their lands, causing substantial losses to many influential Virginians.[54]

At the same time, the Constitution, if adopted, would greatly reduce the influence of state government. Since Virginia was by far the largest and wealthiest of the thirteen states, this consideration was an especially important factor in that state's deliberations over ratification. By insuring to the United States an adequate revenue through a broad-based taxing power,[55] and by prohibiting the states from taxing either imports or exports[56]—theretofore the prime source of revenue for most states —it placed a practical ceiling on state operations. By giving Congress the power to regulate foreign and interstate commerce[57] and the currency,[58] and by prohibiting the states from issuing paper money[59] and from passing laws affecting the performance of contracts,[60] it placed off-limits significant areas of regulation.

Related to the reduction in state governmental power was the imminent loss of state control over members of Congress. Under the Articles of Confederation, the members of the Continental Congress were not the representatives of the people of their respective states but instead the agents or delegates of the state legislatures that appointed them. As agents, they were on short leash. They could serve no more than three in any period of six years and were subject at all times to state instructions and recall.[61]

Moreover, to insure that state governments maintained a tight control over policy, state legislatures saw to it that the power they delegated to their congressmen was extremely limited. Under the Articles, each state retained "its sovereignty, freedom and independence, and every Power, Jurisdiction, and right, which is not by this confederation expressly delegated to the United States, in Congress assembled."[62] And to insure that the United States was not to operate as a full-fledged government, the Articles made no provision for a chief executive officer to carry out the laws Congress enacted or for a judiciary to interpret and administer them. Instead, Congress conducted the government when in session and, when out, appointed congressional committees and other ministerial officers to do their work.[63] If the government of the United States was thereby rendered weak and inefficient, that was the states' intention.

The proposed Constitution would end the control of the state legislatures over the new government. State legislatures would not choose the members of the House of Representatives,[64] and while they would continue to choose the senators, a senator's term was long—six years—and he was not subject to recall.[65] Nor would the state legislatures participate in the election of the president.[66] And, critically, they would have no direct influence over the appointment of federal judges, who by their life tenure would be beyond the control of even the president or Congress.[67]

But while the factors mentioned—debtor fears, western lands, the desire for paper money, the loss of state tax revenues and legislative influence—all played a practical part in the spirited opposition to the new Constitution, theoretical opposition to ratification, in Virginia and elsewhere, concentrated on two specific arguments: the absence of a federal bill of rights, dangerous to the liberties of the people; and the grant to the federal government of broad, and therefore consolidating, powers dangerous to the sovereignty of the states, the self-styled protectors of the people. These consolidating powers were sometimes found to inhere in the new government's broad-based taxing power, sometimes within the taxing and spending clause in the provision to provide for the "general welfare," sometimes in the Supremacy Clause, but most often in the Necessary and Proper Clause, derisively referred to as the "sweeping clause."

By any standard, the debate in the state ratifying conventions over the meaning and implications of the Necessary and Proper Clause had the greatest political and constitutional effect on the operations of the new government. The meaning of the clause would determine whether the enumerated powers constituted limits upon the actions of the national government or whether they were merely specific examples of how the government might act in the general interests of the nation, in cases where the states either were incompetent to legislate on their own or where their legislative actions would disturb the harmony of the Union.

The resolution of this question would, after the Constitution was ratified and the new government organized, call forth countervailing theories of constitutional construction—Madison on one side, Hamilton on the other—in a contest for control of the government's operations and the determination of its policies. Political parties would emerge, their principal doctrines and destinies shaped by opposing views of the appropriate meaning of that clause. For Hamilton and the Federalists, "necessary and proper" would be a language of liberation for the new Congress; for Madison and Jefferson, it would be a phrase of almost complete restriction. Ultimately, Madison would rely for his understanding of the appropriate meaning of the language on the assurances and promises that the friends of the Constitution gave to those in opposition during the ratification campaign. What was said at that time regarding the scope of the Necessary and Proper Clause therefore had a most important bearing on the future course of political, constitutional, and governmental development.

The Virginia state convention began its debates early in June 1788. As expected, Henry led the opposition. In lengthy speeches he warned of the dangers to state and citizenry in the absence of a federal bill of rights; he spoke of the probable loss of western lands and navigation rights on the Mississippi; and he conjured up the evils arising from the exercise by the federal government of a wide-ranging taxing power and, not least of all, its employment of the "sweeping clause." Ignoring the assurances of Wilson in Pennsylvania and of Publius in the *Federalist,* he contended that the implications of the last clause were particularly ominous. "Implication is dangerous, because it is unbounded," he said. And he added, "Every implication should be done away."[68]

Unexpectedly, Randolph became the proponents' most effective spokesman. Defending the Constitution, he even supported the Necessary and Proper Clause, despite his earlier publicized reservations about it. In a statement which amounted to a paraphrase of the Wilson-Publius argument, he declared that "the sweeping clause . . . does not in the least increase the powers of Congress. It is only inserted for greater caution, and to prevent the possibility of encroaching upon the powers of Congress. No sophistry will be permitted to be used to explain away any of those powers—Nor can they possibly assume, any other power, but what is contained in the Constitution, without absolute usurpation."[69] When, immediately following Randolph, James Monroe supported Henry and opposed ratification of the Constitution because of, among other reasons, the Necessary and Proper Clause,[70] George Nicholas in defense spelled out in greater detail the Wilson-Publius line, which deemed the clause an incidental, albeit, redundant power:

[I]T WILL BE PERCEIVED] that the Constitution had enumerated all the powers which the General Government should have; but did not say how they were to be exercised. It therefore in this clause tells *how* they shall be exercised. Does this give any new power? I say not. Suppose it had been inserted at the end of every power, that they should have power to make laws to carry that power into execution: Would this have increased their powers? If, therefore, it could not have increased their powers, if placed at the end of each power, it cannot increase them at the end of all. This clause only enables them to carry into execution the powers given to them, but gives them no additional power.[71]

The opposition, however, was not reassured. The indefinite nature of the clause, amplified by Mason's estimate of the intentions of his fellow delegates to the Constitutional Convention, was sufficiently disturbing to the opponents of ratification to cause them to reintroduce the subject toward the close of the convention. The vehicle was a discussion of the clause empowering Congress to "exercise exclusive Legislation in all Cases whatsoever, over such District (not exceeding ten Miles square) as may, by Cession of particular States, and the Acceptance of Congress, become the Seat of the Government of the United States."[72]

Discussion of this clause gave Henry the opportunity to make use of his oratorical skills to instill fear in the hearts of the assembled. In his customary vivid style, he pictured all kinds of horrors taking place within the territory: A man, for instance, could be hanged there without the benefit of clergy. When taken in conjunction with the implications of the sweeping powers of the Necessary and Proper Clause, he added, the new congress, bent on tyranny, might keep a standing army there, as within a stronghold, ready to spring upon the states. In fact, he threw in for good measure, they might achieve the same result, even without the provision for a federal district, through the operations of the sweeping clause alone.[73]

We can only speculate on the effect of Henry's oratory, but in any case Madison, who was in effect the proponents' leading spokesman, immediately rose to reply. In defense of the District Clause, he claimed that no legislature in existence had ever held its sessions at a place over which it did not exercise control.[74] As for the Necessary and Proper Clause, he repeated the line that Randolph and Nicholas had already advanced:

[THE NECESSARY AND PROPER CLAUSE] is only a superfluity. If that latitude of construction which he [Henry] contends for, were to take place with respect to the sweeping clause, there would be room for those horrors. But it gives no supplementary power: It only enables them to execute the delegated powers. If the delegation of their powers be safe, no possible inconvenience can arise from this clause. It is at most but explanatory: For when any power is given, its delegation necessarily involves authority to make laws to execute it.—Were it possible to delineate on paper, all those particular cases and circumstances in which legislation by the General Legislature would be necessary, and leave to the States all the other powers, I imagine no Gentleman would object to it. But this is not within the limits of human capacity.—The particular powers which are found necessary to be given, are therefore delegated generally, and particular and minute specification is left to the Legislature.[75]

Mason came to Henry's support and injected a new reason for fear. Together with the sweeping clause, he seized upon the indefinite character of the phrase "general welfare" in Article I, Section 8, Clause 1, wherein Congress would have the power "to lay and collect Taxes, Duties, Imposts, and Excises, to pay the Debts and provide for the common Defence and general Welfare." Suggesting a situation remarkably prophetic of the circumstances that would enfold in the United States in 1798, he said:

NOW SUPPOSE OPPRESSIONS SHOULD ARISE under this Government, and any writer should dare to stand forth and expose to the community at large, the abuses of those powers. Could not Congress, under the idea of providing for the general welfare, and under their own construction, say, that this was destroying the general peace, encouraging sedition, and poisoning the minds of the people? And could they not, in order to provide against this, lay a dangerous restriction on the press? Might they not even bring the trial of this restriction within the ten miles square, when there is no prohibition against it? Might they not thus destroy the trial by jury?[76]

In this short argument, Mason had incorporated most of his usual reasons for rejecting the Constitution: the absence of a bill of rights protecting freedom of speech, freedom of the press, and trial by jury; and the dangerous and indefinite nature of the powers of Congress, particularly under the Necessary and Proper Clause and the term "general welfare."[77]

He was not far amiss in his remarks. In 1798 the Federalists, over the objection of the Jefferson-led Republicans, in a broad construction of their powers under the Necessary and Proper Clause did enact such a sedition law on the ground that certain speech and writings, critical of governmental policies and personnel, destroyed the general peace, encouraged sedition, and poisoned the minds of the people. What Mason did not foresee was that the Federalists would do so in spite of a constitutional provision for freedom of speech and the press, and not in its absence.[78]

Having roused his supporters, Mason concluded his argument by a call for specific language, later memorialized in the Tenth Amendment to the Constitution, that all powers not granted to the United States were retained in the states.[79] In defense, Nicholas answered that the phrase "general welfare" "was united, not to the general power of legislation, but to the particular power of laying and collecting taxes, imposts, and excises, for the purposes of paying the debts and providing for the common defence."[80] In that reading, the payment of debts would exhaust the meaning of "general welfare."

Randolph as usual complicated rather than simplified matters. Apparently oblivious of what he had said earlier in the convention in defense of the Necessary and Proper Clause—that it had been inserted with a cautionary purpose, lest the enumerated powers of Congress be diminished[81]—he began by saying that he himself had some objections to the clause. Then after a rambling review of the entire Constitution and a refutation of the objections raised to its many provisions, he criticized the opponents' construction of the clause as mistaken and extravagant. While the constructions put upon the clause by both sides were, he said, erroneous, some construction was better than anarchy.[82]

Randolph set forth his own understanding. First he dismissed as too narrow the construction put forth by the friends of ratification in arguing that the clause involved only incidental powers, that is, powers necessary for the implementation of the enumerated powers. This, he concluded, would render the language superfluous. Then, in a rare burst of candor unusual for this careful and consummate politician, Randolph spoke his mind: "My objection is, that the clause is ambiguous, and that that ambiguity may injure the States. My fear is, that it will by gradual accessions gather to a dangerous length. This is my apprehension, and I disdain to disown it."[83] His solution was that they should take the Constitution as proposed and amend it, the only question in his mind being whether they should amend it before or after ratification. The alternative, he declared, was anarchy and confusion.[84]

Presumably neither side liked what he said. Proponents disliked Randolph's opinion because it both admitted the essentials of the Mason-Henry line, that the clause would be a handy device for a gradual increase in the powers of the new government, and dismissed as preposterous their own carefully laid line that the clause meant little or nothing. Nor did they like his solution. They wanted the Constitution approved—certainly without preconditional amendments, which Madison regarded as destructive to ratification, and with the least number of post-recommendatory amendments possible. Opponents might have liked the analysis, but they did not like the solution. Rejection pure and simple was their goal.

Perhaps there was a hint later of Randolph's belated concession in a speech Mason gave, in which he charged that there were "many Gentlemen in the United States who think it right, that we should have one great national consolidated Government, and that it was better to bring it about slowly and imperceptibly, rather than all at once." Whereupon Madison, concerned that by these insinuations Mason might create a belief that everyone at the Constitutional Convention, including himself, was of that opinion, demanded of him that he name the persons to whom he alluded. Mason declined. But persisting in his previous statement that such had been the opinion of many at that convention, he absolved Madison and everyone in the Virginia delegation. The subject was closed.[85]

As the end of convention drew near, those opposed to ratification shifted their tactics. Up to that point they had stirred the convention with their charges that the Constitution, by virtue of the sweeping clause and the power to provide for the general welfare, had created a consolidated government dangerous to the liberties of the people. Now they appealed to a different, perhaps more immediate, fear, that of the danger to their personal safety and their property interests resulting from the abolition of slavery.[86] Henry and Mason charged that Congress, pursuant to its taxing power, might levy such an onerous excise on slaves as would result in their manumission. Madison eventually admitted that this was possible, but argued that since four other states were greatly interested in slave ownership and three northern states tolerated slavery, the imposition of such a tax was unlikely.[87]

Then, following a motion for ratification, Henry again adverted to the dangers to slavery from the adoption of the Constitution. In time of war, he charged, Congress under the provision for the common defense and general welfare could free all slaves who joined the military to fight. Such an act, he warned, would put an end to Virginia's peace and tranquility. To forestall that eventuality, he said, he proposed a second resolution in which he set forth a series of amendments to the Constitution for the convention's approval, and for subsequent transmittal to the other states in the confederacy prior to ratification. The first of these amendments, similar to one offered by the dissenters to the Pennsylvania convention, and patterned on the provision in the Articles of Confederation concerning congressional powers, declared that the states would retain all powers "not by this Constitution expressly delegated to the Congress of the United States."[88]

Randolph undertook the first reply to Henry's speech. To the statement that Congress could emancipate the slaves under the provisions in Article I, Section 8, Clause 1, for the common defense and general welfare, Randolph repeated Nicholas's earlier explanation of the general welfare language—that it was not a regulatory power, but, as part of the Taxing Clause, it constituted a purpose for which taxes could be laid and collected. Madison, following Randolph, said that the congressional action Henry conjured was completely unjustified under the Constitution and would amount to a usurpation of power. Furthermore, Madison added, since such an act would alienate five-thirteenths of the Union, he considered its adoption incredible.[89]

Randolph termed the first of Henry's proposed amendments impractical. The Continental Congress, he explained, had been deterred from issuing passports during the Revolutionary War because of the "expressly delegated" provision in the Articles of Confederation, even though the power to do so had been a necessary means of carrying on the war.[90] What Randolph seemed to suggest was that had the Articles contained a Necessary and Proper Clause, Congress, under the Madison-Nicholas interpretation, could have issued the passports. The adoption of the Henry amendment therefore would amount to a repudiation of that interpretation and render the Necessary and Proper Clause totally meaningless.

Madison regarded the reservation of enumerated rights, which Mason and Henry had attached to the amendment, as dangerous: "If an enumeration be made of our rights, will it not be implied, that every thing omitted, is given to the General Government? . . . Does it follow from the omission of such restrictions [on the exercise of government power], that they can exercise powers not delegated? The reverse of the proposition holds."[91]

Henry replied. In a highly emotional declamation—which appropriately ended in a violent thunderstorm—he defended his proposed amendment. The power to emancipate the slaves, he said, would be implied unless implication was prohibited.[92]

Finally, the convention was ready for a vote, first on Henry's motion, that a declaration of rights along with other recommendatory amendments to the Constitution "be referred . . . to the other States in the American confederacy for their consideration." This was seconded by Theodorick Bland, a future colleague of Madison's in the House of Representatives in the First Congress of the United States. The motion was defeated by a margin of eight votes, eighty-eight to eighty.

Then the convention, by a margin of ten votes, approved a motion to ratify the Constitution, along with a resolution authorizing the preparation of a series of recommendatory constitutional amendments for consideration for adoption by the First Congress pursuant to the procedures set forth in Article V of the Constitution. James Monroe and William Grayson, future United States senators in the First Congress, voted with Henry on both motions.[93]

Virginia had ratified. In the end, despite the fiery oratory and fine argumentation, Washington's firm support for the Constitution and the prospect that he would become the first president of the United States had proved decisive in the Virginia convention, as it had elsewhere.[94] But the spirited attacks on the sweeping clause, the repeated intimations that the Constitution somehow threatened the maintenance of slavery, and the narrow margin of approval vindicated the judgment of Madison and Randolph during the Constitutional Convention: Unless the large states could control both branches of Congress, Virginia would not approve a provision that would allow the Congress to legislate in matters of general concern to the country.

But what were the powers of the new Congress and the new president? What was the meaning of the Necessary and Proper Clause and the provision for spending for the general welfare in Article I, Section 8? Had the state ratifying conventions determined anything besides the basic question of approving the Constitution and the organization of the new government? Had their deliberations fixed the meaning of those indefinite clauses? Did "necessary and proper" mean that Congress had only incidental powers—the powers Wilson, Madison, and Nicholas in debate and Publius in the *Federalist* had attributed to it? Or did the language mean more, as Henry and Mason had argued? In ratifying the Constitution, the Virginia convention seemed to be rejecting the Henry-Mason arguments and accepting the view that the Necessary and Proper Clause included only incidental powers. That was the explanation Randolph offered in his passport example during the debate over Henry's amendment.

Henry and Mason might have been better served if they had first proposed a more restrictive amendment whereby they would have made the Randolph interpretation explicit. In place of the ambiguous Necessary and Proper Clause, they could have proposed that the Constitution read as follows: "To make all laws incidental to the execution of the powers enumerated in this section and all other powers vested by this Constitution in the government of the United States, or in any department or officer thereof."

Such a measure would have incorporated the Wilson-Nicholas-Madison-Publius version of "necessary and proper," while at the same time, by removing those enigmatic words, ridding the Constitution of any "sweeping" implications. The measure would have carried into effect the motion Pierce Butler had wanted to make in the Constitutional Convention, but didn't,[95] and would have pinned the Federalists down to a doctrine of incidental, that is, ancillary, implication.

If that motion carried, Henry and Mason then could have followed it with their proposal that the states would retain all powers not expressly delegated. Since by the adoption of the first proposed amendment all merely incidental powers would be expressly delegated, the second would have the effect of prohibiting the delegation of more than incidentally implied powers.

The motion they had offered, however, was overbroad. Their failure to narrow it allowed those controlling the convention to reshape it by deleting the word "expressly" and substitute instead the following language, the forerunner of the present Tenth Amendment: "1st. That each State in the Union shall respectively retain every power, jurisdiction, and right, which is not by this Constitution delegated to the Congress of the United States, or to the departments of the Federal Government."[96]

Undoubtedly the recommended amendment meant to authorize the assertion of those incidental powers that in the convention Madison and Nicholas had said were subsumed in the Necessary and Proper Clause. But the amendment also left the Constitution open to the assertion that other, more than incidental, powers were also implicit in the text. That this was Madison's intention would become clear during the debate in the First Congress over the phraseology of what eventually became the Tenth Amendment. He would then propose that "the powers not delegated to the United States by the Constitution, not prohibited by it to the States, are reserved in the States respectively, or to the people." But on the basis of what had transpired in the Virginia ratifying convention, he would successfully oppose a motion to insert in the text of that amendment the word "expressly" before the word "delegated."[97]

While committing himself to a narrow construction of the Necessary and Proper Clause, Madison wanted to be free to argue the existence of important, albeit implicit, powers elsewhere in the Constitution. Thus, in the first session of the First Congress, he would argue for a presidential power to remove important executive officers, a power he found implicit in the general provisions of Article II.

Moreover, to have proposed to the Virginia convention, and subsequently to the First Congress, a constitutional amendment that would have foreclosed the argument—namely, that the powers implicit in the Necessary and Proper Clause were more than merely incidental to the execution of the enumerated powers—would have undone the compromise regarding the scope of congressional power crafted in the Committee of Detail and approved by the Constitutional Convention. Madison could not have done this.

The consent of Virginia, the leading southern state, proved crucial. With Virginia committed, the state of New York, faced with the prospect of a commercial blockade by the new Union and of a secession by the city of New York with its commercially valuable port, also capitulated. The new government began to organize. Only North Carolina and Rhode Island continued to hold out: the former, in league with Henry and hoping that that resourceful politician might yet wreck the new government; the latter, intent on its own independence and on the retention of its paper money and seaport duties for as long as possible.[98]

Eventually, as will be discussed in the next chapter, Henry's outright opposition to the Constitution proved fruitless and North Carolina belatedly ratified.[99] A few months later, Rhode Island, confronted with an actual threat of a commercial boycott by the new Congress, reluctantly followed.[100] In the meantime, without North Carolina or Rhode Island, the other eleven states were ready to organize the new government of the United States under the Constitution with a bicameral Congress and a president.

Virginia Interests: Madison's Shifting Canons (First Congress, First Session, 1789)

After ratification, Henry continued to work against the Constitution and to limit the powers of the new government. Quickly he gave notice that anyone supporting the Constitution was likely to enjoy an early retirement from public life. His primary target was Madison. Using his influence in the Virginia legislature, Henry blocked Madison's appointment to the United States Senate and instead obtained senatorial positions for Richard Henry Lee and Grayson, ardent opponents of ratification. And, in an endeavor to keep Madison out of Congress entirely, Henry stirred up Baptist sentiment against him in his congressional district, on the ground that as a strong supporter of a Constitution containing no provision against an established church and for the free exercise of religion, Madison was no supporter of religious liberties. Henry then prevailed upon Monroe, a strong candidate and opponent of ratification, to stand against Madison. Monroe, Lee, and Grayson could all be counted on to work conscientiously to limit the powers of the new government.[1]

Madison, however, foiled Henry's strategy as it applied to his own immediate political future. His long-standing support in the state legislature for religious freedom and disestablishment enabled him to convince the Baptists that he was indeed their true friend and would, if elected, work in the First Congress for a bill of rights through amendments to the Constitution. On his record and with those promises, he was elected.[2] Henry maintained his opposition to Madison. When during the first session of the First Congress Grayson died, the Virginia legislature, still operating under Henry's influence, appointed Monroe in Grayson's place.[3]

In addition to his maneuvers to reward those who had voted against ratification and punish those who had voted for it, Henry also took measures to limit the powers of the new government under the Constitution by pursuing a suggestion that had emanated from the New York State ratifying convention. John Jay and Hamilton, in order to win ratification, had there proposed circulating among the states a letter calling for a second constitutional convention to consider the adoption of the constitutional amendments recommended by the New York convention. Those amendments, thirty-two in number, repeated many already recommended by the Massachusetts and Virginia conventions. On this understanding New York had ratified, and thereafter Governor George Clinton of New York had circulated the letter.[4]

A Preliminary Skirmish

Henry, in response, persuaded the Virginia legislature to adopt a resolution requesting the First Congress, when it met, to call for the second convention to consider the amendments the state conventions had previously recommended. Theodorick Bland of the Virginia congressional delegation was primed to present the resolution to Congress in its first session in New York City.[5]

When Congress convened, however, Madison, outmaneuvering Bland, once again foiled Henry's strategy. Moving in the House before Bland did, Madison obtained an order assigning a day later in the session for consideration of a series of constitutional amendments for adoption and referral to the states.[6] His subsequent campaign for the adoption of what later came to be known as the Bill of Rights would remove from controversy the question whether the Constitution had given adequate protection to basic liberties. While its adoption did not put an end to fears regarding the federal government, it did deprive opponents of their most effective issue: the protection of civil liberties.

The business of organizing the new government, however, necessarily took immediate priority over the adoption of the Bill of Rights. While Madison was thus delayed in achieving his objectives, Henry met with even less success in the new Congress. His goal of eliminating implication and confining the government to expressly delegated powers found little support. On the contrary, government by implication soon became the modus operandi. Ironically, in the first item of organizational business, it was Henry's principal agent, Theodorick Bland, who led the way toward construction of the Constitution by implication.

The matter for consideration was a bill prescribing the official oath of office to be taken by members of Congress and executive officers of the United States to support the Constitution, as required in Article VI, Clause 3. Madison, objecting to an amendment by Richard Bland Lee of Virginia that would have required state legislators to take the same oath,[7] raised the question of congressional power to do this. He doubted the power, he said, and added he was not persuaded that the Constitution had placed any such obligation on the states. He admitted that in this view, "the Constitution may be chargeable with . . . [a] defect." But, he concluded, Congress had "no right to supply it . . . [and] it follows that [they had] no right to carry [this amendment] into execution."[8] In case of doubt, he seemed to be saying, deny the power.

Madison's position was consistent with that which he had taken in the Virginia convention: The powers of Congress were limited to those specifically enumerated in the Constitution, and the Necessary and Proper Clause conferred only such powers as were incidental to the execution of the enumerated powers. His position was also consistent with those he would take later in the First Congress and thereafter.

Of course, he could have remained silent. The matter was comparatively unimportant. But out of concern for his state's and his region's long-range interests, he may have deemed it advisable to quickly put his fellow congressmen on notice as to the limits of their power. Moreover, he may have felt that, as slight a matter as it was, a federal statute imposing the form of oath on state legislators might not sit well in Virginia. And having just waged a difficult campaign for election to Congress, he may have been unwilling to allow the proposal to pass unchallenged.

Perhaps alluding to Virginian sensibilities, he gave an additional reason for opposing the amendment: the requirement was not expedient. Others, including Alexander White of Virginia, agreed. The amendment was defeated, and the bill was passed without reference to any requirement for state officials.[9]

In the Senate, however, the debate was renewed under a proposal requiring not only state legislators but all state executive and judicial officers to take the prescribed oath within a specified period.[10] Senator William Maclay of Pennsylvania, doubting both the power and the expediency of requiring the oath, repeated Madison's argument. But although Senators Richard Henry Lee of Virginia and Oliver Ellsworth of Connecticut agreed with him,[11] the amendment carried. The bill as amended passed and was returned to the House.[12]

There, Elbridge Gerry of Massachusetts repeated Maclay's objection to the Senate's amendment. The power, he said ironically, must originate, if anywhere, in the sweeping clause, that is, the Necessary and Proper Clause. The use of that power to justify the bill, he added, reminded him of the prophecy made during ratification that persons in the new government would make use of the clause to do as they pleased. Gerry modestly omitted mentioning that he, among others, had made that charge.[13]

Surprisingly, it was Henry's man, Theodorick Bland, who came to the amendment's rescue. Not only did he say that the power to adopt it was implied in the Constitution and that it was expedient for Congress to do so, but, astonishingly, he invoked in its support the argument of its necessity: "If the state legislatures were to be left to arrange and direct this business, they would pass different laws, and the officers might be bound in different degrees to support the Constitution."[14]

In essence, Bland's reasoning was an echo of the proposition that Gunning Bedford had advanced in the Constitutional Convention and that Edmund Randolph, on behalf of the Virginia delegation, had opposed: Congress shall have the power "to legislate in all cases for the general interests of the Union, and also in those to which the States are separately incompetent, or in which the harmony of the United States may be interrupted by the exercise of individual legislation."[15]

It is hard to understand why Bland made such a statement. He had been present at the Virginia convention and, along with Henry, had opposed ratification and joined in the fight against the doctrine of powers implicit in the Necessary and Proper Clause or anywhere else in the Constitution. And he had come to Congress under orders from the Virginia legislature to propose a call for a second constitutional convention for the purpose of securing assurances against the assertion of implied powers.[16]

Now, just days after Madison spoke against House power to adopt such a proposition, Bland was saying that despite the lack of an enumerated power, Congress could pass a uniform law since it was a case in which the states were not competent to act. Was Bland trying to entrap Madison into making a similar statement? If he was, Madison, who certainly realized the implications of Bland's argument, remained silent. Support had to come from elsewhere, and it did.

On Bland's side and in direct contradiction of Gerry, John Laurance of New York found a basis for the amendment in the much belabored Necessary and Proper Clause, arguing it was necessary and proper that Congress carry into execution the oath required in Article VI of the Constitution. Roger Sherman of Connecticut, who had earlier opposed Representative Richard Bland Lee's amendment, changed his position and supported the Senate amendment on the same ground that Theodorick Bland had urged: A uniform law to establish the form of the oath and the time and manner of its taking was necessary, and "no other legislature [than Congress] is competent to all these purposes." When Elias Boudinot of New Jersey pointed out that Richard Bland Lee's amendment had provided for a penalty, while the Senate's amendment did not, he saved the House from inconsistency. The amendment and the bill were approved handily.[17]

The debate was a skirmish. But by its approval, Congress—if first hindered by the less than helpful doubts of James Madison, then saved by the unexpected support of Theodorick Bland—signaled that it intended to adopt legislation required for the swift implementation of the Constitution, notwithstanding the difficulties concerning its authority under the enumerated powers.

Maclay and Gerry in their respective houses, however, had given notice that, jealous of state power and on the alert for any unwarranted extension of national power, they had not abandoned the cause of a limited construction of the Necessary and Proper Clause. For a time their cause was without prestigious leadership. The matter at issue was not substantial enough to arouse public opinion or to affect vital state and regional interests. But it was a cause awaiting the right issue, and Madison had given notice that under appropriate circumstances he might serve as its champion.

The Removal Bill and Broad Construction

A far more important controversy regarding the use of implied powers arose in the House during debate of a bill to establish the Department of Foreign Affairs and, within it, the office of secretary of foreign affairs. The controversy centered on a provision in a bill to invest the president with the power to remove the secretary without the consent of the Senate. This time, just as he had in the later stages of the Constitutional Convention, Madison maneuvered to increase the powers of the presidency, doing so on the principle of efficient administration and sound governmental practice.[18] Forgetting his doubts concerning the use of implied power to justify the imposition of a standard oath on state officials, he took the lead in positing an implied presidential power of removal.

As was well known in Congress, Madison's advocacy of an extended executive power was more than a matter of principle. He was at the time the president's private counselor, his prime confidant, if not his prime minister, advising him on a wide range of appointments and helping him in the draft of his inaugural address and other papers. Madison's stand could only be interpreted to mean that Washington wanted the removal power.[19]

Nevertheless, despite Madison's backing and despite the appearance that the very popular president wanted it, the opposition, sounding the theme of "Country versus Court," characterized both the bill and the supporting arguments as dangerous. James Jackson of Georgia deemed that any ensuing governmental good would be more than outweighed by the probable resulting danger to liberty. The power to dismiss officers, he said, was based on European practice, where it flourished under the monarchical principle of divine right.[20]

John Page of Virginia, reflecting the Mason-Henry line, charged that the bill contained the seeds of royal prerogative, and conjured up images of unbridled regal tyranny. He declaimed, "[The plea for energy in government] has led many patriots to the Bastille, to the block, and to the halter. If the chief magistrate can take a man away from the head of a department without assigning any reason, he may as well be invested with power, on certain occasions, to take away his existence."[21]

Later, in the Senate, Maclay played on the same theme, if on a somewhat more subdued note, declaring that the measure would lead to dependence in office and an abject servility among officeholders, unfailingly productive of despotism and tyranny. Richard Henry Lee and Grayson also opposed it, Grayson exclaiming that Henry's prediction had come to pass: Consolidation, he had foretold, was the object of the new government, and the destruction of the Senate, as the representative of the state legislatures, its first business. By placing in the president instead of in the Senate the power to remove officers, the bill, in Grayson's view, represented the initial step toward the accomplishment of this first business. Others called the bill a step toward the establishment of an aristocracy surmounted by Washington as its de facto monarch.[22]

The issue of the competing prerogatives of the president and the Senate provoked the first major constitutional debate. Those opposed to the bill asserted that the constitutional provisions governing impeachment and the appointment of superior executive officers invalidated it. They also questioned the authority of Congress to pass such legislation.

Representative William Loughton Smith of South Carolina opened the debate by suggesting that since the only method which the Constitution had provided for removing officers was by impeachment, a person must remain in office until convicted through that process. Jackson agreed.[23]

The suggestion was quickly dismissed as untenable. Madison pointed to the consequence of Smith's position: Even subordinate officers would have tenure during good behavior and could be removed only for cause. Others said that impeachment was an extraordinary remedy, intended as a punishment for a crime, and to be used only in cases where the president failed to remove an officer charged with a serious offense. It was not meant to apply to cases of ordinary misconduct because the impeachment process was too cumbersome, and would necessitate the Senate's sitting in continuous session, engaging in protracted trials.[24]

Later, White presented a more serious challenge to the bill when he argued that the provision conferring upon the president the sole power of removing the secretary of foreign affairs was contrary to the requirements of Article II, Section 2, Clause 2, of the Constitution. The secretary as a department head, he declared, was not "an inferior officer," whose appointment, pursuant to that provision, Congress could by law "vest . . . in the President alone." Rather, he was "an officer of the United States," whose appointment required "the Advice and Consent of the Senate." Because the power to remove must, by implication, reside in whoever had the power to appoint, White concluded, the Senate must share in the removal.[25]

Smith, perhaps convinced that his argument for impeachment as constituting the sole method for an officer's removal could not gain sufficient backing, supported White. He read from an essay by Hamilton in the *Federalist,* in which the latter had extolled the merits of Senate participation in the removal of executive officers:

IT HAS BEEN MENTIONED AS ONE OF the advantages to be expected from the co-operation of the senate, in the business of appointments, that it would contribute to the stability of the administration. The consent of that body would be necessary to displace as well as to appoint. A change of the chief magistrate therefore would not occasion so violent or so general a revolution in the officers of the government, as might be expected if he were the sole disposer of offices. Where a man in any station had given satisfactory evidence of his fitness for it, a new president would be restrained from attempting a change, in favour of a person more agreeable to him, by the apprehension that the discountenance of the senate might frustrate the attempt, and bring some degree of discredit upon himself. Those who can best estimate the value of a steady administration will be most disposed to prize a provision, which connects the official existence of public men with the approbation or disapprobation of that body, which from the greater permanency of its own composition, will in all probability be less subject to inconstancy, than any other member of the government.[26]

The position taken by White and Smith was not grounded in strict construction because, as all would shortly acknowledge, the Constitution had not expressly addressed the issue. Rather, it rested on the supposedly inherent purpose of a specific provision in Article II, which they, according to the custom of common law lawyers, inferred from the letter of the text and supported with the authority of the *Federalist*.

But it was an argument of more limited range than the one Madison was to present. Madison, ignoring the supposed purpose underlying the specific provision of Article II requiring advice and consent for certain appointments, divined in the entire article an overriding intent to vest executive power exclusively in the president. Such a vesting, he reasoned, was evidence of a broader constitutional principle, the separation of the powers of the federal government among its various branches: the legislative, in Article I; the executive, in Article II; and the judicial, in Article III.[27]

Since the removal of an executive officer was an exercise of executive power, Madison reasoned, it could not be shared with the legislature. And since the provision for senatorial participation in the appointment of certain executive officers was a specific exception to the principle of the exclusive vestment of executive power in the president, he reasoned further, it should be narrowly construed and not extended. If the practice were otherwise, he contended, it would lead to bad government—to the continuation in office of incompetent, insubordinate, or perhaps even corrupt persons, whom the president could not convince the Senate to remove or whom members of the Senate, for their own reasons of intrigue, might wish to retain in office, against the best interests of the country.[28]

Gerry, in response to Madison, denied his premise that the powers of appointment and removal were inherently executive, a premise, he said, that could not have been deduced from any American precedent. It was contrary to the practice of the states, where in many cases the legislatures made executive appointments.[29]

Samuel Livermore of New Hampshire, jealous of the prerogatives of the smaller states whose influence in the Senate was much greater than in the House, and concerned that the logic of Madison's position would exclude senatorial participation in the termination of treaties, supported Gerry. Just as the provisions of Article II, Section 2, Clause 2, required the consent of the Senate to the appointment of superior officers, he said, so they also required its consent to treaties. If, therefore, senatorial consent were not needed for an officer's removal, it would not be needed for the termination of a treaty.[30]

A few years later, Hamilton would be happy to accept the logic of Livermore's position, although not in the manner the latter had envisioned, and would argue under Article II for the sole presidential power to terminate a treaty, and against the authority of the Senate to participate in that decision. By that time, Madison, no longer the supporter of broad presidential powers, would adopt Livermore's position and distinguish his own argument favoring an exclusive presidential power of removal.[31]

The constitutional arguments pro and con the bill's provision for the removal of a superior officer of the United States offset one another. None was conclusive, for the simple reason that the Constitution had not expressly provided for such a removal, except by impeachment under Article II, Section 4. And yet, as Fisher Ames of Massachusetts said, hardly anyone accepted the view that in the ordinary case impeachment was the proper remedy. Generally, it was agreed, removal was.[32] The question, he asked, was by whom?[33]

In the search for an answer to that question, a second more fundamental inquiry emerged: Was Congress competent to supply the answer? Early in the debate, Madison had said that Congress could declare in favor of a presidential power of removal. Since it could establish offices by law, he concluded, it had the discretion to state the terms on which an office should be held—whether during good behavior or at the pleasure of the president.[34]

Those opposing the bill, however, believed that Madison had overstated the extent of congressional power. While under the provisions of Article II, Section 2, Clause 2, Congress did have such discretion with regard to the creation of inferior offices, it did not have it with regard to the creation of a superior office, such as the secretary of foreign affairs. Under that provision and in that case, the opposition maintained, senatorial advice and consent was required for both the appointment and removal.

Probably in recognition of that contention, Madison restated his own position later in the debate. Rather than saying forthrightly that Congress had the power to settle the question and that it was proper for it to do so, he equivocated and said it was not improper for Congress to do so: "There was no impropriety in the legislature settling this question. It could affect none of the principles of the constitution. If the clause [providing that the president might remove the secretary of foreign affairs] was nothing more than a declaration of the constitution, it could do no harm; if it related to a doubtful part, an explanation would come more properly from the whole legislature, than any branch; and if the constitution was totally silent, Congress might use its discretion."[35] Madison did not specify the power that gave Congress the discretion. Nor did he do so when in concluding he said, "But if it [the clause under discussion] was a doubtful point, it was properly the duty of the legislature to examine and decide upon it."

Smith promptly challenged him. The construction of the Constitution, he said, was for the judiciary, not Congress.[36] Disagreeing with Smith, Ames restated Madison's thought more directly: "The power of removal is incident to government; but not being distributed by the constitution, it will come before the legislature, and, like every other omitted case, must be supplied by law."[37] Ames, however, also failed to mention the power pursuant to which Congress could supply the deficiencies of the Constitution. There seemed to be a constitutional vacuum.

Endorsing the substance of the Madison-Ames arguments, but perhaps desirous of filling the vacuum, Thomas Hartley of Pennsylvania the next day adopted the previous position of the House in passing the bill for a uniform state oath: If it was an omitted case, Congress could act under the Necessary and Proper Clause.[38]

Laurance, following Hartley, said that if it was an omitted case, the people would want Congress to supply the omission, and the judges would support Congress unless it was wrong. Since Congress had the power to establish offices, it could under the Necessary and Proper Clause adopt such measures as were required to carry into effect the general powers of the president.[39]

Madison, however, seeking to distance himself from Hartley and Laurance, retracted what he had said earlier. Conceding that a construction of the Constitution which postulated "that the power of displacing from office is subject to a legislative discretion . . . [was a]t first sight . . . considerably plausible," he now held that the presidential power of removing officers was required by the true meaning of Article II. The consequence of admitting a congressional discretion to vest the power in the president, he maintained, would have dire consequences: Congress could also divest him of the power and give it to the Senate or to the Senate and the House. Such a course would lead to intrigue and executive irresponsibility.[40]

Yet, because he needed Hartley, Laurance, and those who agreed with them, Madison labored to accommodate their views. Conceding that "this is perhaps an omitted case," he urged the House to approve a declaration that the president had the removal power. In this way, he repeated, Congress would state its sense of the Constitution, a statement which, he predicted, would then become the permanent construction of the Constitution.[41]

Meeting Smith's criticism, Madison conceded that the ordinary exposition of the Constitution was for the judiciary. But, he added, this did not mean that, where pertinent, the other departments should not declare their sentiments. In fact, since the subject before them bore on the powers of the respective branches of the government, those branches should determine it. Once again, however, he did not cite the power pursuant to which Congress could make such a declaration.[42]

It escaped comment that earlier in the session Madison had been against the provision imposing a uniform requirement on state officials to take the oath supporting the Constitution because, he had said, he doubted the Constitution had provided for it, and that if this was a constitutional defect, he doubted Congress had the power to supply it.[43]

But Gerry, commenting on Madison's position in the present debate, did cut through the latter's elaborate phraseology to say that if it was an omitted case, any congressional attempt to supply the omission would constitute an attempt to amend the Constitution in derogation of Article V, respecting the procedures for the effectuation of constitutional amendments.

The constitutional system, Gerry conceded, was undeniably obscure. During the ratification process, he added, "[it had] been a strong objection to the constitution, that it was remarkably obscure; nay, some have gone so far as to assert, that it was studiously obscure, that it might be applied to every purpose by congress." If Congress could explain what the Constitution meant in that case, Congress could make the Constitution say whatever it pleased in any other case. This, he concluded, would only confirm the suspicions of those who had opposed ratification.[44]

Smith, following Gerry, declared that all the arguments the bill's supporters had advanced for a sole presidential power of removal showed only what the Constitution ought to have said, not what it did say. Since the president's power of removal had not been included in the Constitution, he added, it could be inferred that the framers "never intended to give it to [the president]."[45]

John Vining of Delaware, responding to Gerry and Smith, summarized the arguments for the bill: Since the Constitution did not say that the president did not have the sole power of removal, and since it did provide for a separation of powers, the president either had the power as an incident to the executive power—the Madison view—or Congress could give it to him under the Necessary and Proper Clause— the Hartley-Laurance view.[46]

Vining's remarks elicited from White a spirited attack against reliance on the Necessary and Proper Clause. Speaking as a staunch defender of Virginia's views on the limited powers of the federal government, White insisted that the authority of Congress was restricted to the enumerated powers. Vining's invocation of a doctrine of general, unenumerated powers, he declared, was contrary to the sense of the Virginia ratifying convention, which had prepared a specific amendment prohibiting the implementation of such a doctrine. North Carolina had yet to ratify the Constitution, he added, because of similar misgivings.[47]

Madison did not respond to White's characterization of the sense of the Virginia convention. But both he and Ames did address the impractical consequences arising from a strict construction of the enumerated powers of Congress that Gerry, Smith, and White had advanced.

Ames, speaking first, argued in effect for a double necessity: that the president have the power and that Congress say so. Admitting that the Constitution did not explicitly speak to the point at issue, Ames maintained that unless the president were to have the power, he would be unable to control his officers and insure that the laws were faithfully executed. If he were not to have the power, Ames stated, "You virtually strip him of his authority; you virtually destroy his responsibility."[48] Since the clause in controversy was calculated to support the president's authority and responsibility, he supported it.[49]

Madison also spoke in practical terms, albeit more circumspectly. Returning to the position he had taken at the outset of the debate, he pointed out that under the Constitution Congress had the power to establish offices by law. But, he said, before establishing an office, the membership should know the period for which it was to be held and the identity of the person or body who would authorize the officer's removal: the president alone or together with the Senate. Depending on the answers to those questions, he reasoned, the members might in certain cases decide to limit the office to a time certain. To settle these questions, he concluded, Congress must declare its sense that the Constitution required that only the president had the power of removal.[50]

In appealing to the requirements of government and to the necessity of construing the Constitution in the light of those needs, both Ames and Madison confirmed the views set forth in the *Federalist* a year and a half earlier. There Hamilton had written that experience had taught "how unequal parchment provisions are to a struggle with public necessity. . . . [N]ations pay little regard to rules and maxims calculated in their very nature to run counter to the necessities of society."[51]

Madison, also writing in the *Federalist,* and defending the Continental Congress's assumption of power in its governance of the western territories despite the absence of such an authority under the Articles of Confederation, had echoed Hamilton's views: "The public . . . necessity of the case, imposed upon them the task of overleaping their constitutional limits."[52]

Neither Ames nor Madison in the House, however, was willing to admit a constitutional limit on congressional or presidential power running counter "to the necessities of society" or to "the public necessity of the case." Such a concession would have required a resort to the difficult amending process of Article V, and that course was out of the question. An early appeal to the amendment procedures would have undermined public confidence in the adequacies of the Constitution and the new government; more practically, supporters of an exclusive presidential power of removal would not have been able to muster the two-thirds majority required for an appropriate amendment in the Senate.

Rather than deny a constitutional limit on the powers of Congress and of the president, Ames and Madison argued instead for a construction of the Constitution whereby Congress would have the authority to declare that the president had the power to remove, and the president, irrespective of any congressional declaration, would have such a power. In other words, without saying so directly, the powers for which they argued were implied. And while mildly denying the contention that the authority of the president could be supplied by Congress pursuant to the Necessary and Proper Clause, Madison accepted the support of those who made the contention. He prevailed. Unsatisfied with the impractical alternatives presented by the opposition, a majority of the House decisively voted down the motion to strike the clause enabling the president to remove the secretary of foreign affairs without consulting the Senate.[53]

But there was one critical weakness in Madison's finely spun argument: If the constitutional principle of the separation of powers required that the Senate not participate in the removal of officers in the executive branch, how was it that the legislative branch had the power to undertake the nonlegislative function of declaring the constitutional powers of the executive branch? As Smith put it, if the president had the sole power to remove officers under the Constitution, Congress did not have the power to say that he had.[54]

Smith's remarks led to the ultimate resolution of the controversy. Egbert Benson of New York and Madison, acting as floor managers for the bill, decided on a change in the controversial clause. To counter Smith's latest position and yet secure to the president the right to remove, while at the same time fulfilling the Vining criteria—that either the president had the right as an incident to presidential power or Congress could give it to him under the Necessary and Proper Clause—Benson moved to amend the bill to provide that whenever the secretary was removed by the president, the chief clerk in the Department of Foreign Affairs should administer the office until a successor was appointed.[55]

If his motion was approved, Benson said, he would then "move to strike the words . . . 'to be removable by the president'—which appeared somewhat like a grant." This method, he said, would establish a legislative construction that the president had the power according to the Constitution. Madison, seconding the motion, declared, in a departure from Benson's statement, that the words of the pending motion might certainly "be construed to imply a legislative grant of the power."[56] Thus between them, Benson and Madison were proposing a legislative solution broad enough to satisfy both the Madison position and that of Hartley and Laurance.

Actually, as Theodore Sedgwick of Massachusetts explained, it was not that simple. While some like Madison would support the pending motion on that ground, others such as himself considered the subject of presidential removal solely "a matter of legislative determination; and that they must give it to the president on the principles of the constitution." The clause the motion proposed would not give the president the desired power. But later, after Sedgwick had second thoughts, he, Hartley, Laurance, and their supporters voted for the amendment because, he said, it would do no harm; while Gerry, White, Smith, Page, Sherman, and others like them, who thought that the Senate must share in the removal process, voted against it. The amendment was approved, thirty to eighteen.[57]

Then, Benson, as he said he would, moved to strike the provision that the secretary "be removable by the president." Again Madison supported the motion. Everyone, he said, should be happy. It would satisfy those who thought the subject was not one for legislative determination, while those who wanted a vote on "the sense of this house upon the doctrine of the constitution" should have been satisfied by the vote on the previous motion.[58] But in fact the motion did not satisfy Sedgwick, Hartley, Laurance, and those who agreed with them. Because they thought that the president would not have the power without enabling legislation, and that the clause to be stricken was the very provision which would give it to him, they voted against it. For the very same reason, Gerry, White, Smith, Page, Sherman, and those who agreed with them voted for it. With that realignment—Madison and his supporters voting with Gerry, White, and the others—the amendment carried, thirty-one to nineteen. Ames voted with Madison.[59]

Opposition in the Senate to the provision for the exclusive presidential power of removal was naturally more intense, since it directly affected the Senate's interests. The substantive arguments followed those of the House. The senators opposing the Benson-Madison accommodation were apparently unconvinced that the proposal had no bearing on their constitutional powers. But what proved decisive was not senatorial but executive influence. During the debate, Vice-President Adams, who hoped in time to succeed to the presidency, repeatedly spoke in favor of an exclusive presidential power. And off the floor, during recesses, the uncommitted were solicited for support. Paterson from New Jersey and Ellsworth, future Washington appointees to the United States Supreme Court, joined the presidential party. In the end, the Senate divided equally, and Adams broke the tie in favor of the president.[60]

If the provision for the removal of superior officers was an omitted case, and everyone seemed to realize that it was—the framers had not provided for it and therefore could not have intended anything concerning it—Congress nevertheless decided that the president could, without consent of the Senate, exercise the power, and the president himself signed the bill into law.[61] As far as the executive and the legislative branches of the new government were concerned, they would supply the omission without regard to the amending process of Article V.

In the final analysis, this was not an implied construction of the Constitution according to the practice of the common law, which, as one shrewd opponent of ratification had warned, would interpret a text by recourse to its purpose rather than to its letter. While Madison on one side and White on the other had each employed such an interpretation, Hartley and his supporters had relied on a much broader construction against which the same opponent of ratification had also warned: Deficiencies in the written text would be supplied to carry out the presumed intent of the draftsman "according to the reasoning spirit of [equity]."[62] Without the votes of Hartley and those who agreed with him, Madison's position would have foundered.

Moreover, as Smith had pointed out, the proponents' constructions of the Constitution were contrary to the authority of the *Federalist,* and, as Gerry had argued, to American practice.[63] Last, but perhaps not least, the proponents' constructions added to the Constitution a provision for removal which it did not specify, in derogation of the provision for impeachment which it did specify. Whether this result was one the framers would have approved, had the problem presented itself to them, is impossible to know.

What we do know is that Washington as president apparently wanted that result, and that Madison, one of the most influential of the framers and probably the most influential member of the House of Representatives, worked in the House, as Adams worked in the Senate, to get it for him. To that end, they tolerated a broad exercise of legislative power, including a liberal interpretation of the Necessary and Proper Clause. They also went so far as to brush aside suggestions for supplying constitutional deficiencies through the formal processes of Article V, and used instead the indirect technique of a legislative "recognition" of the president's constitutional power. How the legislature, whose own powers were supposed to be limited by and enumerated in the Constitution, could do this was assumed but never adequately explained. Under Madison's leadership, the president's party, "the federal party," as he called it, was indeed daring and resourceful.[64]

By this time, it was clear that although Madison would not himself invoke an implied grant of congressional power under the Necessary and Proper Clause in justification of legislation, he would not hesitate to call on other unexpressed congressional powers in such justification. He would not be so indelicate, however, as to characterize those powers as implied.

Consistent with this position, later in the first session when Madison presented the proposal for what is now the Tenth Amendment as part of the Bill of Rights, he deftly omitted any reference to "clearly" or "expressly" delegated powers, even though four of the ratifying states—Massachusetts, New Hampshire, South Carolina, and New York—had requested that qualification.[65] Instead, he proposed that "the powers not delegated by the constitution, nor prohibited by it to the states, are reserved to the states respectively."[66] And when a motion was made to insert the word "expressly," he objected. "Because it was impossible to confine a government to the exercise of expressed powers, there must necessarily be admitted powers by implication, unless the constitution descended to recount every minutiae [*sic*]."[67] Continuing in this vein, he said that "the word 'expressly' had been moved in the convention of Virginia, by the opponents to the ratification, and after full and fair discussion was given up by them, and the system allowed to retain its present form."[68]

Madison's recollection of that convention was correct as far as it went. Influenced by the fear that following ratification Congress would use the Necessary and Proper Clause to justify the assertion of sweeping general powers, the motion had been introduced, despite the many assurances given that the clause contemplated only the exercise of incidental powers.

The object of Henry and Mason in proposing the motion, however, had been wider: to rid the Constitution of any kind of implication. But because their motion was overbroad, the proponents of ratification had been able to defeat it by pointing out that, as Randolph said, it would preclude the assertion of essential powers, namely, those incidental to the exercise of the expressed powers.[69]

If Madison's recollection was only partially correct, his conclusion was unqualifiedly correct: because the motion was rejected, "the system [had been] allowed to retain its present form." He did not expatiate on the scope of that system. As stated in the *Federalist* and in the Virginia convention, that system clearly permitted the adoption of legislation incidental to the execution of the legislature's enumerated powers under the Necessary and Proper Clause. And as he himself pointed out in the presidential removal debate, the system also contemplated an implied presidential power to remove department heads, incidental to his execution of the laws pursuant to Article II. And as Madison had also advocated in the same debate, the system further contemplated an implied legislative power to declare the sense of Congress concerning the president's removal power, incidental to the sound exercise of the congressional power to establish offices.

Retention of "the system . . . [in] its present form" had also permitted a substantial number of congressmen to argue under the Necessary and Proper Clause for a power to grant the president the removal power.[70] (In fact, the Hartley-Laurance contingent had outvoted the Madison contingent by a three-to-two margin in favor of the clause empowering the clerk of the Department of Foreign Affairs to administer the department after the secretary had been removed by the president, until a successor was appointed.)[71] And although Madison had been unwilling to say so, such a use of the clause could have been said to be suitable because the measure was incidental to the faithful execution of the laws by the president.

A similar argument, however, could not be made with regard to the statute imposing a standard oath on state officers. That law was neither authorized by one of the enumerated powers nor was it incidental to the execution of a law adopted pursuant to one of these powers. Nevertheless, "the system [in] its present form" had countenanced the use of "necessary and proper" in that instance as well.

In sum, the system that had been retained, following the defeat of the Henry-Mason motion, tolerated the assertion of many kinds of implied powers, at least one of which was more than incidental to the execution of an enumerated power. Madison made no reference to any of these considerations in his discussion concerning the proposed wording of the Tenth Amendment.

Against this background, the House rejected the use of the word "expressly." After that, with the addition of the final reservation "or to the people," the House and the Senate approved the proposed constitutional amendment.[72] When ratified, it became the Tenth Amendment. The amendment did not change the "present form" of the Constitution. It did not affect the meaning of the Necessary and Proper Clause. After its ratification, as before, House members would feel free to argue for the existence of implied powers, incidental or otherwise, inherent in the language of the clause.

As the First Congress approached the end of its first session, it appeared, from Madison's work in drafting the text of what is now the Tenth Amendment and his outstanding advocacy on behalf of the presidential removal power, that he was a committed "federalist." He had been a proponent and ardent worker for strong presidential powers, and the most skillful of advocates in construing the Constitution broadly to achieve those ends. He had artfully fended off attempts to limit the powers of Congress. Any doubts about his commitment to federalist goals, which may have been caused by his brief misgivings concerning the power of Congress to impose an oath on state legislators to support the Constitution, should have been forgotten.

Location of the Nation's Capital and Strict Construction

While Madison usually assumed positions appropriate to a national figure during the first session of the First Congress, he was careful at the same time to advance his own interests and those of his state. In pushing for the exclusive presidential power to remove a departmental head, he had furthered the interests of Washington, his fellow Virginian. In securing the Bill of Rights, he served the cause of civil liberties, the interests of the new government, and the Constitution. At the same time he had fulfilled his campaign promise to the Baptists and no longer needed fear their opposition to his reelection. And by successfully opposing the insertion of the word "expressly" in the future Tenth Amendment, he had preserved the assertion of implied powers.

National interest, if it existed, had to yield to the interests of Madison's state and region in one case, however: the location of the seat of the new government. Southerners chafed at the decision of the Continental Congress, sitting in New York City, to keep that city as the meeting place for Congress under the Constitution and as the temporary seat of the new government.[73] New York was not centrally located, and they had to travel long distances at great expense, at inopportune times, and under difficult conditions. Locating the capital in New York, Madison worried, would adversely affect southern representation in Congress, discourage southern participation in the executive branch, and, all in all, substantially diminish southern influence in the government. Moreover, southerners realized that if the capital were located in the North, they would lose the business generated by the national government and connected with its administration.[74]

Virginians considered their own state, the most northerly of the southern states, the most appropriate location for the new capital, and the location of the capital in their state the single most important condition for their continued support of the new government and the Constitution. Madison became the leading spokesman for his state and region in the matter, fashioning his arguments, constitutional and otherwise, accordingly.[75] Not surprisingly, the quality of his advocacy suffered, and along with it his reputation.

The issue came to a head in the last month of the first session when Pennsylvanians, with northern support, moved a resolution confirming the sense of the House that the permanent seat should be located at the center of wealth, population, and territory, a placement favoring a site on the Susquehanna. In response, Richard Bland Lee moved a competing resolution placing the permanent seat at the center of the states, near the Atlantic and open to the western territories, a location favoring a site on the Potomac.[76] To Madison's distress, the Pennsylvania motion prevailed. If Virginians had foreseen the day, he lamented, they would not have ratified the Constitution.[77]

The debate then focused on whether to specify a location on the Susquehanna or on the Potomac as the permanent site. For the time being, it was agreed that the temporary seat would continue in New York City. The House voted for the Susquehanna. Proposals were then made, with southern support, to change the temporary seat from New York to either Wilmington or Philadelphia, and failed.[78] But before a final vote on a bill to implement those decisions could be taken, and just eight days before the scheduled day of adjournment, Madison moved to strike the provision continuing the temporary seat in New York on the ground that, placed as it was in a bill, it was irreconcilable with the spirit of the Constitution.[79]

His argument was complicated. Under Article I, Section 5, Clause 4, he pointed out, an adjournment "for more than three days . . . [or] to any other place than that in which the two Houses shall be sitting" required the concurrence of both houses. Therefore, he reasoned, matters covered by an adjournment, whether of time or place, were not properly the subject of a bill but of a joint resolution. This, he continued, was confirmed by the provisions of Article I, Section 7, pertaining to procedures governing the adoption of bills and joint resolutions.[80] The first two clauses of that section, pertaining to the introduction and passage of bills, were not directly in point but, he argued, the third clause, pertaining to joint resolutions, was. It provides: "Every Order, Resolution or Vote, to Which the Concurrence of the Senate and House of Representatives may be necessary (except on a question of Adjournment) shall be presented to the President of the United States; and before the Same shall take Effect, shall be approved by him, or being disapproved by him, shall be repassed by two thirds of the Senate and House of Representatives, according to the

Rules and Limitations prescribed in the Case of a Bill." Madison contended that because the provision for the continuation of the temporary seat of government in New York City pertained to the place of reassembly following an adjournment, it could be effected only by joint resolution under Article I, Section 5.[81]

Now came the reason for his nice distinctions. Because such a resolution, as confirmed by Article I, Section 7, Clause 3, did not require the president's approval, he continued, it would be a wrong and dangerous experiment for Congress "to attempt to give to the president a power, the constitution expressly denied him." While he supposed such an attempt would not absolutely convey such a power, the charges of unconstitutionality it might raise in the Senate might, he warned, impede its adoption there.[82]

Was Madison's argument a signal to Congress that publicly or privately he would advise the president—who was after all a fellow Virginian and just as interested as Madison in the permanent location of the seat of government on the Potomac—that if the bill was passed, he should not approve it because it improperly included a place of adjournment within the form of a bill?

Madison's position, if based on strict construction, rested on substantial grounds. In the Constitutional Convention during a discussion of a committee report on the subject of congressional adjournments—later incorporated in the Constitution in Article I, Section 5, Clause 4—Madison had at first supported a provision requiring that any action effecting an adjournment to a new place be accomplished by law. But when Richard Spaight, a delegate from North Carolina, objected that this would fix the seat in New York, especially if the president was a northerner, Madison moved an amendment allowing Congress on its own, during its very first session, to determine the place at which its future sessions were to be held, but thereafter to determine this by law. When several delegates expressed their opposition that even as amended the proposal placed too much power in the president, the motion to effect an adjournment to a new place by law was withdrawn, and the original committee report, empowering Congress alone to fix the time and place of adjournment, was adopted.[83]

A few days later, during the discussion of the procedures governing the presentation of bills to the president for approval under what is now Article I, Section 7, Clause 2, Madison again moved to amend the committee report to include a provision for joint resolutions, excepting those pertaining to adjournment. He reasoned that if the veto was confined to bills, it "would be evaded by acts under the form and name of Resolutions, votes &c."[84] His motion was adopted when cast in different form and placed in the following paragraph of the section.[85]

The president and those in Congress who had also been delegates to the Constitutional Convention were aware of the soundness of Madison's position. Nevertheless, his opponents properly charged him with inconsistency: After first supporting a bill that would place the temporary seat either in Wilmington or Philadelphia, he then challenged the constitutionality of a second bill which would continue it in

New York. They further questioned why, if Congress could properly fix the permanent seat of government by legislation rather than by joint resolution unapproved by the president, as Madison had apparently admitted in his support of a bill placing the permanent seat on the Potomac, it could not do the same with regard to the temporary seat.[86]

Laurance pointed out that the seat of government was determined by the residence of the president, the great offices of the government, judges, foreign ministers, and the public archives. Ames argued that the seat had to be determined by bill, precisely so as to require the approval of the president. They both suggested that matters affecting the operations and placement of the executive and judicial branches of the government, under Articles II and III, went beyond the bounds of the simple resolution concerning the place of legislative adjournment contemplated in Article I, Section 5, and thus were properly incorporated in the form of a bill, under Article I, Section 7, Clause 2.[87]

In effect, the opposition agreed with the Madison of the Constitutional Convention that the matter of the seat of government should require the participation of the president of the United States and be fixed by law. An arrangement that would allow Congress to settle this on its own was bad government, smacking of unbridled legislative supremacy.

The opposition objected to the way Madison invoked a constitutional argument to advance the interests of his state and region but opposed it when it did not. In that context, Madison's position bordered on pettifoggery. By obstructing passage, in the dying days of a legislative session, of a bill that would permanently seat the government on the Susquehanna River, he was calculatingly kicking constitutional dust in the eyes of his fellow representatives in an attempt to confound them.

Madison's tactic failed and served only to diminish his personal authority. On the floor of the House, Ames said that while he admitted Madison's abilities and "doubted not but the constitution was the better in consequence of those abilities having been employed in its formation; . . . [I am] not disposed to pay implicit deference to that gentleman's expositions of that instrument. There were but few on this floor, who were in convention, and who could say what was the intention with which every clause was inserted; . . . [I am] content to take it as [I find] it."[88]

A majority in the House then, including Madison at first, were willing to disregard the framers' intention in favor of its own sense of what the constitutional text should mean, at least in a matter involving the housekeeping details of the federal government. Since this interpretation resulted in the enhancement of presidential power at congressional expense, it could be said to advance, rather than frustrate, the overall constitutional principle of checks and balances: The federal legislature was yielding rather than extending its power, and pronouncing at the same time that the framers' scruple regarding excessive executive power was itself, at least in that case, excessive.

The determination of Congress to confer upon the president a share in the location of the temporary and permanent seat of the new government is the earliest example of the substitution of a legislative sense of what the Constitution should mean, irrespective of any supposed authoritative exposition based on an insider's putative knowledge of the framers' intent. This substitution of the legislative sense of the Constitution went beyond the previous provision recognizing an exclusive presidential power of removing superior executive officers. That had supplied a deficiency in the constitutional text. As Ames suggested, the substitution of the congressional sense of the Constitution with regard to the location of the government ignored both the text and the word of a framer, namely, Madison.

In taking these positions—recognizing or establishing the president's removal power, fixing by law the seat of government, and, a minor matter, imposing a uniform oath for state officials—Congress had determined that, practically, they would do whatever had to be done to make the new government work. Considerations of framers' intent, of expressed versus implied powers, were not irrelevant to their final determination. They were not, however, controlling.

Insofar as Madison personally was concerned, his shifting tactics, his manipulation of an otherwise sound argument, had tarnished his reputation as a disinterested expositor of the constitutional text. He would have been a most unusual politician if, when friends of his state and region had supported the bill for Wilmington or Philadelphia, he had publicly stated a construction of the Constitution unfavorable to their and his interest. While no one could have realistically expected such behavior, what might have been expected was a fair measure of consistency. If he withheld his expert knowledge concerning the constitutionality of place-of-adjournment resolutions when it would hurt his cause, he should not have belatedly made use of it, against New York, when it would help his cause.

By his exhibition of artful constitutional manipulation in the first session of the First Congress, Madison placed the membership on notice that when the interests of his state and region, and—the shadow cast by Patrick Henry was always present— of his own career, were involved, and when the stakes were high enough, he was capable of subtle, sometimes substantial, shifts in constitutional positioning. He was after all an advocate for the state he represented, not a disinterested scholar. He would reveal this flexibility again in the second and third sessions of the First Congress and thereafter, when, arguing in favor of state and regional interests, he would establish his position as the country's foremost advocate of a consistently narrow construction of federal legislative and executive powers.

In the matter immediately before the House, the temporary and permanent locations of the seat of the new government, Madison, as we know, prevailed. The capital is on the Potomac, and not on the Susquehanna. This came about through a series of maneuvers. On September 22, 1789, the House passed a bill fixing the permanent location on the Susquehanna with the temporary location in New York.[89]

Because of a subsequent split in the Pennsylvania delegation, however, the Senate four days later voted to designate Philadelphia as the permanent seat.[90] Two days after that, the House over southern objection voted to concur in the Senate's decision.[91] This time Madison saved the day for the South by moving a seemingly innocuous amendment, which the House approved,[92] declaring the laws of Pennsylvania to be in effect in the district to be ceded and accepted, until Congress should otherwise provide. As Madison hoped, the Senate, caught in the rush to adjourn, postponed further consideration of the amendment until the next session.[93] The next day Congress adjourned.[94]

The matter would become a vital part of the business of the second session. When, through the famous compromise of 1790, Congress designated by bill a location on the Potomac as the permanent seat of government, Madison did not raise a constitutional objection to the form of designation.[95] In the end he achieved his substantive position.

That was in the future. By the end of the first session of the First Congress Madison had shown that although he was not a completely disinterested exegete of the Constitution, he was nevertheless the leading man in the House, the most influential person in the government next to Washington, and a resourceful advocate of broad powers, at least for the president.

CHAPTER FOUR

Madison and Strict Construction (First Congress, Second and Third Sessions, 1789–91)

By September 29, 1789, the day the First Congress adjourned its first session, Madison's influence was already on the wane. Among the other accomplishments of the session had been the organization of the executive offices, following which Washington on September 11 had sent to the Senate the name of Alexander Hamilton as his nominee for secretary of the treasury. The Senate promptly confirmed him. During the recess, in Madison's absence, Hamilton prepared a report for the support of public credit, in which he advocated payment in full of the unpaid debt of the United States and assumption and payment in full of the unpaid debt of the states incurred on behalf of the Revolution. Hamilton modeled his proposals on those advanced by Robert Morris to the Continental Congress in 1782 and 1783, when he was acting as superintendent of finance during the Revolution.[1]

The report, submitted to the House during the second session, was very unpopular in the South, particularly in Virginia. Originally much of the debt had been issued in long-term paper to soldiers during the Revolution in payment for their service. But due to the lack in revenue, the interest had long been in arrears, and the value of the principal had severely depreciated because of doubt about the ability of the United States or the states to repay it. In those circumstances, speculators had been able to buy the paper at a substantial discount.[2]

Therefore, when a proposal was made during the Constitutional Convention for the assumption of the debt of the United States, Pierce Butler of South Carolina, moved to discriminate between the amounts paid the "Blood-suckers who had speculated on the distresses of others, . . . [and] those who had fought & bled for their country."[3] Under Butler's plan, the "Blood-suckers" would receive only what they paid, while the original holders, if they still held the paper, would receive payment in full. Mason, in his concern that a bill for assumption might "beget speculations and increase the pestilent practice of stock-jobbing," supported the motion.[4]

As it turned out, Mason's concerns were realized. Prior to publication of the secretary's report, speculators, mostly from the North, acting on inside information from the Treasury about its forthcoming plan and looking forward to a considerable windfall, bought up large amounts of state debt from its holders. When the public realized what had happened, indignation erupted, especially in areas of high victimization—the back country, Virginia, and the South. Despite the circumstances, Hamilton determined that discrimination in payment would damage the public credit of the United States in the eyes of the moneyed class, whose opinion, he considered, had to be respected in view of the future financial needs of the United States.[5]

Virginians were against the proposed assumption of state debt on a second ground: Their state had for the most part already paid its war debt, and they feared being taxed a second time to pay the expense of assumption. While it was true that the federal government had begun a settlement of accounts under which the United States would reimburse states for the payment of debts incurred on behalf of the Union during the Revolution, Virginians were also afraid that their state might not be given full credit for the claims it had submitted, and that once the United States had assumed the obligations of the debtor states, the latter would oppose the settlement of Virginia's claims to its satisfaction. For all these reasons Virginia's delegation, almost to a man, opposed both the decision to pay the debt of the United States in full and to assume state debt.[6]

Madison was particularly affected. He had led the campaign for ratification in Virginia against strong opposition and had in the process earned the enmity of Henry, whose influence in the state legislature had almost cost Madison a seat in the new government. He was still in correspondence with Monroe, whom he had defeated in the election for his seat in the House, and could feel Monroe's breath on his neck as the latter wrote about assumption's unpopularity, its unfairness to Virginia, and the threat it would pose to state sovereignty if it were adopted. The consolidation of state debt, Monroe predicted, would lead to greater federal taxation and, since the federal tax would fall on the same property that the states wished to tax, would inevitably diminish state power and initiative. With a consistency proper to an opponent of ratification, Monroe deplored the prospect.[7]

For the same reasons that Monroe deplored assumption, a supporter of the federal government should have welcomed it. As Hamilton argued, by consolidating the debt of all the states, assumption would eliminate the necessity for thirteen separate, complicated, and conflicting systems of finance and assure vigor and order in the national system. And it would strengthen the new government at the expense of the states.[8]

Because Madison was a long-standing advocate of a strong national government and had advocated, in the Continental Congress, both the assumption of state debt and the payment in full of the United States debt to holders of record, Hamilton expected his support.[9] He did not get it. Instead, reflecting the prejudices and interests of his state and region, Madison now opposed assumption and favored discrimination in payment.

He moved for discrimination;[10] the motion was overwhelmingly defeated.[11] He next proposed that along with assumption credit should be given states for their wartime expenditures, to insure that the citizens of states that had already paid their debt would not be taxed again to pay the unpaid debt of the delinquent states.[12] When this proposal was also defeated, he spoke against assumption.[13]

During the debates, constitutional issues again came to the fore. Because of his past positions, Madison was not free to argue that Congress lacked the power to assume state debts because that power was not enumerated. Hamilton later claimed that during the convention Madison and he had had a long talk in which they agreed that while it would be expedient and proper to assume state debt, "it would be more advisable to make it a measure of administration than an article of constitution; from the impolicy of multiplying obstacles to its reception on collateral details."[14]

If this was so, then both had already contemplated the post-ratification employment of a rather broad construction of the expressed powers of the United States, whereby the provision to pay the debt of the United States would include both the debt of the general government and that of the individual states. In addition, since Madison desired that Congress reimburse Virginia and other states for the debt they had already paid, his position necessarily was based on the premise that Congress had the implied power to do so.

But Michael Stone of Maryland, unlike Madison, was not constrained by previous positions. Early in the debates he said that he doubted the United States had the power to assume state debts. In response, Roger Sherman of Connecticut stated flatly that the United States did. Gerry, siding with Sherman, declared that debts contracted by the states for the common defense were in effect the debt of the United States and that therefore Congress had the power to pay them. More surprisingly, Gerry, abandoning his past suspicions regarding the sweeping character of the Necessary and Proper Clause, contended that if Congress did not have the power to pay the state debts as debts of the United States, it could do so under that clause.[15] (Gerry's departure from the position he had previously taken with regard to the Necessary and Proper Clause during the Constitutional Convention and ratification, and during the first session of the First Congress when he spoke out against a presidential power of removing department heads, may be explained by his personal interest in assumption: he held a substantial amount of Massachusetts debt.)[16]

The following day, Gerry, responding to statements that the assumption of state

debt had never been contemplated, went further and relied on his own personal recollections of the Constitutional Convention:

> WHEN THE PRESENT CONSTITUTION WAS UNDER consideration, in
> the general convention, a proposition was brought forward, that the
> general government should assume and provide for the state debts, as well as
> the debts of the union: It was opposed, on this ground, that it did not extend
> to the repayment of that part which the states had sunk, as well as that which
> remained unpaid; had it not been for this objection, I believe the very provi-
> sion, which gentlemen say was never expected, would have been incorporated
> in the constitution itself. If I recollect right, it was also contended in conven-
> tion, that the proposition would be useless, as congress were authorised, un-
> der other parts of the constitution, to make full provision on this head. From
> this anecdote gentlemen will see, that it was in contemplation from the very
> commencement of the new government.[17]

Madison did not immediately respond to Gerry's statement, but almost two months
later—during a later phase of the debate—he did so in the following terms:

> IF AS WE HAVE BEEN TOLD, the assumption originated in the convention,
> why were not words inserted that would have incorporated and made the
> state debts part of the debts of the United States? Sir, if there was a majority
> who disapproved of the measure, certainly no argument can be drawn from
> this source; if there was a majority who approved of it, but thought it inexpe-
> dient to make it a part of the constitution, they must have been restrained by
> a fear that it might produce dissentions and render the success of their plan
> doubtful. I do recollect that such a measure was proposed, and, if my mem-
> ory does not deceive me, the very gentleman . . . who now appeals to the con-
> stitution in support of his argument, disrelished the measure at that time, and
> assigned for a reason, that it would administer relief perhaps exactly in pro-
> portion as the states had been deficient in making exertions.[18]

Some time later, Sherman replied to Madison's statement: "It is objected that this [the
assumption of state debts] is a new project—and not mentioned in the constitution. . . . It was mentioned in the general convention—but it was not thought *necessary* or *proper* to insert it in the constitution, for Congress would have sufficient
power to adopt if they should judge it expedient."[19]

Sherman and Gerry's recollections of the Constitutional Convention were more
accurate than Madison's, if we refer to the latter's own notes on the debates in the
convention. The convention had contemplated the assumption of state debt. A formal resolution to that effect had been presented and Sherman had spoken in its

favor and for a formal authorization for Congress in that respect. It had been Gerry, according to Madison's notes, who had raised the difficulty concerning a provision for the assumption of state debt, "that as the States had made different degrees of exertion to sink their respective debts, those who had done most would be alarmed, if they were now to be saddled with a share of the debts of States which had done least."[20] But Madison, if we can credit Hamilton's recollections, had correctly stated why a provision for assumption had not been expressly included: the fear that it might raise objections to ratification.

In any case, Madison's position in the second session of the First Congress was that the lack of a specific constitutional authorization—for whatever reason—when combined with his recollection of the convention, rebutted Gerry's earlier argument that the framers had intended Congress should assume the payment of state debt. He did not take the next step, however, and conclude from the lack of specificity in the enumerated powers of Congress and from his own recollection of the convention a lack of constitutional power in Congress to assume state debts.

But as in the case of the bill for uniform state oaths in the first session, he was certainly giving notice that he would worry about the lack of a specific constitutional authority for Congress to legislate. In a case against the interests of Virginia he would not search for implications of legislative power in the grants of specific powers. In fact, in such a case he would suggest there was no such implied power.

Late in the debate, James Jackson, asserting his conviction that the convention had not intended that Congress should have the power to assume state debts, pushed Madison's argument to the conclusion the latter had not made and reasserted the contention Stone had advanced at the beginning: assumption was unconstitutional.[21] In response to Jackson, Gerry again resorted to his own recollections of the Constitutional Convention:

S O FAR WAS THE CONVENTION FROM DOING this [rejecting the proposition for assuming state debts], that there was no opposition to the measure. It was urged by some of the members, and I confess myself to be of the number, that at the same time the debts were assumed provision should be made for those states who had exerted themselves to sink their debts, and it was observed by the gentleman from Connecticut (Mr. Sherman) that as the constitution gave sufficient power to Congress to assume the debts, they undoubtedly would assume them, and make the other provision mentioned. He thought it eligible therefore to refer the whole matter to Congress, and his proposition met the approbation of the convention.[22]

Not coincidentally, the various recollections of the convention's proceedings supported the rememberers' present positions in the ongoing debate over the manner of assumption. Yet although both Gerry's and Sherman's versions differed from

Madison's, and indeed from his notes of the Constitutional Convention, in one respect Gerry's was more favorable to Madison's position. States, Gerry asserted, should be given credit for the war debts they had already paid.

On the jurisprudential question whether it was proper for a congressman during a debate over the allocation of power under the Constitution to use his recollection of what had occurred at the Constitutional Convention, Gerry, it should be noted, had changed his position from the preceding session. (This change coincided with the shift of his position regarding the scope of the Necessary and Proper Clause and with the intrusion of his personal interest in the outcome of assumption.) He had then taken issue with Abraham Baldwin of Georgia when the latter had summoned up his sense of the framers' intention as to the presidential power of removal. On that occasion, Gerry would have left the intention of the framers to the judiciary.[23] This year, a framer's recollections were in order.

Eventually, however, there was a compromise. The formula for assumption was changed to reimburse Virginia and other states for the debt they had already paid. At about the same time it was agreed that beginning in 1800 the seat of the new government would be permanently located on the Potomac and, until then, would be transferred from New York City and located in Philadelphia. On that basis, four congressmen from Maryland and Virginia, whose districts bordered on the Potomac, shifted their positions and supported assumption. Assumption carried. Although Madison privately approved the arrangement, he would not, as the leader against assumption, vote for it. At the same time, his opposition would be a help, not a hindrance, in seeking reelection in his own district.[24]

Washington also favored the compromise. He very much wanted the nation's capital located on the Potomac, for he had long promoted the construction of a canal connecting that river with the Ohio to spur the economies of Virginia and Maryland. He also supported Hamilton's financial scheme: As commander in chief, he had witnessed the distress resulting from the inability of the Continental Congress to clothe, feed, and pay the Continental Army. He understood that to support the military a government must have either hard money or credit, and that to borrow, a government must have satisfied its creditors. Public virtue, Washington understood, must support private interest.[25]

As a result of the compromise, northern interest had obtained what it wanted most: payment in full of state and continental debt for the benefit of its public creditors. Southern interest had what it wanted most: the permanent location of the nation's capital in their region and the settlement of state claims against the United States for moneys expended on behalf of the Revolution.[26] The compromise had come, however, only after a bitterly contested six-month struggle that had the effect of raising public sentiment in the South against the federal government, even among those who had theretofore been strongest on its behalf.

In Virginia, the most ardent opponents to ratification became enthusiastic about Madison because of his outspoken opposition to government policy. He in turn began to reflect his state's common opinion that government policy, through Hamilton's influence, had passed into the control of northern money and commerce to the detriment of the agricultural economy of the entire region and the political interests of the state.[27] Reflecting assumption's unpopularity and Henry's continuing influence, the Virginia House of Delegates on December 16, 1790, passed a resolution declaring assumption unconstitutional.[28]

The concern of Virginians and other southerners over the consolidation of debt, the consequent strengthening of the federal government, and the weakening of state power was exacerbated by fears concerning the presidency. Washington, it was known, disliked the office. In the spring of 1790 he had been dangerously ill, and it was uncertain that he would submit to a second term. If he did not, the candidates to succeed him would be, Madison believed, Vice-President Adams, the choice of New England, Chief Justice John Jay, the favorite of the middle states, and Secretary of State Jefferson, the candidate of the South.[29]

Southern concern in this matter emerged in the third session of the First Congress during the consideration of a bill to specify the officer who, in the unlikely case of vacancy by death, removal, or disability in the offices of both the president and vice-president, would act as president. In January 1791, Representative William L. Smith of South Carolina, desirous of testing Jefferson's strength on behalf of his region, moved that the secretary of state be the succeeding officer. Supporting Smith were Madison and William Giles of Virginia, Daniel Carroll and Stone of Maryland, and Baldwin. New Englanders, preferring a nonentity whose office would not by itself constitute him a likely alternative to Adams, opted for the president pro tempore of the Senate, whoever he might happen to be. A few members preferred Jay.[30]

The fate of Smith's motion ultimately became involved with the deliberations over Hamilton's proposal to establish a national bank, which he had presented earlier in the session as the next installment in his plan to structure a sound national fiscal system. The principal advantages accruing to the country from the bank, Hamilton wrote, were several. The bank would secure for the country an adequate national money supply through the medium of a privately issued, governmentally sanctioned paper currency. In sudden emergencies, it could make loans to the government. By increasing the quantity of money and quickening its circulation, it would facilitate the payment of taxes.[31]

The establishment of the bank would have additional advantages, Hamilton continued. The displacement of gold and silver as the ordinary medium of domestic monetary exchange would enable the government to make use of specie to pay its foreign debt. In addition, their displacement would enable the merchant to support his credit and to undertake new enterprises, which would ultimately promote the prosperity of trade and the augmentation of the precious metals.[32]

Finally, Hamilton wrote, the introduction of bank paper as an equivalent to gold and silver would enable the government to pay the interest on its debt at thirteen different locations, which would spare the economy the strain of withholding a considerable part of the country's specie from circulation and relieve the government of the expense and risk of transporting it to the places where payments were to be made.[33] In advancing his proposal, Hamilton again followed a recommendation Robert Morris had made to the Continental Congress when serving as superintendent of finance during the Revolution.[34]

A bill incorporating Hamilton's proposal was introduced first in the Senate, where it quickly passed. Opposition was confined to the South, southern senators complaining that the legislation would establish a banking monopoly for the chief benefit of northern merchants.[35] For this reason, they moved an amendment to strike from the bill a provision prohibiting the creation of another bank for the period of the bank's charter. The motion was overwhelmingly defeated.[36]

Southern senators were also concerned that the provisions of the bill locating the bank in Philadelphia and extending its charter of incorporation until 1811 were designed to accustom the public to a concentration of finance and government in Philadelphia. They feared that subsequently northerners might attempt to undo the decision by which, under the Residence Act passed in the previous session, the nation's capital would be moved to the District of Columbia in 1800.[37] To block such an attempt, they moved an amendment limiting the duration of the bank's charter to 1800. That motion was also overwhelmingly defeated, and the bill passed.[38]

Although some in opposition to the bill said in passing that it was unconstitutional because it created a monopoly, Maclay, that ardent foe of unauthorized and aggressive national power, thought its purposes sound and its validity unquestionable, and voted with the majority.[39] And at that time, the bill's validity was not generally disputed in Virginia.[40]

While the Senate was debating the bank bill, the House was considering the presidential succession bill. After much discussion, it deferred action. Sedgwick, in an apparent reference to southern support for the secretary of state, expressed his regret over the "zeal" and "personal interest in the question."[41] He could afford to say that. The waters had been sufficiently tested to show that New Englanders in their preference for Adams would and could block Jefferson. Madison and Jefferson were duly alerted that as matters then stood, the person to succeed Washington was likely to be Adams. They blamed their defeat partly on Hamilton, who later admitted that he had helped block Jefferson, although, he said, not as much as the latter thought.[42]

Regional differences intensified when the House took up the bank bill. Hamilton's plan had provided for the organization of the bank through a private subscription of four-fifths of its stock, for which a one-fourth payment could be made in gold or silver and the balance in the continental debt certificates that the United States had assumed the previous year.[43] Because southerners held significant amounts of the state debt certificates that the United States had assumed and because the greatest part of the continental debt had "travelled Eastward of the Potowmack,"[44] southern interest lay in the adoption of an amendment permitting the acceptance of state debt certificates in payment of the subscription.

William L. Smith therefore moved to recommit the bill to frame an amendment extending the time for the reception of subscriptions. Such a provision, Smith said, would permit persons living farther from the capital additional time to tender. Two days later, Hugh Williamson of North Carolina also moved for recommittal, to frame an amendment "for the purpose of altering the time or manner of subscribing, so that the holders of state securities assumed to be paid by the United States, may be on a footing with the holders of other securities formerly called national securities."[45]

Southerners in the House, as in the Senate, were also suspicious of the provisions extending the bank's charter for a term of twenty years and locating it in Philadelphia. Their suspicions were strengthened by the fact that in the Senate the bank's friends were blocking consideration of a bill to amend the Residence Act to change the boundaries of the territory bordering on the Potomac in minor, though necessary, respects. Feelings ran so high, Smith reported, that off the floor Madison threatened bank supporters with the charge that the bill would be unconstitutional if they did not reduce the term of the bank's charter from twenty years to ten.[46]

The southerners' belief that New England and the middle states wanted control of the government and the presidency for their own benefit was confirmed when, following the deferral of the proposal to fill the vacancy in the presidency, the Smith and Williamson motions were both defeated by northern votes.[47]

The day after the rejection of the Smith motion and before the rejection of the Williamson motion, Madison opposed the bank on both policy and constitutional grounds.[48] It was a turning point in the history of constitutional law. A short time later, Jefferson, who in his private correspondence had previously been unconcerned about the financial consequences of the bank's operations, complained to George Mason of the subservience of southern agricultural interests to "the stockjobbers." And writing to New York's Robert Livingston, who the month before had joined with Gov. Clinton to oust Hamilton's father-in-law, Philip Schuyler, from the United States Senate in favor of the Anti-Federalist Aaron Burr, Jefferson mentioned southern discontent with the national government and inquired whether New Yorkers felt the same.[49] After the bank bill passed, he and Randolph, when asked by Washington for their opinion, followed Madison's position and declared the bill unconstitutional.

Thereafter, for the next ten years, Jefferson and Madison would join in a policy of systematic opposition to Hamilton and to northern political and financial domination in "the federal party." Their goals would be the diminution of federal power—and, within the federal government, the power of the executive branch, particularly that of the Treasury—and the increase of state power. To achieve these goals, Madison would abandon the tactic he had employed in the first session of the First Congress on behalf of the presidential removal power: advocacy of implied constitutional powers. Instead, he and Jefferson would assume a position of strict constitutional construction, approaching that of Maclay and Gerry in the first session. Organizing a party of opposition, they would ally themselves with those who had been against ratification and would in the end advocate a modified theory of confederated con-stitutionalism.

Madison's opposition to the bank, which he revealed only on the bill's third read-ing, was based on a close interpretation of the enumerated powers of Congress.[50] Those powers, he declared, did not include that of establishing a corporate bank. His views, he added, were especially strong "because he well recollected that a power to grant charters of incorporation had been proposed in the general convention and rejected." He did not add that it was he who had made the proposal. In fact, he had done so twice.[51]

Basing his argument on the premise that the federal government had been granted "particular powers only, leaving the general mass in other hands," he con-tended that the bill did not fall within the "only clauses under which such a power could be pretended." He went down the list of the particular powers and dismissed each of them in turn: The bill did not fall within "the power to lay and collect taxes to pay the debts, and provide for the common defence and general welfare," because it did not lay a tax. The provision for defense and welfare had reference only to statutes laying taxes for those purposes. Nor did the bill fall within the borrowing power, because it did not borrow money. And, finally, the bill was not authorized under the Necessary and Proper Clause, because the clause merely enabled Congress to execute the specified powers. He expanded his interpretation of that provision: "Its meaning must, according to the natural and obvious force of the terms and the context, be limited to means *necessary* to the *end,* and *incident* to the *nature* of the specified powers. The clause is in fact merely declaratory of what would have re-sulted by unavoidable implication, as the appropriate, and as it were, technical means of executing those powers. In this sense it has been explained by the friends of the constitution, and ratified by the state conventions."[52] The bill did not fall within the clause, he concluded, because, although it might create an institution from which the government might one day borrow, it did not directly concern the power to borrow.[53]

Madison's argument was momentous. By excluding the exercise of federal power in the absence of a specific authorization, even though the proposed legislation might be in the best interests of the government or country, he definitively repudi-ated the original formula of the Virginia Plan whereby Congress could legislate "in all cases to which the separate States are incompetent, or in which the harmony of the United States may be interrupted by the exercise of individual Legislation."[54]

His argument thus completed the work he had begun in the Constitutional Con-vention and continued during ratification: to limit the powers of Congress. In the convention, he had warned that if the states were awarded equal representation in the Senate "every effectual prerogative would be withdrawn or withheld, and the New Govt. wd be rendered as impotent and as short lived as the old." He had also warned that the large states "would probably accede to no Govt. which did not in great measure depend for its efficacy on their voluntary cooperation; in which case they would indirectly secure their object."[55]

Following those warnings, Virginia had voted against the modification of its proposal empowering Congress to legislate in the general interests of the country. And although Madison had accepted the inclusion of the Necessary and Proper Clause among the enumerated powers of Congress, he had labored in the Constitutional Convention to limit its meaning so that it could be used to adopt only such measures as were incidental to the execution of the enumerated powers.[56]

During ratification, Madison had continued that strategy. He had assured the readers of the *Federalist* and the delegates to the Virginia convention that the powers of the new Congress were limited and that the powers implicit in the clause were purely incidental.[57] After ratification, in the first session of the First Congress, during debates of the bills to require a uniform state oath and to recognize a presidential power of removal, he had been careful to maintain that position.[58] During the debate of the bank bill, he determined that the time had come to make manifest the stand he had held in reserve ever since Virginia had lost the fight in the Constitutional Convention for a Senate based on population, namely, that Congress did not have the authority to legislate for what it considered to be in the general interests of the country.

But Madison must have understood that this position did not go far enough, and that his opponents, to justify the bill, did not need to maintain that its provisions would promote the general interests of the country. They could offer a more limited argument, namely, that the bank's operations would be incidental to the execution of two of the specific powers of the government: the collection of taxes and payment of the national debt. As Hamilton had pointed out in his report, the bank, when organized, would in its many offices constitute a convenient depository for government revenues; and it could facilitate their interstate transfer so that the Treasury might pay interest on the debt in whichever state it might be due. In addition, by substituting paper for gold and silver, the bank would enable the Treasury more easily to pay the foreign debt.[59]

Therefore, to convict the bill of unconstitutionality, Madison had to go beyond a simple position that the creation of a bank was not incidental to the execution of a specified power. He had to bring forth additional arguments, the first of which he based on a purported constitutional principle forbidding "the exercise of any power, particularly a great and important power, which is not evidently and necessarily involved in an express power." Such a power, he explained, was one "necessary and proper for the government or union," as distinguished from one merely "necessary and proper for executing the enumerated powers." That the Constitution required the specification of an important power, he continued, was manifest in its provisions for punishing counterfeiters and raising armies even though they were incidental to the powers of regulating the value of coins and declaring war.

Applying his constitutional principle to the case at hand, Madison asserted that the power to charter a corporation was great and important because it created an artificial person, delegated to it the quasi-legislative power of making by-laws, gave it the power to purchase and hold lands, and involved a monopoly. Therefore, it followed—Madison did not spell it out—that despite the advantages that the services of a corporate bank might offer to the government in its ordinary operations or to the country, Congress could not create one.[60]

Madison's position reflected the viewpoint of a traditional agricultural society, under the influence of the English "Country" opposition, toward a then highly controversial subject: the relation of corporations to the economic and moral well-being of the new United States. To that society, a corporation was a suspect monopoly whose franchise, conceded by a high act of sovereignty, had been obtained by corrupting the government and diverting it from the public good. A corporation therefore connoted a great and largely uncontrolled trading company, an exotic and immoral creature, such as the East India Company or the South Sea Company, to which Madison referred during the course of his remarks. Reflecting that view, four states had recommended specific constitutional amendments to prohibit Congress from creating commercial corporations. To urban, merchant capitalists, on the other hand, the monetary advantages of national and international investment, business, and trade were obvious, and the corporation was a convenient instrument of normal business life.[61]

Madison briefly advanced a second argument against the proposition that since the bank would afford a convenient depository for the government's revenues and would facilitate the payment of its debt, its establishment could be justified as a necessary and proper measure. The means incident to the execution of a specified power, he insisted, had to be literally necessary to the government's operations, not merely convenient: that is, the means had to be essential to their accomplishment.

Having posited a stricter test for what was necessary and proper, Madison argued (Jefferson in his opinion to Washington would follow him at greater length) that since state banks and individuals could offer the same depository and discounting services to the United States, the government could conduct its business without a national bank. The proposed bank was therefore not necessary, and the provision for its establishment was accordingly not necessary and proper.[62]

In a final appeal to his listeners, Madison reminded them of the assurances that supporters of the Constitution had given to those who had opposed it in the state ratifying conventions: the new government was to be one of limited powers. Indeed, he said, in a reference to what are now the Ninth and Tenth Amendments, the recently adopted Bill of Rights had contained such an assurance in two of its amendments: "the former, as guarding against a latitude of interpretation—the latter, as excluding every source of power not within the constitution itself."[63]

Madison, however, had misrepresented the extent of the assurances that friends of the Constitution had given during ratification. They had not discussed the breadth of the means that Congress could employ in providing for the execution of a specified power. Rather, the assurances they had given had been in refutation of the charge that the Necessary and Proper Clause was sweeping, conferring general powers on the new government.

At the Pennsylvania convention James Wilson had stated that necessary and proper meant "no more than that the powers . . . [specified in Article I, Section 8] shall be effectually carried into execution."[64] Writing in the *Federalist,* Hamilton had followed Wilson's explanation: "And it is *expressly* to execute these powers [i.e., those specified in Article I, Section 8], that the sweeping clause, as it has been affectedly called, authorises the national legislature to pass all *necessary* and *proper* laws."[65]

Madison himself used similar language in the *Federalist.*[66] And in the Virginia convention, he had said the following: "[The Necessary and Proper Clause] only enables them [i.e., Congress] to execute the delegated powers. . . . For when any power is given, its delegation necessarily involves authority to make laws to execute it. . . . The particular powers which are found necessary to be given, are therefore delegated generally, and particular and minute specification is left to the legislature."[67]

Madison's reference to the ratification campaign in support of his construction of the Necessary and Proper Clause had a sound basis, therefore, only insofar as it substantiated the thesis that the clause had not conferred general powers of legislation on Congress. But no one during ratification had mentioned the distinctions on which Madison now relied in discussing the meaning of the clause: between important incidental powers and unimportant ones; or between necessary incidental means and merely convenient ones. His distinctions, moreover, were unrelated to the purpose of the clause: the authorization of measures designed to carry into operation laws passed pursuant to the enumerated powers. Nevertheless, House supporters of the bill were unwilling to challenge Madison directly and say that its provisions did accord with the construction of the clause that proponents of the Constitution had advanced in the state conventions and in the *Federalist:* that the operations of the bank would facilitate, and therefore be incidental to, the collection of taxes and the payment of the debt.

Although Ames did say—as part of a much more ambitious argument in support of the bill—that the bank would facilitate the payment of the debt,[68] he disregarded what was said during ratification and argued instead for a construction of the Necessary and Proper Clause that would allow Congress general, as opposed to incidental, powers of legislation. Taking the lead for the party that Madison had deserted, he contended "that construction [of the clause] may be maintained to be a safe one which promotes the good of the society, and the ends for which the government was adopted, without impairing the rights of any man, or the powers of any

State."[69] Advancing the principal reasons for establishing the bill that Hamilton had set forth in his report, Ames said that since the bank would enhance trade and the collection of taxes and enable the government to borrow in time of war, the bill would promote the ends of the government and facilitate the execution of its powers.[70]

These contentions, however, avoided the thrust of Madison's argument that since the bill did not constitute a regulation of commerce, did not provide for the government's collection of taxes, and did not authorize a government loan, it did not constitute an execution of an enumerated power. Instead, Ames was advocating a reading of the Necessary and Proper Clause that confirmed the interpretation that Randolph, Mason, and Gerry had given the clause toward the conclusion of the Constitutional Convention, and that Mason, Gerry, and others, including the Federal Farmer, had given it during ratification: the clause was a sweeping one. It would grant Congress broad powers to legislate for what it considered to be in the best interests of the country.[71]

In further support of the bill, Sedgwick recalled that two years earlier Madison had argued for an exclusive presidential power to remove a department head under a broad and implied construction of the executive article of the Constitution; he properly charged him with inconsistency.[72] (He could have added that the power to remove was an important one and that under Madison's new view of the Constitution, it could not, unless it was expressed, be ascribed to the president or even to the Senate.) But this was the limit of Sedgwick's rebuke. He did not mention that others in that debate, including himself, had, without protest from Madison, relied on the doctrine of a power implicit in the Necessary and Proper Clause to invest the removal power in the president.[73] Instead, Sedgwick characterized Madison's reading of the clause as too narrow and impractical. Congress, Sedgwick said, had to be the judge of what was necessary and proper. Otherwise, to make government work effectively the Constitution would have to be amended at length and become an extended code.[74]

Smith, who had earlier moved to recommit the bill for purposes of amendment, opposed Madison's opinion of the bill's unconstitutionality. He reasoned that since the bank's operations involved matters of a fiscal nature, it was necessary for the federal government to establish it.[75]

The arguments of Ames, Sedgwick, and Smith were made to rebut Madison's contention that the establishment of the bank was not justified under the Necessary and Proper Clause. Gerry, a bank supporter and former delegate to the Constitutional Convention, next challenged Madison's rules of constitutional construction. In doing so, he disregarded his own prior position on this subject and said, "His [Madison's] rules being made for the occasion, are the result of his interpretation, and not his interpretation of the rules: as they are not sanctioned by law exposition, or approved by experienced judges of the law; they cannot be considered a criterion for regulating the judgment of the house."[76]

Conveniently forgetting that in the prior session he himself had referred to the proceedings in the Constitutional Convention as supportive of the proposal to assume state debts,[77] Gerry criticized Madison for his reference. In the construction of written documents such as the Constitution, Gerry said, the House should proceed according to the rules set down by William Blackstone in his *Commentaries,* wherein the text of a written document was to be interpreted according to the usual meaning of its words, their use in context, and their effect and consequence. A construction leading to an absurd or trivial meaning was to be disregarded.[78]

Words, Gerry continued, again following Blackstone, should be construed according to their reason or spirit, which was to be found in the cause that moved their enactment. In the case of the Constitution, the cause could be found in its preamble. This of course was an explicit statement of the prevailing canon of the federal party: the Constitution should be broadly construed according to its spirit.[79] What Gerry did not say was that he had spent his energies during the Constitutional Convention and afterwards in Massachusetts during ratification inveighing against such a construction of the powers of the federal government in general, and of the Necessary and Proper Clause in particular.[80]

Disregarding the inconsistencies between his past and present versions of the proper method of constitutional construction, Gerry now embarked on an attack on the argumentation Madison used to support his constitutional construction. He scored the impropriety of a framer's recollection because—as had already been witnessed, he said—memories differed. Even if they did not, he added, they should not be considered. Then, in order not to allow Madison the advantage of his supposedly improperly utilized recollection, Gerry offered his own: The motion to which Madison had referred concerned the power to establish commercial corporations generally, and not a banking corporation specifically.[81] Gerry's recollection tended to support Madison rather than to confute him, but Gerry was never nice about his arguments.

Next, he proceeded to attack the use of the reports of the proceedings of the state conventions. Those reports, he maintained, were unreliable, partial, and mutilated. Pennsylvania's, for instance, omitted the arguments of opponents to ratification. Besides, he added with brutal honesty, the speeches in support of the Constitution were intended only to obtain ratification. They should not be regarded as the speakers' genuine sense of what the text meant. Under the circumstances, the words of even great men were not to be considered authoritative. They should be ignored.[82]

Shifting his grounds, Gerry said that the best proof of the bank's legitimacy was the fact that when Congress under the Articles of Confederation established the Bank of North America and referred the matter to the states, the states did nothing.

On the other hand, he argued, the constitutional amendments that the state ratifying conventions had proposed—for restraining Congress from establishing commercial corporations—amounted to an admission that under the Constitution Congress had the power. (Gerry, it should be added, was a practical man. When the bill became law, he plunked down about $12,000 to buy thirty shares of the new bank's stock.)[83]

One final set of arguments should be mentioned. Early in the debate Jackson, attacking the constitutionality of the bill, invoked several passages from the *Federalist* to support his contention that the bill was not authorized under the Necessary and Proper Clause. Later, Elias Boudinot of New Jersey quoted a different passage from the same essay to support his contention that the bill was authorized under the clause. Although Jackson, rather than Boudinot, was faithful to the meaning and intent of the essay, that fact probably had little effect on the outcome.[84]

There were many reasons for the opposition to the bank: underlying fears concerning the permanent site of the capital, concerns about the bank as an engine for the economic and political domination of southern agriculture by northern money, southern disappointment regarding the failure to secure the acceptance of state debt certificates in payment of bank stock or to have the secretary of state named in the line of presidential succession, the need for a graphic political issue, and perhaps, as Madison wrote privately to some of his political associates, concern about the political and constitutional direction of the United States government.[85] Yet Madison and his supporters lost. The bill carried.[86]

Confronted with this basic constitutional disagreement in the House, Washington asked his cabinet for their opinions concerning the bill. Jefferson, supporting Madison, embellished his arguments, even to the point of reminding the president that "the very power now proposed *as a means,* was rejected *as an end,* by the Convention which formed the constitution."[87]

Randolph followed Jefferson. Forgetting that toward the close of the Virginia convention he had dismissed as too narrow the construction of the Necessary and Proper Clause put forth by the proponents for ratification—that the clause involved only incidental powers[88]—Randolph in his opinion to Washington counseled that the word "necessary" meant incidental, and that the phrase "'and proper,' if it has any meaning, does not enlarge the powers of Congress, but rather restricts them." Then also forgetting that both during and after the Constitutional Convention he had cautioned against the indefinite powers of Congress and the "ambiguities of expression" in the Constitution, he wrote that the clause as a whole should be considered "as among the surplusage which as often proceeds from inattention as caution."[89]

Hamilton in his opinion to Washington first addressed the objection which Madison had raised: that the chartering of a corporation was an important matter which, since it had not been expressly provided in the Constitution, Congress could not undertake. Hamilton did not claim for the United States unlimited sovereign powers, but, foreshadowing Chief Justice Marshall's opinion in *McCulloch v. Maryland*,[90] he argued that under the Supremacy Clause of Article VI of the Constitution the United States possessed the sovereign authority to choose the means requisite to the exercise of its enumerated powers. More specifically, he wrote, the government as an incident to its sovereign power had the authority to create a corporate bank as an expeditious means to the accomplishment of those objects entrusted to its management.[91] Reflecting an urban mercantile point of view in contrast to the agricultural mind-set of Madison, Hamilton denied that the corporate form was "some great, independent, substantive thing." Rather, he wrote, it was simply an ordinary means to an end.[92]

After responding to Madison's argument, which Jefferson and Randolph had followed, Hamilton next addressed their primary argument: the bill was not authorized under the Necessary and Proper Clause. Avoiding the broader construction that Ames had placed on the clause—that through it Congress could legislate for the good of society and the ends for which the government was adopted—he hewed to the more narrow meaning which proponents of the Constitution had advanced during ratification: the clause authorized the adoption of "*all laws* necessary & proper to carry into execution those [i.e., the specified] powers."[93]

But when he applied this standard to the bill, Hamilton proceeded to repeat what he had written in his report and what Ames had said in the House: The bank would secure for the nation an adequate money supply through the medium of a privately issued, governmentally sanctioned paper currency. Under public direction, Hamilton wrote, the bank's bills would continue to circulate even in times of stress involving substantial drains of gold and silver from the country. In this manner, the bank would preserve the orderly collection of taxes and prevent widespread private and, ultimately, public defaults. The bank, he added, would also facilitate the government's ability to borrow, especially in emergencies, and thereby aid in the defense of the country. Finally, a bank, through its creation of credit, would enhance commerce.[94]

Everything that Hamilton had stated was true. He had a keen understanding of the vital role that the control of credit plays in the private economy and public finances of a country. The disastrous consequences of ignoring that understanding and following the Madison-Jefferson rule of governance would be demonstrated during the War of 1812 when, in the absence of a national bank to control the amount and quality of the bills and notes emitted by state banks, the national government was compelled to default on its debt.[95]

Nevertheless, it was also true that the Constitution had made no provision for the control of credit or for the supply of a paper currency. Instead, in its Coinage Clause it had specifically provided for the issuance of a metallic currency, that is, one based on gold and silver. That had been deliberate. At the convention, the framers had rejected a reliance on a national paper currency when they defeated a motion expressly permitting the emission of federal bills of credit.[96]

Hamilton, however, strongly believed that the country's finances and economy could not subsist with a circulating currency limited to gold and silver. Yet, as he stated in his report, "The emitting of paper money by the authority of Government is wisely prohibited to the individual States, by the National Constitution. And the spirit of that prohibition ought not to be disregarded, by the Government of the United States." His solution was to create an agency that could do for the government what it could not do for itself: emit paper which would circulate as money and thus supply the medium essential for a prospering commerce, the payment of taxes, and the prevention of private bankruptcy and a default on the public debt. The establishment of a national bank for this purpose was absolutely necessary.[97]

It must be said, however, that under the meaning of the Necessary and Proper Clause to which Hamilton nominally subscribed, the establishment of a bank to assure an adequate money supply was not incidental to the execution of a specified power. Indeed, it seemed to run counter to the constitutional provision for a metallic currency. Hamilton's application of the clause therefore was more than incidental. It was sweeping.

Elsewhere in his opinion Hamilton, rebutting Jefferson, deprecated the latter's reference to the proceedings of the Constitutional Convention: "What was the precise nature or extent of this proposition, or what the reasons for refusing it, is not ascertained by any authentic document, or even by accurate recollection."[98] Different persons gave different accounts. Hamilton summarized his position: "Whatever may have been the intention of the framers of a constitution, or of a law, that intention is to be sought for in the instrument itself, according to the usual & established rules of construction. Nothing is more common than for laws to *express* and *effect,* more or less than was intended."[99]

Ironically, during the debate in the Fourth Congress over the powers of the House affecting the implementation of ratified treaties, it would be the Republicans who, led by Albert Gallatin and Madison, would make the argument advanced by Hamilton concerning the impropriety of employing a framer's recollections to interpret the meaning of the Constitution. And it would be the Federalists who would make the argument advanced by Madison and Jefferson of the propriety of such employment.[100]

Washington, in considering the arguments for and against the constitutionality of the bill, was faced with a quandary. The difficulty with Hamilton's position was that through the bank he would deliberately create a governmental agency whose function it would be to create paper money and with government sanction circulate it as currency in disregard of the Constitution's Coinage Clause, which envisioned an official currency based on metal. But in practical terms a purely metallic currency could not adequately serve the American economy. As Hamilton had ably demonstrated in his report, the country did not have the mines to produce the gold and silver which the United States required to pay its foreign debts and collect its revenues, and which the private economy needed in the ordinary course of its operations. Nor did the country have a favorable trade balance whereby it could add to its gold and silver supply instead of depleting it.[101] And as Hamilton had also ably demonstrated in his report, the then existing state banks were in no position to supply the country's monetary deficiencies.[102] Only a national bank could do that.

It followed that a national bank was crucially important to the sound administration of the United States government and to the future prosperity of the country. Madison had been right—the power to establish the bank was important—but not for the reasons he had given: as a corporation, the bank would be an artificial person and have the extraordinary powers of a corporation. A bank was important because through the extension of credit and the issuance of its paper it created money. Hamilton wanted the bank precisely because it would have those powers. And it was because the bank's importance lay in those powers that both Hamilton and Ames chose not to rely on what was for them an inconsequential reason for its establishment: its usefulness in the collection of taxes and the payment of the debt.

Yet Madison, in opposing the bank, avoided any discussion of its true importance or the reasons for its establishment. In effect, he admitted them. One may suppose that it was because of his understanding of the importance of a national bank that he had twice moved in the Constitutional Convention to confer on Congress the specific power to establish one.

Washington was neither an economist nor a constitutional lawyer. But he was able enough to read Hamilton's report, to consider the arguments for and against the creation of the bank in the light of that report, and to contemplate the consequences to the American economy of a veto. He also had close friends in the Philadelphia mercantile community, including Robert Morris, with whom he could have consulted.

From his own experience at the Constitutional Convention, Washington knew that Madison's second motion to confer the power to establish a bank had failed only because it was feared that a specific authorization would provoke the New York and Philadelphia banks into opposing the Constitution. He must have also understood that it was the general sentiment among the delegates that Congress would have such a power without the need for saying so.

Washington had presided over the compromise that led to the adoption of the Necessary and Proper Clause, and he had heard Mason, Randolph, and Gerry charge it with a general and indefinite meaning. This protest, Washington must have known, grew out of a conviction that the clause would be used to justify legislation such as the bank bill. For the same reasons, he must have known that Madison's opposition to the bank bill really arose from the fact that, despite its merit, its constitutionality had been defended by a recourse to a construction of the clause broader than Madison considered essential to the protection of the interests of Virginia and the South.

The president must have realized that in the vacuum resulting from the absence of a national bank, the states would establish new banks. Without a federal banking control, these banks would through the extension of their credit create their own paper, which passing as money would in turn circulate as currency, and lead to the growth of a national economy perilously based on state paper. Eventually, the Madison-Jefferson system would lead to monetary chaos. The country needed a national bank.

As president of the United States, responsible for the establishment of the first principles of its government and the creation of institutions and practices that would ensure its success, he must have concluded that under those circumstances it was impossible for him to side with Virginia. Instead, he sided with Hamilton and signed the bill into law.[103] When the bank's charter expired in 1811, Madison, then president, did what Washington had done before him. He also decided in favor of a national bank and sought renewal of its charter.

Washington's approval of the bank bill did not end Madison's and Jefferson's discomfiture. To their dismay, national and northern interest and Hamilton's influence also predominated in the area of foreign policy, on the critical question of whether, in retaliation for British discrimination against American shipping and their closing of their colonial markets to American produce, the United States should commercially discriminate against British shipping. This was a course that both Madison and Jefferson had long favored. As far back as 1783 in the Continental Congress Madison had advocated it, purportedly to encourage American shipping but actually to help the South by fostering competition in the transportation of agricultural exports and consumer imports. The following year Jefferson in Congress had given Madison his support.[104]

Madison's and Jefferson's position, however, was also based on more fundamental concerns—on the perennial governmental problems of insuring to the citizens of the republic the availability of full and useful employment and the maintenance of a classless society. Appalled by the social and economic conditions in Britain and France, they wished to avoid the growth of an American landless poor, who in order to survive would consent to the mind-deadening routine of factory work. Piecework, they thought, was not the proper environment for the development of good republicans.

America, they considered, could avoid this situation only so long as large areas of unsettled land suitable for farming were available to its expanding population, and so long as sufficient numbers of people at home or abroad were willing and able to consume American farm products. Madison and Jefferson decided that to ensure the availability of those markets the United States must insist on a policy of free trade. This in turn required that the United States do everything necessary to open markets closed to American produce, including the adoption of the policy of retaliatory discrimination against those countries closing their markets to such produce.[105]

Pursuant to this analysis, Madison in the first session of the First Federal Congress took the initial step of offering a bill that would impose a duty on tonnage carried in foreign ships at rates substantially higher than those in domestic. This was done to encourage New England shipping and secure that region's support. But, seeking to force the British into a treaty of commercial accommodation, he also provided in his bill that shipping from countries with commercial treaties with the United States (like France) would pay lower rates. Both proposals ran into opposition. The former displeased the South because, as the country's primary importing region, the burden of higher duties would fall mostly upon it. The latter displeased the merchants of New England and New York City because they feared that discriminatory duties might antagonize their best customers and even provoke a disastrous war. For these reasons, although the bill passed the House, where anti-British sentiment was high, it failed in the Senate.[106]

Madison did not give up. In the second session, he reintroduced his bill. He was encouraged by an initial success to go even further and move that the ships of countries not having commercial treaties with the United States be prohibited from transporting American farm produce. With this, he lost southern support, and his bill failed once again.[107]

During the third session, while the fate of the bank bill was pending, Jefferson as secretary of state, reporting to the president on the state of the New England fisheries, joined Madison in recommending a policy of commercial retaliation to compel Britain to end its discrimination against American shipping. After Washington submitted the report to Congress,[108] Madison once again moved a bill for commercial discrimination against the British.[109]

At this point, Hamilton intervened. If he were consistent and followed the course he had advocated in the *Federalist,* he would have supported Jefferson's and Madison's policy. There he had argued for ratification of the Constitution on the ground that the new government, with its power to regulate foreign commerce, would be able to compel the British to desist from its discriminatory practices against American shipping by excluding British shipping from American ports.[110]

But Hamilton was not consistent. He now opposed the Jefferson-Madison policy as running the risk of precipitating a war that he thought the country was financially and militarily unable to wage. The policy, he now considered, would disrupt the country's trade, alienate northern merchants, and ruin the government's revenues, most of which derived from duties laid on imports—mainly from Britain. Making up the deficit would require the imposition of excise taxes, which would severely burden the country's commerce and make both the Treasury and the government very unpopular.[111]

Hamilton recommended deferring significant legislation until the imminent arrival of a new British envoy to the United States, who, he said, would probably seek to adjust the countries' differences. His influence and reasoning helped carry the day in Congress.[112] The influence of the Treasury, as is often the case, significantly affected foreign, as well as domestic, policy.

In consequence, by the end of the First Congress, the secretary of the treasury had become the most important man in government after the president. He, not Madison or Jefferson, had become the president's unofficial prime minister. Washington certified as much when he accepted Hamilton's formal opinion in favor of the bank bill's constitutionality, and when he signaled his acceptance of the wisdom of establishing a national bank by signing the bill into law.[113]

From that time on, Madison, in opposition to Hamilton's policies and influence, would contend repeatedly that the expanding powers of the federal government were working toward a rapid consolidation of all governmental powers, to the detriment of state sovereignty and the people's liberties. In the shadow government of opposition, he would be Jefferson's prime minister.

The Emergence of Opposition

As the First Congress closed, the view from Virginia was bleak. In theory, its personnel dominated the new administration. Its own president was in command, and it was represented in two of the four cabinet posts. In the House, its delegation was the most numerous and, as the leader of the South, carried great weight. Yet its influence and counsel were ineffective. Under Hamilton's leadership, administration policy advanced northern financial interests and favored British rather than French commerce. His interpretation of the Constitution prevailed.

No change from Hamilton's policies or constitutional interpretation seemed likely. In Congress his opinion had proved decisive. As for the presidency, although Washington was popular and, if he chose, would be elected for another term, his reelection would probably insure the continuation of Hamilton's influence. And if Washington chose not to stand for reelection, Adams would receive the backing of New England, his own region, and probably that of the middle states. As matters stood, the South would be outvoted. If Adams was elected, he would most likely continue the policies his supporters wanted, and the South, with its agricultural economy, would share the burden of import duties but few of the benefits from the Hamilton system of trade and finance.

Jefferson and Madison sought a way out of this predicament. While consolidating their political base in the South, they looked to conclude alliances with disaffected persons in the North. These comprised political enemies of Hamilton in New York, as well as farmers and merchants disgruntled by his policies and at odds with the prevailing Federalist mercantile class in New York, Pennsylvania, and elsewhere. The Virginians hoped to separate the House from Hamilton and persuade its membership to follow their own leadership.[1]

The New "Republicans"

In working toward this end, however, they formulated a program calculated to appeal to more than just economic interest. Working on widespread public hostility to all things British, they accused the vice-president and the secretary of the treasury, as well as their followers in Congress, of a deep-seated bias in favor of British institutions and practices, which, the accusation went, they were foisting on the federal government. Indeed, Jefferson and Madison asserted, "crypto-aristocrats" would by stages attempt to impose on the government of the United States an aristocratic-monarchical form. Only fidelity to the principles of true republicanism could save the country from this danger. The true republicans of course were the Virginians themselves and those who took up their cause.[2]

It was not difficult to convict Adams, Hamilton, and their supporters of a bias in favor of British institutions. During the opening days of the first session of the First Congress Adams, in championing an ill-conceived attempt to confer lofty titles of respect and address on the president, had shown advanced signs of Anglophilia (the attempt had foundered in the House). Hamilton had followed English practice when he sponsored legislation providing for an almost permanent system of taxation to insure redemption of the national debt. Similarly, in establishing the Bank of the United States and advocating a dependence on the paper it would issue as a circulating medium of national currency, he had followed methods used in the creation and operations of the Bank of England.[3] And while Hamilton might base his preference for British commerce on the Treasury's pragmatic need for a dependable source of revenue, it was true as well that Federalist merchants and politicians favored British trade.

Jefferson and his allies could also plausibly charge the Federalists with British-style methods of governance, claiming that as in Britain, the United States government, with the connivance of a corrupt legislature, operated for the benefit of the monied interests. Here is what Jefferson said he told Washington early in 1792:

THAT A SYSTEM HAD THERE [i.e., in the Treasury Department] been contrived, for deluging the states with paper-money instead of gold and silver, for withdrawing our citizens from the pursuit of commerce, manufactures, buildings, and other branches of useful industry, to occupy themselves and their capitals in a species of gambling, destructive of morality, and which had introduced it's poison into the government itself. That it was a fact . . . that particular members of the legislature, while those laws were on the carpet, had feathered their nests with paper, had then voted for the laws, and constantly since lent all the energy of their talents, and instrumentality of their offices to the establishment and enlargement of this system: that they had chained it about our necks for a great length of time; and in order to keep the game in their hands had from time to time aided in making such legislative constructions of the constitution as made it a very different thing from what the people thought they had submitted to.[4]

Thus warning of a corrupting, aristocratic-monarchical federal government dangerous to the liberties of the people, Jefferson and Madison, the new, self-styled republicans, appealed to the country's tradition of political opposition. They allied themselves with Madison's former opponents in the presidential removal bill, and preempted the Anti-Federalist movement.[5] Gerry could not join them. That erstwhile Anti-Federalist, republican, and fierce opponent of "Court" machinations against the liberties of the people had deserted the cause and supported—and profited from—the fiscal policies of Hamilton. But if Jefferson and Madison could not gain his support, they could, without naming names, denounce the "monarchist" methods by which the Treasury had secured his vote. In "Country" terms, "the Court" had corrupted Gerry.[6] Such a denunciation would prove particularly effective with those in both North and South who made a living by the sweat of their brow or the brows of their slaves.

The first step in the plan to reduce Hamilton's influence in the House and to hamper Adams's eventual candidacy for the presidency was taken in early March 1791, even before the First Congress adjourned. Through Madison, Jefferson offered a position in the State Department to Philip Frenau, Madison's classmate at Princeton, a writer, Frenchman, and staunch republican enemy of monarchy. Madison and Jefferson also promised to help him start a newspaper in Philadelphia as a platform for republican principles against what they termed the monarchical tendencies of administration policies. The new paper was to rival one already subsidized by Hamilton. When Frenau accepted, they worked assiduously to build his subscription list. The publication, *The National Gazette,* became the Treasury's most virulent critic. Madison, under a pseudonym, became one of its chief contributors.[7]

In a series of essays Madison sounded a favorite theme of Patrick Henry: The encroachments of the national government would lead to a consolidation of the national and state governments and eventually—in violation of constitutional principle—to a hereditary monarchy and the endangerment of the people's liberties.[8] The monarchists, Madison stated, could be identified by the techniques they used to influence federal policy: the bribery of congressmen, the disbursement of subsidies to interest groups,[9] the systematic accumulation of federal debt, and the insidious exaction of taxes.[10] Anticipating the accusation that those opposing the administration were no more than political factions motivated by the desire for power, he developed a justification for an opposition party based on principle.[11]

In May 1791 another event helped further the campaign against the policies of the administration and its supposed aristocratic-monarchical tendencies. A Philadelphia printer, publishing an American edition of Thomas Paine's *The Rights of Man,* included excerpts from a Jefferson note which endorsed the work as a refutation of certain "political heresies." The endorsement had all the marks of a gibe against the so-called royal tendencies supposedly revealed by Adams in his recently published *Discourses on Davila.* Jefferson's popularity, as a defender of true republican sentiments, rose while Adams's declined. Writing privately to Washington, Jefferson explained that he had not known that his endorsement would be published. Washington apparently did not believe him.[12]

A few weeks later Jefferson and Madison pursued their cause in person. Meeting in New York City, the pair traveled upstate through Albany and through western New England, ostensibly on a holiday. Mixing political business with pleasure, they conferred in New York City with Chancellor Livingston and Aaron Burr, close supporters of Governor Clinton and outspoken opponents of Hamilton. In recent correspondence Jefferson had inquired of Livingston whether New York was content with the conduct of the federal administration; presumably on this occasion he pursued his query in person. As the Virginians traveled through the state, British agents in New York City reported that they were seeking support for a commercial war with Great Britain. Next the two proceeded easterly into Vermont and met there with politicians who opposed the federal administration.[13]

On the completion of their "holiday," Jefferson returned to Philadelphia, but Madison remained in New York City to confer with John Beckley, clerk to the United States House of Representatives, a fellow Virginian and his and Jefferson's close confidant. Beckley had just returned from Boston, where he and Madison had originally planned to go together. He had good news, which Madison happily passed along to Jefferson: Adams was generally unpopular in Boston.[14]

Eighteen months later, when Washington agreed to a second term, Madison would work with Beckley in an attempt to stop Adams from being reelected vice-president. Together they would join with Monroe, Madison's rival in the 1789 election and one of Henry's chief lieutenants in the campaign against ratification, to solicit votes for Governor Clinton, who had headed the fight against ratification in New York. The alliance between disaffected Federalists and Anti-Federalists would then be complete.[15]

Second Congress, First Session, 1791–92

Limits on Federal Power

In spite of all the signs warning of an impending opposition, and in spite of the constitutional challenges Madison had raised against the Bank of the United States in the First Congress, Hamilton in the first session of the Second Congress advanced another controversial scheme, the subsidization of manufactures. In his report on the subject, Hamilton's analysis of the American economy mirrored that of Jefferson and Madison: An increasing domestic agricultural surplus would not be able to find a market either at home or abroad. His prescription for a remedy, however, was entirely different: Since the prospect for free trade was dim and the United States lacked the power to open foreign markets, the nation should develop its own factories, whose products would supply its domestic needs and whose laborers would consume the domestic farm surplus. His advocacy of an early establishment of the European factory system alarmed many.[16]

As in the case of the Bank, there was no specific constitutional provision for Hamilton's plan, although, as in that case, the idea was not novel. During the Constitutional Convention, Charles Pinckney had proposed granting Congress the authority to establish public institutions for the promotion of manufactures, agriculture, commerce, and trades, but his suggestion had not been included in the final list of enumerated powers. The Constitution as drafted, however, did authorize Congress, after collecting taxes, "to pay the Debts and provide for the common Defence and general Welfare of the United States."[17] Hamilton now argued that provision for the general welfare included the power to spend for the promotion of manufactures.[18]

Hamilton had more immediate support for his argument. Washington, in his address to the second session of the First Congress, had followed the substance of Pinckney's proposal and recommended legislation in aid of agriculture, commerce, manufacturing, science, and literature, as well as of institutions of higher learning. We may suppose that Washington believed, as a framer, that the substance of the Pinckney motion had been included within the scope of the spending power. Washington's suggestions in the First Congress had not gone unchallenged, however. When a motion was made there to refer his recommendations to committee, Representatives Stone and Sherman both questioned the authority of Congress to implement the president's proposals. Sherman observed that the Constitutional Convention had rejected the proposition to vest Congress with the power to establish a national university. It was thought, he added, that the power should be left to the states. No further action was taken in the First Congress.[19]

After Madison's attack on the Bank, moreover, the administration was probably aware of the conceptual difficulties in arguing under the Constitution for the support of manufactures. The likelihood of a constitutional attack was heightened by the southerners' practical reservations about Hamilton's proposal. Because manufactures were invariably a northern activity, their subsidy would yield no direct benefit to the agricultural South. At the same time, because federal taxes were chiefly exacted from manufactured imports, and southern agricultural interests relied heavily on those imports in trading with the British, the money needed to finance the subsidy would constitute an additional fiscal burden on the South.

Perhaps in view of all this, Hamilton made one important concession to the scrupulous in his argument that the promotion of domestic manufactures was for the benefit of the country as a whole and "for the general Welfare of the United States" under Article I, Section 8, Clause 1. Mindful that the Constitutional Convention had, besides rejecting motions enabling Congress to charter a bank or establish a national university, also rejected a motion authorizing the construction of canals,[20] he expressed a doubt as to a congressional power to build either roads or canals.[21]

It was against this background that the House on February 3, 1792, in the first session of the Second Congress, took up a bill for government subsidies or, as it was termed, "bounties" in aid of the fishing industry. Congressmen from Massachusetts, who were strong supporters of both Hamilton and the fishing industry, led the fight for approval. In reply to Giles's charge that the bill was invalid because the power to provide subsidies was not enumerated in the Constitution, they contended that the subsidy in question was not really a bounty but in the nature of a rebate to the revenue laws.[22]

But when Laurance invoked the spending power as constitutional authority for the bill, Madison protested. He was willing in that particular case, he said, to regard the expenditure not as a bounty but rather a "modification of a drawback" in revenue, but he was opposed to a bounty based on the theory of spending for the "general welfare."[23]

Characteristically well prepared for the occasion, Madison delivered his classic argument against a broad reading of the spending power. Reasoning from the overall design of Article I, Section 8, he maintained that Congress might spend only for the purposes set forth in the list of powers enumerated in that section, for instance, to raise armies and provide a navy. For Congress to go beyond those purposes would be absurd, because such a construction would virtually convert the United States into "a Government without any limits at all." If Congress could spend for the general welfare as it pleased, he reasoned, it could provide for a jurisdiction for the federal courts throughout the United States without regard to citizenship or the type of case involved. It could, according to Madison, "take the case of religion" into its own hands, assume the cost of education, or provide for the press and the regulation of all roads, over and above post roads. All the objects of state legislation would consequently fall within its power. Laurance's suggestion, Madison said, was not only novel, it was contrary to the practice of the Continental Congress under the Articles of Confederation, which had its own general welfare provision. It was also against the intention of those who proposed the Constitution and, more materially, against the intention of those who in state conventions ratified the Constitution. The government of the United States, he concluded, was limited "to the specified powers which explain and define the general terms."[24]

In essence, this was a repetition of his argument concerning the meaning of the Necessary and Proper Clause in the debate over the Bank: The general or indefinite character of its language had to be read in the light of the specific and definite provisions of Article I, Section 8, and in the light of the concessions made to the opponents of the Constitution during the state ratifying conventions.

There were, however, important differences. Textually, the Necessary and Proper Clause appears in the final paragraph of Section 8 and therefore, as a matter of internal design, could plausibly be said to sum up the preceding paragraphs and be interpreted in their light. The term "general welfare," however, appears in the very first clause of the section, as part of a specific power to collect taxes and pay the debts and provide for defense and welfare. As a matter of textual design, therefore, and despite the argument Madison made in the *Federalist*,[25] it does not constitute a summary of the specific authorizations in the subsequent paragraphs of the section.

In addition, as the first in the list of specifically enumerated powers, the provisions of Clause 1 might be said to assume a primacy of importance. That the power of Congress to lay and collect taxes and pay the debts of the United States was the single most important power that the national legislature could possess, everyone, including Madison, had agreed. What then was the meaning of the additionally included power in this provision: to provide for "the common Defence and general Welfare of the United States?" Why did not that phrase mean literally what it said?

Essentially, Madison's argument was based as much on the practical effects of a literal construction as on logic. Under such a construction Congress, through the adroit use of the spending power, would be able to accomplish what it could not under the subsequent paragraphs of Article I, Section 8. The course of constitutional history, subsequent to the Supreme Court's vindication of the Hamilton interpretation of the clause, has proved Madison correct.[26]

But it was not true, as Madison claimed, that assurances had been given supporting his version of the term "general welfare" in the state conventions. Opponents to ratification had not questioned the spending implications of the clause. Rather, Mason in the Virginia convention had interpreted it as an alternate regulatory power, a second Necessary and Proper Clause allowing Congress to legislate in any way it pleased, and in that light opposed it. At the same time, he admitted that Congress should have the power to provide for the general welfare of the Union, a concession that seemed to include a power to appropriate money for that purpose.[27]

To meet Mason's argument that the term "general welfare" was part of an all-purpose regulatory provision, George Nicholas and Randolph had assured the Virginia convention that the clause, of which it was part, would authorize Congress only to pay the debts of the United States.[28] At the least, therefore, it can be concluded that the issue of whether Congress, in spending for the general welfare of the United States, was limited to the subjects set forth in the specifically enumerated powers of Article I, Section 8, was not before the Virginia convention. And certainly a literal construction of the clause, to the effect that Congress generally could spend for the prosperity of the United States, was not contrary to the sense of that convention, or of any other convention. In presenting an argument to the contrary in the Second Congress, Madison was advancing a position that, in all logic, opponents to such a broad congressional power should have raised during the ratification campaign, but hadn't.

If we have a good idea of what was said and written during ratification regarding the meaning of the term "general welfare," the evidence we have of what the framers intended by the language is circumstantial. There had been some discussion during the convention about conferring on Congress the power to legislate or to provide for the general welfare of the country. And during the debates concerning the payment of the war debt, references had been made to the obligations and expenses incurred for the common defense and general welfare.[29]

Madison, late in life, maintained that the clause was included in order to make a special provision for the payment of the war debt. It was not needed to provide for the debts the new Congress would incur, he wrote, because "a power to provide money, and a power to perform certain acts of which money is the ordinary & appropriate means, must of course carry with them a power to pay the expence of performing the acts."[30]

But Congress already had that power under the Necessary and Proper Clause. Therefore, according to Madison's explanation, the general welfare phrase was redundant. (This would be so whether one regarded the Necessary and Proper Clause as merely conferring the power to execute the specifically enumerated powers or as enabling Congress to legislate in the general interests of the country.)

Having convicted the general welfare provision of redundancy, Madison labored to make that point. The phrase had its origins in the Articles of Confederation, wherein "all charges of war and all other expences that shall be incurred for the common defence or general welfare, and allowed by the united states, in congress assembled, shall be defrayed out of a common treasury."[31] Turning to the words used in the Constitution, Madison wrote: "With this addition [i.e., "to provide for the common Defence and general Welfare"] indeed the language of the clause being, in conformity with that of the clause in the Articles of Confederation, it would be qualified, as in those Articles, by the specification of powers subjoined to it."[32]

Madison's explanation of the general welfare provision, twice rendering it redundant, assumed the validity of his explanation of the Necessary and Proper Clause—that the clause's operation was limited to the execution of the specified powers. His explanation also assumed that the practice of the Continental Congress accorded with his interpretation of its powers under the Articles. In fact, that body had made a number of expenditures for purposes for which it could not legislate, including education and road construction, as he admitted.[33]

If Madison's understanding of the general welfare provision is correct, why, it might be asked—as John C. Calhoun did in the House in 1817—had not the framers written, "and provide for the implementation of the powers hereinafter more specifically enumerated," instead of the language they had used?[34] The answer is that they could not. Contrary to Madison's version of convention history, the framers had not decided to limit the legislative powers of Congress to those specifically enumerated. Rather, leaving the matter of legislative power unresolved, they had settled on the compromise language of the Necessary and Proper Clause. The framers had left it to Congress to determine whether, pursuant to that clause, they could legislate in the general interests of the country or whether they could merely implement the specifically enumerated powers.

Had the framers, when formulating the general welfare language, authorized Congress to "provide for the implementation of the powers hereinafter more specifically enumerated," they would have undone the earlier compromise and, in effect, adopted the position that Madison pursued on behalf of Virginia and the South against Gunning Bedford and the northern states: that Congress could not legislate in the general interests of the country, but only in execution of the specifically enumerated powers. Since that compromise could not be undone, the convention, in shaping a provision for congressional spending, had to employ language as indefinite as the Necessary and Proper Clause, and equally ambiguous.

The general welfare provision, therefore, constituted a second compromise. Other considerations point to this conclusion. References to the general welfare of the United States at the Constitutional Convention had not, as Madison would have it, been confined to the payment of the war debt. In his recounting of convention history and the origins of the general welfare provision, he selectively omitted references connecting the provision with proposals to legislate or to provide for the common or general interests of the country.

During the debate over the scope of legislative powers, Roger Sherman had unsuccessfully moved that Congress be authorized to make laws concerning "the common interests of the Union" in matters that did not affect the internal affairs of the states and "wherein the general welfare of the United States is not concerned."[35] Later, the Committee of Detail, picking up on Sherman's language, had recommended that Congress provide for managing "the common property and general interests and welfare of the United States in such manner as shall not interfere with [the internal affairs of the states or in which the states might not] be competent."[36]

The convention did not directly act upon that recommendation. It is not improbable that the same considerations that prompted Detail to advance its proposal—and Sherman to move that Congress be authorized to legislate for the general welfare—influenced the framing and adoption of the general welfare provision as it appears in the Constitution. Some formula was needed to allow those in the majority to argue, as Hamilton and his northern allies in Congress later did, that Congress through its spending power could indeed provide for the general interests of the country. At the same time, the formula that the convention approved had to permit the minority to argue, as Madison and his southern cohorts did, that it was in effect redundant. The compromise was framed; the provision for spending for the general welfare, as we know it, was proposed and approved.

None of these considerations surfaced in the Second Congress. The House avoided the issue of the meaning of Congress's spending power by amending the bill to provide for an "allowance" for the fisheries rather than a "bounty," and on that basis the bill passed.[37] For decades to come, however, Madison's argument and Jefferson's influence would be the primary obstacles to federal funding for any purpose that could not be made to fit within the confines of one of the enumerated powers.

By this argument, Madison and his supporters in effect crossed the Rubicon, or, perhaps we should say, the Potomac. From then on, he committed the South to a construction of the Constitution whereby—regardless of almost all exigencies except those of unavoidable and overwhelming necessity—the federal government would be confined within narrow channels of authority. To achieve this result, the spending power would not be construed literally. Instead, it would be read according to the spirit of confederation and Anti-Federalism, whereby national power would be systematically limited and state power, if not expanded, would be systematically maintained. Madison's opposition to Washington's nationalist aspirations could not have been made plainer.

The Limits of Executive Power

In advancing a strict construction of both "necessary and proper" and "general welfare," Madison assumed the leadership in the House of the "Country" forces in their effort to limit the powers of the federal government. His principled argumentation legitimized their opposition and assured it a respectful audience.

He next joined in their attacks on executive power. Moving to thwart Hamilton's influence, opponents spoke out against proposals to extend the power of departmental heads. "Country" themes—fears of corruption and the establishment of a monarchy—colored their construction of the Constitution. They invoked legislative prerogatives and charged that Hamilton and others were violating the principle of separation of powers.

The first attack against executive power arose during the discussion of a bill to organize the Post Office. At issue was a provision empowering the postmaster general, under the direction of the president, to establish post offices and post roads he considered necessary. Objection had been initially raised to such a proposal in the First Congress, on the ground that it would constitute an improper delegation of legislative authority to the executive. The claim was made that disbursement of revenues would be centered in the executive's hands, leading to the widespread corruption and servility of the people and the destruction of their liberty. Moreover, the argument went, because Congress was expressly authorized to establish post offices and post roads, the provision was unconstitutional.[38]

Those who sounded the corruption theme in that instance were concerned that the postmaster general would use his power to influence legislative votes on matters important to him or to the administration. Executive power would increase and congressional independence decline. Legislation might be approved, not because Congress considered it meritorious, but because the executive branch wanted it. Private interests might benefit, while the public interest would suffer. Since at that time the Post Office was placed in the Treasury Department and the postmaster general would be subject to Hamilton's supervision, and since Treasury influence had been at work in the passage of the legislation effecting the assumption of state debt and the establishment of the national bank, "Country" fears were rampant.[39]

The bill to organize the Post Office had foundered in the First Congress. While Madison had voted with those who opposed investing the postmaster general with discretionary power, he had not participated in the debates.[40] The bill, with its controversial provision, was revived in the Second Congress. Its supporters, stressing its practicality, observed that in adopting the excise law, the House had left it to the president to delineate excise districts, a task they said was fairly comparable to the designation of post roads.[41]

Madison now spoke out publicly against the provision for the first time. The delineation of post roads, he said, was distinguishable from that of excise districts, because the latter rested on an "exigency." (What constituted the exigency or why it made a difference, he did not say, or if he did, it was not reported.) If the postal bill were to provide differently, he added, it would violate the Constitution. As in the First Congress, the proposal was defeated.[42]

Another provision, authorizing stage coach proprietors employed in carrying the mail to carry passengers as well, was similarly attacked as unconstitutional, and its justification under the Necessary and Proper Clause impugned. It too was defeated.[43] The bill to organize the Post Office finally passed with a provision that its profits—instead of being paid into the general revenues of the United States and administered by the Treasury, as formerly—be specifically earmarked for the activities of the Post Office. The anti-Hamiltonian purpose of such a change was soon revealed.[44]

In the administration, Jefferson called Washington's attention to the provision respecting the dedication of postal profits and suggested that the president move the newly organized Post Office from the Treasury Department. Because the Treasury was no longer to administer its revenues, and because Treasury had "already such an influence as to swallow up the whole Executive powers," Jefferson said, it would be advantageous to place the office in the State Department, that is to say, under his own control.[45]

It was on the following day that Jefferson reportedly unburdened himself to Washington and gave him his views, quoted earlier in this chapter, on how the Treasury was corrupting Congress and the country. For good measure, he told the president of his fears that Hamilton's construction of the spending power would lead to an unlimited government. Jefferson did not report the president's reaction, but since Washington failed to shift the Post Office from Treasury to State, we can assume that he did not share Jefferson's concerns about undue Treasury influence. And from the president's subsequent message to the Fourth Congress repeating his call for legislation to promote manufactures and agriculture, we can deduce that he did not share Jefferson's interpretation of the Constitution.[46]

Back in the House, the opposition leveled a second constitutional attack on executive powers, this time in response to a proposed resolution directing Hamilton to report to the House "his opinion of the best mode for raising the additional [revenue] . . . requisite for the ensuing year."[47] John Page of Virginia sounded a "Country" theme when he argued that in view of the constitutional provision for the origination of revenue matters in the House, the resolution permitting a member of the executive branch to initiate revenue suggestions would constitute an intrusion upon legislative powers and would introduce a monarchical system of government.[48]

Page's argument closely followed the line he had taken in the First Congress when, during debate over the bill to organize the Treasury Department, he had opposed a provision authorizing the secretary of the treasury to "report plans for the improvement and management of the revenue." Madison at that time had spoken in favor of the provision. The small probability that an officer might "have some degree of influence upon the deliberations of the legislature" was, he had said, outweighed by "the danger and inconvenience of not having well formed and digested plans." "Inconsistent, unproductive and expensive schemes," he had continued, "will be more injurious to our constituents than the undue influence which the well-digested plans of a well-informed officer can have. From a bad administration of the government, more detriment will arise than from any other source. The want of information has occasioned much inconvenience and unnecessary burthens under some of the state governments."[49] Madison had concluded with a constitutional argument: "If the power of reporting plans can be construed to imply the power of originating revenue bills, the constitution is inconsistent with itself in giving the president authority to recommend such measures that he may think expedient or necessary." His position had prevailed. The statute as finally passed directed the secretary to prepare and report to the House his estimates of the revenues.[50]

By the Second Congress, however, Madison had joined with Page in his fears of an executive intrusion on legislative powers and of a gradual introduction of a monarchical system of government. Accordingly, he voiced his opposition to the resolution directing the secretary of the treasury to report to the House his opinion on the best mode of raising revenue. In its place he advocated a complicated procedure by which the secretary would first present the facts as to revenue needs to the House; the House would then form its opinion as to how revenues should be raised and inform the secretary, who next would devise an arrangement of their opinions and send it back to the House.[51]

The process seemed likely to produce the "inconsistent, unproductive and expensive schemes" Madison himself had deprecated three years before. In his zeal to stifle Hamilton's influence with Congress, he seemed to have abandoned the interest in an efficient administration that he had exhibited in the First Congress when he had led the movement to win for the president the power to remove departmental heads. An apologist in his defense might say that the change in his position had been dictated by his belated discovery of the strength of that influence. But this would overlook the fact that the source of Hamilton's influence lay not so much in his willingness to initiate revenue recommendations as in his ability to reward those who voted for them.

In addition, Madison's proposal ignored what he had earlier pointed out: The Constitution authorized the president—and through him, his departmental heads —to recommend to Congress such measures as he judged necessary and expedient. In sum, Madison's proposal not only worked against good government, it also distorted the constitutional plan. Washington could not have been happy with Madison's newly adopted positions.

Indeed, as Hamilton later wrote, Madison had more in mind than the proper management of the government's fiscal policies and the maintenance of the constitutional plan for the appropriate separation of the powers of government. In opposing the resolution directing the secretary to report his opinion of the best mode of raising revenue, Madison's intention was that the vote on the resolution should be in effect a vote of confidence in Hamilton himself. On its failure, Hamilton would have to resign.

The evening before the vote, Madison, according to Hamilton, believed that a great majority supported his position. But Hamilton, realizing his danger, took certain "measures of counteraction." The resolution, despite Virginian opposition, carried by a narrow margin. Nevertheless, Jefferson was satisfied. The outcome, he wrote, "shewed that treasury influence was tottering."[52] The president's reaction was probably a good deal different.

A few weeks later the House, apparently still possessed by fears of monarchical usurpation, rejected a provision the Senate had included in the mint bill to impress Washington's image on a coin. The provision, Page declaimed, was reminiscent of the days of Nero or Caligula. This time Madison and his colleagues from Virginia were in the majority.[53]

The campaign against monarchy and administrative corruption, and against Hamilton specifically, would continue in the second session of the Second Congress and culminate in a fierce and bitter personal attack on Hamilton in a determined effort to drive him from office. Jefferson and Madison would lead the attack.

Reapportionment and the Presidential Vacancy Bill

Much of the remainder of the first session was devoted to two political matters: the reapportionment of the House—the more important to the membership, since it affected them personally—and the resolution of the previously debated measure to fill the presidency in the event of a vacancy in the office of both the president and vice-president. Again, state and regional interests animated the discussions and influenced the various constitutional positions. Again, Madison and Jefferson labored to further the interest of their state and region.

The competing positions regarding apportionment can quickly be summarized. The Constitution, after enumerating the number of representatives to which each state was entitled in the new government, directed that Congress should reapportion representation in the House after taking a census of the country's population within three years of the first meeting of Congress. The time for such action came during the first session of the Second Congress.[54]

The Constitution also commanded that "Representatives and direct Taxes shall be apportioned among the several States . . . according to their respective Numbers."[55] Pursuant to this mandate, the House first established the ratio of representation, that is to say, the number of persons a member of the House would represent. (Under the Constitution as it then read, slaves counted as three-fifths of a person.) The House next divided the population of each state by the ratio to determine the state's representation. The total of each state's representatives constituted the total membership in the new House. Fractions were disregarded.[56]

The Senate followed a different method. Applying the principle of the Constitution that the apportionment of representation was tied to the apportionment of direct taxes, they followed the same procedure for the former as they would have for the latter. Just as in apportioning taxes they would have first determined the total amount of taxes to be collected, so in reapportioning representation they initially determined the total membership of the House. They aggregated the total population of the individual states and divided the total by the ratio of representation the House had used. Only then did they repeat the House procedure of dividing each state's population by the ratio. As in the case of apportioning taxes, fractions were not disregarded. Instead the residue of unapportioned representatives resulting from the Senate's method was distributed among those states having, under the previous step, the largest fractional remainders. The Senate's approach, dominated by northern and middle states, in effect favored those regions at the expense of Virginia and the southern states.[57]

After a prolonged interbranch dispute, the House agreed to the version of the bill the Senate had adopted.[58] When the bill was presented to the president, he asked his cabinet for their opinion. Characteristically, since the bill favored the northern states, Hamilton supported it and argued for its validity. The Constitution, he wrote, did not specify a method according to which an apportionment should be made. Since the method the Senate followed was reasonable, it should stand. The necessary consequence of the Senate's procedure was an unapportioned fractional residue, which had to be distributed by some rule. The provision the bill had adopted—for giving preference to the states having the largest fractions—was, he concluded, the most consistent with equality.[59]

Against Hamilton, Jefferson, as usual, supported the southern side, and argued that contrary to the requirements of the Constitution no single ratio had been applied to all the states. Focusing on the eight states that, because of their large fractional remainders, had been allotted additional representatives, he determined that the ratio of their representation—the total of each of their populations divided by the number of their allotted representatives—was smaller than that of those of the remaining states. As his argument suggested, he urged that fractions be disregarded.[60]

Jefferson also sought support in the text of Article I, Section 2, Clause 3. Since reference there was made to the states in their separate capacities, Congress, in apportioning their representatives, should treat with the states separately. In so arguing, Jefferson echoed a statement Madison had made earlier in the House: "[The requirement for reapportionment] refers to the respective numbers of the states, and not to any aggregate number. The proposition [implicit in the Senate's method] breaks down the barriers between the State and General Governments, and involves a consolidation."[61]

In response to these opinions, Washington leaned toward a veto of the bill on constitutional grounds, but held back. He was aware, as he told Jefferson, that division on the construction of the Constitution followed geographical lines, and that if he vetoed the bill he would be seen as following the southern side.[62]

But there may have been other reasons for his reluctance to veto, which he did not disclose to Jefferson. The text of Article I, Section 2, Clause 3, as Hamilton pointed out, tied together the apportionment of direct taxation and representation, and the effect of the Jefferson-Madison position would be to undo that linkage. Washington, as a participant in the Constitutional Convention, knew the circumstances in which the linkage had occurred and might well be uneasy about changing it.[63]

The connecting link was slavery. While northern delegates had not been unwilling to allow a slave to count as three-fifths of a free person for purposes of representation, some, particularly those from Pennsylvania with its large Quaker constituency, had insisted on coating the proposition in a way that would induce their voters to swallow it. As James Wilson put it, "Less umbrage would perhaps be taken agst. an admission of the slaves into the Rule of representation, if it [the formula] should be so expressed as to make them indirectly only an ingredient in the rule, by saying that they should enter into the rule of taxation: and as representation was to be according to taxation, the end would be equally attained."[64]

On that basis, representation had been proportioned according to taxation and the approved apportionment formula, including its complicated provision that, in addition to the whole number of free persons, including those bound to service for a term of years and excluding Indians not taxed, there be added "three fifths of all other Persons," that is, slaves.[65] Thus supporters of the Constitution, following the convention, could go to a trusting public in the North and sell the inclusion of slaves for representation as a device by which people in the South would pay more taxes and they less. This is exactly how Madison sold it in the *Federalist*.[66] And to make the deception more complete, the framers had agreed among themselves that, despite the apparent linkage, fractions should be disregarded in apportioning representation only, not taxation.

In vetoing the bill the president faced the prospect of compromising himself. He would show himself to the world as an accomplice in the separation of the Constitution's apparent linkage of representation and taxation. That linkage, his veto would say, had really been a charade designed to deceive a gullible public, and he, George Washington, had played a primary part in it. His recollection of the defense of the provision in the *Federalist* cannot have made his decision easier. (Madison, it should be pointed out, apparently had no such qualms: He advocated the separation despite his statement in that publication.)

Yet in the end Washington did veto the bill. Jefferson's description of how he came to do so is revealing:

H E WENT HOME, SENT FOR RANDOLPH the Atty. Genl. [,] desired him to get Mr. Madison immediately and come to me, and if we three concurred in opinion that he should negative the bill, he desired to hear nothing more about it but that we would draw the instrument for him to sign. They came. Our minds had been before made up. We drew the instrumt. Randolph carried it to him and told him we all concurred in it. He walked with him to the door, and as if he still wished to get off, he said, "and you say you approve of this yourself." "Yes, sir," says Randolph, "I do upon my honor." He sent it into the H. of Representatives instantly.[67]

When the veto was sustained, both chambers quickly agreed on a compromise, which Washington signed into law. As a result, New England lost five representatives from the number allotted in the previous bill, the Middle Atlantic states four, and the southern states six.[68]

If in the end no section fared worse than another, and if Jefferson's victory was more formal than substantial, the controversy nevertheless served to heighten states' rights consciousness, to impress upon the nation that there were indeed constitutional limits upon the powers of Congress, and to increase the likelihood that the Virginia mode of constitutional construction would thereafter be adopted. At the same time, it gave Madison the opportunity to label the position of his and Virginia's adversaries as, in language worthy of Patrick Henry, "consolidation." Washington had more than one reason to be unhappy.

The second political subject that concerned the first session of the Second Congress and exacerbated regional differences was the proposal to fill the presidency in the event of a vacancy in the offices of both the president and vice-president. The question, raised and deferred in the final session of the First Congress, was particularly important in the Second Congress, because 1792 was a presidential election year. If Washington chose not to run, a vote on the vacancy bill would prove a test of the strength of the respective candidates.

This time the question was decided. Once again, as in the First Congress, Madison and his colleagues pushed for Jefferson and moved that the vacancy be filled by the secretary of state. They carried the House. But the Senate, standing by Adams, voted instead for the President pro tempore of the Senate or the Speaker of the House. In conference, the House again yielded in favor of the Senate version. In Congress, at least, Adams's supporters prevailed.[69]

Second Congress: Recess

Following adjournment Madison and his friends looked forward to the presidential election and discussed alternate strategies. If Washington did not stand for reelection, Jefferson would be their candidate. If, however, Washington did stand, practically they would have to support someone other than Jefferson. The Constitution under Article II, Section 1, Clause 3, then provided that in voting for a president and vice-president the electors in their respective states should cast a ballot for two persons, at least one of whom must not be an inhabitant of the same state as themselves. Because electors in Virginia balloting for Washington would be prohibited from voting for Jefferson, the latter, deprived of the votes of his own state, could not realistically be elected vice-president.

Madison and his friends therefore decided that if Washington was a candidate, they would urge southern electors to cast one of their votes in favor of New York's Governor Clinton instead of Adams.[70] The merger of disaffected members of the federal party and the erstwhile Anti-Federalist opponents of ratification in defense of state sovereignty was effectively accomplished.

In fact, it had progressed so far that in the fall of 1792 Jefferson, the almost complete confederate in matters of domestic concern, could write to Madison that persons who recognized the authority of the Bank of the United States in the state of Virginia were in effect recognizing a foreign legislature in a matter belonging to the state. As such, they were guilty of an act of treason against the state and should suffer death by judgment of the state courts![71]

To advance their strategies, Jefferson and others visited Washington in Virginia during his summer vacation to educate him on what they termed the disenchantment of loyal members of the federal party with Hamilton's views on the powers of the federal government, his broad constructions of the Constitution, and his policies. If those complaints did not induce the old general to throw up his hands and retire from office, thus hastening the day when Jefferson's candidacy for the presidency would be viable, they might at least serve to diminish Hamilton's influence.

Jefferson summarized the many grievances against the administration, the substance of which Washington transmitted to Hamilton in a lengthy letter.[72] Bearing all the aspects of a formal legal declaration, down to the separation of its allegations into twenty-one separately numbered paragraphs, the letter requested from Hamilton a detailed answer so arranged as to correspond with the paragraphs of the complaint.[73]

Most of Jefferson's charges were directed to Hamilton's system for funding the payment of the national debt and his fiscal system, especially his reliance on bank paper money. The familiar accusations against him were set forth: Paper money encouraged speculation, corrupted the citizenry, including members of Congress, and prepared the way for a change from the present republican form of government to that of a monarchy based on the British model. The accusations, again, were the common stuff of Country versus Court polemics.

As though in acknowledgment of his ideological alliance with the remnants of Anti-Federalist sentiment, Jefferson went on to say that, out of fear of administration policies, republican federalists, who wished to preserve the present form of government, had joined, as the lesser of two evils, with "the two, three, or half dozen antifederalists, who, tho they dare not avow it, are still opposed to any general government." This explanation was probably included to justify the tactics Madison had employed and the alliances he had forged in the recently concluded first session of the Second Congress, and the forthcoming rapprochement between Jefferson's supporters and Governor Clinton. In the meantime, the complaint continued, republican federalists looked forward to the next Congress, where, it was hoped, the great increase in the membership would lessen the pernicious influence of the Treasury in the adoption of legislation.[74]

The complaint then shifted to constitutional considerations. As matters stood, Jefferson's letter continued,

THE ANTIFEDERAL CHAMPIONS ARE NOW strengthened in argument by the fulfilment of their predictions; that this has been brought about by the Monarchical federalists themselves, who, having been for the new government merely as a stepping stone to monarchy, have themselves adopted the very constructions of the constitution, of which, when advocating it's acceptance before the tribunal of the people, they declared it insusceptible; that the republican federalists, who espoused the same government for it's intrinsic merits, are disarmed of their weapons, that which they denied as prophecy being now become true history.[75]

This was of course a reference to the warnings of Henry and Mason in the Virginia ratifying convention and of Gerry in Massachusetts. The complaint ended with the disquieting question: "Who can be sure that these things may not proselyte the small number which was wanting [at the time of ratification] to place the majority on the other side?" This, he concluded, "is the event at which I tremble."[76]

Hamilton answered at even greater length, devoting the bulk of his answer to the criticism of the funding system and the arrangements he had made for the payment of the debt. To his opponents' constitutional arguments he gave short shrift, accusing them of begging the question. They took it for granted, he wrote, "that their constructions of the constitution are right and that the opposite ones are wrong, and with great good nature and candor ascribe the effect of a difference of opinion to a disposition to get rid of the limitations on the Government."[77]

Those who advocated the construction which had prevailed, he continued, argued fairly and considered they had refuted their opponents. Some things the United States government clearly could do, some clearly it could not. But there was "a good deal of middle ground, about which honest & well disposed men may differ." Congress had occupied some of this middle ground. That, he commented, was not evidence of a disposition to get rid of the limitations in the Constitution.[78]

Then Hamilton revealed the substance of his position, which he could be sure would appeal to Washington's desire for an energetic and efficient administration. If one wanted to accomplish "the essential business" of the nation, one had to resort to a liberal construction. Those against his position, Hamilton continued, were so from disaffection, overweening jealousy, and for party and personal reasons.[79] The specific charge, that his construction of the Constitution had fulfilled the prophecy of the Anti-Federalists made before ratification, he adroitly turned on his opponents. Perhaps the true state of the case was, he suggested,

THAT THE ANTIFŒDERAL CHAMPIONS HAVE been encouraged in their activity, by the countenance which has been given to their principles, by certain fœderalists, who in an envious and ambitious struggle for power influence and preeminence have imbraced as auxiliaries the numerous party originally disaffected to the Government in the hope that these united with the factious and feebleminded fœderalists whom they can detach will give them the prœdominancy. This would be nothing more than the old story of personal and party emulation.[80]

Hamilton's response was skillful. Like a good lawyer composing a brief for the defense, he attacked the complainants' weakness while parrying, if not avoiding, their strength. Jefferson's and Madison's weakest point was that they had "imbraced" the Anti-Federalists, had echoed the rhetoric of consolidation and monarchy, and had labored to reduce the power of Congress and the influence of the presidency. If their words and actions were successful—here Hamilton touched on Washington's fears —they would revive the pre-Constitutional conditions of state competition with the federal government for the primary loyalties of the people. The triumph of state power would in turn lead once again to the diminution of the central government. The nation's finances, influence, and ability to govern effectively would falter and the country would slowly sink back into the morass of the old Confederation. To avoid all this, a broad construction of the Constitution was, in the eyes of Hamilton and the Federalists, a matter of national necessity.

Nevertheless, the Jefferson-Madison doctrine of limited government and their canon of strict construction was, as Madison and Hamilton both knew, based on more than an idle gloss of language. It was plausible and therefore effective. Whatever private understandings the framers may have had among themselves—that proponents of a strong national government could be free to argue, for instance, that the Necessary and Proper Clause included an undefined bevy of congressional and presidential powers, as Mason and Gerry charged and as Randolph conceded in the Virginia convention—the supporters of the Constitution had for the most part publicly disavowed such understandings both in the *Federalist* and in the state conventions in their campaign to secure ratification.

Therefore, when Madison, after his break with Hamilton, steadfastly maintained that the Constitution should be read in the light of the discussions of the state ratifying conventions, his position had the ring of honesty in government: his side was keeping the campaign promises of ratification. It appealed to those against whom and to whom the promises had been made, and it secured their support. It eliminated any reference to private understandings of the framers, which in amplification of the text were bound to go against his side.

All of this served as the background to the quarrel that Washington was called on to resolve: personal rivalries,[81] charges of speculative excesses and monarchical tendencies, constitutional and fiscal disputes, the clash of state and federal interest, and the divergence of northern and southern, commercial and agricultural, concerns. He had in hand Jefferson's multiparagraphed complaint and Hamilton's lengthy answer. He did not pursue the matter further. He did not repudiate Hamilton's policies or the doctrine of liberal construction. Instead, in what amounted to an endorsement of those policies and that doctrine, he stood for reelection.

The republicans employed their alternate strategy: They supported Clinton for whom they were able to garner fifty electoral votes in opposition to Adams's seventy-seven.[82] The message of the 1792 election was clear: The republicans were organized for business and were a going concern. They had become a functioning party, perhaps not a full-fledged political party as we know it today, but a party nonetheless. Against Hamilton's leadership and the press he had financed, the republicans, under their own leadership and with their own subsidized press, had formed a base for themselves at the state and regional levels and had fashioned a well-developed line of ideological and constitutional opposition.[83]

Second Congress, Second Session, 1792–93

While waiting for the election returns in the second session of the Second Congress that began in November 1792, the republicans renewed the struggle against Hamilton and executive power. The previous year a military expedition against the Indians had ended in great defeat. When a motion was made to invite the secretaries of the treasury and war to attend the House and furnish information shedding light on the investigation of the defeat, Madison, without being specific, objected on constitutional grounds that such an invitation would constitute an innovation with embarrassing consequences.[84]

Although it would appear that the matter went to the question of House prerogatives rather than constitutionality, Madison's speech revealed the quickness with which unwelcome measures had come to be called unconstitutional. The motion was defeated, and it was agreed that instead the cabinet officers should send to the House such written information as they thought pertinent.[85]

A week later Madison attempted to follow this victory by opposing a resolution directing the secretary of the treasury to report his proposals for reducing the public debt. In a repeat of his support for the Page motion in the first session, that the secretary should not give his opinion to the House as to the best mode of raising revenues, Madison said the House should desire information, not proposals. Whether the debt should be reduced by new taxes or by varying the burdens through new loans, he declared, was for the House to deliberate and decide, not the secretary. Madison stopped short of saying that the resolution was unconstitutional, leaving it to Baldwin to suggest it, and Giles and John F. Mercer of Maryland to say it outright. After Ames defended the resolution, it was approved by a greater margin than that on the resolution in the first session.[86]

The last and most formidable attack on Hamilton came early in 1793 in the final week of the second session, when Giles introduced a series of nine resolutions, prepared by Jefferson, censuring Hamilton's official conduct as secretary of the treasury, with such wording as to carry the innuendo of moral turpitude. The ultimately personal thrust of all the republican maneuverings—to get Hamilton—was revealed. Madison in a lengthy speech supported the resolutions. They were overwhelmingly defeated. On that bitterly partisan note, the second session of the Second Congress ended.[87]

CHAPTER SIX

Opposition and Foreign Policy

When war broke out between France and Great Britain in 1793 during the recess between the Second and Third Congresses, regional and party divisions were extended to questions of foreign policy. New and profound differences quickly developed in constitutional theory concerning the appropriate allocation between Congress and the president of responsibility for war and peace. Hamilton naturally argued for a broad range of presidential power, Madison, now a committed advocate of legislative rather than executive power, for a far more restrictive scope.

In July 1789, while the First Congress in its first session was undertaking the organization of the United States government, revolution had erupted in France, convulsing the government. In the spring of 1792, with a system of parliamentary government and a hereditary monarchy in place, France went to war with Austria and Prussia to vindicate and spread republican ideals. That summer its king was deposed, and in September the Republic of France was established. American republicans, now self-styled Republicans, supported the new government enthusiastically, the Federalists less so.

Then the Reign of Terror began. In January 1793 King Louis XVI was executed, followed by thousands of others. When, on the news of the king's death, Great Britain went to war with France, the applicability of the treaty between the United States and Louis, made in consideration of his help during the American Revolution, was called into question. Although under its terms the United States was obliged to side with France in a war with the British, practicality required neutrality. In great debt from the Revolution and heavily taxed to pay the debt, the United States was not financially or militarily able to wage another war. The revenue of the United States came primarily from tariffs on imports, and 90 percent of the imports came from Great Britain.[1]

As a continuing legacy of the American Revolution, however, the public disliked the British, were likely to side with the French, and thus would favor the commitments of the treaty. For this reason, Jefferson as secretary of state considered that at the least the British might be induced to pay a price for neutrality. He also had serious misgivings about the president going beyond a bare declaration of peace until such time as Congress, in his view the proper constitutional authority in the matter, could act. He therefore proposed that the president limit himself to advising American citizens that it was their duty to behave as neutrals with respect to the warring countries.[2]

Jefferson's approach had one serious flaw. While the decision whether to honor the treaty had to be made in mid-April, the Third Congress would not convene until the beginning of December and thus was in no position to act. Yet Jefferson agreed that the president should not alarm the country by calling Congress into special session.[3] His position seemed impractical: In default of Congress, the president had to decide.

Hamilton, the soul of practicality, recommended an instant and definitive decision in favor of neutrality. Because the country could not afford to go to war, he thought it fatuous to pretend otherwise and recommended that the president make the decision. Typically, Randolph, participating as attorney general, devised a compromise: The decision should be published as part of a presidential proclamation. In form it would constitute a statement to the American public concerning the state of affairs in light of the European crisis; as such, it would not be an official paper directed to the French, the other party to the treaty, and would therefore take no position on whether its terms were operative.[4]

Washington, following this advice and, out of deference to Jefferson, avoiding the use of the word "neutrality" altogether, proclaimed to the citizenry in Randolphian language that the country was at peace.[5] Since this did not amount to a formal repudiation of the treaty, it avoided the question whether the president under the Constitution had the authority to make such a repudiation without a reference to Congress or whether, because a determination as to a treaty's operability amounted to a declaration of war or peace, the question was one for Congress alone.

Washington's proclamation was not widely popular at first. What no one in the administration, including Jefferson, had anticipated was the depth of public feeling against the British remaining from the American Revolution and the widespread support for the French as the European repository of republicanism against the execrated British monarchy. The previously small group of republican adherents suddenly found themselves the spokesmen for an emotional popular cause: international republicanism. At last they had an issue, a movement, that had the solid potential to enable them to challenge Hamilton successfully and, in their view, his policy of British appeasement.[6]

When Citizen Edmond Genêt, the French minister to the United States, completed a crowd-rousing tour of the east coast northward from Charleston to Philadelphia, anti-British sentiment peaked. A series of articles in Frenau's *National Gazette* attacked the proclamation and Washington himself for having presumed to issue it in disregard of the people's feelings.[7] Hamilton responded with a series of newspaper essays under the pseudonym of Pacificus,[8] in which he took the position that the proclamation constituted a statement of neutrality. Despite the form of its address—to the citizens of the United States rather than to the Republic of France—it was designed, he wrote, to make known to both the American public and France that this country was "in the condition of a Nation at Peace with the belligerent parties, and under no obligations of Treaty, to become an *associate in the war* with either of them."[9]

Hamilton defended the president's authority to make the decision and in doing so considered where under the Constitution the responsibility lay for passing on the question of neutrality in time of foreign war. This was not an easy assignment. Although Hamilton did not say so, the Constitution seemingly gives little guidance concerning either the powers of the federal government in foreign affairs or the allocation of power within the federal government as to the conduct of foreign policy. For the founders, foreign relations appeared to consist of treaty making—the president having the duty of negotiating and approving treaties with the advice and consent of the Senate—and the reception of foreign ministers. And the presidential function in the performance of the second matter, Hamilton had already written in the *Federalist,* was perfunctory: "[The authorization for the president] to receive Ambassadors and other public Ministers . . . is more a matter of dignity than of authority. It is a circumstance, which will be without consequence in the administration of the government; and it was far more convenient that it should be arranged in this manner, than that there should be a necessity of convening the Legislature, or one of its branches, upon every arrival of a foreign minister; though it were merely to take the place of a departed predecessor."[10]

At the time he published that commentary, Hamilton had felt the need to reassure the public that the new executive would be no more than the obedient servant of the federal legislature, the agent of its policy and will, rather than, like a British king, the creator and executor of his own policy. In much the same way, influenced by the need to reassure the public about the limited powers of the federal government, Hamilton in the *Federalist* had minimized the scope of the Necessary and Proper Clause.[11]

But despite his protestations regarding the minimal extent of executive powers, Hamilton had not always cast the president in a supine role. "Energy in the executive," he also wrote in the *Federalist,* "is a leading character in the definition of good government." By way of emphasis he added: "A feeble executive implies a feeble execution of the government. A feeble execution is but another phrase for a bad execution: And a government ill executed, whatever it may be in theory, must be in practice a bad government."[12]

In keeping with that viewpoint, once the Constitution had been ratified, the president's most trusted adviser concerned himself with making the government of the United States work energetically and effectively. In 1791, moved by the need for a national agency empowered to extend credit, he had disregarded his *Federalist* statement concerning the narrow limits of "necessary and proper" and advocated instead the establishment of a national bank under a broad reading.[13] So in 1793, moved by the need to assert an executive prerogative in foreign affairs, he disregarded his narrow *Federalist* position regarding presidential power and advocated instead a broad range of executive powers.

Past assurances had to yield to the present demands of diplomacy. In a world of monarchical and despotic governments with long-standing executive prerogatives, the president had to act on equal terms. In those circumstances, Hamilton proclaimed a new jurisprudence of presidential power, supporting his assertion that as a matter of constitutional law only the president had the power to determine the operability of the treaty.

Developing a constitutional argument to support his new position, Hamilton followed those taken by Jefferson and Madison, his political opponents. Three years earlier Jefferson as secretary of state had occasion to advise Washington regarding the extent of senatorial power in the matter of diplomatic appointments. After considering the Constitution's division of federal power into three separate branches, Jefferson concluded: "The transaction of business with foreign nations is Executive altogether. It belongs then to the head of that department, *except* as to such portions of it as are specially submitted to the Senate. *Exceptions* are to be construed strictly."[14]

Jefferson's opinion had been patterned in turn on the argument Madison had used in the First Congress when he had spoken in favor of an exclusive presidential power to remove a departmental head and had contended that exceptions to the broad executive powers conferred by Article II should be construed strictly. Since that article had conferred on the Senate only the power of consenting to the presidential appointment of certain officers, the Senate did not, Madison reasoned, have the power of passing on their removal.[15]

Hamilton therefore had only to refashion the Jefferson-Madison premises to suit his purpose, apply them to the case before him, and draw his conclusions. Echoing his predecessors, he began his Pacificus essays with the proposition that by virtue of Article II the executive branch was the organ of intercourse between this country and foreign nations. As such, the executive should properly interpret treaties in cases in which the judiciary is not competent, that is, in cases between one government and another. Furthermore, Hamilton wrote, it was appropriate that the executive should interpret treaties because it is the branch charged with the application and execution of the laws—of which treaties form a part—and with the command of their enforcement.[16]

His view of the subject, "so analogous to general theory and practice," Hamilton maintained, was grounded in the text of the Constitution. The provision in Article II, Section 1, Clause 1, that "the executive Power shall be vested in a President of the United States of America," evinced a constitutional principle of broad executive powers. And the later enumeration of certain executive powers in Section 3—the powers to "receive Ambassadors and other public Ministers; . . . take Care that the Laws be faithfully executed"—were so many specifications of "the principal articles implied in the definition of Executive Power."[17]

Disregarding his previous argument in the *Federalist* that the specification of the president's power to receive ambassadors should properly be construed as defining the exact limits of his authority in such respect, Hamilton now contended that such a construction was not only inconsistent with the general principle established in the first section of the article but textually impractical, owing to the difficulty of a complete enumeration of all cases of executive authority.

Next, Hamilton—again following Jefferson in his opinion concerning senatorial power and diplomatic appointments, and Madison in his argument during the debate over the presidential removal power—maintained that the broad range of executive power as established in Article II, Section 1, was subject only to the "*exceptions and qu[a]lifications . . .* expressed in the instrument,"[18] and that, as exceptions and qualifications to a general principle, they should be strictly construed. In the two such instances appearing in Article II, Section 2, Clause 2—the power to appoint officers and to make treaties—the Constitution had provided for a senatorial participation. In the first case Congress itself, he continued, had already recognized, in the statute governing the removal of departmental heads, that the exception and qualification with respect to the appointment power should be strictly construed. Just as the removal of executive officers had effectively been admitted to be an inherently executive act and, as such, beyond the requirement of senatorial participation, so, Hamilton argued, the interpretation of the treaty with France, including the proclamation of neutrality, should be similarly recognized as an inherently executive act, not requiring senatorial participation.[19]

But Hamilton, not satisfied with the case he had made for the president, inserted in his argument, as though in passing, a much more audacious position: that the power vested in Congress "to declare war and grant letters of marque and reprisal," was also by way of exception to the "general doctrine of our constitution . . . that the EXECUTIVE POWER of the Nation is vested in the President." It followed, he asserted, that the war power also was an exception to the executive power, and as such was to be strictly construed and extended no further than essential to its execution.[20]

Hamilton, however, had unwisely departed from the text of the Constitution: Unlike the provisions for senatorial participation in the treaty-making and appointment powers, which appear as a restriction on executive power in Article II, the war power is set forth as a legislative power in Article I. Since his argument was not based on the text, Hamilton left himself open to the charge that he was importing British monarchical principles into the Constitution. When Madison assumed the task of responding to Hamilton, he would make the most of his opportunity.[21]

Continuing his argument, Hamilton conceded, as he had to, that under the Constitution it was the province of Congress to declare war, but, he asserted, that until war was declared it was the duty of the president to preserve peace. In fulfilling that duty the president necessarily had to judge and state the obligations treaties placed on the nation. The president had fulfilled this duty with respect to the treaty with France in proclaiming the country's neutrality.[22]

Hamilton returned to the subject of the constitutional provision for the president's reception of foreign ministers, which he had discussed in the *Federalist*. Without specifically mentioning the position he had taken there, he dismissed the view that the provision was an example of limited executive powers. Instead, he took the stand that, falling as it did within the broad-ranging scope of Article II, the provision implied a presidential power to recognize foreign governments and, incidentally, a power to decide whether to give effect to preexisting treaties.

Indeed, Hamilton went so far as to say, the provision implied a general power and competence in foreign affairs so extensive and vital to the government that the president might even properly lay Congress under the obligation of declaring war. He then admitted, as if in concession to constitutional form, that Congress was thereafter free to make its own decision, but, he warned, it must in so doing consider the president's antecedent conduct.[23]

Hamilton really did not need to go that far. In the case before him, as he argued at length in his next Pacificus essay,[24] the treaty did not require the United States to go to war with Great Britain. By its terms, it was a defensive alliance. Therefore, he concluded, since the French had attacked the British, and not vice versa, the treaty did not bind. Washington's decision was one for peace, not war.

Hamilton's interests, however, went beyond the instant controversy. He had a penchant for general principles and for extending the powers of the presidency as far as he could take them. For this reason he read Article II's brief statement of presidential duties as encompassing a broad prerogative in the exercise of foreign affairs, subject only to such congressional limits on the president's authority as were specifically written into the Constitution.

The Pacificus essays, when published, made a favorable impression on the public. Jefferson, despite his concern, apparently felt he could not respond to them. Having already been on record as agreeing with two of Hamilton's basic premises—that under Article II the transaction of business with foreign countries was a matter exclusively for the executive branch, and that exceptions to presidential power in such matters were to be construed strictly—he perhaps did not feel safe taking public issue with Hamilton, even under a pseudonym. That he agreed with a corollary of Hamilton's first premise—that the executive is the organ of intercourse between the government and foreign nations—is evidenced in a letter he sent four months later to Genêt:

HE [THE PRESIDENT OF THE UNITED STATES] . . . being the only channel of communication between this country and foreign nations, it is from him alone that foreign nations or their agents are to learn what is or has been the will of the nation, and whatever he communicates as such they have a right and are bound to consider as the expression of the nation, and no foreign agent can be allowed to question it, to interpose between him and any other branch of government under the pretext of either's transgressing their functions.[25]

As a way out of his dilemma, Jefferson turned to Madison and asked him to take up his pen in reply: "Nobody answers him, and his doctrine will therefore be taken for confessed. For god's sake, my dear Sir, take up your pen, select the most striking heresies, and cut him to pieces in the face of the public. There is nobody else who can and will enter the lists with him."[26]

But what was Madison to write? That the responsibility for the interpretation of treaties was for the Senate, or for the Senate and the president jointly? Should he who had fought so hard in the Constitutional Convention for the cause of presidential power at the expense of the Senate now argue on behalf of senatorial prerogatives? There he had argued that the president, as the elected representative of a majority of the people, rather than the Senate, which "represented the States alone," was the proper agent in making treaties; should he now argue that the interpretation of the nation's treaties should be shared with the representatives of tiny Rhode Island and Delaware?[27]

Of course, in the convention Madison had wanted to exclude the president from participating in the approval of peace treaties, on the ground that a president "would necessarily derive so much power and importance from a state of war that he might be tempted, if authorized [to concur in the approval of a peace treaty], to impede [its conclusion]."[28] But in this case Washington, involving himself as president in the interpretation of the treaty with France, had decided on a policy of neutrality and peace. His determination seemed hardly to afford Madison the opportunity of belaboring the warmongering propensities of the chief executive.

Furthermore, it was one thing for Madison to attack the scope of executive power vested in a departmental head, such as Hamilton; it was another to attack the scope of power to make and interpret treaties, which affected the prerogatives of the president directly. But Madison this time was no longer working for the president and the cause of his power. He was working with Jefferson against Hamilton, and for the cause of their newly formed Republican Party against the policies of the Hamilton-led Federalists.[29] Taking up his pen, Madison followed Jefferson's request and replied to Hamilton's theses in a series of newspaper essays appearing under the pseudonym of Helvidius.[30]

If Hamilton had argued for implied executive powers so extensive as to render Congress little more than the president's accomplice in determining whether to declare war, Madison in response continued the practice he had begun in the Second Congress of strictly construing executive power in the federal government. Indeed, he argued for such a broad power in the legislature and such a narrow scope for the president as to render the latter a robot in the execution of congressional foreign policy: a ceremonial figure in the reception of foreign ministers, a mere presiding officer in the conduct of foreign affairs and, all in all, a person of no constitutional competence, with little, if any, prerogative in the determination of the great issues of war and peace. If the country needed an administration of energy and efficiency, Madison's copy of the Constitution did not supply it.

Conceding Hamilton's argument that the general principle of Article II was to posit all executive powers in the president, Madison took issue with his thesis that the power to make treaties and—Hamilton's overextended position—to declare war were incidents of executive power. Skillfully stirring the political pot of anti-British sentiment against Pacificus, and at the same time reviving party insinuations of a Federalist penchant for aristocracy and monarchy, Madison admitted that in Britain the power to make treaties and declare war were matters of royal and executive prerogative. But, he argued, it was otherwise with the United States, which had a republican, not a monarchical, form of government.[31]

Having thereby impugned the motives of his adversary in relying, as he said, on British practice, Madison addressed the merits of the issue. As a general rule, he argued, the powers to make treaties and to declare war could not, from their nature and operation, be properly called executive, because the action of the president in executing the laws presupposed the existence of laws to be executed. A treaty, he added, did not execute laws, but on the contrary had itself the force of law and looked to the chief magistrate for its execution. Similarly, a declaration of war did not execute laws or suppose preexisting laws to be executed. In fact, he maintained, a declaration of war was legislative in nature and, when employed, had the effect of repealing laws inconsistent with a state of war. Both powers, then, were not executive but legislative in nature; if not strictly legislative, they were more legislative than anything else, and should be so considered. It followed, according to Madison, that the rule of strictly interpreting exceptions which Pacificus had employed against the legislature and in favor of the executive, served in fact to narrow executive pretensions rather than enlarge them.[32]

After positing that the powers to make war and peace were essentially legislative rather than executive, Madison next contended that the Constitution supported his position. He began with his stronger argument. Just as in Article II, the Constitution had vested executive powers in the executive, so in Article I, he wrote, it had vested legislative powers in the legislature. From the placement of the provision authorizing Congress to declare war in Article I, Section 8, he reasoned, the Constitution had manifested a determination that the power was legislative in nature. This conclusion, he asserted, was buttressed by the principle of the separation of powers consistently followed in the Constitution, whereby no power that was legislative in nature was placed among the executive powers and vice versa.[33]

But the very strength of his first argument weakened his second. For the Constitution had placed the power to make treaties in Article II and, following Madison's reasoning, this should have proved conclusively that such a power was executive in nature. Madison attempted to avoid that conclusion by characterizing its placement there as an aberration from the usual legislative process, whereby the Senate's ratification of a treaty by a two-thirds vote instead of by the customary majority compensated for the exclusion of the House which, because of the size of its membership, could not be conveniently included.[34] This explanation, however, did not explain why the process, if it was strictly legislative in nature, was not placed in a separate section in Article I. Pushing past this dubious point, Madison found in the specific language of Article VI the (for him) conclusive argument for the legislative nature of the treaty-making power. According to the provisions of that article, a treaty is to operate as law and, like any other federal law, constitutes the supreme law of the land.[35]

Returning to his original contention, Madison dismissed as inappropriate contrary arguments from precedents of international law and the established practices of the British and other monarchies, because the Constitution, he declared, had deliberately changed the long-standing practice of placing the treaty-making and warmaking powers in the executive, and for good reason:

W AR IS IN FACT THE TRUE NURSE of executive aggrandizement. In war a physical force is to be created, and it is the executive will which is to direct it. In war the public treasures are to be unlocked, and it is the executive hand which is to dispense them. In war the honors and emoluments of office are to be multiplied; and it is the executive patronage under which they are to be enjoyed. It is in war, finally, that laurels are to be gathered, and it is the executive brow they are to encircle. The strongest passions, and most dangerous weaknesses of the human breast; ambition, avarice, vanity, the honorable or venial love of fame, are all in conspiracy against the desire and duty of peace.[36]

In those circumstances, war and peace were too important to leave to one man. The Constitution had therefore placed the power to declare war fully and exclusively in Congress and joined the Senate with the president in the power to make peace through treaties.[37] Therefore, it could not be allowed that the president as the person charged with the execution of the laws had the authority to interpret treaties and to judge of their obligations. If it so happened that he should judge that a treaty obliged the country to go to war, it might be said with equal force that he was authorized to carry those obligations into effect by the employment of public force.[38]

As to Pacificus's supporting reference to the presidential power to receive foreign ministers, that procedure, Madison wrote, was not really a power at all but a mere matter of ceremony, involving no power to question the legitimacy of the government the minister represented. He bolstered his position with a reference to Hamilton's statement in the *Federalist* on the subject.[39] Madison concluded from this statement that should an extraordinary case of an illegitimate foreign despotism present itself, the Constitution did not intend that "so limited an organ of the national will as the Executive of the United States" should decide it.[40]

Equating executive discretion with prerogative and prerogative with monarchy, Madison returned with a Republican oratorical flourish to the position from which he started. Placing in the executive the power to declare war would impose on the country the substance of a monarchical government under the form of a constitutional republicanism, with results dangerous to the liberties of the people.[41]

A commentator could tweak Hamilton, as Madison did without mentioning him by name, for the inconsistency in the positions advocated under his various pseudonyms, Publius in the *Federalist* and Pacificus in the ongoing controversy, but he could also tweak Madison for similar inconsistencies. As mentioned, he had led the debate in the First Congress for a sole presidential power to remove departmental heads without the consent of the Senate—led it in the face of the provision in Article II, Section 2, Clause 1, requiring senatorial consent in their appointment. He had then disregarded the argument that his position would permit the executive to terminate a treaty without the consent of the Senate, despite the provision in the same clause requiring a two-thirds approval for its ratification.[42]

Madison would soon be guilty of an additional inconsistency. As Helvidius, he contended that the Senate acting without the House was performing a legislative act in ratifying a treaty with a two-thirds majority. Yet two years later, during the House debate on Jay's Treaty, he would argue that the House, as part of its legislative power under Article I, had the right to withhold support of such part of a treaty as conflicted with preexisting law.[43]

It should also be pointed out that, *pace* Madison, the placement of the treaty-making power in Article II reveals a constitutional acknowledgment: although the final product (the treaty) is law, as stated in Article VI, the process by which it is made differs significantly from the ordinary method of lawmaking. With treaties, the draftsmen are not the members of a congressional committee but the president or his surrogate and the foreign government. Moreover—although Madison might have disputed this at that time (before he and Jefferson became presidents)—the power to make law through a treaty is, as we know today, broader than that of Congress under Article I.[44] And while the treaty itself has the force of law, the process by which it is made, approved, and ratified is neither legislative nor executive in nature, as Hamilton stated elsewhere in the *Federalist:*

THE ESSENCE OF THE LEGISLATIVE AUTHORITY is to enact laws, or in other words to prescribe rules for the regulation of the society. While the execution of the laws and the employment of the common strength, either for this purpose or for the common defence, seem to comprise all the functions of the executive magistrate. The power of making treaties is plainly neither the one nor the other. It relates neither to the execution of the subsisting laws, nor to the enaction of the new ones, and still less to an exertion of the common strength. Its objects are CONTRACTS with foreign nations, which have the force of law, but derive it from the obligations of good faith. They are not rules prescribed by the sovereign to the subject, but agreements between sovereign and sovereign. The power in question seems therefore . . . to belong properly neither to the legislative nor to the executive.[45]

And finally, Madison's position with regard to the role of the president in the government of the country was inconsistent with that which he had taken during the Constitutional Convention. The Madison of the convention would never have referred to the president as "so limited an organ of the national will." At that time he considered the president—the only person elected by all the people, albeit indirectly—to be the supreme representative of the national will.[46]

Setting aside considerations of consistency, the primary factor in determining whether the president had acted properly in issuing the proclamation of neutrality was whether, practically, there was any alternative. Even in so important a matter as committing the country to war, the delegates to the Constitutional Convention, on Madison's motion, had amended a proposal conferring power on Congress "to make war" to read "to declare war" so that the president could repel a sudden attack.[47]

Thereby, in effect, the framers had allowed the president a residual power, that is, a prerogative to be exercised in emergencies or, if we may extend the power, in situations where it was not prudent to call the Congress into session to decide for itself whether to go to war or to remain at peace. Jefferson had agreed that such was the situation confronting the president in April 1792. The president, he recognized, could not prudently call Congress into special session to resolve the question of the treaty's operability. This position was not too far from the one Hamilton took in his Pacificus essays, although the latter may have allotted the president more discretion in his foreign relations than the framers had contemplated, and certainly more than he had allowed in his statement in the *Federalist* concerning the reception of ministers.

In fact, presidential prerogative in foreign affairs extended even further than the narrow limits of the controversy regarding the neutrality proclamation. And had Hamilton not so restricted executive action in his essay concerning the reception of foreign ministers, he could have relied on broader views of presidential power set forth in the *Federalist*. As Jay in one of his infrequent essays wrote, Congress is unable to control the day-to-day operations of foreign policy. International affairs change too quickly, so that of necessity the country must work through the president, who, as John Marshall would later say—in affirmation of Jefferson's official positions as secretary of state and of Hamilton's position in the Pacificus essays—"is the sole organ of the nation in its external relations, and its sole representative with foreign nations."[48]

While Congress may very well initiate some aspects of foreign policy and effectively oppose the pursuit of others, in practice, "the actual conduct of foreign negotiations," as Hamilton wrote elsewhere in the *Federalist,* falls peculiarly within the province of the executive department.[49] It is the president and the State Department which must execute policy and, in so doing, modify it or initiate a new one. And as Jay pointed out, effective foreign relations require secrecy and a continuity in execution impossible in a multiperson entity with intermittent sessions, although of course presidential action must be subject to monitoring by that entity.[50] These qualities, Hamilton later wrote, are "indispensable in the management of foreign negotiations, [and] point out the executive as the most fit agent in those transactions."[51]

However, as Hamilton qua Pacificus conceded, the last word was with Congress. In the case at hand, it could, if it desired, have declared war on Great Britain in support of France in disregard of the president's proclamation and even in disregard of a presidential decision to terminate the treaty with France. True, Congress would have had to overcome the obstacle of the implication in the president's proclamation that the treaty did not oblige. But if public opinion was sufficiently aroused and considered his position wrong, Congress could and most likely would dismiss the presidential position as a makeshift in aid of a repudiated policy and do what the public wanted.

All of this is speculative. The question that Pacificus and Helvidius discussed at such great length was, after all, moot. It was moot because in form the proclamation had not repudiated the treaty obligation and because in practice, however it was phrased and however much it irritated ardent Francophiles, it had become—while Madison was composing his Helvidius essays—overwhelmingly popular. The reason was that Genêt had in a few short months so infuriated public opinion by his arrogant and insulting behavior to Washington that sympathy had shifted in favor of neutrality and the presidential proclamation. As a result, after having first persuaded Madison to compose the reply to Hamilton, Jefferson now counseled him to avoid attacking the proclamation and "little cavils about who should declare [neutrality]." In view of the change in public opinion, Madison discontinued his essays after the fifth installment.[52]

The question, although moot, was symptomatic of the ongoing political and institutional struggle between Hamilton and Jefferson. Hamilton, whose policies, domestic and foreign, Washington adopted, wished to advance the executive's claims of predominance and to forfend a rival claim by Congress. On the other hand, Jefferson and Madison, prevented from determining administration policy and limited by Hamilton's influence, sought to effectuate their policies through Congress, the only governmental institution open to them.

Inextricably interwoven with the constitutional and institutional questions was the struggle over the policies and fortunes of the two emerging political parties and the fortunes of Great Britain and France. Hamilton, because of his economic and fiscal policies, favored good relations with Britain.[53] Madison and Jefferson favored the French, because, among other reasons, they hoped that France would advance the cause of republicanism in Europe and therefore the world, as opposed to the prevailing monarchical systems. Support of the French also gave them the opportunity to display their own commitment to the cause, and at the same time to attack Federalist support of the British as indisputable proof of the supposed Federalist desire to convert the United States into a monarchical system.[54]

As in the case of most questions involving the respective powers of Congress and the president, that of the president's power unilaterally to terminate a treaty[55] or to interpret one[56] has never been resolved. Whether the actions are executive or legislative in character is still not clear.[57] In any case, some of the powers granted to Congress under Article I, such as the spending and appropriation powers, are not legislative in nature.

For Hamilton and Madison, however, the definitive resolution of the issue of the president's power to terminate a treaty was not necessarily an end in itself. The immediate end was the control of policy and public opinion. In this battle, the Constitution became the ultimate political weapon by means of which one's adversaries could be depicted as usurpers wielding power in contravention of the limits set down in the supreme law of the land. In Hamilton's terms, the adversary was seen as interfering for selfish purposes with the executive's administration of the affairs of government, and rendering it ineffective. In Madison's terms, the adversary was seen as clearly lawless: acting, at best, above the law like an unprincipled, prerogative-ridden royal monarch, or at worst, in utter disregard of the law, like a grand or petty tyrant, but in either case, threatening the liberties of the people. As a result, foreign policy became yet another battleground for domestic partisan politics.

CHAPTER SEVEN

Strict Construction: Impracticalities and Trivialities

With the development of the Helvidian argument for a narrow reading of presidential power in the conduct of foreign affairs, the essentials of Madison's thesis of constitutional construction were in place. Conceived as a political strategy to advance the interests of state and region, person and party, through the systematic advocacy of interpretation according to the strict letter of the law, the thesis also apparently fulfilled the ancient ideal of rule by law and not by men.

Overall, Madison's system was brilliant. It had the virtues of simplicity and consistency. He argued from the premise that the powers of the United States and the powers of the president were both strictly limited. Then, following the laws of deductive logic with a great display of intellectual strength, he applied this premise with rigor, reasonableness, and authenticity and unfailingly arrived at his desired conclusions. Since the practical effect of his exercise was to deny his adversaries the constitutional authority to act, it pleased his followers.

The man who could conceive such a system, make it appear plausible and workable, yet know when to keep silent or secretly abandon it would become politically indispensable. He could help mold opinion, construct a political party, and make someone president. Sooner or later, of course, if Madison's system had been implemented, the requirements of doctrinal consistency would have led to impractical and unsound results. Very soon, if Washington had followed Madison's arguments and vetoed the bill chartering the Bank of the United States, the economy of the country would have foundered for want of a centralized paper currency. And without a presidential prerogative in the conduct of foreign affairs, the political fortunes of the country would have faltered as well.

For Madison, out of power and in opposition, the necessities of practicality were not so insistent. How long in his more relaxed circumstance he could maintain the purity of his doctrine would depend on the flexibility of his own positions and his ingenuity in accommodating doctrine to political results. As the events of the following year proved, Madison was both supple and ingenious. With those qualities and with his intelligence, he prospered.

Third Congress, First Session, 1793–94

In the summer of 1793 and into the fall, an epidemic of yellow fever swept Philadelphia. Reportedly, more than three thousand died. Thousands more fell sick; much of the city's population fled. Only a few were left to run the government's offices. In mid-October, Washington, worried about the safety of the Third Congress, scheduled to convene in Philadelphia on the first Monday in December, consulted with Jefferson, Hamilton, and Madison. Setting the problem before them, he asked them about the practical and constitutional alternatives open to him.[1]

Madison was of the opinion that under Article II, Section 3, of the Constitution, which authorized the president to call Congress into session on "extraordinary Occasions,"[2] his power was limited to the call for special sessions.[3] Therefore in the case at hand the president was authorized to change only the time but not the place of the next congressional session.

His interpretation, Madison wrote, was confirmed by other parts of the Constitution, in which its "solicitude . . . to appease [the] jealousy [in anything concerning the location of the federal government] is particularly marked by the 1st paragraph of section 6th & the 3d. paragraph of section 7th. of article I." The former provision, which prohibited the questioning of a member of Congress "in any other Place" for a speech made in Congress, was intended to prevent the president from following the practice of the British crown—before their civil war—of subjecting members of Parliament to criminal penalties for remarks made in Parliament.[4] The latter provision concerned the propriety of presenting to the president a joint resolution regarding "a question of Adjournment."

In the first session of the First Congress Madison had invoked that provision during the discussion of the propriety of providing for the temporary seat of government by bill rather than by joint resolution. At that time he had argued that the section must be read in connection with Article I, Section 5, Clause 4, wherein each House was prohibited from adjourning "to any other Place than that in which the two Houses shall be sitting" without the consent of the other. The purpose of those sections, he had contended, was to bar the president from any participation in the decision concerning the place of adjournment. In advancing that contention, Madison was reflecting the opinion of the framers of the Constitution, who had been jealous, excessively it would appear, of the powers of the executive.[5]

The subsequent passage of the Residence Act, placing the permanent seat of government on the Potomac,[6] could have supported the claim that thereby Congress had recognized the propriety of the president's participation in determining where

Congress meets. Madison in his letter to Washington, however, dismissed the idea, warning that such an exercise of power might in the future lead another executive to use the precedent as a pretext to change the seat of government. Since Washington shared his passionate commitment to the location of the capital on the Potomac, near Virginia, Madison must have known that his warning was likely to make the president cautious about asserting the power.[7]

From this reasoning, Madison should have concluded that the president was powerless to act. But recognizing the necessity of an intervention under the circumstances, he suggested that Washington inform members of Congress of the dangerous condition in Philadelphia and "recommend that the several members assemble at ———— in the State of ———— at which place I shall be ready to meet them." The president was to fill in the blanks with the name of the city and state he deemed the safest, most commodious, and most politically acceptable to southern and northern members.[8]

By such advice, Madison worked to reconcile the demanding requirements of, on the one hand, fidelity to the intent of the Constitution and strict construction of its letter, which kept the channel of executive power within a narrow, literal scope, and, on the other hand, the practical necessities of government whereby the chief officer of the executive branch, the only branch of government always in session, could solve the emergent problem of a meeting place for Congress, a problem which, in adjournment, it could not solve for itself.

The strictest of strict construction would of course never have tolerated such a practical, but devious, bypass of literal provision: The concession that the president had the unwritten right or power to suggest to Congress a different time and place of meeting implied a whole reservoir of other unwritten rights or powers, reminiscent of the prerogatives of the British crown. Madison, however, was too intelligent to take his doctrine to the logical, but impractical, conclusion that the president was, by the terms of the Constitution, powerless to divert Congress from sickness and death in its impending meeting in malarial Philadelphia. Besides, the question at issue was purely nonpartisan. If solved in the manner he suggested, so as not to upset either southern or northern members, practical avoidance of the strictures of the Constitution need not be troublesome.

Not surprisingly, Jefferson, writing to Washington, supported Madison. It just so happened, Jefferson told the president, that Madison had dropped by his house the day before and informed him of his constitutional advice to the president. He, Jefferson, agreed. The president did not have the authority to change the place of the meeting. Showing, however, that his construction of the Constitution was even stricter than Madison's, he added: "I think we have nothing to do with the question, and that Congress must meet in Philadelphia, even if it be in the open feilds [sic], to adjourn themselves to some other place."[9]

Hamilton also agreed with Madison, reaching the same result, however, by way of broad construction. Once again, he read the provisions of Article II as conferring extensive powers on the president, whereby in effect he had the prerogative to do what was best under the circumstances. The president under Section 3 of the Article, he wrote, could on extraordinary occasions convene both Houses. And, he added, because the Constitution was silent as to time and place, the president could in his discretion reasonably specify both the time and place.[10]

Uncharacteristically, however, Hamilton doubted that the matter before the president constituted such an extraordinary occasion. It was, he wrote, unlike the case of an enemy occupation of the seat of government or its destruction by earthquake. Hamilton, who had himself fallen victim to malaria in Philadelphia, may have felt it a shame to deprive members of Congress of such an interesting experience. More probably, he may have felt disinclined to expend the jurisprudential capital of the broad construction of presidential powers on such an issue, the resolution of which was for the benefit of Congress and not for the office of the president. At any rate, along with Madison, as opposed to Jefferson, he suggested that the president recommend another place where the members might rendezvous prior to the scheduled date and settle the matter for themselves.[11] In the end, insofar as the president was concerned, the problem resolved itself. At the first frost, the epidemic ceased, and by the beginning of December it was safe to return to Philadelphia.[12]

But in a matter affecting their health and life, the members of Congress had no qualms about broad construction. During its first session the Third Congress—not caring to run the risk of convening when "from the prevalence of contagious sickness, or the existence of other circumstances, it would, in the opinion of the President of the United States, be hazardous to the lives or health of the members to meet at the place to which the Congress" had appointed—passed a bill authorizing the president, by proclamation, to convene Congress at the place he thought proper. No debate was reported. Madison did not object. Constitutional scruples regarding framers' intent, presidential power, congressional prerogatives, and an impermissible delegation of legislative authority, all yielded to the practical necessity of self-preservation. In this respect at least, the system had to work.[13]

In the meantime, Jefferson, weary of being the odd man out in cabinet disputes and weary of losing to Hamilton, had decided to retire.[14] Before he did, he and Madison agreed on a strategy whereby, following the prior year's reapportionment, they might be able to take advantage of the greatly enlarged membership in the House and commit the Third Congress to the policy of retaliatory discrimination against British shipping that they had unsuccessfully pursued in the First Congress.

Hamilton, it will be recalled, had at that time been able to thwart them by persuading Congress to await the arrival of the newly appointed British minister and the commencement of negotiations between the countries on the many issues that troubled their relations.[15] Since then the minister had arrived, the negotiations had taken place, but nothing had changed. It remained official British policy to exclude

American shipping from trade with the British West Indies. And the British, contrary to the provisions of the Treaty of Peace, continued to occupy their western frontier forts.[16]

In December 1793, Jefferson, in his last major act as secretary of state, submitted a report to Congress summarizing the unsatisfactory state of British-American trade relations. He again recommended the adoption of a policy of retaliatory discrimination.[17] The following month Madison introduced a series of resolutions in the House which, if adopted, would effect the recommendations.[18]

The resolutions had western and southern support. The British had irritated the West by failing to withdraw from their forts in New York and in the Northwest Territory. Through those forts, they controlled navigation on Lake Champlain and on the Great Lakes and continued a profitable fur trade with the Indians, whose frequent attacks on western settlers they were suspected of supporting, if not instigating.[19] The British had also irritated the South by failing, in violation of the treaty, to compensate for the damage inflicted on southern plantations during the Revolution, particularly for the slaves they had taken and later freed.[20]

As the main excuse for their failure to withdraw from the western forts, the British pointed to the supposed continuing inability of British subjects to collect their American debts in American courts, owing to the interposition of obstructive state laws and the alleged unwillingness of state courts to disregard them. The difficulty was especially vexing, they asserted, because of specific provisions in the Treaty of Peace mandating the resolution of these matters, and because the adoption of the Constitution was supposed to have put an end to the problem of obstructive state laws. This claim, however, was specious. In fact, the complaint was true only with respect to Virginia, where, due to state law, British debts were still uncollectible. Elsewhere, as Jefferson as secretary of state was able to point out, both state and federal courts enforced the collection of British debts, and even in Virginia a test case was pending for their collection.[21]

In theory, Madison's resolutions should also have pleased the Northeast. The previous year the British navy, enforcing the official policy of closing West Indian ports to American shipping,[22] had seized American ships serving those ports, confiscated their cargo, and impressed American seamen into the British navy; and the British government had failed to satisfy demands for compensatory damages and for a termination of their impressment practices.[23]

But in reality, because of the war in Europe, the British had been compelled to permit the governors of their West Indies colonies to admit American shipping. In consequence, as Ames told the House during the debate on Madison's resolutions, business was thriving, and no shipping or commercial state would support Madison's position. Supporting Ames, William Loughton Smith informed the membership that Americans exported twice the value of goods to Britain as they did to France, and imported more than seven times as much. The first statistic revealed the importance of British trade to the American consumer and merchant, the second—since United States revenues were strongly dependent on import duties—the importance of British trade to the United States Treasury.[24] The votes required for the policy of retaliatory discrimination did not materialize.

Opposition to Madison's resolutions was placed largely on economic grounds, but one congressman, Abraham Clark of New Jersey, succeeded in throwing doubt on the validity of the last resolutions on the basis that, under Madison's own reading of the Constitution, Congress lacked the power to adopt it. That proposal, designed to redress the grievances of American shippers, made provision "for liquidating and ascertaining the losses sustained by citizens of the United States, from the operation of particular regulations of any country contravening the Law of Nations . . . such losses [to] be reimbursed, in the first instance, out of the additional duties on the manufactures, productions, and vessels of the nation establishing such unlawful regulations."[25]

In advancing this proposal, Madison made no mention of a constitutional authority pursuant to which Congress could expend the funds of the United States in compensation for its citizens' losses. It is true that under Article I, Section 8, Clause 10, to which he later referred, Congress has the power "to define and punish Piracies and Felonies committed on the high Seas, and Offences against the Law of Nations." But he had not said that Congress should adopt a law defining the British policy of discrimination against American shipping as an offense against the law of nations. Such a proposal would have constituted a serious provocation. Yet in the absence of such a definition, he advanced the proposition that Congress should make monetary provisions for losses that victims had sustained by reason of another country's "regulations . . . contravening the Law of Nations."[26]

While debate on the resolutions for retaliatory discrimination was pending, Samuel Smith of Maryland, introducing an unrelated matter on behalf of a special House committee, suggested that the House appropriate money for the relief of some three thousand French refugees from the Island of Saint-Domingue, present-day Haiti, who had fled to Baltimore following the revolt of the slaves under the leadership of Toussaint L'Ouverture. The refugees, he reported, had until then been supported by private funds raised in that city and by money advanced by the executive department of the United States.[27]

Madison objected, as if glad of the opportunity of educating the new members of the Third Congress in the principles of sound Republican constitutional doctrine. Without alluding specifically to his opposition in the Second Congress to a proposal to authorize bounties to New England fisheries as beyond the enumerated powers of Congress,[28] he objected to the proposal as introduced, saying: "[I cannot] undertake to lay . . . [a] finger on that article in the Federal Constitution which granted a right to Congress of expending, on objects of benevolence, the money of their constituents. And if once they [break] the line laid down before them, for the direction of their conduct, it [is] impossible to say to what lengths they might go, or to what extremities this practice might be carried." [29]

He did not protest, he said, against whatever the executive department had already done. That was an emergency, he declared, as though recognizing the need for a presidential prerogative in matters of emergency, as in the case of a sudden attack on the United States. The matter before the House was different. [30]

Once again, however, Madison reconciled doctrinal consistency with practical solution. Not wishing to appear mean-spirited, especially before the new members of Congress, he suggested that they advance the money for the refugees against the installment shortly due on the payment of the United States' debt to France, and leave it to the French ministry to decide whether or not it would accept the "advance." [31]

It was then that Congressman Clark interposed to say that the Smith provision for refugee relief was no more unconstitutional than Madison's attempt to reimburse American victims of British discriminatory trade practices. [32] In response, Madison suggested a distinction. American ships sailed under the American flag and were protected under the law of nations by the American government, while the French refugees unquestionably were not. This, however, seemed a distinction without significance: To use his own figure of speech, he had not laid a finger on the article in the Constitution that granted Congress the right to expend money for losses arising out of an incident that Congress had not previously defined as an offense of the law of nations. Declining to say anything further of substance, he observed that his proposal was not before the House at that time, and that he did not wish to be misunderstood: He had the warmest sympathy for the refugees and would support their aid if a proper way for their relief could be found. [33]

Finally, the funds were approved in the form of an "advance," as Madison had suggested. [34] Again, not the strictest of strict construction, but practical. No one could rightly accuse Madison and his friends of heartlessness, nor for that matter of rigid consistency. If they were ready to bar the doors of the United States Treasury against the importunities of widespread welfare and subsidy, they could somehow bend consistency and alleviate the sufferings of refugees and, as part of their ongoing campaign against the British, the losses of American shipowners.

But before a vote was taken on the merits of Madison's resolutions, the British navy took action that threw the entire United States, North and South, into an uproar. Proceeding pursuant to an order-in-council, the navy seized approximately 250 American ships bound for the French West Indies, condemned 150 of them, and once again impressed many of the sailors into their navy on the grounds that they were in fact British seamen. At about the same time, reports were received in New York and forwarded to the president in Philadelphia that British officials in Canada were inciting the Indians on the northwestern frontier to attack American settlements. [35]

In the ensuing crisis, Federalists in the House introduced legislation to arm the country's military forces in a national show of strength. These measures took center stage. The Madison resolutions now seemed meaningless. A bill to expand the navy quickly passed.[36] Before a bill to augment the army was debated, however, the immediate crisis passed. Washington received word from London that the British had revoked the offending order-in-council, set aside the condemnation of American vessels made pursuant to it, given assurances that ample compensation would be afforded to those suffering from its execution, and replaced the old order with a new and milder one. It appeared that, contrary to what Washington had feared, the British were not intent on going to war with America.[37]

The Federalists nevertheless continued their efforts to increase the army, confirming in Madison's mind the suspicion that he had privately expressed to Jefferson: The Federalists would use the crisis as an opportunity "for accumulating force in the Government."[38] Accordingly, the Republicans opposed a provision in a bill to grant the president discretion to raise an army of 10,000. Madison argued that the measure was not only unnecessary but unconstitutional. The Constitution, he maintained, had vested in Congress the power to raise an army, and in the president the power to command it. In the bill under consideration powers that should be kept separate would be mingled.[39]

In this argument there was an echo of Hamilton's explanation in the *Federalist* of the president's power as commander in chief. There Hamilton, reassuring his readers as to the limits of the president's military authority—as he had done when discussing his authority to receive foreign ministers—had written to defend the presidency against the charge that it had been invested with monarchical powers: "[The president's military power] would amount to nothing more than the supreme command and direction of the military and naval forces, . . . while that of the British King extends to the *declaring* of war and to the *raising* and *regulating* of fleets and armies; all which by the Constitution . . . would appertain to the Legislature."[40]

In Madison's eyes, the danger was that a president who had both the power to assemble an army and the power to command it might wish to assemble it for the sake of the influence he acquired by the command. For Congress to authorize the president to raise an army without the clear prospect of an enemy to fight amounted to giving him both powers.[41]

Madison's fear of the potential for a presidential abuse of military power was deep-seated. It pervaded his recent position in the Helvidius papers, in which he had read Pacificus's assertion of the president's power to interpret the treaty with France in favor of peace as a potent precedent for a presidential power to interpret a treaty in favor of war.[42] And in the Constitutional Convention his suspicions regarding the military proclivities of the executive had led both to his unsuccessful attempt to exclude the president from the conclusion of peace treaties and to his support of Mason's last-minute motion, decisively defeated, to insert language in the Constitution labeling peacetime standing armies as dangerous.[43] Indeed, Madison's fears were not unfounded. Even Hamilton, that far-from-pacifist-minded statesman, had written in the *Federalist:* "It is of the nature of war to increase the executive at the expence of the legislative authority."[44]

At the same time Madison's opposition to the delegation to the president of the power to raise a peacetime standing army had a political dimension. Fear of standing armies was a dominant "Country" theme, one that had moved many during ratification to propose amending the Constitution to either prohibit or make difficult the maintenance of such armies. (Jefferson was among those who had favored the former course.)[45] Madison's position then reflected the strong influence of "Country" thinking in the new Republican Party.

Madison's argument of the bill's alleged unconstitutionality might have provoked the Federalists under other circumstances to cries of impracticality: If the British dispatched an army to Canada after Congress adjourned, there would be insufficient time for the president to call Congress into special session, for Congress to assemble and pass legislation authorizing the president to raise an army, and for him then to raise the army and organize it to resist an invasion. The alternative—that Congress before adjourning authorize the president to raise an army that probably would not be needed—would be considered a waste of time, money, and manpower.

A British invasion from Canada at that time, however, was most unlikely, and Madison could plausibly make the argument against a greatly expanded standing army. For the same reason the Federalists could not appeal convincingly to the need for national security. Besides, many in the party, worried that the expense of supporting the army would require the imposition of new taxes, withheld their support. As a result, the bill to strengthen the army and the federal government, and within it the executive branch, failed. If the bill had passed, Washington, who had recommended to the Continental Congress the formation of a professional army, would probably have signed it.[46]

A few years later, in the Fifth Congress, when the Federalists were intent on war against the French, they would revive the proposal to confer upon the president a discretionary power to raise an army, defend it with their own constitutional arguments, beat back counterconstitutional arguments by Madison's successors in the Republican Party, and pass the bill.[47]

In the Third Congress, after defeating the army proposal, the House considered a bill to pay the expense for expanding the navy through the imposition of excise taxes on particular objects, such as carriages. Since carriages were generally used only in the South, Virginians and southerners objected to their inclusion, arguing, on constitutional grounds, that the tax was direct and therefore invalid unless, as required by Article I, Section 2, Clause 3, it was apportioned among the several states according to their respective numbers.[48]

Again the House debated a question which Hamilton had discussed in the *Federalist.* Faithfully tracking the deliberations in the Constitutional Convention,[49] he had stated that indirect taxes pertained to duties and excises on articles of consumption. The term "direct taxes," as used in the Constitution, principally pertained to levies on lands and buildings.[50]

John Nicholas of Virginia, taking the lead for the Republicans, argued that a tax imposed directly on a consumer was, for constitutional purposes, "direct."[51] William Vans Murray of Maryland, speaking for the Federalists, termed the argument impractical and unjust. If the carriage tax were direct, he pointed out, carriage owners in Connecticut would as a class have to pay as large a tax as carriage owners in Maryland, even though in all of Connecticut there were only two carriages and the state had one less representative in the House than Maryland.[52] Next, Sedgwick, without attribution, adopted Hamilton's reasoning in the *Federalist*.[53] The Federalist arguments were persuasive. The bill passed with decisive margins, Madison intervening only at the last moment to announce his opposition on unreported grounds of unconstitutionality.[54]

The constitutional validity of the tax so distasteful to the South would supply an ongoing political issue for use against the Federalists. Having lost in Congress, Republicans in Virginia, in now time-honored political fashion, shifted their fight against the tax to a different forum, the federal courts, where they repeated their argument that the tax was direct and therefore invalid for having been imposed without an apportionment among the states according to population, as required by the Constitution.[55]

For Republicans, the commencement of such a suit constituted an anomaly. The theory of their action depended on the assumption that federal courts had the power of judicial review, for which, however, the Constitution had made no provision. What constitutional argument could Virginia Republicans, under the leadership of Madison and Jefferson, have made that federal courts nevertheless had the power to set aside an act of Congress and refuse to enforce collection of the tax? The power could arise only by implication.

Virginia Republicans were not compelled to make the argument, because neither their adversary, the government of the United States, nor the courts raised the issue. Eventually, and not surprisingly, the case was decided on the merits against the taxpayers. The Supreme Court, to which the case was appealed, sustained the constitutionality of the tax.[56]

That was in the future. In the meantime, in the Third Congress, the crisis with Great Britain was brought to a head when the House adopted a resolution terminating trade with that country as of the following November unless by then the British had made restitution for the losses sustained by the seizure of American vessels and had surrendered the northwest forts.[57] To forestall adoption of the resolution in the Senate, Washington, after consultation with a small committee of Federalist senators, decided to send a special envoy to London for the purpose of negotiating and settling all aspects of the troubled British-American relations. He named as his envoy John Jay, who had served as secretary of foreign affairs under the Continental Congress.[58]

In a clear signal that the president had allied himself with the Federalists against the Republicans in the Senate, Washington left it to the same committee of Federalist senators, with the aid of Hamilton, to draft the instructions which he was to present to Jay and which were to govern his negotiations. Then, contrary to past practice, the president decided not to submit the instructions to the Senate for their advice and comment. And when the Republicans attempted to elicit from the Senate a request that the president inform the body of his instructions, the Federalist-dominated Senate declined.[59] The influence of partisan politics on the practical construction of the constitutional requirement of advice and consent with respect to treaty making could not have been clearer.

Jay, who was chief justice of the United States, took leave of the Supreme Court to carry out the assignment, in part, he said, because he considered it his duty, and in part because he was tired of the bench. At that time the justices of the Supreme Court, besides sitting as appellate judges in Philadelphia had to sit as trial judges when the Supreme Court was not in session. In the latter capacity, Jay had to ride the circuit of trial vicinages from Vermont to Virginia. He cordially disliked the traveling.

Republicans, however, and not without reason, attributed his acceptance of the assignment to political ambition. In 1792, while chief justice, he had allowed himself to be a candidate for governor of New York and had narrowly lost the election. And while he was in London negotiating the treaty with Great Britain, his friends would once again advance his gubernatorial candidacy. Indeed, upon his return to the United States following the conclusion of his negotiations, he found himself elected governor, and promptly resigned from the Court.[60]

It was probably because of these political adventures that Madison considered Jay a possible successor to the presidency. And it was probably because of this possibility that Monroe and other Republicans in the Senate attacked his ministerial appointment as, among other things, contrary to the spirit, if not the letter, of the constitutional principle of the separation of powers. A sitting judge, they said, should not engage in executive-appointed duties. And it was probably in part because of Jay's potential presidential candidacy that, when the contents of the treaty he concluded with the British were published, Republicans expended so much energy in attacking it.[61]

In the short run, Jay's appointment and mission had the effect of forfending the adoption of Madison's retaliatory discrimination resolutions in the Senate.[62] Washington had bought time. On this note, the first session of the Third Congress ended. The House never did vote on the Madison resolutions for retaliatory discrimination.

Third Congress, Second Session, 1794–95

Party wrangling carried over into the second session; but this time constitutional disputation, with one marked exception, sank to the level of triviality, if not cynicism. The level of disputation may have sunk because, on the Republican side, Jefferson was now in retirement in Virginia and Madison, a recently married man, may have lost some of his former zest for argument,[63] and because, on the Federalist side, Hamilton, leaving the Treasury in the middle of the session, gave increasing attention to his own domestic needs.[64]

The marked exception to the lower level of constitutional argument arose in reaction to a proposal to censure "certain self-created societies" for their alleged participation in the Whiskey Rebellion. During the recess between the first and second sessions of the Third Congress, farmers in western Pennsylvania had resisted collection of federal excise taxes on whiskey, prompting Washington to call out the militia of four states to suppress the resistance. Exacerbating the problem and giving it a highly political tone, some self-styled Democrat-Republican societies announced their moral support for the farmers and criticized Washington for his action. The groups, formed at the outbreak of war between the French and the British, had generally been critical of the administration for its neutrality policy, and supportive both of France and of the Republican Party.[65]

Washington was angered, and in his address to Congress at the opening of the second session included a reference to "certain self-created societies [which] assumed the tone of condemnation."[66] The Senate, dominated by Federalists, quickly concurred in a responding address, which, in emulation of British Parliamentary practice, it was then the custom of both houses to compose. In concurring, the Senate defeated a motion offered by Aaron Burr of New York to expunge from the response the words "open resistance to the laws . . . has been increased by the proceedings of certain self-created societies." In presenting his motion, Burr was acting on behalf of his Republican constituency, which had reacted strongly against the rebuke.[67]

In the House, Madison also intervened to shield the societies. Because what they had done was not illegal, he said, it was not the business of Congress to censure them or any private individuals for their opinion, no matter how obnoxious. Opinion, he added, was not the object of legislation. Indeed, in an oblique reference to what is now the Ninth Amendment, he said that the people in forming the Constitution had retained rights that they had not expressly delegated and that the right to express an opinion was one of them. If Congress continued in this fashion, it might extend its censure to matters of speech and press. Censure, he went on, was a form of punishment and as such constituted a bill of attainder.[68] The last objection may not have been stated with his usual precision, but overall his argument had the desired effect. He had raised a substantial constitutional issue, one calculated to arouse public support. The House agreed to drop the phrase "certain self-created societies" and referred instead to "combinations of men." Thus amended, the House's address was narrowly approved.[69]

But thereafter the level of discourse sank. When, during the course of House consideration of a bill to amend the naturalization law, Giles proposed that before becoming a United States citizen an alien should first renounce a hereditary title or title of nobility of another country, the Federalists, in a marvelous switch of constitutional advocacy, denied that Congress had the power to make such a law, it not being within the enumerated powers. And in an equally marvelous switch, Giles for the Republicans said the power was implied, and Madison agreed. Following this display of bipartisan constitutional cynicism, the proposed amendment was approved and the naturalization bill passed.[70]

A few weeks later, things became worse. The Virginia delegation objected to the House receiving a message from the president enclosing a copy of a letter from the secretary of war on Indian conditions in the Southwest Territory. Nicholas, Giles, and Madison, in a fit of utter triviality, all argued the impropriety of both the message and the letter, on the ground that the House had not asked for them. The president, they objected, had sent them on his own. Their motion to refuse reception was defeated by a large majority.[71]

Finally, in February 1795, one member in the House, objecting to a Giles argument, expressed his surprise "at the way in which the Constitution was introduced into every subject. . . . Whenever a gentleman is at a loss for an argument, the Constitution is brought forward." The circumstances of the remark are obscure. The reporter did not catch Giles's original words, and later Giles denied making any reference to the Constitution; but considering the extent to which it had been used as an instrument of partisan attack, the accusation was inevitable.[72]

The truth was that although the Republicans had a substantial majority in Congress, Hamilton's influence, now exerted through his correspondence with the president and the members of his cabinet, was still dominant. The Republicans, despite their numbers, were denied influence and, without Jefferson's leadership, were frustrated.[73] Snatching at whatever issue was at hand, they attempted to turn it into one that might fatally undermine Federalist control.

They were a party waiting for a major opportunity, a major confrontation. They would have their moment, at last, in the debates in the Fourth Congress over the implementation of Jay's Treaty. Since by then constitutional interpretation had become the chief weapon in partisan disputes, constitutional issues would predominate.

CHAPTER EIGHT

Jay's Treaty and the Withering of Madison's Authority (Fourth Congress, First Session, 1795–96)

Just after the Third Congress had adjourned, Washington received the treaty Jay had negotiated with the British. From a long-range perspective, the treaty was a success, but in the short-term it presented serious problems. To his credit, Jay secured the definite withdrawal of British troops from their fortifications in the territories ceded to the United States in the Treaty of Peace and arranged for the arbitration of certain rather vaguely defined boundaries in those territories.[1] He also arranged for the arbitration of American claims against the British for their past illegal maritime seizures,[2] and opened the British East Indies and, to a limited extent, the British West Indies to American shipping.[3]

But, on the downside, and against southern interest, he failed to obtain compensation for the manumitted slaves and agreed to the arbitration of American debts to British creditors before joint commissioners in London.[4] Moreover, in abandonment of the Madison-Jefferson policy of retaliatory discrimination, and against the interest of the American shipping industry and of France, he conceded that, contrary to an existing act of Congress, British goods need no longer pay an additional 10 percent tax when carried in British ships, and he agreed that British trade be placed on a most-favored-nation basis.[5] Worse, from both the American shippers' and the French points of view, he abandoned the principles to which the United States had previously committed itself in treaties: that neutrals were entitled to trade freely with belligerents in noncontraband goods and that the list of contraband must be narrowly confined to war-making items. Instead, Jay agreed to the inclusion of timber and other raw materials for shipbuilding as contraband, and to the right of the British to deflect American vessels from blockaded enemy ports and remove enemy property from the vessels.[6] Finally, the treaty omitted any reference to the impressment of American seamen.[7] Viewed as a whole, the treaty so offended Virginia interest that its publication was bound to cause a partisan Republican uproar.

Washington did not like the treaty and anticipated both the vehement political criticism he and his administration would be subjected to if he accepted it and the probable mischievous effect that criticism would have on relations with France. But at the same time he considered that the country's relations with Britain would be even worse if he did not accept it. Consequently, ever the prudent administrator, he proceeded cautiously. He did not publicize the treaty's contents but instead, acting formally and in accordance with the Constitution, called the Senate into special session in June 1795, and without comment submitted the document to it for the purpose of obtaining its advice and consent.[8]

By a narrow margin and after a lengthy and secret debate, the Senate approved the treaty with one amendment.[9] Soon after, Stephens T. Mason, a Republican senator from Virginia, delivered a copy of the treaty to the *Aurora,* which published it. From the North and South, from both Federalists and Republicans, widespread opposition developed immediately.[10] Jay's Treaty, as it was called, had apparently delivered the perfect campaign issue into the hands of the Republicans.

In the face of this opposition, Washington continued to proceed cautiously. With his cabinet he considered the constitutional implications of the Senate's amendment, which amounted to a rejection of Article XII of the treaty governing the renewal on limited terms of American trade with the British West Indies. The cabinet decided that the president could ratify the treaty without the article and on that basis send it to Great Britain for its approval, and that if the British approved it on those terms, the treaty would take effect without the need of further reference to the Senate.[11]

While Washington deliberated as to whether to sign the treaty, Hamilton, writing under the pen name of Camillus, with the president's encouragement, published a series of essays in defense of the treaty. These proved so effective as to elicit from Jefferson a mingled exclamation of admiration for Hamilton's ability and concern that the essays might convince the public the treaty was good, and lead to a Federalist victory in the next election.[12]

In the meantime, the British disclosed to the administration a report they had intercepted from Joseph Fauchet, French minister to the United States, to his government. Washington, alarmed at the contents of the report and indignant at the evidence of Randolph's acceptance of a French bribe and of French influence the previous year in instigating the Whiskey Rebellion, forced Randolph, who had succeeded Jefferson as secretary of state, to resign and summarily signed the treaty.[13] The disclosure served only to convince influential Federalists in and out of the administration that French-minded Republicans could in all likelihood be traitors.

Despite Hamilton's successful defense of the treaty, the Republicans judged that it remained widely unpopular and considered that the first session of the Fourth Congress, beginning in December 1795 and running late into the spring of 1796, would give them a platform from which they could attack it and rally the country around their party. Since 1796 was a presidential election year, they would have a good chance, they felt, to persuade the electors, should Washington decline to run, to choose Jefferson as the next president of the United States.[14]

Accordingly, in early October Madison, in consultation with Jefferson, drafted an anonymous petition to the Virginia General Assembly in which he set forth various objections to the treaty and requested the legislature to take appropriate action. Among the objections was the charge that the treaty was incompatible with the Constitution. More particularly, the petition stated: "The President and Senate by ratifying this Treaty, usurp the powers of regulating commerce, of making rules with respect to aliens, of establishing tribunals of justice, and of defining piracy."[15] The petition did not disclose the constitutional basis for its charge.

Such a basis was unexpectedly furnished the following month when in the Assembly John Marshall, who had recently entered the legislature, spoke against a proposed resolution disapproving the treaty. Leading the Federalist minority opposition, he argued that the parts of the treaty affecting commerce could not take effect until the House of Representatives ratified them. The regulation of commerce, as a subject committed to the legislative powers of Congress under Article I, Section 8, of the Constitution, Marshall contended, required the joint concurrence of House and Senate. Pending House approval, the treaty was a mere inchoate act.

Marshall's tactic, intended to defeat the adoption of the resolution at the state level, was unwise because it furnished opponents at the national level with a credible constitutional ground for blocking the implementation of the treaty in the House of Representatives. Under the leadership of more perceptive politicians, the Republican-controlled General Assembly could have defeated its own resolution and substituted another, based on the Marshall thesis, calling on the House to use its supposed constitutional power and withhold its support of the treaty.

However, neither Jefferson nor Madison were in Richmond at the time. Consequently, the Assembly, under less astute leadership, rejected Marshall's argument as contrary to the history of the Virginia ratifying convention: There Henry had unsuccessfully opposed ratification on the very ground that the Constitution permitted, without the participation of the House of Representatives, the approval of a treaty whose terms might be dangerous to the interests of a state or region. Accordingly, the Assembly, playing into the hands of the Federalists on the national level, resolved to disapprove the treaty and proposed a series of four constitutional amendments, one of which would have required that future treaties containing any provision subject to regulation by Congress pursuant to Article I, Section 8, be approved by the House of Representatives before ratification.[16]

When he heard of the Marshall argument, Jefferson, writing to Madison, told him he liked it.[17] What he did not mention, however, was that the question of the rights and duties of the House of Representatives with respect to the implementation of a ratified treaty had come before the president during his own tenure as secretary of state. At that time Washington had under consideration the negotiation of a pact with Algeria and the ransoming of Americans Algeria held captive. Nor did he mention that the Marshall thesis was inconsistent with the construction he, Jefferson, had given the Constitution and with the position the president had subsequently taken.

According to memoranda which Jefferson recorded, his advice to the president had been practical: not to proceed without first obtaining the approval of both houses. Just as the Senate, whose consent to a treaty was needed, ordinarily expected to be consulted ahead of time, he had cautioned, so the House, whose consent would be needed for an appropriation to pay the ransom, might also expect to be consulted ahead of time. The president, Jefferson reported, had at first followed his advice.[18]

But although the Senate, when approached, had approved the substance of the president's proposal—that he ransom the captives and negotiate a treaty with the Algerians—they had disapproved his consulting the House. The Senate had thought, Jefferson reported, "that to consult the representatives on one occasion would give them a handle always to claim it, and would let them in to a participation of the power of making treaties which the constitution had given exclusively to the President and Senate." Whereupon the president had asked him whether a treaty providing for money to be paid the Algerians, to which the Senate consented and which he ratified, "would not be good under the constitution and obligatory on the Represent. to furnish the money?" Jefferson had answered: "It certainly would, and that it would be the duty of the representatives to raise the money: but that they might decline to do what was their duty, and I thought it might be incautious to commit himself by a ratification with a foreign nation, where he might be left in the lurch in the execution."[19]

Jefferson added that he had told the president: "It was possible too to concieve [sic] a treaty which it would not be their duty to provide for." To which the president had reportedly replied "that he did not like throwing too much into democratic hands, that if they would not do what the constitution called on them to do, the government would be at an end, and must *then assume another form.*" He had then instructed Jefferson that in preparing questions for future consultation with the Senate he strike out any intimation that the presidential seal would not be put on the treaty until both houses had voted the appropriation.[20]

We do not know whether Madison was privy to this information. If he was, he might have known that in view of the president's strong feelings on the subject it would be imprudent to espouse the argument that the House did not have a duty to implement a ratified treaty, especially when the underlying purpose of such an argument was to bring into disrepute the merits of a treaty the president had already ratified.

In any case, Madison must also have reflected that the Marshall thesis contradicted not only the sense of the Virginia ratifying convention, as the Virginia General

Assembly had pointed out, but also that of the Constitutional Convention, during the course of which the Pennsylvania delegation had moved unsuccessfully first that "no Treaty shall be binding on the United States which is not ratified by a Law" and later that the House of Representatives, as well as the Senate, should be included in the treaty-making process.[21] He should have suspected that if the Republicans in the House were to advance the Marshall argument and he were to concur in it, he, as a participant in both conventions, would in particular be open to the accusation that he was repudiating the plain text of the Constitution and the sense of both conventions.

Had he had any doubt about his vulnerability on this score, it should have been dispelled when early in January 1796, Hamilton, in response to the charge in the petition to the Virginia legislature that the president and Senate in ratifying the treaty had usurped their powers, renewed his defense of the ratification. Following his contention that under the Supremacy Clause in Article VI the House was required to implement a treaty,[22] he asserted it to be a fact that it was the sense and intention of the Constitutional Convention that a treaty should control and bind the legislative powers of Congress. For this reason, he continued, the requirements for making a treaty were "carefully guarded: the cooperation of two thirds of the Senate with the President being required." Then, with typical Hamiltonian audacity, he continued: "I appeal for [a corroboration of] this with confidence to every member of the Convention—particularly to those in the two houses of Congress. Two of these, are in the House of Representatives, Mr. Madison & Mr. Baldwin. It is expected by the adversaries of the Treaty that these Gentlemen will in their places obstruct its execution. However this may be, I feel a confidence that neither of them will deny the assertion I have made. To suppose them capable of such a denial were to suppose them utterly regardless of truth."[23]

In the face of this open challenge, Madison could not have looked forward to a debate on these matters. Such an opportunity was not immediately forthcoming. In his opening address to the House the previous month, Washington had deprived that body of a quick chance to challenge the treaty by announcing simultaneously its conclusion, the Senate's approval with the exception of the one amended article, his own approval, and his intention, when he received notice of British agreement to the amendment, of referring the matter to Congress without delay. In fact, it was not until March 1796 that Washington chose to inform Congress of the British agreement.[24]

But by then the nation's economy was booming. In the East, exports were expanding and there was an upsurge in shipbuilding. Settlers, cheered by Anthony Wayne's victory over the Indians in Ohio and by the news that the British would vacate their forts by June 1796, poured westward across the Alleghenies. The public had begun to enjoy and appreciate the beneficial results of Jay's Treaty.[25]

Despite the surging economy and the danger that an attack on the treaty based on the supposed constitutional powers of the House would pose to Madison personally, however, the Marshall thesis appealed to some Republican newcomers in Congress as well as to Jefferson. One of these was Albert Gallatin of Pennsylvania, who in a short time proved to be a constitutional theorist of the first order and, by virtue of his ability, one of the leaders for the opposition in the House. Like Jefferson but unlike Madison, Gallatin was not a founding father and therefore was not encumbered by a history of prior public positions in the Constitutional Convention, in a state ratifying convention, or in Congress. True, he had been active in the state politics of Pennsylvania during the ratification period and later in the state legislature, but in the main his record was a blank.[26] Thus he had no inhibition about arguing that in a sense the Constitution itself was blank: the proverbial tabula rasa, upon which a person could write anything he chose so that the text could mean anything he wanted it to mean. Gallatin's manner of constitutional construction was freer than Madison's; but that freedom could come only at Madison's expense.

Thus, it was Gallatin who, after Washington referred the treaty to Congress for its consideration, advanced the Marshall thesis during the course of a House debate brought on by a motion of another newcomer, Edward Livingston of the formidable New York clan. The debate was precipitated when Livingston, confident of his powers and disdainful of Madison's caution, decided on his own to introduce a motion requesting the president to lay before the House treaty documents, including copies of his instructions to Jay and of all related correspondence, excluding, however, any papers whose disclosure might be improper because of existing negotiations.[27]

When asked the specific purpose for which he sought the papers, Livingston admitted he could not tell without first seeing them. (This was misleading. In fact, as he later conceded, he already had access to the papers in his capacity as chairman of the Committee on American Seamen.) He ventured that they might be useful in an impeachment proceeding but then added, almost as an afterthought, that principally they might assist the House in the conduct of its discretionary power whether to carry the treaty into effect. A supporter explained that the House might have a constitutional responsibility to consider the matter.[28]

When Federalists, following the Hamiltonian line of defense, objected that under the Constitution the treaty-making power had been assigned to the president and the Senate and that in consequence the House had no power to deny effect to the treaty,[29] Gallatin assumed effective leadership for the Republicans in place of Madison, whose knowledge of the convention proceedings and whose past public positions on the question had made him peculiarly vulnerable. Closing party ranks, Gallatin came to Livingston's support and suggested in the vaguest of terms the various ways recourse to the papers might be relevant to the legitimate purposes of the House. The information, he said, would be useful for whatever purpose the president had in mind when he laid the treaty before the House. Or it might be useful in the future deliberations of the House if the treaty should contain a provision conflicting with existing law. (Later he would charge that in fact it did.) Or the information might be useful in an impeachment proceeding, since the House, Gallatin stated loftily, was "the grand inquest of the nation." He admitted, however, that he did not then contemplate the exercise of that function.[30]

A full-scale constitutional debate ensued. Once again, as in previous congressional debates, result-oriented considerations determined the content of the arguments, the canons of construction employed—strict or broad—and the decision whether resort should be had to sources of interpretation contemporaneous to the adoption and ratification of the Constitution, either in the Constitutional Convention itself or in the state conventions. But this time, the political stakes could not have been higher: control of the presidency following the election of 1796 and, with it, control of appointments and influence upon, if not control of, public policy.

In avid pursuit of those prizes, each side forsook whatever intellectual and political integrity it had left and, regardless of consistency, advanced the most immediately useful argument in the battle for public opinion and votes. On the general question—of the use of extraneous materials in the construction of a text, whether that of a treaty or of the Constitution—each side adopted contradictory positions. And on the specific question—of the use of such materials in the construction of the Constitution—each side changed the position it had customarily taken in prior debates. All in all, the debate conclusively demonstrated the debilitating effect that the desire for partisan advantage had on the quality of constitutional argument in Congress. Madison's contributions were no exception.

Opening the debate in opposition to Livingston's motion, the Federalists charged that the unconstitutionality of a treaty must be apparent from the face of the document. Robert Goodloe Harper of South Carolina stated their thesis: If a treaty was constitutional on its face, the previous negotiations and the instructions under which it was framed were irrelevant, and knowledge of their contents could not make it otherwise. So, on the other hand, if it was unconstitutional, the defect could not be cured by instructions set forth in previous correspondence.

Harper placed great reliance on judicial practice: In the courts, it was the constant and invariable legal maxim, he said, that "every deed, every law, every written instrument of any sort, was to be judged of and explained by itself, and not by recurrence to other matter." In construing a statute, he declared, the judges never resorted to the debates which preceded it or the opinions of individual legislators concerning its meaning, but rather inspected the act itself and interpreted it by its own evidence. From this it followed that the House could not resort either to the correspondence or to the journals of the negotiations for the purpose of ascertaining the treaty's meaning. The body must take the treaty on its face and do everything necessary under the Constitution to carry the treaty into effect, including voting the necessary appropriations.[31]

The applicability of this legal maxim to the proper method of construing the Constitution was not then in point, and Harper did not consider it. Had he done so, he might have realized that the argument tended to cut against his own and his party's ultimate position. But having posited the impropriety of any reference to correspondence, instructions, or negotiations, Harper concluded that the call for papers had no competent purpose and was therefore improper. He conceded, however, that in an extreme case the House might withhold an appropriation for carrying a treaty into effect.[32]

Harper also placed his opposition to Livingston's motion on practical grounds. Livingston, he charged, already knew what was in the papers for which he called. As chairman of the Committee on American Seamen, he and his entire committee had been allowed access to them. The same privilege, Harper supposed, would probably be given to any other member of the House who requested it. Since this was so, Livingston should be required to state the exact purpose for his call, and in the absence of such a specification the House should reject his motion.[33]

So far the debate had turned on the relevance of the papers to a purpose within the constitutional competence of the House. Gallatin, perceiving the weakness of the Republican position, shrewdly seized on Harper's concession regarding the constitutional powers of the House in an extreme case and shifted the debate from the immediate question—the right to inspect the papers—to the broader and, in any view of the case, purely speculative constitutional issues of House powers with respect to treaties. One such issue was whether the House should give effect to a treaty inconsistent in one of its provisions with the Constitution or with the requirements of a preexisting law. Another was whether the House was obliged to accept a treaty whose provisions affected subjects such as the regulation of commerce, which by Article I of the Constitution were consigned to the lawmaking powers of both branches of Congress.[34]

Interested in advancing House powers at the expense of those of the president and Senate, and in the process advancing the Republican cause of maligning the treaty on the merits, Gallatin argued for the strict limitation of the treaty-making power—in which the House did not participate—and the broad vindication of congressional power—in which it did. Gallatin's first thesis was that a treaty inconsistent with the Constitution or preemptive of the laws of Congress was invalid; his second thesis was that, as Marshall had argued the preceding year in the Virginia General Assembly, a treaty purporting to cover matters of commerce, which under Article I of the Constitution were the subject of the lawmaking powers of both branches of Congress, was, insofar as its commercial provisions were concerned, an inchoate act, requiring the sanction of the House before it could take effect.[35]

Gallatin buttressed his second thesis with the assertion that if it were otherwise, the president and the Senate could subvert the Constitution by employing the treaty-making power, for example with Indian tribes, to deprive the House of a participation in lawmaking. He probably had in mind a pending administration bill that, in implementing an Indian treaty, would seriously affect the interest of settlers in lands the state of North Carolina had earlier ceded to the United States. He and Madison were bent on blocking the proposal in an effort to protect that interest and, as a result, gain southern and western support.[36]

Returning to the debate on the call for the president's papers and on the incidental question of the House's right to participate in the treaty-making process, Gallatin contended that since the Constitution had empowered the House to participate in the appropriations process, it could—to ensure its participation in treaty making—withhold an appropriation from a treaty's implementation. This interpretation of the Constitution, he observed, was consistent with British practice, whereby the crown in asking for a treaty's effectuation submitted it together with all relevant papers to the House of Commons. He underscored the irony of the case: The chief executive of Great Britain, the other participant to the treaty, and a king at that, submitted papers to the House of Commons, the representative of the people; while in a republic under the Constitution of the United States the House of Representatives, according to the Federalists, was excluded both from an examination of the relevant papers and from the exercise of an independent judgment. Gallatin concluded with an enumeration of the treaty's specific provisions that affected existing laws: those generally prohibiting the importation of goods by land, and requiring the imposition of an additional duty for goods carried in foreign vessels.[37]

Gallatin's argument was ingenious, but he had not shown its relevance. No one contended that the treaty conflicted with a provision of the Constitution. Moreover, the practice of the crown under the unwritten British Constitution was not pertinent to the requirements of the written United States Constitution. And according to what Hamilton had written in the *Federalist,* Gallatin's understanding of British practice was erroneous. Hamilton had said:

THE KING OF GREAT BRITAIN IS THE SOLE and absolute representative of the nation in all foreign transactions. He can of his own accord make treaties of peace, commerce, alliance, and of every other description. It has been insinuated, that his authority in this respect is not conclusive, and that his conventions with foreign powers are subject to the revision, and stand in need of the ratification of Parliament. But I believe this doctrine was never heard of 'till it was broached upon the present occasion. Every jurist of that kingdom, and every other man acquainted with its constitution knows, as an established fact, that the prerogative of making treaties exists in the crown in its utmost plenitude; and that the compacts entered into by the royal authority have the most complete legal validity and perfection, independent of any other sanction. The Parliament, it is true, is sometimes seen employing itself in altering the existing laws to conform them to the stipulations in a new treaty; and this may have possibly given birth to the imagination that its co-operation was necessary to the obligatory efficacy of the treaty. But this parliamentary interposition proceeds from a different cause; from the necessity of adjusting a most artificial and intricate system of revenue and commercial laws to the changes made in them by the operations of the treaty; and of adapting new provisions and precautions to the new state of things, to keep the machine from running into disorder.[38]

Finally, even assuming that Gallatin was correct—that the House had the right to withhold an appropriation in implementation of the treaty and that certain provisions in the treaty conflicted with existing federal legislation—the conflict appeared on the face of both the treaty and the preexisting laws. The contents of the papers that Livingston sought, unilateral communications between the president and his envoy, would shed no light on the intent of the parties to the treaty and therefore could not influence its interpretation.

Gallatin's argument then was a diversion, probably intended as such, to cover the inherent weakness in Livingston's position and to save him and the Republican Party from his blunder. The diversion was successful at that. The debate continued for an additional two weeks, touching on the constitutional powers of the president, Senate, and House, Republicans arguing systematically for the extension of House power, Federalists for the powers of the president and the Senate.

Madison, as his party's resident constitutional expert, could not very well sit out the discussion of those important constitutional questions, and so he had to participate, doing his best to keep the House off track. Acting the party man and admitting that the question was incidental,[39] and the subject not clear, he proceeded to speak at great length in support of Gallatin's position, as though the question were not after all incidental. Essentially, he relied on one of his favorite constitutional themes, that of the separation of the respective powers of the legislature, the executive, and the judiciary in Articles I through III.

The gist of his argument was that the terms of Article II, whereunder the treaty-making power had been expressly placed in the president and Senate, were in apparent conflict with the terms of Article I, whereunder certain legislative powers had been placed in both branches of Congress. The conflict, he declared, should be resolved in the light of the overall constitutional principle of a separation of powers and thus in favor of the power of both branches, including that of the House, in order to maintain the system of checks and balances the Constitution was designed to ensure. Without the participation of the House, the treaty-making power would tend to be absolute and dangerous: It would enable the president and the Senate to make the United States a party to a foreign war, furnish troops for overseas use, stipulate subsidies and borrow money to pay for them, and keep up a standing army in time of peace for mutual security projects—all without the need of House support.[40]

Madison's current position was not inconsistent with a statement he had made in the *Federalist:* "And although the house of representatives is not immediately to participate in foreign negotiations and arrangements, yet from the necessary connection between the several branches of public affairs, those particular branches will frequently deserve attention in the ordinary course of legislation, and will sometimes demand particular legislative sanction and cooperation."[41] Here Madison had not specified the respect in which the powers of the House would be called into play. But in a paper written shortly thereafter he referred only to the appropriations power. He reminded his readers that the House "can not only refuse, but they alone can propose the supplies requisite for the support of government."[42]

His position in the debate over the Jay treaty papers, however, was inconsistent with that which as Helvidius he had advanced in his essays against the sole presidential power to terminate a treaty. There he had written that the treaty-making power under Article II, in requiring a two-thirds consent of the members of the Senate present, served as a compensation for the vote of the House, which could not conveniently be made a party to the function. In addition to clearly implying that the House was excluded from any aspect of treaty making, he had further argued that by virtue of the Supremacy Clause of Article VI of the Constitution a treaty had the force of law.[43] Since this was the case, it should follow that the terms of the treaty should supersede those of preexisting laws. Fortunately for him, because he had written those essays pseudonymously, he could not be publicly charged with the inconsistency.

In any event, as the Federalists quickly demonstrated, Madison, with his long record of public participation in discussions of constitutional interpretation, was on shaky ground in speaking out on the issue. Sedgwick, in an allusion to Madison, reminded the House that theretofore it had been warned repeatedly against the dangers of construction by implication. Here, Sedgwick said, the Constitution expressly gave to the president and the Senate the power to make treaties, and yet it was now contended that by the implication of the lawmaking power the House also had a share in treaty making.

He went on to expose the fundamental flaw in Madison's argument: Although a treaty operated as law, it was not a mere exercise of the lawmaking power. It was a compact with a foreign country whereby each party could agree to arrangements for mutual security and mutual benefits, including the exchange of commerce; to the adjudication of disputes, including the settlement of boundaries; and, most important of all, during wartime, to the conclusion of peace.[44]

Aiming at the weakest point in Madison's position and using the constitutional argument that Madison himself most habitually employed, Sedgwick appealed to constructions of the Constitution advanced during the ratification process as among the best of guides in finding its true meaning. Those who opposed its ratification had then argued, as Madison now did, that the president and Senate alone had the power to make treaties and that the failure to include the House was dangerous. Sedgwick recalled, for instance, that Mason had warned of this danger in the Virginia convention and had charged that under the treaty-making power the president and Senate might do what in England the king could not. Henry, he recalled, had also warned that a mere two-thirds of a Senate quorum might cede territory and agree to the concession of most valuable commercial advantages.

On the other side, Sedgwick further recalled, it had been contended that it was not prudent to include the House in the treaty-making process because the large number of representatives would make it impossible to conduct business in secrecy. Whereupon Henry had countered that it was improper to exclude the House and that they must amend the Constitution by requiring the House's consent. When such consent is necessary, Henry had concluded—Sedgwick quoted him—"there will be a certainty of attending to the public interests." To this, Madison had replied—again, Sedgwick quoted him—that the treaty-making power had been properly placed "in the new Constitution as it was in the Confederation."[45]

Madison, Sedgwick pointed out, had changed his position: When participating in the Virginia debate in support of ratification, he had set forth the checks on the treaty-making power that the Constitution had in fact provided, but he had not then claimed a share for the House in that power, although that position would have been a sufficient answer to both Henry and Mason. Rather, in confirmation of the construction that the House would not share in the power, Sedgwick went on, the Virginia convention had agreed that the treaty-making power with all its effects and consequences was vested solely and exclusively in the president and Senate. It had therefore requested a constitutional amendment requiring treaty approval by two-thirds of the entire Senate, instead of two-thirds of a quorum.[46]

In similar vein, William Smith, charging Gallatin with a change of position, recalled his participation in a Harrisburg meeting during ratification, at which, on the assumption that the House had no part in treaty-making, a constitutional amendment had been proposed that no treaty should affect the operation of state or federal law until approved by the House. In practice, Smith added, treaties had theretofore been enforced without regard to the House. As a consequence of this practice and on the assumption that, after the Senate's consent to Jay's Treaty, the president alone could withhold government sanction, petitions had been sent to him asking him not to sign the treaty. A recent action of the Virginia legislature proposing a constitutional amendment to give the House a participatory power in treaty making was, he concluded, based on that assumption.[47]

Benjamin Bourne of Rhode Island introduced a further consideration. Expressing concern at any move that would enlarge the powers of the House at the expense of the smaller states, he referred to the Constitution where, he maintained, the power to consent to treaties had been placed in the Senate as the representatives of the respective states. Without this power, which followed the plan of the Articles of Confederation in requiring the consent of two-thirds of the Senate, the smaller states, he claimed, would not have ratified the Constitution. Then in a thrust at the usual line of Madison and his Virginia colleagues, he hailed the Senate's participation in treaty making as a means whereby the smaller states could prevent consolidation of their governments into the mass of the United States, which would be dominated in the House by the larger states. This, he said, had been the construction placed on the Constitution in the Virginia, Massachusetts, and North Carolina ratifying conventions. To construe the Constitution otherwise, he charged, constituted a trick on the smaller states.[48]

Finally, Murray delivered the Federalists' coup de grace. Pursuing the line that Hamilton had set forth in his newspaper defense of the treaty, Murray openly twitted both Madison and Baldwin over their failure to recall the proceedings of the Constitutional Convention of which they had been members. Taking special aim at Madison, with language dripping with sarcasm, he said:

THE GENTLEMAN FROM VIRGINIA [HAS] BORNE an exalted rank among those who framed . . . [the Constitution]. To his genius and patriotism, in a great degree, [I have] always understood, were we indebted for the Constitution. Would it not be expected that he who had helped to speak through the Constitution would be well prepared to expound it by contemporaneous opinions? Would it not be desirable that, if there are doubts, if we wander in the dark, the gentleman should afford us light, as he has it in abundance? If the Convention spoke mysterious phrases, and the gentleman helped to utter them, will not the gentleman aid the expounding of the mystery? If the gentleman was the Pythia in the temple, ought he not to explain the ambiguous language of the oracle? To no man's exposition would [I] listen with more deference. If any cause could justify the intrusion of curiosity upon a deposite [sic] of secrets in a very sanctuary itself, it would be this doubt, and he should almost feel at liberty to open the Journals of the Convention, to see at least what they meant who spoke a language to others ambiguous, but to himself plain, incontrovertibly plain.[49]

The Journals of the Constitutional Convention had been preserved, Murray continued, and on the very question before them a vote had been taken. If in such a short space of time doubts could arise as to what the framers intended, he wondered, what was likely to happen in a hundred years? With a pointed reference to Madison and with consummate irony, he asked: "One hundred years hence, should a great question arise upon the construction [of the Constitution], what would not be the value of that man's intelligence, who, allowed to possess integrity and a profound and unimpaired mind, should appear in the awful moments of doubt, and, being known to have been in the illustrious body that framed the instrument, should clear up difficulties by his contemporaneous knowledge? Such a man would have twice proved a blessing to his country."[50]

Madison could not very well accept the challenge, and did not. Instead, Gallatin, who in defense of Livingston's call for the papers had succeeded in diverting the House's attention from that subject by the introduction of the incidental and then irrelevant question of the powers of the House, now came to Madison's defense. In a wide-ranging speech supporting the Republican position on the incidental question—during the course of which he also responded to the textual arguments of Sedgwick and Bourne[51]—Gallatin rejected as entirely inappropriate Murray's reliance on the history of the Constitutional Convention and the proceedings of the state ratifying conventions.

Gallatin first belittled any reference to the history of the Constitutional Convention and any appeal to the individual memories and private opinions of congressmen who had been delegates to the convention. Calling such recollections unreliable, he asked whether Murray had been fostering suspicions, which could not with propriety be directly resolved, that some members of the House were acting inconsistently. And he wondered whether the House was to be told that a construction of a text different from what it naturally bore was to be found in secret journals left under seal and preserved for use on a supposedly proper occasion.[52] Essentially, Gallatin's was the argument Harper had made against Livingston's call for papers extraneous to the text of the treaty. In defending Madison on the incidental question of House power, Gallatin was weakening Livingston on the main question.

In any case, Gallatin said, continuing his attack on the proceedings of the Constitutional Convention, consideration of a supposed framers' intent was pointless. The framers, he said baldly, were not the persons who made the Constitution. They were like clerks employed to draft a bill. It was the people and the state conventions who made the Constitution. They were the only parties whose intentions might be investigated with propriety.[53]

Gallatin's remarks somewhat resembled an argument that in a different context Madison had advanced in the *Federalist*. There Madison had set out at length to defend the delegates to the Constitutional Convention against the charge that in framing and proposing for ratification a Constitution in place of the Articles of Confederation they had gone beyond their commission. The commission was to prepare a set of alterations to the Articles which would render the federal government adequate to the requirements of government and the preservation of the Union. After explaining at great length why the delegates had decided that this could not be done, and why in good conscience they had instead framed and submitted a new constitution, Madison reminded his readers:

THAT THE POWERS [OF THE DELEGATES] were merely advisory and recommendatory; that they were so meant by the States, and so understood by the Convention; and that the latter have accordingly planned and proposed a Constitution, which is to be of no more consequence than the paper on which it is written, unless it be stamped with the approbation of those to whom it is addressed. This reflection places the subject in a point of view altogether different, and will enable us to judge with propriety of the course taken by the Convention.[54]

Madison concluded that if the delegates had exceeded their powers, they had done so because they had to. Their work was good. But far from denigrating them as lowly clerks, Madison praised them as responsible and intelligent servants whose work the people, their master, should ratify.[55]

In refuting Murray and the Federalists, Gallatin, however, had to move beyond a denigration of the framers' status. Since the Federalists had relied on the reports of the Virginia ratifying convention, he had to belittle a resort to their proceedings as well. Thus, having said that it was the intention of the people and of the state conventions that counted, he argued that no great weight should be given to the views of those who opposed the Constitution.[56] Besides, he continued, the records of the state ratifying conventions supported his position: Justice James Iredell, a delegate in the North Carolina convention, had argued that the House's authority over appropriations would act as a limit to the treaty-making power; and Justice James Wilson, a delegate in the Pennsylvania convention, had said that the House might balk a treaty by refusing to repeal a law.[57] A treaty therefore was an inchoate act, requiring the House's concurrence before it could become effective. Without that concurrence the treaty-making power would be subject to abuse, and—he closed with the usual Republican peroration—it would be dangerous to the liberties and welfare of the people.[58]

William Cooper of New York ended the debate by picking at the flaw in Gallatin's reasoning and the Republican position: If the House must rely on the text of the Constitution and not call on the recollection of House members who were also at the Constitutional Convention as to the construction that body had placed upon the treaty-making power, why should they in the House now ask for the papers from which the treaty had arisen? Why not instead, in accordance with Gallatin's principles, explain the treaty by the instrument itself?[59]

Cooper had indeed made a valid point, but his point worked against the Federalist position as well. To achieve their desired results, both sides had worked at cross-purposes: In support of the call for the papers by Livingston, Gallatin, his fellow Republican, had introduced the incidental question of House power and then proceeded to argue a principle of construction inconsistent with that which Livingston had advanced on the main motion. Similarly, Harper, in opposing the main motion, had argued a principle of construction inconsistent with that employed by Sedgwick and Murray, his fellow Federalists, on the incidental question. If Harper was correct in insisting on the irrelevance of correspondence to the construction of the treaty text, could Sedgwick and Murray also be correct in insisting on the relevance of contemporaneous opinion as expressed in both the Constitutional Convention and the state conventions, particularly in Virginia?

But in addition to the internal contradictions in the respective party positions, there was another, and more significant, contradiction in the guidelines the parties adopted for the resolution of constitutional issues in this debate. In purporting to resolve the question of House power with regard to the implementation of treaties, party positions had been reversed. Formerly the Republicans, when arguing against the assertion of federal power at the expense of state power or against a presidential prerogative or the authority of the executive branch at the expense of the powers of Congress, had relied either expressly or implicitly on the history surrounding the adoption and ratification of the Constitution, including the proceedings of the Constitutional Convention itself, the essays in the *Federalist,* and the proceedings in the state ratifying conventions.

For example, during the debate over the establishment of the national bank, Madison in opposing a broad construction of the Necessary and Proper Clause had expressly referred to the decision of the Constitutional Convention rejecting a motion to enable Congress to authorize corporate charters, and had invoked the common understanding of the state conventions. To the same end, his supporters in that debate had invoked the authority of Hamilton's remarks in the *Federalist.*[60] Similarly, Madison in opposing a broad construction of the spending power had argued for a reading of the Constitution consistent with the reasons advanced by the proponents of the Constitution when they sought ratification in the state conventions.[61] In striving to limit presidential participation in the arrangements for the placement of congressional sessions, he had based his arguments, without expressly saying so, on the proceedings of the Constitutional Convention.[62] And in general, when writing as Helvidius against an overall presidential competence in the conduct of foreign affairs and speaking in the House against a presidential competence in the raising of an army, he had relied on his understanding of the convention's sentiment and on the explicit statements of Hamilton in the *Federalist.*[63]

Conversely, in each of these cases, it was the Federalists who had disregarded history and argued instead for a construction of the Constitution that would in their view take care of the practical needs of the nation. Hamilton based the power to create a national bank on the need to make available a paper currency to facilitate tax collection, government borrowing and commercial enterprises, and, in an emergency, military preparations.[64] Similarly, in recommending the promotion of congressional subsidies to manufacturers and in espousing presidential primacy in the conduct of foreign affairs, Hamilton—in disregard of history—had advocated a broad reading of the spending power and of presidential powers under Article II.[65] In all these cases, Hamilton had argued, a broad construction of the Constitution clearly advanced the good of the country, a strict construction would have unduly constricted governmental or presidential operations.

Now, on the issue of a House power to withhold the implementation of a treaty made, confirmed, and ratified by the joint action of the president and the Senate, it was the Federalists who stood strongly on the record of the history of the Constitutional Convention and the Virginia ratifying convention. And it was Madison and the Republicans who fixed upon the Constitution a construction in disregard of history.

As a result of this sudden reversal of constitutional jurisprudence, Madison's mortification was shortly at hand. The House, apparently expecting the president to accommodate them, overwhelmingly approved the Livingston resolution and formally requested from the president the papers relating to Jay's Treaty.[66] They seriously miscalculated. As would appear from the president's message of rejection, Washington was annoyed.

First of all, the Republican leadership had chosen to mingle the question of the House's right to have the papers with its right to withhold approval of legislation or appropriations for the implementation of a treaty. As Livingston, who moved the question, said toward the end of the debate: "[I am] not unwilling . . . to consider the decision of this motion as declaratory of the sense of the House on that important question, whether it is constitutionally bound to give its sanction to every Treaty that may be formed by the other branches; and to provide all the sums necessary to fulfil every stipulation they may make; for, to this extent, did all their arguments go."[67]

The House call for the papers consequently implied a right to review the treaty, and probably, in view of Republican hostility to its terms, to attack it. But the House could not attack the treaty without attacking Washington. He had sent Jay to England, had committed the treaty to the Senate for its consent, and, when it consented, had sanctioned the treaty by signing it. By that time, he was accountable for its contents. In addition, there was the loose talk of impeachment, as though someone in the administration were guilty of venal conduct—if not Washington, then someone Washington should have dismissed and hadn't.

Furthermore, the attack on the merits of Jay's Treaty must have seemed to the president a House and Republican power play at his and the Senate's expense on constitutional grounds. In the light of his personal experience, including his prior discussions with Jefferson regarding the Algerian treaty, he must have considered those grounds not only unsound but false and unprincipled. To the president it must have seemed that constitutional advocacy had been debased, constitutional history repressed, and constitutional arguments distorted and misrepresented. Within a week, he rejected the House resolution and sent a message basing his rejection on carefully reasoned constitutional grounds.[68]

Adopting the arguments supporters of the treaty had advanced in the House, Washington first based his noncompliance on the nature of foreign relations, whose conduct, he wrote, required caution and whose success depended on secrecy. A disclosure of negotiations to the House with its large membership would be impolitic and perhaps dangerous. Besides, he wrote, it did not appear that the papers were relevant to any purpose within the jurisdiction of the House excepting that of impeachment, and that purpose had not been mentioned in the request.[69]

Such was the gist of the president's refusal, but he did not stop there. Following the House example, he indulged himself and expressed an opinion on the impertinent question of House power with regard to treaty making—in flat opposition to Gallatin's and Madison's positions. The Constitution, he declared, had vested the power to make treaties exclusively in the president with the advice and consent of the Senate. Treaties thus made were the law of the land and obligatory. The House had previously acquiesced in this construction and, even more, had carried treaties into effect.[70]

Then, and in direct contradiction of Gallatin's methodology, Washington based his position on the records of the Constitutional Convention and of the state conventions. He prefaced his remarks with a statement of his own participation in the Constitutional Convention and knowledge of the principles on which the Constitution had been formed. He further supported his construction with a reference to the deliberations of the state conventions, in particular to those of Virginia, in which objection had been raised to the treaty-making power because in commercial treaties the consent of two-thirds of the entire Senate membership had not been required, and because in treaties affecting territories and other rights the concurrence of three-quarters of both Houses had not been required.[71]

Washington also adopted Bourne's argument that the exclusion of the House had been in a spirit of concession to the smaller states.[72] And, finally, he referred to "the plain letter of the Constitution itself" and, in a clear rebuke to Madison for his departure from his customary canon of strict construction, appealed to the Journals of the Constitutional Convention, deposited in the State Department, from which it appeared that a proposal "that no Treaty should be binding on the United States which was not ratified by a law" had been made and explicitly rejected. The presidential message was a clear vindication for Murray, who during the House debates had twitted Madison for his failure to recall the proceedings of the Constitutional Convention.[73]

Madison's reputation was in shreds. Ames regarded him as "deeply implicated by the appeal of the President" to those proceedings. "Most persons," he wrote a friend, "think him irrecoverably disgraced, as a man void of sincerity and fairness." Representative Jonathan Trumbull, Jr., of Connecticut considered Madison's conduct "insidious and uncandid in a high degree." Undoubtedly, Madison felt keenly this change in his colleagues' opinion. A week after the delivery of the president's message, he wrote Monroe that he meant the Fourth Congress "to be my last here." Shortly thereafter, Adams wrote home that Madison was looking "worried to death. Pale, withered, haggard."[74]

Madison in his misery was convinced that the president's reply was all Hamilton's fault, that such enthusiasm for presidential prerogative, such hard-hitting argumentation of the Federalist position on behalf of executive and senatorial power, could only have emanated from the pen of that partisan disciple of high Federalism. But Madison was wrong. From Philadelphia, Washington had written to Hamilton in New York City for his opinion; but his reply, though in substance agreeing with the contents of Washington's message, was received too late to be of use. Although Washington received help from Timothy Pickering, his secretary of state, in drafting his message, the decision to reject the resolution of the House and to send it the message he did was his own.[75]

Nevertheless, the Republicans were not daunted. Still expecting favorable results in the upcoming elections, they renewed the attack. A series of resolutions was presented to the House reaffirming its constitutional authority, its duty to deliberate on the expediency of measures designed to carry a treaty into effect, and its consequent right to receive information from the president without a statement as to its relevance, as long as it related to the constitutional functions of the House.[76]

In support of the resolutions, Madison voiced regrets concerning the president's reference to the constitutional powers of the House, since, he said, the prior debates on that question had been only incidental to the main question of obtaining the papers.[77] Madison's regrets seem disingenuous, to say the least, for three reasons: Discussion of the incidental question had quite overshadowed that of the main question; it was Gallatin who, with Madison's considerable help, had succeeded in diverting attention from the dubious merits of Livingston's original motion to those of the incidental question; and Livingston himself had said that a vote in favor of his motion would be a vote in support of the constitutional right of the House to withhold legislation or appropriations in implementation of a treaty.[78] In any event, Madison claimed that he looked to the people to apply the appropriate remedy at the polls, where, manifesting their will, they would choose candidates eager to further the House's cause.[79]

These statements prepared the way for Madison's riposte. Accepting the fact that the president's use of constitutional history was an implied rebuke of himself, Madison proceeded to attack both the substance of the president's position and the propriety of his use of history. He began by protesting that it was too far in the past for him to rely on his memory of the convention without the aid of written notes left home in Virginia. In any event, he stated, it was hardly possible to speak with authority about the convention. Many of the delegates had never spoken, so that neither he nor Baldwin nor anyone else could say what the sense of the body had been.[80]

Echoing a theme that Gallatin had propounded earlier in the session, Madison stressed the unreliability of a framer's recollections and their unsatisfactoriness as an aid in ascertaining constitutional meaning. On this very subject, he pointed out, different framers had different recollections. During the Pennsylvania convention Justice Wilson, and more recently others in South Carolina and Wilmington, had given versions of the convention proceedings differing from the president's. It was for this reason, Madison recalled, that he himself had been chastised when he had referred to the debates of the Constitutional Convention during consideration of the bill to establish the Bank of the United States.[81]

Having disposed of the recollections of an individual delegate to the Constitutional Convention, Madison next addressed the reliability of the Journals of the Constitutional Convention, to which the president had also referred in his message. As the contents of a written document could not so readily be labeled untrustworthy, their quick dismissal was not possible. Therefore, Madison was forced to go further. After first characterizing the Journals as inconclusive in import, he repeated another aspect of Gallatin's earlier argument, namely, that "the sense of that body [i.e., of the delegates to the convention] could never be regarded as the oracular guide in expounding the Constitution." It was but a plan, Madison said, a dead letter only given life by the people through the state conventions.[82]

But even this position did not help Madison, because the president, following Federalist arguments in the House, had relied on the proceedings of the Virginia convention. Therefore, to cover his tracks completely, he went beyond Gallatin and disparaged the use of the state convention reports. Only the reports of the proceedings of the Pennsylvania, Virginia, and North Carolina conventions were relevant, he argued, and even those had been imperfectly preserved. In fact, he added by way of complete disparagement, the arguments based on those proceedings were inconclusive.[83]

Finally, Madison protested, the fears of the smaller states were groundless; the weight of precedent as to the prior implementation of treaties was irrelevant, because they had all been concluded with Indian tribes and Jay's was the first foreign treaty negotiated since the Constitution.[84] In short, the president's reasons were either spurious or mistaken. Constitutional history and past practice were no guide to the proper meaning of the Constitution.

Madison's argument was thoroughly devastating, both to the proper course of constitutional construction, and to the meaning of his own career. If all past history were irrelevant, and the Constitution indeed a tabula rasa, why had he taken such pains, almost working himself to death, to preserve the debates of the Constitutional Convention?[85] His own personal authority as a reliable expositor of the Constitution, grounded in his role and observations in the convention and in the belief that his view of the Constitution reflected the overall sense of the convention's deliberations, was then ultimately baseless. In his own words, he was not especially qualified after all. If Gallatin was correct, if Madison's response to Washington was correct, his references in previous debates to the assurances given in the state ratifying conventions of a federal government of limited powers had been idle, if not misleading; and the Journals of the Constitutional Convention, the published proceedings of the state conventions, the *Federalist,* and his own notes wherever they were—all were dross.[86]

If Gallatin and Madison were correct, strictures on the Constitution should be forbidden to historians: the Constitution could mean whatever the politicians said it meant. In short, the new Republican politics ultimately destroyed the necessity for the old Madison, since his experience and knowledge of the past were only inhibiting handicaps to contemporaneous creative theorizing. It was appropriate therefore that the Fourth Congress was Madison's last. As far as congressional debates were concerned, he had used up his political capital.

The resolutions Madison supported, which had political but no substantive effect, quickly passed.[87] The main issue was reached a month later when, after much political maneuvering, the House took under consideration a motion made by Sedgwick calling for the implementation of Jay's Treaty.[88] By the time the motion came to a vote, however, the Republican position in the House had eroded and, in a crucial series of votes, the implementation resolution was adopted, and resolutions critical of the treaty as injurious to the country were defeated. In several key votes, Peter Muhlenburg of Pennsylvania, the Speaker of the House and an otherwise stalwart Republican, broke the tie in favor of the administration.[89]

The Republicans had suffered a major legislative defeat and, more important, as Madison wrote Jefferson, the whole affair had hurt them politically: "A crisis which ought to have been so managed as to fortify the Republican cause, has left it in a very crippled condition; from which its recovery will be the more difficult as the elections in N.Y. Massachusets & other States, where the prospects were favorable, have taken a wrong turn under the impressions of the moment. Nothing but auspicious contingencies abroad or at home, can regain the lost ground."[90] The burgeoning economy, Republican miscalculations, and the maladroit use of Jay's Treaty had turned the 1796 election around. If Washington should retire, Jefferson, the Republican choice for the presidency, lacking northern support, could not be elected. While the controversy had eliminated Jay, it would help elect Adams.

What was worse for the party and ultimately for the country was the fact that, lured by the 1796 presidential election and their first real chance of gaining power, the Republicans had repudiated Madison's usual constitutional arguments in a headlong pursuit of what they considered winning policies. They had thoroughly compromised his integrity and eroded his authority.[91]

During the remainder of the first session of the Fourth Congress, Republican integrity was further compromised when, in an effort to consolidate party strength, their leaders engaged in what is now the standard political technique of logrolling sectional interests. As intersectional cooperation increased, constitutional arguments became guided less and less by the lessons of history, national needs, or the sense of constitutional text, and more and more by the requirements of politics.

Logrolling and Constitutional Construction

While the resolution to implement the provisions of Jay's Treaty was still before the House, a second proposal, the implementation of a series of previously concluded Indian treaties, aroused Republican political and constitutional opposition. An administration bill would mark the boundaries of Indian lands fixed in the treaties and penalize settlers for entering upon the Indian lands. The provision, if adopted, would directly affect the interest of would-be plantation owners in Tennessee and of would-be free-soil settlers in the cheap lands north of the Ohio River in the Northwest Territory.[92]

Once again interest preceded the formulation of partisan position and constitutional theory. Just as Republican desire to win the votes of northern shipowners and southern slaveholders had led to the decision to repudiate Jay's Treaty and argue on constitutional grounds for the expansion of House power at the expense of that of the president and the Senate, so now a Republican desire to win the votes of white settlers north and south of the Ohio River led to the decision to attack this second proposal on the constitutional ground of a lack of federal power. This time, however, the attack was not based on the usual Republican line that under a strict construction of Article I the proposed legislation did not fall within the enumerated powers. Instead, Republicans argued that the bill offended a broad construction of the provision in Article III governing forfeitures.

The controversy arose as follows: North Carolina had deeded land to the United States, subject to specific reservations of hunting tracts for the Indians and of acreage assigned to the claims of white settlers. To preserve the second exception, the deed to the United States stipulated that no obstruction should be made to grantees staking their claims, and that the state could for a time execute deeds in furtherance of those claims. The subject was complicated, however, by the fact that the territory North Carolina had ceded was covered in previous and subsequent treaties between the United States and the Cherokees.

The entry of whites on the lands for the purpose of staking their claims had provoked Indian retaliation against settlers in the area, and to protect them from the ensuing murder, mutilation, and widespread destruction of property, the United States had been compelled to raise and maintain a succession of armies at substantial cost. To restore and maintain peace the administration proposed that the United States mark the boundaries of Indian property and keep white settlers off it.[93]

The dispute centered around a motion made by Thomas Blount of North Carolina to strike from the bill a provision that would forfeit the rights of anyone entering on land included in the treaty for the purpose of claim staking.[94] In the course of a lengthy review of state property law, James Holland of North Carolina, speaking for the motion, argued that the provision was unconstitutional. He contended that under British law before the Revolution, title to all land was vested in the crown, since Indians, as savages and conquered peoples, were considered tenants at will, who were unable to convey a fee simple without the crown's permission. Therefore, when in the 1783 Treaty of Peace it was acknowledged that the respective states were the free sovereigns of all land within their provincial charters, it had the effect of placing in them title to land in fee simple.

From this Holland concluded that when North Carolina sold its citizens interests in part of the land and later deeded the land to the United States with the reservations already mentioned, the United States did not receive a title in fee simple and could not defeat the claimants' interest without in effect constituting a forfeiture in contravention of Article III, Section 3, Clause 2, of the Constitution.[95] That section, which relates to the punishment Congress can prescribe for the crime of treason, after placing limits on punishment by "Attainder of Treason," prohibits "Forfeiture except during the Life of the Person attainted." He did not specify in what respect the section applied, inasmuch as the bill had not referred to the prohibited offense as treason and could not plausibly be said to have done so. His construction was rather strained and unnecessarily so in view of the more readily applicable provisions of the fair compensation clause of the Fifth Amendment.[96]

In reply, James Hillhouse of Connecticut denied that before the Revolution the Indians had been nothing more than tenants at will of the lands they occupied. They had been owners in fee simple, he asserted, given this title by the "God of Nature," and recognized as such by the United States in the treaties they made with them. In any event, he said, the bill's provision for property forfeiture as punishment for a violation of the law was constitutional. Referring to past provision for forfeitures in the revenue laws, he cited one case in which an East Indian ship and cargo valued at $100,000 had been subject to forfeiture. The value of the property subject to forfeiture in the proposed bill, he pointed out, would in many instances be less.[97]

Madison in response maintained that Hillhouse's position regarding Indian land rights was at odds with the understanding of all European nations holding territory on the American continent. In support of Holland's constitutional argument, Madison stated that the bill was against the letter, if not the spirit, of the provision against forfeiture. If Congress could provide for the forfeiture of real estate in any case other than treason, he reasoned, it might also do it in the case of treason by giving it another name. Moreover, he stated, the term "forfeiture," as used in that clause, referred only to real property. That the value of the real property affected by the proposed bill might be less than the value of personal property forfeited under the revenue laws was therefore, for constitutional purposes, not pertinent.[98]

In an argument of the broadest construction Madison had in effect converted the section's specific proscription against forfeiture for treason into a general and total proscription against any forfeiture of real estate. It was an astonishing display of forensic power at the service of North Carolina settlers and slaveholders and the Republican Party cause—and at the Indians' expense. On this bathetic note, Madison delivered his last exposition of the Constitution in Congress. Gallatin, who represented a frontier district in Pennsylvania, agreed with him. Indians, being Indians, would always go to war, he said, either against Americans or against one another.[99] In the end, the motion to strike the forfeiture provision was defeated and the bill passed. The use of federal power was sustained.[100]

The Republican tactics, nonetheless, signaled the party's growing strength in matters of intersectional interest. In the name of the Constitution, Gallatin, representing the interests of free-soilers north of the Ohio, and Madison and his southern colleagues, representing the interests of settlers and slave owners south of the Ohio, could work together for the benefit of the several states against the federal government. Fittingly enough, when Tennessee was admitted into the Union that same year, its electorate chose Andrew Jackson as its first representative to the House.[101] Many years later, as president of the United States, he would work for the substantive and constitutional policies that his first mentors in government and constitutional law, Gallatin and Madison, had taught him—at the Indians' expense and to the detriment of the Bank of the United States.[102]

These mentors had one further constitutional lesson to pass on to Jackson in the Fourth Congress: their application of the canon of strict construction to the Commerce Clause, in aid of state power at the expense of national. This time when the Republicans raised objections to another administration bill, Pennsylvanians took the lead and Madison was silent. The bill would authorize the president to fix the time and place near ports of entry in the United States to which vessels arriving from foreign ports might be directed to undergo quarantine.[103] Daniel Heister of Pennsylvania objected, and Gallatin agreed, that the bill was unconstitutional. The bill, Heister said, was a health measure and as such was a matter reserved to the states. In addition, he charged, the bill would place too much power in the president and the port collectors.[104]

However, those favoring the bill argued for its practical necessity on the grounds that only a federal military officer had the authority and force to forbid a vessel from entering a port, and that some states had no quarantine facilities at all.[105] John Swanwick of Pennsylvania answered that the first difficulty could be overcome by a presidential order directing the federal officer to aid state governments in the performance of quarantine. Gallatin agreed.[106]

To the proponents' claim that the regulation was commercial in nature and as such the business of the federal government, the opponents repeated—Gallatin taking the lead—that a quarantine regulation had nothing to do with commerce and everything to do with health. The prevention of pestilence was accordingly a matter of internal police. Whether persons came by land or water, for commerce or pleasure, was of no importance.[107] The section authorizing the president's action was stricken by a wide margin.[108] Practically speaking, the House under Republican leadership had voted for a narrow reading of federal power and the Commerce Clause.

Subsequently, the bill became law along the lines suggested: The federal government would stay within its narrow limits, but the president was authorized to direct revenue and military officers "to aid in the execution of quarantine, and also in the execution of the health laws of the states, respectively, in such manner as may to him appear necessary."[109] No one raised the question as to why this authorization was not an unconstitutional delegation of legislative powers, as in the case of a proposal in the bill organizing the Post Office to confer upon the president the authority to establish such post offices and post roads as he considered necessary.[110] Nor did anyone inquire which of the enumerated powers Congress had authorized the president to make such directives in aid of state quarantine laws. Apparently, since the federal government had become the servant of the states, much as under the Articles of Confederation, a broad construction of federal power was admissible. When he was president, Jackson would follow that precedent, and John C. Calhoun, as leader of the southern states' rights contingent in the Senate, would attempt to follow it more systematically.[111]

It was evident from this vote that the party of Jefferson, Madison, and Gallatin was committed to the role of systematic opposition to the establishment of an efficient federal government organized to recognize and regulate national problems. In aid of that role, Republicans had come to advocate a philosophy of states' rights, under which the Constitution would be strictly construed so as to limit as much as possible the powers of the federal government and within it the powers of the president, and would be broadly construed to advance the interests of state governments. In effect, construction had become a weapon whereby, as Sedgwick would later say, the United States was rendered a confederation and the Constitution its governing compact.[112] In a competition for power, a sovereign State would be victorious over the union.

In counterpoise, construction of the Constitution also became a weapon for the Federalists, whereby the powers of the federal government and the power of the president, broadly read, could be expanded at the expense of the states, and state powers, strictly read, could be limited as much as possible. In any case, in a competition for power the Union would be victorious over the individual states.

The events of the next few years would disclose the extremities of constitutional argumentation and political positioning that both sides would embrace in pursuit of ambition, partisan triumph, and national and sectional interest.

Turbulence, Aliens, and Sedition

The second session of the Fourth Congress, running from December 1796 through the following March, gave no sign of the bitter rancor to come in the Fifth Congress. Short and uneventful, the session was completely overshadowed by the election of 1796. The Republicans deemed it pointless to duel with the Washington administration, then on its way out. The state elections that would choose the presidential electors and determine the new administration for the next four years had been almost completed; and party leaders, Madison among them, were chiefly interested in hearing the day-to-day news of how the various states had voted and in speculating about returns from states yet to vote. It was not until February that it was definitely known that Adams, with seventy-one electoral votes, and Jefferson, with sixty-eight, had been elected president and vice-president respectively.[1]

This anomaly, the president from one party, the vice-president from the other, reflected both the peculiar nature of Washington's presidency and the parties' hitherto loose organization, in which personal and regional considerations played a greater part than factional solidarity. In consequence, the country's vice-president had been chosen almost at random. On the Federalist side, New York's preference for president had been not Adams but Thomas Pinckney of South Carolina, who had served successfully as a foreign minister under Washington. Hamilton, who considered Adams difficult to work with, supported a strategy, in which some New Englanders concurred, of soliciting votes nationwide for Adams and Pinckney alike. But others in New England who were close to Adams—and Adams himself—suspected a Hamiltonian plot to cut Adams and advance Pinckney; and some in the South who were close to Pinckney did cut Adams, perhaps confirming those suspicions.[2] On the Republican side, personal and regional rivalries had produced similar results. When Aaron Burr presented himself as New York's candidate, Republicans, desirous of making inroads in the North, quickly agreed to solicit votes nationwide for Jefferson and Burr equally. But as it turned out, Virginia's electors cut Burr completely.[3]

In the end, Adams took New England and New York and gathered just enough votes elsewhere to be elected, but the maneuvering had lasting consequences.

Adams deeply resented the strategy whereby Federalists promised to vote for him and Pinckney equally, blamed it for his narrow victory, and blamed New York and Hamilton in particular for advancing it. Ultimately this resentment would color his administration and perhaps cost him reelection. Burr, in turn, blamed Jefferson for his defeat; and four years later, before he would commit New York's vote to the Republican cause, he would insist on a strict understanding that Republican electors in Virginia and the South vote for him on equal terms with Jefferson. So successful was the arrangement that their election would eventually have to be determined in the House of Representatives. Strict party organization was to have its drawbacks.[4]

Fifth Congress, First Session, 1797

Adams, on assuming the presidency, had no honeymoon. During the last days of Washington's administration, relations with France had seriously weakened. Treating the United States as an underdeveloped country, France did not hesitate to interfere in its politics. It was Citizen Adet, French minister to the United States, who had arranged for the publication of Jay's Treaty after its approval in the Senate.[5] Franco-American relations had become further strained when, in retaliation for the ratification and implementation of the treaty, France had proclaimed the suspension of full diplomatic relations and the commencement of a naval policy of search and seizure of all neutral shipping bound for British ports.[6]

In November, Pierre Adet, hoping to sway the presidential election, had publicized the proclamations in the Republican press in Pennsylvania, where he resided, and appealed to the state's electorate to vote for Jefferson as a means of restoring the United States to the good graces of France. Afterwards, the French had intensified the pressure, seizing American shipping and refusing to accept the credentials of the new United States minister to France, Charles Cotesworth Pinckney—brother of Thomas Pinckney—whom Washington had appointed when he recalled Monroe.[7]

Adams, therefore, considering relations between the two countries dangerously explosive, called the Fifth Congress into special session on May 15, 1797, set the state of affairs before it, and asked for an increase of both the army and navy.[8] Jefferson, now both vice-president and leader of the Republican opposition in the place of Madison, who had retired from Congress, regarded Adams's speech as an invitation to Congress to declare war.[9] If it was, Congress did not accept.

As the session was about to end without decisive action, Adams decided on a new diplomatic tack. Over the protests of his cabinet, but—unknown to him—with the private support of Hamilton, he sent Marshall and Gerry to join Pinckney in France as extraordinary envoys to negotiate a treaty of amity and commerce. The new diplomatic overture, however, quickly foundered. In France, the envoys became involved in the notorious XYZ affair, in which agents of Talleyrand, the French foreign minister, unofficially solicited a bribe to induce him to negotiate. The Americans refused, and negotiations to begin negotiations dragged on through March 1798.[10]

In the meantime, the publication in a New York newspaper in May 1797 of a private letter written by Jefferson the previous year to Philip Mazzei, a European friend, caused the political differences between the parties to deepen into bad feeling. In the letter, Jefferson had been so indiscreet as to characterize the Federalists as "an Anglican, monarchical, & aristocratical party . . . whose avowed object is to draw over us the substance, as they have already done the forms, of the British government." Worse still, in a reference generally taken to include Washington, he wrote about "apostates who have gone over to these heresies, men who were Samsons in the field & Solomons in the council, but who have had their heads shorn by the harlot England."[11]

Following publication of the letter, Washington broke off relations with Jefferson.[12] Federalists were furious. Political passions, Jefferson reported to another friend shortly afterwards, had by then reached the point where in Philadelphia men crossed the street to avoid saying hello. Disingenuously, he did not mention that to a considerable extent his own views and indiscretion had brought about the situation.[13]

At about the same time another incident occurred in Virginia which, further roiling the political climate, showed that if a prominent Republican officeholder could speak or write improperly, so could a Federalist federal judge. Since the matter concerned the conduct of Samuel J. Cabell, the congressman for the district including Albermarle County, where Jefferson lived, it was bound to affect the latter personally and receive his close attention.

A federal grand jury in Richmond, following the directions of the presiding judge, had returned a presentment against Cabell, charging that he, in circular letters to his constituents, had attempted during a time of public danger "to disseminate unfounded calumnies against the happy government of the United States" and to effect a ruinous foreign influence.[14] When Jefferson heard of it, he complained about the perversion of the federal grand jury from a legal to a political institution, and the tendency of those juries, under the direction of their presiding judges, "to become inquisitors on the freedom of speech, of writing & of principle of their fellow-citizens."[15]

Jefferson was correct. The Cabell affair was not an isolated instance. The charges of federal judges to their grand juries, of which he complained, were not confined to legal matters. Justice James Iredell, for instance, had given a grand jury his personal views about the merits of Jay's Treaty and warned the citizens of Philadelphia, a center of French sentiment, against assisting any European country at war. Later, Justice William Cushing would advise jurors in Virginia to be on guard against the wily French, and Justice William Paterson would characterize the administration's opponents as discontented Jacobins bent on the disorganization of the country.[16]

This time Jefferson, acting on the well-founded belief that Congress under the influence of the Federalists would do nothing, decided to do something. He prepared a petition for the consideration of the Virginia House of Delegates, in which he denounced the presentment and called on the delegates to take remedial action. The theory upon which Jefferson based his address was, however, to say the least, novel, and, coming from the vice-president of the United States and his party's candidate for the presidency in the last election, startling in its implications.

Terming the criticism of the correspondence between Cabell and his constituency an interference with the latter's natural right to be informed by their chosen representative of political events at large and in the government of the United States, the petition declared the protection of that right one of the objects for which local laws had been created. Therefore, the petition declared, only Virginia and its state courts, as expressed in the Tenth Amendment, had jurisdiction of an infringement of the right of citizens of the state of Virginia to be informed. To make the point abundantly clear, the petition further stated that since the right of free correspondence between a federal congressman and his constituency was not one of those enumerated in the United States Constitution and did not arise under its laws or treaties, the federal government and its courts did not have jurisdiction of such an infringement. While interference with the right in the federal courts was not proscribed by any state statute, it was, the petition concluded, a crime "of the highest and most alarming nature," and subject as such to impeachment under the Virginia constitution. In conclusion, the petition formally requested the impeachment and punishment of the grand jurors who had returned the offending presentment and who were also citizens of the state of Virginia, for infringement of the state-given right of free correspondence.[17]

In sum, in the name of natural law principles, and following the broadest construction of state powers, Jefferson had taken the extraordinary course of asking a state legislature to impeach federal grand jurors for interfering with the relation between a federal congressman and his constituency on the theory that, by strict construction of the United States Constitution, such a relationship was not and could not be protected by federal law.

Jefferson, assuming thereby the coloration of the most ardent of his states' rights supporters, had moved into the shadowy realm of confederation. He had never been a federalist in matters of domestic concern, which, he had believed, should remain under the control of the state.[18] Now he would extend that control even to the internal relations of a federal congressman and his federal constituency. Madison, formerly the ardent nationalist in matters of foreign and domestic concern, joined him. When Jefferson submitted the petition to him for comment, he approved it with only minor suggestions.[19]

Jefferson received better advice from Monroe, who considered it improper to make federal officials amenable to state tribunals for misconduct in office. While Jefferson shrugged off this criticism, he at least deleted from his final draft a demand for the grand jurors' impeachment. The petition in amended form was circulated in the various counties of Cabell's constituency and then forwarded to the Virginia House of Delegates, which the following December approved the sentiments but went no further.[20] While the probable effect of all this was to rouse Republican sentiment throughout the state and to boost Republican morale in Cabell's district, it also had the effect of convincing Federalist supporters in Virginia and throughout the country that the tenor of Republican rhetoric was undermining the Union and promoting anarchy, and that the mind-set of official Virginia had regressed to the era of the Confederacy. If they had known that it was Jefferson who had drafted the petition, the Federalist majority in the House might have moved an impeachment.

Fifth Congress, Second Session, 1797–98

Turmoil and the Debate on Foreign Missions

With Jefferson as vice-president and only two electoral votes away from the presidency itself, the Republicans under his leadership could be expected to speak and act aggressively in the second session of the Fifth Congress beginning in December 1797. Their chief concern was a breakdown in negotiations with France, which —because of their habitual support of the French—they feared the Federalists would use against them. Their main hope was that without the popular Washington as president, they could at last convince a majority of the American public that the Federalists in both the executive and the legislative branches were a corrupt lot and should be thrown out of office.

On the other hand, the Federalists were still smarting from the publication of Jefferson's letter to Mazzei the previous spring and from the more recent publication of the astonishing, albeit anonymous, petition to the Virginia House of Delegates in support of Cabell, the vice-president's congressman. Thus, with the balance of power almost evenly distributed between the parties, the session opened in a highly charged atmosphere.

Almost immediately the Republicans went on the offensive, mounting a fresh onslaught against the use of executive power. John Nicholas of Virginia, objecting to the size of the appropriations an administrative spokesman had proposed for the salaries of foreign ministers, moved to reduce the diplomats at Berlin, Madrid, and Lisbon from the grade of minister plenipotentiary to minister resident and to limit the salary to be paid each grade. Sounding a favorite "Country" theme, he said that he was acting to stop the recent practice of increasing the number of foreign ministries and staffing them with Federalist personnel recruited from Congress. The practice, he charged, served to corrupt congressmen by dangling before them the prospect of serving abroad in exchange for their vote on legislation.[21]

The Nicholas motion raised constitutional questions regarding the respective powers of the president, the Senate, and the House with respect to diplomatic appointments, questions which, although not theretofore debated in Congress, had been discussed in private within the executive branch during the Washington administration. At that time, in response to an inquiry from the president as to whether the Senate had the right to disapprove "the *grade* he may think it expedient to use in a foreign mission, as well as the *person* to be appointed," Jefferson as secretary of state had answered that it did not.[22]

Analyzing the problem in the light of the constitutional principle of separation of powers, Jefferson wrote: "The transaction of business with foreign nations is Executive altogether. It belongs then to the head of that department, *except* as to such portions of it as are specially submitted to the Senate. *Exceptions* are to be construed strictly."[23] In fact, Jefferson wrote, the Constitution itself had carefully circumscribed the presidential power of appointment. It gave to the president the power to nominate and commission foreign agents, and to the president and the Senate jointly only their appointment. But, he said, there were other actions that the Constitution had not enumerated. In the natural order of making a diplomatic appointment, the acts of determining, first, "the destination of a mission to the particular country where the public service calls for it" and, second, "the character, or grade to be employed in it" precede those of nomination, appointment, and commission. He reasoned that if the power of appointment, which the Senate shared with the president, did not comprehend "the neighboring acts of *nomination,* or *commission,* . . . still less can it pretend to comprehend those previous and more remote of *destination* and *grade.*" From this, he concluded: "The Senate is not supposed by the Constitution to be acquainted with the concerns of the Executive department. It was not intended that these should be communicated to them; nor can they therefore be qualified to judge of the necessity which calls for a mission to any particular place, or of the particular grade, more or less marked, which special and secret circumstances may call for. All this is left to the President. They are only to see that no unfit person be employed."[24]

Jefferson admitted the Senate might, by successive rejection of the persons whom the president nominated, effect what amounted to a rejection of the grade of the mission and so indirectly defeat the right of the president. But, he said, "This would be a breach of trust, an abuse of the power confined to the Senate, of which that body cannot be supposed capable. . . . If the Constitution had meant to give the Senate a negative on the grade or destination, as well as the person, it would have said so in direct terms, and not left it to be effected by a sidewind. It could never mean to give them the *use* of one power thro the *abuse* of another."[25]

The logic of Jefferson's analysis could be applied to the amount of salaries the diplomats receive. Under the appropriations power, certainly the Senate and the House could jointly control the salary level that each diplomatic grade was to receive, as Jefferson conceded when he appeared before a conference committee in the First Congress.[26] But if either used that power to attempt to control the subject of destination and grade, that, in Jefferson's understanding of the Constitution, would constitute a breach of trust and an abuse of one power in usurpation of another.

But in practice, Jefferson did not push his logic that far. During the Second Congress, in the face of a Senate disinclination to confirm presidential nominations to the ministries of Great Britain, France, and the Netherlands without knowledge of the specific reasons for maintaining those ministries at that time, he did not stand on his opinion that the Senate did not have the right to such information, and gave them the reasons. Whereupon the Senate confirmed the appointments.[27]

Therefore, when in the Fifth Congress Nicholas moved that the House go beyond the question of fixing the amount of ministers' salaries to one of reducing the grade of the ministries in Berlin, Madrid, and Lisbon, and then argued for the elimination of all foreign ministers plenipotentiary, he was, under Jefferson's analysis, improperly advocating the intrusion of the House in the determination of the destination and rank of the diplomatic corps and into the conduct of foreign affairs. Nicholas's position, that the House use its appropriations power to gain control over this subject, was in effect a breach of trust and an attempt to usurp functions that the Constitution had placed in the "Executive altogether." Nevertheless, neither Jefferson, now the vice-president, nor Madison, who had supported him in his opinion to Washington,[28] protested the position of their fellow Virginian and Republican.

Understandably, then, the Nicholas motion provoked a new constitutional debate, similar to that in the previous Congress over the Republicans' request of the president that he submit to the House his instructions governing the negotiations of Jay's Treaty. Since the motion affected patronage—and one of the choicest bits of patronage at that, the appointment of foreign ministers—the debate was heated. Republicans, advocating a House power over appropriations, again appealed to the self-interest of the membership to assert a role in the conduct of foreign affairs, which under Article II of the Constitution had been largely placed in the president and the Senate. And desirous of asserting control over the appointments for the benefit of their fellow Republicans, they also appealed to the self-interest of the party membership.

Since the Federalists controlled the presidency and, therefore, following the practice of the last years of the Washington administration, were the beneficiaries of foreign appointments, they naturally objected to the Republican proposal and presented constitutional grounds for their objection. Adopting, albeit without attribution, Jefferson's opinion to President Washington and Hamilton's argument in the Pacificus essays, they argued for a broad presidential prerogative in the conduct of foreign affairs.[29] Citing the provision of Article II, Section 2, of the Constitution whereunder the president has the responsibility for appointing ambassadors and other public ministers, with the advice and consent of the Senate, they deduced from it the further presidential responsibility for determining the requisite number of foreign ministers and their mission and grade.

Again, as in the controversy over the implementation of Jay's Treaty, the Federalists argued that it was the constitutional duty of the House, once the Senate had confirmed the officers, to vote the necessary appropriations for their support, just as it was its constitutional duty to appropriate the money required for the support of the federal judiciary. While admitting that Congress could lower the salaries allowed to ministers, they contended that a failure to appropriate in a case where a foreign government had already decided upon a minister to the United States would also, in evident disregard of the design of Article II, place in the House rather than in the president the decision whether to enter into diplomatic relations with that country. If this design afforded the executive too much influence over the legislature, they concluded, Congress should amend the Constitution.[30]

Then, departing from the strictly constitutional basis of their defense, the Federalists charged Republicans with leveling a partisan attack. The partisan nature of this attack, they said, was openly disclosed in the additional ground for Republican opposition, that the president intended to restrict the appointments to persons from his own party. Robert Goodloe Harper reminded the House of the recent failure of a foreign minister to carry out the president's policy. (Federalists considered that Monroe, while serving as minister to France, had failed to support Washington's sanction of Jay's Treaty.) In light of this experience, he defended Adams's intention to appoint only members of his own party. Making such appointments was sound and proper: Only in that way could he expect his policies to be followed rather than frustrated. The Republicans' opposition, he bluntly declared, arose from their failure to wrest power for themselves, whereby they could conduct foreign policy the way they wanted.[31] In any case, Samuel W. Dana of Connecticut added, fears of executive patronage and cries of economy were exaggerated, since the matter was not one of money—the motion, he declared, would serve to save only the miserable sum of $13,000—but of political interference.[32]

Dana's accusation that politics and policy, not money, were at the heart of the Republican position required a rebuttal. Thus Gallatin, in support of the contention that the executive policy of selecting Federalist congressmen would corrupt the integrity of the federal legislature, interjected a more high-minded consideration: The practice violated the spirit of Article I, Section 6, Clause 2, of the Constitution, prohibiting the appointment of a senator or representative to any civil office "which shall have been created, or the Emoluments whereof shall have been encreased during [the time for which he was elected]."

Intimating that fear of executive patronage was the purpose of this provision, he asked why "the framers of the Constitution inserted a clause of this kind." Answering the question, he argued for a liberal application of the text, whereby the powers and prerogatives of the president might be further limited to the prohibition of appointment of a senator or representative to any civil office, regardless of whether it had been created or its emoluments increased during his term.[33] A liberal construction of the Constitution by Republicans was here in character because its effect was to advance their interests and hurt those of the Federalists in Congress.

The partisan appointments, Gallatin continued, were an attempt to influence Congress unduly. Citing the fact that four of the five most recent ministers to Europe had come from Congress, he claimed that the president, to further his influence, was creating missions that were either unnecessary or larger than necessary. In consequence, the House had the right and the duty to check presidential powers when it was convinced that the purposes for which they were used were improper or subject to abuse.[34]

The challenge the Republicans presented as a matter of policy was not without merit and, in view of the history of the proceedings of the Constitutional Convention, must have nettled some Federalists. The constitutional provision Gallatin had invoked, Article I, Section 6, Clause 2, had been narrowly approved in the convention only after an extended and heated debate during which another proposal, absolutely prohibiting the appointment of a member of either House to any federal office during his legislative term of office, had just as narrowly been rejected. In addition, the more restrictive proposal had been advanced largely out of resentment over the practice of the Continental Congress of appointing many of its own members to diplomatic and executive positions. Pierce Butler had feared that the new government might follow the practice in Great Britain "where men got into Parlt. that they might get offices for themselves or their friends. This was the source of the corruption that ruined their Govt."[35]

Especially embarrassing to Federalists from Connecticut was the fact that during the convention the Connecticut delegation, led by Roger Sherman and Oliver Ellsworth, had been among the most steadfast supporters of the more restrictive proposal. Now, however, the state's Federalists were disregarding their state's previously held principles and defending the actions of their president, who had made it clear that he intended to confine his appointments to the diplomatic corps to members of his own party. And interestingly, Ellsworth, who then was serving as chief justice of the United States, would soon accept a diplomatic appointment to France.[36]

But politically embarrassing as Gallatin's contentions were, ultimately they fell short of the mark. For, as was known to the two remaining members of the House who had been delegates to the Constitutional Convention, Abraham Baldwin on the Republican side and Jonathan Dayton on the Federalist, Gallatin's contentions were a misrepresentation of the framers' intent. Not only had the convention specifically rejected the substance of what was now Gallatin's proposal, it had done so at the instance of Madison and Charles Pinckney, among others, who had argued that such a severe limitation on eligibility to appointment to nonlegislative office would discourage the more talented from service in Congress.[37]

Gallatin's contentions therefore were a continuation of the kind of constitutional argumentation he had advanced in the Fourth Congress during the debate over the power of the House to withhold implementation of a ratified treaty. In disregard of any question of framers' or ratifiers' intent, he based his construction of the Constitution on the text and the supposed reason underlying its formulation. Republican exegesis had indeed entered a new phase.[38]

The Republican challenge should have been irritating, but hardly likely to push tempers over the brink. The Federalists in control of patronage could afford to defend on temperate grounds. Ugly feelings, however, erupted during a recess when Representative Matthew Lyon of Vermont, a Republican and a native of Ireland, stated loudly on the floor of the House that congressmen from Connecticut, all Federalists, were in the habit of furthering their own personal interests rather than those of their constituency. This remark perhaps went too close to home, reminding the Connecticut delegation that they were not standing by the principles that had animated their state in the Constitutional Convention. Thus, Roger Griswold, one of their number, responded with a biting reference to Lyon's having been discharged from the army during the Revolution, to which Lyon replied by spitting in his face.[39]

A House committee, formed to review the incident, moved for Lyon's expulsion.[40] Protracted hearings and debate ensued, during which Gallatin, again taking the lead for the Republicans, asked for a vote of censure instead of expulsion.[41] A motion for expulsion, although approved by a margin of eight votes,[42] did not carry, since the number in favor was less than two-thirds of the members present, as required by the terms of Article I, Section 5, Clause 2.[43]

Three days later, Griswold, entering the House just before it was called to order, beat Lyon over the head with a walking stick. Lyon, picking up fire tongs, swung them at Griswold's head.[44] The following day a motion to expel them both was made and then subsequently dropped. The House returned to the consideration of pending matters.[45]

But by then political passions had been deeply aroused. Joshua Coit, one of the Connecticut delegation whose integrity Lyon had impugned, attacked the Nicholas motion to reduce the appropriations for foreign ministers and to downgrade the rank of certain ministries, calling it the annual Republican phillipic against the president. Referring to Jefferson's letter to Mazzei, Coit denounced the prevailing Republican bias against the administration's positions as reason enough not to consider any of Jefferson's supporters as worthy of appointment in the executive branch.[46]

The public attack on their leader touched a sensitive Republican nerve in turn, and demanded a response. Gallatin, coming to Jefferson's defense, yet unable to explain away his offensive language, repeated his leader's charges, openly throwing them in Federalist faces. There was, he affirmed, a Federalist plot to recreate a monarchic-aristocratic form of government patterned on the British, and, he added, when Republicans objected they were called disorganizers, subverters, and Jacobins.[47]

Inevitably, Federalists abused Republicans in return, Harper calling them lunatics, fanatics, and dangerous, albeit unwitting, anarchists bent on tearing down the executive branch and concentrating powers in the House. Going further, in a reference to Jefferson, he charged that a system of alliance with the French against the British had been imported into the United States by means of a missionary, "a citizen of our own [country], who was recalled from a public employment in that country [France], to fill a high official station here."[48]

Partisan hatred filled the air, and little was needed to set off another explosion. After twelve days of debate, the Nicholas motion to affect the appropriations for ministries lost by a margin of four votes, reflecting the almost equal division of the parties.[49] Jefferson's principle of executive autonomy in the matter of ministerial appointments, which he had advanced in the Washington administration and which was now impugned by his political friends, had been vindicated by his political foes.

The Federalist Advantage: War Measures

Thereafter each party waited on events for the opportunity to increase its advantage. When quite by chance the opportunity arose, however, Adams did not take it. When finally he received notice of the XYZ affair and the consequent impasse in the French negotiations, he considered himself bound to inform Congress and ask its advice as to the appropriate action. But out of concern for the safe return of the three American envoys still in France, he was reluctant to state publicly that the reason for the impasse was the attempted bribe.[50]

Unwittingly he had laid a trap for the Republicans who, thinking the history of the Jay papers was repeating itself, wanted to see the envoys' dispatches. Believing that they were being deprived of valuable information that would damn the administration, they proposed a resolution requesting the president to submit the dispatches. Instead of pleading executive privilege, as Washington had, Adams complied.[51]

On seeing the papers, the Federalists in Congress, realizing the political ramifications, quickly emulated the action of the Republicans in the case of Jay's Treaty, and leaked the papers to the press. Publication of Talleyrand's solicitation led to a swift and sharp rise in anti-French sentiment. The Republicans, as the party of French sympathy, were driven on the defensive. For the first time in years, Federalists had the whip hand and they used it.[52]

In a show of strength, they passed in rapid succession bills that Adams had vainly sought in the special session the preceding year: creating the Department of the Navy separate from the War Department and raising a provisional army in case of war or invasion or, in the president's opinion, of imminent danger of invasion. Later, to protect American shipping, Congress authorized the president to provide an armed escort for commercial vessels and to increase the army.[53]

The Republican leadership in the House opposed the measures for a provisional army on policy grounds: The bill was premature and unnecessarily expensive. Such danger as existed from a land invasion could better be handled by the militia. But they also raised the constitutional argument that Madison had successfully used against a similar measure in the Third Congress: Since Article I, Section 8, Clause 12, conferred on Congress the power to raise an army, the bill constituted an improper delegation of legislative power to the president.[54]

This time, however, the Federalists were prepared. Samuel Sewall of Massachusetts, defending the bill, applied the usual Federalist canon of broad construction in favor of a general power of delegation of authority to take the proposed action. He cited in reliance a bill the House had recently passed authorizing the president to provide for armed escorts when he deemed necessary, and pointed to the broad language of Article I, Section 10, Clause 3, prohibiting states from keeping troops in time of peace unless "in such imminent Danger as will not admit of delay." If the Constitution had contemplated the exercise of state discretion in cases of emergency, so Congress could contemplate the exercise of presidential discretion in similar circumstances.[55] Dana, backing Sewall, reasoned that if under the Constitution Congress could delegate to the president the power it had under Article I, Section 8, Clause 15, "for calling forth the Militia to execute the Laws of the Union," it could also delegate the authority it had under Clause 12 to raise an army.[56]

But Gallatin in opposing the bill for a provisional army had another constitutional string to his bow. The Constitution, he said, envisioned two kinds of military service, a militia operated under state control and a regular standing army. The bill instead impermissibly provided for something in the middle. On the one hand, by allowing men to stay at home until their call, it would make it difficult for the state militia to recruit, and on the other, it would in effect convert the militia into a standing army and transfer the power of appointing military officers from the states to the president.[57]

This seemed more an argument against the manner of recruitment than against its constitutionality, and Harrison Gray Otis of Massachusetts, for the Federalists, dismissed it as such. Republicans, he said, on all occasions made the Constitution a stumbling block: "Instead of forming any safe rule of conduct, it proves a mere cobweb—a mere jargon of political maxims, and is the foundation of sophisms in almost every debate."[58]

Undercutting the constitutional argumentation and getting down to the essence of Republican opposition, Thomas T. Davis of Kentucky protested that while easterners knew the president, trusted him, and would volunteer, southerners didn't and wouldn't. As a result, the army would be dangerously composed of and staffed by easterners.[59] He seemed to suggest that an eastern president might turn an eastern standing army on the South. Considering the bad feelings between the parties and the fact that Republican strength was largely based in the South and Federalist strength largely in the "East," this fear was not misplaced. In fact, considering Hamilton's subsequent statement for use of the eastern army, when he was named its commander—to enter Virginia on a pretext and suppress Republican "rebellion"—the fear was not without foundation.[60] But Federalists in the House, intent on raising an army, dismissed the suggestion and passed the bill.[61]

The Federalist Advantage: Naturalization and Aliens

Having prepared for the external dangers arising from what was feared would be a probable war with France, the Federalist majority in the House next voted to suspend all commercial intercourse with that country. It then turned to prepare for what it perceived as internal dangers.[62] Those dangers, in Federalist eyes, might come from foreigners, from naturalized citizens, or, generally, from any citizen who continued to show sympathy with the French. In particular, they first had in mind the leaders of the Republican Party: Jefferson, whom they considered an apostolic missionary from France, was seen to present the greatest threat to national security; Gallatin, a naturalized Swiss francophile, and Lyon, the party's naturalized Irishman, were close behind.

The Federalists next had in mind the Republicans' close allies in the party press, which was dominated by recent political refugees from Ireland, Scotland, and England, such as the Irish Matthew Carey, James Carey, and William Duane, the Scottish James Thomson Callender, and the English Thomas Cooper. They all had been deeply influenced by the egalitarian polemics of Thomas Paine against the British establishment, and regarded Federalist policies as a carbon copy of those of the British government.[63]

The first need, in the Federalist estimation, was to shore up the country against the dangers presented by the foreign-born. The previous year, as part of a revenue bill, the House had approved a five-dollar tax on certificates of naturalization in order to discourage immigration.[64] Indeed, at one point, the House had considered a motion to fix the tax at ten dollars.[65] Otis had spoken warmly in support:

> T HE AMENDMENT . . . WOULD NOT AFFECT those men who had already
> lands in this country, nor the deserving part of those who might seek an
> asylum in it. Persons of that description would easily pay the tax; but it would
> tend to foreclose the mass of vicious and disorganizing characters who could
> not live peaceably at home, and who, after unfurling the standard of rebellion
> in their own countries, might come hither to revolutionize ours. . . . [I do] not
> wish to invite hordes of wild Irishmen, nor the turbulent and disorderly of all
> parts of the world, to come here with a view to disturb our tranquillity, after
> having succeeded in the overthrow of their own Governments.[66]

The Federalists now determined it was necessary to go further than merely imposing a tax to stem immigration. In a move calculated to discourage the Irish and other undesirables and to weaken the Republican Party, to which those immigrants had become largely attached, they proposed amending the naturalization law so as to increase the preliminary residency requirement for United States citizenship from five to ten years.[67]

Otis, wishing to go still further, moved an amendment barring any future naturalized citizen from holding federal office.[68] This would serve to exclude both a future Gallatin and a future Lyon. In support, Otis argued that if Congress had a plenary power over naturalization, it might choose to grant the privilege of citizenship on such terms it deemed proper.[69] Otis's theory was not completely novel. In the Constitutional Convention and in the First Congress Madison had been of the opinion that the power to naturalize would include the power to increase the civil rights of a naturalized citizen to correspond with the increase in the years of his residence.[70] But Otis's position went beyond a step-by-step increase in the rights of naturalized citizens. He would have relegated them to a permanent status of second-class citizenry.

Harper, going even further than Otis, moved that any future naturalized citizen be denied the right to vote in either a state or federal election.[71] But someone questioned whether the Constitution would allow Congress to affect the power of the states to admit as state citizens such persons as they saw fit. Someone might also have pointed out that under Article I, Section 2, Clause 1, of the Constitution, pursuant to which persons eligible to vote for "the most numerous Branch of the State Legislature" are eligible to vote for members of the House of Representatives, the states determine voter qualifications.[72] In any case, Harper withdrew his motion.[73] And when a short while later someone else questioned the constitutionality of the Otis motion, as seemingly providing for different classes of citizenship, his motion was also withdrawn.[74]

To satisfy those who felt that the Harper and Otis proposals had some merit, however, the proposal to increase the preliminary residency requirement from five to ten years was amended to fourteen years. So amended, it passed by a majority of one vote.[75] While this legislation undoubtedly gave the Federalists great emotional satisfaction, it was not particularly intelligent. Since the states controlled the franchise—as the Federalists themselves recognized—and in fact had already allowed aliens the vote, the new provisions would solidify for the Republicans the vote of almost all the resident aliens in states permitting them the franchise: citizens of France, if that country was not at war with the United States; Irish immigrants, their numbers growing with refugees from that year's latest failed revolt against British rule; English and Germans, and others migrating for political or economic reasons. Thereafter, all these would have the greatest incentive to vote Republican and secure the repeal of this onerous provision. The new law amounted to a perpetual write-off of their vote. No wonder the Federalist Party came to take on the appearance of an exclusive country club and ultimately failed due to declining membership.[76]

Having made the door of naturalization more difficult to open for the future Gallatins and Lyons, Duanes and Callenders, the Federalists next brought forth a bill directed at enemy aliens, empowering the president, in case of war or threatened invasion, to secure or remove from the country all citizens of an enemy country resident in the United States. It was eventually adopted.[77]

Then, concerned that the French might not formally declare war, but instead undermine the United States through the infiltration of what today would be called fifth columnists, the Federalists in the House next considered a Senate bill authorizing the president to deport "such aliens as he shall judge dangerous to the peace and safety of the United States, or shall have reasonable grounds to suspect are concerned in any treasonable or secret machinations against the Government thereof." The bill further provided that a person subject to a deportation order could nonetheless be permitted to remain in the country if he proved that no injury or danger to the country would accrue from his continued residence. Otherwise, anyone found in the country after having received a deportation order would be subject to a three-year jail sentence and be permanently disqualified from American citizenship.[78]

Given Federalist assumptions that the country was already at war with the French at sea, and that the French might soon either formally declare war or employ sympathizers in the United States—especially among the resident French or the wild Irish or both—to undermine the country's war efforts, the bill's purposes were not amiss. Of course, given those premises, certain additional measures should properly have been taken even against citizens of the United States. Those measures would shortly be brought forth in yet another bill, the features of which were then being debated in the Senate. That bill was directed at sedition.

But the sweeping scope of the alien bill and its draconian procedures provoked the Republicans. Espousing the cause of their alien constituency and fearing a total government censorship and repression of their own speech and of their party's publications, they struck out against the constitutionality of the bill. Understandably, Gallatin, as a naturalized citizen, led the attack.

Gallatin, however, did not attack the bill primarily on the grounds on which today's constitutional lawyers would place their principal reliance: that the Federalist proposal dealt unconstitutionally with an alien's personal and property rights. The civil rights argument was only Gallatin's secondary defense, and one he did not develop at great length—that the proposed legislation made no provision for habeas corpus as required by Article I, Section 9, Clause 2, and violated the due process clause of the Fifth Amendment.[79]

Livingston in support did contend that the bill, by concentrating power in the president, violated the constitutional principle of the separation of the powers of the federal government.[80] But because he too did not develop his contention, the Federalists in response gave those arguments short shrift. (Later, Madison, in his report to the Virginia House of Delegates on the constitutionality of the Alien Act, would make the argument based on the violation of the separation of powers one of his primary grounds for opposition.)[81]

Gallatin's primary argument, to which we would give scant notice today, afforded the Federalists the most difficulty and sent them scouring the Constitution in search of a plausible text upon which to justify their proposal. That argument was in essence the familiar Republican staple, that since the power to exclude friendly aliens did not fall within the delegated powers, Congress lacked the power to legislate. What gave the Republican argument greater force, however, was that it accorded with the then current practice: Until that time it had been the states, not the federal government, which had controlled the flow of immigration. History, which had deserted the Republicans during the dispute over Jay's Treaty, was now on their side.

Gallatin opened his remarks against the proposal to deport aliens by pointing out that since the House had already legislated against the citizens of an enemy country, the provision in question must be directed against citizens of friendly countries. Under its war powers, he said, Congress could legislate against the former but not against the latter. Applying the canon of strict construction, he argued against any federal power over friendly aliens. Since the power to admit or exclude them did not fall within the enumerated powers of the Constitution, it had been reserved to the states, as memorialized in the Tenth Amendment.[82]

Appealing to history, Gallatin recalled that the power to admit aliens had been reserved to the states under the Articles of Confederation. In September 1788, he said, when the Constitution had been adopted by nine states and was soon to come into operation, the Continental Congress, in accordance with that reservation, had passed a resolution recommending to the states the adoption of laws preventing the admission of transported criminals from foreign nations. In response, Pennsylvania, among other states, had passed such a law while the First Congress was in session. This, he reasoned, Pennsylvania could never have done had it been considered that under the Constitution Congress possessed such a power.[83]

In furtherance of his argument that the states, and not the federal government, had exclusive power to admit or exclude aliens, Gallatin might also have mentioned the reason Congress had been given the power to establish a uniform rule of naturalization. As Madison explained in the *Federalist*, it was to provide protection to an individual state, which, under Article IV, Section 2, Clause 1, of the Constitution, was required to afford to the citizens of the other states all the privileges and immunities it afforded its own citizens. By assuring the participation of all states in the naturalization process through the agency of Congress, the Constitution had ended the anomalous situation that had prevailed under the Articles of Confederation whereby, under its privileges and immunities clause, the state with the highest standards of citizenship had to afford even to the citizens of the state with the lowest standards the same rights and protection it afforded its own citizens.[84] In this light, the naturalization power dealt only with the transformation of aliens into citizens, not with their entry into or exclusion from the individual states.

Gallatin's position was the natural development of the principle of the strict construction of the enumerated powers that Madison had invoked in the First Congress against the establishment of a national bank.[85] It was the position that Madison himself would adopt the following year in his report to the Virginia House of Delegates in discussing the constitutionality of the Alien Act.[86] The power of Congress to determine whether an alien—one whom a state had by right already allowed to enter the country—would be admitted to citizenship was simply that and nothing more.

Pushed this rigorously, the United States could have no countrywide immigration policy. Coastal states, combining with states bordering on foreign lands, could effectively control the flow of immigrants by barring aliens from entering their territory, to the detriment of those inland states which might desire the benefit of their immigrant labor or wealth to promote their own internal development.

It was this very consideration which in 1849 led a majority of the Supreme Court in *Passenger Cases* to decide that taxes imposed by coastal states on immigrants entering the country were unconstitutional.[87] But in 1798 the Republican construction of the Constitution was shaping that instrument into a modified version of the Articles of Confederation, whereby less and less power was made available to the federal government, and more and more power was reserved to the states. As in the case of the attempt to pass an effective quarantine law in the Fourth Congress, the logic of Republican reasoning rendered the federal government less a union of states than a limited confederacy of the several states.[88]

Gallatin's argument necessarily drove the Federalists to a broad construction of the Constitution in support of their proposal and to reliance on a medley of arguments in support of an implied congressional power. Sewall, taking the lead, set forth the position ultimately accepted by the Supreme Court almost one hundred years later, namely, that the federal government holds general sovereign powers deducible from various provisions in the Constitution, its general nature, and its preamble. From the expressed power in Congress to regulate commerce with foreign nations, the power in the president to appoint foreign ministers, and past congressional practice, Sewall deduced in the government of the United States an implied grant of national sovereignty including a power to conduct foreign relations. The power to regulate commerce, he declared, included the power to regulate the conduct of foreigners who generally came to the country for commercial reasons. From the combination of those powers, he inferred a federal jurisdiction over aliens.[89]

Next he advanced the argument, a staple of Federalist theory based not on any specific provision in the Constitution but on an overriding principle of good government, that where no one state could effectively legislate on a subject, Congress must have, and indeed did have, the power.[90] Of course this had been one of the central elements of the Virginia Plan, which Madison had prepared and Randolph proposed at the beginning of the Constitutional Convention, but opposed when, after the decision to give the states an equal representation in the Senate, Gunning Bedford of Delaware sought to keep the principle in the Constitution.[91]

Obviously, the Constitution on its face had not expressly incorporated the principle of the Bedford resolution. But it was Sewall's position that implicitly it had. It is impossible to know who or what inspired Sewall. Perhaps it was Jonathan Dayton, the only remaining Federalist member of the House who had been a delegate to the Constitutional Convention. Or someone else friendly to the Federalist side who had been at the convention and was still in Philadelphia might have suggested the argument. In any case, Sewall allied himself with the position of those in the convention who remained silent in the face of charges by Randolph, Mason, and Gerry that the Necessary and Proper Clause or some other provision in the Constitution conferred upon Congress the power to legislate generally.[92]

But that history was hidden behind the veil of secrecy: Madison's notes were still unpublished. Whatever the framers had intended, Sewall and his friends had to find words of confirmation in the text of the Constitution. Sewell looked to the purposes of the preamble and its provision for promoting the general welfare.[93] James Bayard of Delaware looked to the two clauses that had been the target of opposition in the Virginia convention: the general welfare language in the Taxing and Spending Clause, and the Necessary and Proper Clause.[94] William Gordon of New Hampshire said that the bill to exclude aliens, like the bank bill, fell within the implied powers of Congress.[95]

In rebuttal, the Republicans objected to Sewall's invocation of the preamble as in effect swallowing up all the reserved powers of the state governments.[96] In reply to Bayard, they properly pointed out that the power to spend for the common defense and general welfare did not involve a power to regulate for those purposes, and they confined the application of the Necessary and Proper Clause to the exercise of powers incidental to one of the enumerated powers. They flatly repudiated the thesis that the federal government had unenumerated powers over matters which concerned the nation as a whole.[97]

For good measure, Gallatin quoted at length from an essay in the *Federalist* in which Madison had rejected the argument that the general welfare provision in Article I, Section 8, Clause 1, implicitly contained general legislative powers.[98] Then, in complete repudiation of the position he had taken two years before in the Fourth Congress,[99] Gallatin went beyond the text of the Constitution and purported to rely on the inside knowledge of one of the delegates to the Constitutional Convention. Gallatin said he was well informed

THAT THOSE WORDS HAD ORIGINALLY been inserted in the Constitution as a limitation to the power of laying taxes. After the limitation had been agreed to, and the Constitution was completed, a member of the Convention, (he was one of the members who represented Pennsylvania.) being one of a committee of revisal and arrangement, attempted to throw these words into a distinct paragraph, so as to create not a limitation, but a distinct power. The trick, however, was discovered by a member from Connecticut, now deceased, and the words restored as they now stand.[100]

The source of Gallatin's information—or perhaps misinformation—is not known. From the records of the convention that we have, no such trick was attempted: Madison did not mention any such incident in his notes of the proceedings of the convention, nor did he allude to it in his lengthy letter of November 17, 1830, to Andrew Stevenson in which he set forth a detailed summary of the progress of the general welfare provision through the convention. All in all, Gallatin's remarks constituted a striking illustration of the dangers of using a framer's recollections of the proceedings of the Constitutional Convention in explication of the text.[101]

But in his original statement opposing the proposal for federal control over friendly aliens, Gallatin had not been content with the simple argument of strict construction of federal powers. He had advanced an alternate argument based on the language of Article I, Section 9, Clause 1, which provided: "The Migration or Importation of such Persons as any of the States now existing shall think proper to admit, shall not be prohibited by the Congress prior to the Year one thousand eight hundred and eight." Perhaps concerned that the Federalists might make the argument that the clause extended only to the admission of slaves and not to free persons, and that by implication therefore it suggested a general federal power to control the immigration of the latter, he may have determined upon a preemptive strike.

In any case, Gallatin boldly contended that the bill was contrary to Article I, Section 9, Clause 1. The term "importation" in the clause, he said, referred to slaves, the term "migration" to free persons. Therefore, he concluded, a state had the right to permit free persons as well as slaves to enter its jurisdiction until 1808; and until then Congress and the president might not exclude them.[102]

The argument did not hold. It was well known, as Madison had written in the *Federalist,* that the provision for the year 1808 had been included as an accommodation to the most southern states, where slaveholders had insisted on the right to continue the importation of slaves, although the other states considered the practice objectionable. Indeed, he had there specifically rejected a construction of the provision that would have had it apply to "voluntary and beneficial emigrations from Europe to America."[103] Madison's commentary is borne out by his notes from the proceedings of the Constitutional Convention.[104] Moreover, no sensible reason existed for withholding from Congress until 1808 the power to adopt legislation affecting free persons. Whatever reason might exist for the power after that date would also exist before it, as Chief Justice Taney pointed out in his opinion in the *Passenger Cases.*[105]

The Federalists, however, strove for the most part to rebut Gallatin's second argument on other grounds. Sewall invoked the principle advanced by Madison in the

First Congress during the debate over the presidential removal bill, and afterwards by Hamilton in his Pacificus essays: that specific exceptions to general powers should be strictly construed.[106] Since under Article I, Section 8, Clause 2, of the Constitution, Congress had the general power to regulate foreign commerce, which included the power to exclude aliens, the provisions of Article I, Section 9, Clause 1— if applicable to free persons as well as slaves—involved commerce, and therefore should be strictly construed.[107]

Otis labeled Gallatin's construction as so impractical and constricting as to prevent Congress from prohibiting even the admission of a French army or from providing against an equally real danger, the notorious French practice of using citizens of other countries to engage in subversive activity on their behalf.[108]

In response to Sewall, Robert Williams of North Carolina countered that persons generally could not be considered a matter of commerce; at best only alien merchants could be so considered. And reflecting southern fears, he conjectured that should Congress have the power under the Commerce Clause to exclude friendly aliens, it could also exclude slaves.[109]

Then, in confirmation of Gallatin's argument, Baldwin, the only congressman other than Dayton to have participated in the Constitutional Convention, proceeded to shed further light on the meaning of the Importation Clause in Article I, Section 9, Clause 1. Disregarding Gallatin's objection in the Fourth Congress to the use of a framer's recollections for that purpose—as Gallatin himself a short while before had done—Baldwin now came to the latter's aid and remembered that although some delegates during the convention had observed that the section, as phrased, would be construed to extend to persons other than slaves, the language had been retained. As a consequence, he concluded that the framers had intended to leave the power of excluding aliens to the states and not the federal government.[110]

Baldwin's statement brought a rejoinder from Dayton, the only one in a position to contradict him, that Baldwin was misrepresenting the proceedings of the convention.[111] But if we can trust Madison's notes of those proceedings, Baldwin had not misrepresented so much as misinterpreted them. According to Madison, during the convention Gouverneur Morris had considered the text of Article I, Section 9, Clause 1, unclear in that it failed to refer explicitly to "slaves." If that word were used, he thought, the clause "would avoid the ambiguity by which, under the power with regard to naturalization, the liberty reserved to the States might be defeated." John Dickinson of Delaware had agreed. But notwithstanding their arguments, the delegates had rejected their suggestions.[112]

Nevertheless, Baldwin's understanding of the proceedings was wrong. The framers, despite Morris's intervention, did intend to foreclose a congressional prohibition of the states' right to permit the importation of slaves only until 1808. The clause did not speak to a congressional power to affect the entry of free persons before or after that date.[113] The Baldwin-Dayton contribution to constitutional history essentially ended the debate, following which approval was given to the provision to authorize the president to deport aliens he deemed dangerous. Thereafter the bill passed quickly.[114]

The Federalist Advantage: The Sedition Act

The House next considered a Senate-approved sedition bill, which made criminal any combination or conspiracy to oppose a federal measure or impede the enforcement of a federal law. The bill also criminalized a wide range of language: libelous writing or speech against the government of the United States, Congress, or the president, or writing or speech that brought the government, Congress, or the president into disrepute or contempt or that excited hatred against them.[115]

To the Federalists the sedition bill was necessary to settle the uncertainty as to whether the administration, in the absence of a specific statutory prohibition against seditious libel, could prosecute such an offense. A few months before, Justice Samuel Chase, sitting with Judge Richard Peters at the trial of a case in the federal circuit court for the district of Pennsylvania, had upheld a motion in arrest of judgment on the ground that the conduct for which defendant Robert Worrall had been charged —an attempt to bribe the United States Commissioner of Revenue into awarding him a government construction contract—had not been designated an offense either under the Constitution or by statute. The federal courts, Chase held, had no common-law jurisdiction of crime. Judge Peters disagreed, stating that such jurisdiction was to be found in the inherent and constitutional power of the federal government to preserve itself and in implied language of Section 11 of the Judiciary Act. Subsequently, defense counsel declined to agree to an order that would have enabled the case to be taken to the Supreme Court, and Chase, reconsidering his position, agreed with Peters to impose a comparatively mild sentence on the defendant.[116] When a short time after, Benjamin Franklin Bache, editor of the *Aurora,* was arrested on a charge of libeling President Adams and the government of the United States, he announced that he would rely on the Chase opinion and argue that there was no federal common law of crime.[117]

The prosecution of indictments in federal courts based neither on the expressed language of the Constitution nor on a federal statute did not begin with the Worrall case, however. In 1790 and 1793 Chief Justice Jay and Justice Wilson had charged federal grand juries that indictments could be grounded in violations of the law of nations. In 1793, at the request of Jefferson acting as secretary of state and in accordance with an opinion of Attorney General Edmund Randolph, Gideon Henfield had been indicted for outfitting French privateers in an American port in violation of the Constitution, treaties with nations with which the United States was at peace, and the common law. And in 1797 an indictment was brought against Thomas Greenleaf, publisher of the *New-York Journal,* for printing a libel of the British consul general. Thus the Chase opinion in *Worrall* had cast doubt on the previous assumption of a federal jurisdiction of crime, based somewhere in the Constitution, a statute, the law of nations, or the common law. It was this doubt that the Senate bill was designed to dispel.[118]

When the bill reached the House, a Federalist speaker made clear at the outset that the bill was directed primarily at the Republicans. Among the expressions the bill would prohibit, he stated, were a speech Livingston had delivered in the House, Cabell's controversial letter to his constituency, and certain newspaper articles.[119] Livingston and Nathaniel Macon of North Carolina immediately protested that the bill was unconstitutional, infringing the First Amendment's guarantees of freedom of speech and the press.[120] Gallatin objected further that most of the newspaper articles cited would be lawful even under the proposed bill, but that in any case they constituted only political opinions about government policy and administration supporters and thus were protected by the First Ammendment.[121]

Then, going beyond a reliance on the express language of the First Amendment, Gallatin argued for a broad construction of its text. Adopting for this debate the constitutional jurisprudence of the Federalists, Gallatin estimated the practical effects of a narrow construction and concluded that good government required his reading. Although broad constitutional construction was not usual with Republican spokesmen, it was not inconsistent with their overall strategy, because such an interpretation of the First Amendment served in this case to limit federal power.

The bill's practical effect, Gallatin declared, would be the suppression of political opinion, which would be subversive of the principles of the Constitution itself. Tying the right of a free press to the right of an informed electorate, he reasoned that restraint of the press concerning measures of government deprived people of information regarding the conduct of elected officials and rendered "their right of electing nugatory." The bill, he charged, would constitute a weapon by the party in power to perpetuate itself.[122]

The Federalists did not attempt to answer Gallatin's broad-based argument. Instead, they concentrated on denying the argument advanced by Livingston and Macon, that the bill offended the express guarantees of the First Amendment. The guarantee of freedom of the press, Dana claimed, did not extend to the offenses the bill proscribed: the utterance of malicious falsehoods injurious to the government. Nor did the amendment protect liars—in proof of which, he observed, the bill did not differ in substance from legislation the states had already approved. Later, Otis, supporting Dana, cited statutes of Virginia and Pennsylvania and legal opinions of the Pennsylvania courts. (In fact, Jefferson, when president, would agree. The states, he would privately write, had the power to punish for seditious libel and in blatant cases should do so.)[123]

John Wilkes Kittera of Pennsylvania adduced a further reason for the bill. In a reference to the proceedings against Bache, he noted that the Adams administration had, without the aid of statute, already commenced criminal proceedings in seditious libel, relying on the federal court's common-law jurisdiction in crime, based on British precedent. Since lawyers for the defense had challenged the jurisdiction, the statute would settle the question.[124]

When Republicans in reply argued the harshness of the British common law, the Federalists amended the bill. In amelioration of the common law, they allowed truth as a defense and permitted the jury, as in other criminal cases, to determine both questions of law and fact under the trial judge's direction. In recognition of widespread fears of overzealous criminal enforcement, the Federalists limited the bill's operation to the period ending March 3, 1801.[125]

The amendments, however, did not placate Republicans. Probably moved by the Federalist argument that the bill corresponded in substance with those of several states, John Nicholas shifted the focus of their attack. Without foregoing the argument based on the First Amendment, he reverted to the Republican canon of strict construction of the original Constitution: Since Congress had no authority under the enumerated powers to pass such a law, the bill violated the provisions of the Tenth as much as the First Amendment.[126]

To this argument, Otis, as befitted a Federalist, responded with an argument based on a broad political principle: Irrespective of the Constitution, the power of Congress to pass the bill rested on the fundamental proposition that every independent government had the right of self-preservation, whereby it could defend itself against attacks endangering its existence; otherwise, the government must either fall or be subordinate to some other government for its protection.

Some of the offenses proscribed in the bill, Otis indicated, were of a nature tending directly to the destruction of the Constitution—for example, forming combinations to oppose government measures, intimidate its officers, and incite insurrections. As guardian of the Constitution, Congress was bound to provide against those offenses and prohibit any means calculated to produce them, whether by speaking, writing, or printing. The national government, Otis reasoned, was, in the nature of things, invested with the power to protect itself, and was doing so.[127]

As if mindful that his argument still needed a direct support in the Constitution, Otis stated that the power of the national government to protect itself emanated from the spirit of the Constitution. Then, as if realizing that he must advance a reason based on some text of the Constitution, he argued for a federal common law in both criminal and civil matters implicit in Article III. More particularly, he purported to discover in the text of that article a common-law jurisdiction in malicious statement against the federal government.

Otis's argument proceeded as follows. The people in the individual states had brought with them the substantive common-law rules of England and used them as the basis for their state's statutes. Additionally, in every state, certain kinds of conduct were designated criminal for which no statute had been passed, because they were crimes under the substantive common-law rules received from England. Thus, for example, each state had a court claiming criminal jurisdiction over the common-law offense of acts against good morals or in opposition to the constitutional authorities. Therefore, he reasoned, when the framers, habituated as they were to the substantive common law of crime in their respective states, provided in Article III, Section 2, Clause 1, for a jurisdiction in the federal courts in "all Cases, in Law and Equity, arising under this Constitution, the Laws of the United States," they must have intended to include within "the Laws of the United States" the substantive common-law rules of crime. The federal common-law jurisdiction thus extended not only to civil but to criminal cases.[128]

It was Madison's belief, however, that the framers had not intended to provide for a federal common law of crime, as is evident from his response to an objection George Mason had raised to the Constitution immediately following the close of the Constitutional Convention. Mason had complained of the convention's failure to provide for a bill of rights and to secure for the people "the Enjoyment of the Benefits of the common-Law," which he regarded as the depository of fundamental rights. Madison, writing to Washington, observed that Mason had brought forward an objection that he had not mentioned in the convention—one that, had he made it then, would have been answered so effectively that he would not have mentioned it afterwards. Madison explained: "If they [i.e., the convention] had in general terms declared the Common law to be in force, they would have broken in upon the legal Code of every State in the most material points: they wd. have done more, they would have brought over from G.B. a thousand heterogeneous & antirepublican doctrines, and even the *ecclesiastical Hierarchy itself,* for that is a part of the Common law. If they had undertaken a discrimination, they must have formed a digest of laws, instead of a Constitution."[129]

In any case, Otis's argument fell short. Even if Article III of the Constitution had provided for a common law in crime, he had yet to explain how under Article II Congress had the power to revise that law. Indeed, as Gallatin pointed out in the debates over the repeal of the Sedition Act in the Sixth Congress, the Otis position led to the anomalous situation that the federal judiciary could decide on subjects upon which Congress, for want of an enumerated power, could not legislate.[130] Furthermore, since the rules of the common law have always been subject to legislative revision, the absence of an enumerated power rendered the Otis argument baseless. Unless, of course, Congress could rely on the Necessary and Proper Clause; but if that were the case, they didn't need Otis's argument.

Nevertheless, his argument and the heated response it generated on the part of the Republicans raised an interesting question: In using the term "cases in law" in Article III, had the framers intended merely to establish the English system of separate courts of civil jurisdiction with their separate forms of civil practice and relief, as Gallatin and his colleagues thereafter contended? It seems more likely that, at the least, they intended the courts to entertain the commencement of civil actions in diversity suits. This necessarily implied the recognition of claims based on the common-law forms of action, along with the substantive causes of action and specific formulary remedies they embodied. The English system of common law, contrary to the Republican argument, could not be separated into discrete compartments of substance and procedure.[131]

Macon, leading the Republican rebuttal, attempted to undermine the Otis historical interpretation with one of his own. The power of the federal government to prosecute for libel, he claimed, had been specifically denied by Justices Iredell and Wilson of the United States Supreme Court when they served as delegates to the ratifying conventions in North Carolina and Pennsylvania respectively. (Macon did not correctly state their positions. Iredell had denied the power of Congress to pass a general crimes law; he had not specifically denied its power to pass a criminal libel law. And while Wilson had denied that Congress had the power to enact legislation affecting the press, he had gone on to say that the new government, like the state governments, would have the power to prosecute libels upon the public in federal court.) The members of the First Congress, Macon further claimed, had shared the views of Iredell and Wilson when the First Amendment had been discussed. He could only hope, he concluded, that if the law were passed, judges would hold it unconstitutional.[132]

Gallatin then attacked Otis's argument on the basis of the text of Article III. The provision upon which Otis relied, he argued, meant merely that federal courts in cases in which they had jurisdiction should refer to the principles of the common law. What these principles involved he did not conjecture, but he did say that they did not embody principles of substantive common law.

Gallatin repeated the argument Nicholas had made earlier, that the bill was unconstitutional because it did not fall within the enumerated powers: Congress did not have an undefined power to legislate concerning crimes, nor did it have a general power to provide for offenses against the government. Rather, he contended, in line with standard Republican doctrine, that the power to legislate concerning crimes was limited to those specified in Article I, Section 8, of the Constitution: piracies, felonies committed on the high seas, and offenses against the law of nations (Clause 10); counterfeiting the coin or securities of the United States (Clause 6); offenses committed in the nation's capital and in forts, arsenals, etc., over which the United States had with the consent of a state acquired exclusive jurisdiction (Clause 17); offenses against the laws or exercise of the constitutional authority of any department, by virtue of the Necessary and Proper Clause (Clause 18); and treason, by implication of Article III, Section 3, Clause 2.[133]

In the past, Gallatin continued, Congress had strictly adhered to these constitutional specifications, citing the two acts previously adopted for the punishment of crimes. The only language in the Constitution that could give color to the authority now claimed, he said, was the Necessary and Proper Clause. But that clause, he said, was strict and precise in its scope. To claim power under it, supporters of the bill had to show that the specific power was given to Congress or the president in some other part of the Constitution, that the power would be carried into effect by the bill, and, finally, that the power could only be effectuated if the bill were passed.[134]

Gallatin summarized the Republican position: As the first instance of a supposed general power to define or punish crimes, the bill justified the suspicions of those who, at the time the Constitution was adopted, had feared that the sense of the Necessary and Proper Cause might be used for that purpose.[135] He may have had George Mason in mind, because the latter during the Virginia convention had specifically prophesied that in the absence of a bill of rights, Congress would use the Necessary and Proper Clause to suppress written and oral criticism of the government.[136] The Fifth Congress, however, was planning to go further than Mason had feared, to enact such legislation under the Necessary and Proper Clause despite, rather than in the absence of, the First Amendment. Gallatin concluded: In the face of that history, in the name of necessity, it was proposed that Congress should adopt a law affecting the press and speech, when the government had existed for more than nine years without it, and by its own terms the law was to take effect for only three years.[137]

To this final argument, Harper responded that the law was necessitated by the emergency with France. It was necessary and proper, and therefore constitutional, for the government to quell sedition.[138] The bill carried by a margin of three votes.[139] A week later Congress adjourned until December.[140]

Sedition and the Kentucky and Virginia Resolutions

Republicans expected that in the long run the corpus of recent legislation was likely to hurt rather than help the Federalists. Eventually, the public would become vexed, not only with the onerous tax on land and houses that the Federalists had imposed to finance the military buildup,[1] but also, Republicans hoped, with the enforcement of the Alien and Sedition Acts. But they knew that this would not happen immediately. In the meantime, the election for the Sixth Congress was imminent and the flood of anti-French sentiment was still against them. They braced for the worst.[2]

Their immediate situation seemed grim. In their view, as recent developments had proved, the Federalists were concerned above all with power, with keeping control of Congress and the presidency, which—without Washington—they had almost lost in the election of 1796. The Alien and Sedition Acts, Republicans believed, had been principally conceived as handy tools of political harassment with which to tarnish Republicans as traitors and throw them in prison, while allowing the Federalists to parade before the country as the party of patriotic fervor. Republicans anticipated that the laws would be zealously justified as constitutional, whether in the name of implied powers, the Necessary and Proper Clause, general principles of government, or a combination of all of these. For Republicans, the Federalist copy of the Constitution was in effect unwritten and without principled limits. The Bill of Rights would afford them no protection.

Events proved them correct: As they had expected, the mere adoption of the Alien Act led to the exodus of many French aliens whom they counted as their supporters; and the enforcement of the Sedition Act led to the systematic prosecution of their leaders, their newspaper editors, and pamphleteers.[3] When Republican defendants, invoking the federal courts' power of judicial review, challenged the constitutionality of the Sedition Act, they quickly found that the courts, manned by Federalist judges, systematically construed the Constitution in the same manner as the Federalist majority in Congress and the president, and upheld the statute's validity.

Even before the adoption of the Sedition Act, the United States had arrested Benjamin Bache, the publisher of the leading Republican paper in Philadelphia, the *Aurora,* indicted him on a charge of common-law sedition and scheduled his trial for late in the year.[4] After the Sedition Act had taken effect, an indictment under the statute was pressed against Representative Lyon in Vermont upon his return from Congress. Lyon was accused of criticizing President Adams for his "continual grasp for power, in an unbounded thirst for ridiculous pomp, foolish adulation, and selfish avarice." Most probably a marked man because of his fight with Griswold, Lyon was quickly tried and convicted. Justice Paterson of the Supreme Court, presiding at his trial, rejected the defense based on the unconstitutionality of the Sedition Act and sentenced him to four months in jail. Lyon's political fortunes, however, did not suffer. While in jail he ran for reelection, and in December he was reelected.[5]

Although Lyon had been the first target, Jefferson regarded himself as the principal one. Reviled as the author of the notorious letter to Mazzei, Jefferson had slipped out of Philadelphia the day after the sedition bill had been introduced in the Senate—the original version provided for the death penalty—and returned to Monticello, where he would remain until well after the opening of the third session of the Fifth Congress. Distrusting the post office, he curtailed most of his political correspondence and carried on the rest under elaborate precautions of secrecy.[6]

Jefferson had little hope that the Alien and Sedition Acts would, if challenged in the Supreme Court, be held unconstitutional. And when Adams appointed George Washington as commanding general of the army created by the Fifth Congress, with Hamilton likely to have the effective command, Jefferson judged the situation menacing and contemplated some kind of public appeal to sustain party morale and rouse opinion in the face of Federalist popularity and imminent sedition prosecutions. He decided upon an appeal to the states as centers of refuge from the threats of usurping federal power.[7]

The Kentucky and Virginia Resolutions: Part One

Taking his inspiration from essays in the *Federalist,* Jefferson determined on a tactic even more audacious than the one used the year before when he had petitioned for the impeachment of grand jurors for their presentment against Cabell: the preparation of a resolution for adoption by a friendly state legislature declaring the Alien and Sedition Acts null and void and applying to other state legislatures for their support in a challenge to the usurpations of the federal government.[8] In the *Federalist,* Hamilton, in an effort to reassure his readers against the threatened excesses of the new government and to secure ratification, had first written: "Power being almost always the rival of power; the General Government will at all times stand ready to check the usurpations of the state governments; and these will have the same disposition towards the General Government. The people, by throwing themselves into either scale, will infallibly make it preponderate. If their rights are invaded by either, they can make use of the other, as the instrument of redress."[9] Then he went further:

I t may safely be received as an axiom in our political system, that the state governments will in all possible contingencies afford complete security against invasions of the public liberty by the national authority. Projects of usurpation cannot be masked under pretences so likely to escape the penetration of select bodies of men as of the people at large. The Legislatures will have better means of information. They can discover the danger at a distance; and possessing all the organs of civil power and the confidence of the people, they can at once adopt a regular plan of opposition, in which they can combine all the resources of the community. They can readily communicate with each other in the different states; and unite their common forces for the protection of their common liberty.[10]

Later, Madison, writing in the *Federalist,* was even more bellicose:

B UT AMBITIOUS ENCROACHMENTS OF THE Fœderal Government, on the authority of the State governments, would not excite the opposition of a single State or of a few States only. They would be signals of general alarm. Every Government would espouse the common cause. A correspondence would be opened. Plans of resistance would be concerted. One spirit would animate and conduct the whole. The same combination in short would result from an apprehension of the fœderal, as was produced by the dread of a foreign yoke; and unless the projected innovations should be voluntarily renounced, the same appeal to a trial of force would be made in the one case, as was made in the other.[11]

Following the prescriptions in the *Federalist,* Jefferson drafted what he considered an appropriate resolution. But while its substance and manner were calculated to stir the hearts of his dedicated followers, it was much too strong both for committed Federalists, whom it infuriated, and for ordinary people, who as usual preferred a moderate course. His resolution, as ultimately adopted by the Kentucky legislature, opened with the premise

THAT THE SEVERAL STATES COMPOSING the United States of America are not united on the principle of unlimited submission to their general government; but that, by compact, under the style and title of a Constitution for the United States . . . they constituted a general government for special purposes; . . . and that whensoever the general government assumes undelegated powers, its acts are unauthoritative, void, and of no force; that to this compact each state acceded as a state, and is an integral party; that this government, created by this compact, was not made the exclusive or final judge of the extent of the powers delegated to itself; . . . but that, as in all other cases of compact among parties having no common judge, *each party has an equal right to judge for itself, as well of infractions as of the mode and measure of redress.*[12]

Specifically, the resolution went on to declare that both the Alien and Sedition Acts were not law but "altogether void, and of no force," and that the state of Kentucky would continue to admit the migration of alien friends irrespective of the "nugatory" provisions of the former statute.[13] The call to the legislatures of the other states was coupled with the ominous advice "to submit to undelegated and consequently unlimited powers in no man, or body of men, on earth." The Alien and Sedition Acts, it warned, "and successive acts of the same character, unless arrested on the threshold, may tend to drive these states into revolution and blood."[14]

The Kentucky legislature had eliminated some of Jefferson's stronger language, such as his statement that "where powers are assumed which have not been delegated, a nullification of the act is the rightful remedy," and his threat that the states will "each take measures of its own for providing that neither these acts, nor any others of the General Government not plainly and intentionally authorized by the Constitution, shall be exercised within their respective territories."[15]

Virginia's resolution, drafted by Madison, was even more temperate, although it too implied a resort to gunpowder. Characterizing the powers of the federal government as resulting from a compact to which the states are parties, it declared "that, in case of a deliberate, palpable and dangerous exercise of other powers, not granted by the said compact, the states, who are parties thereto, have the right, and are in duty bound, to interpose, for arresting the progress of the evil, and for maintaining, within their respective limits, the authorities, rights, and liberties, appertaining to them."[16]

What did "interpose" suggest? The use of a state militia or the show of words? In any event, when the state legislature of Virginia was reported to have authorized the construction of an arsenal at Harper's Ferry, the thorough organization of the state militia, and the levy of additional taxes to meet the increased costs, the Federalists took alarm.[17]

Did the Kentucky and Virginia "plan of opposition" involve the right of a state's secession? The resolutions of both states had characterized the Constitution as a compact to which the states were parties. Both resolutions had either stated or implied that as parties the states had the right to judge for themselves when the compact was violated and what action they should take in redress of those violations.[18] This sounded as though, in the judgment of the Kentucky and Virginia legislatures, the Constitution was, like the Articles of Confederation, a league or treaty among the states.

If that were the case, it followed, as Madison had stated during the Constitutional

Convention, that "a breach of any one article by any of the parties, frees the other parties from their engagements." On the other hand, as Madison had then said, "in the case of a union of people under one Constitution, the nature of the pact has always been understood to exclude such an interpretation."[19] It was to emphasize the distinction between a league or treaty and a constitution, as well as to avoid the inherent difficulty in obtaining an agreement from the requisite number of state legislatures, that the Constitutional Convention had decided upon a plan by which the Constitution would be referred for adoption to the people in their respective states. And it was to emphasize the essential character of the Constitution that its preamble began with the words "We the People of the United States." As Madison had then concluded, "The people were in fact, the fountain of all power, and by resorting to them, all difficulties were got over."[20]

In apparent disregard of that distinction, the legislatures of Kentucky and Virginia had adopted their resolutions; and the governors of Kentucky and Virginia, following the instructions of their legislatures, sent copies of the resolutions to the other states, asking for their endorsement.[21]

Jefferson, returning belatedly to Philadelphia during the third and final session of the Fifth Congress, was encouraged in the apparent success of his campaign by the large numbers of petitions Congress had received from New York, New Jersey, and Pennsylvania, demanding the repeal of both laws. The country, he was sure, was on the verge of a swing to the Republicans.[22]

Fifth Congress, Third Session: Clear and Present Danger

In the final session of the Fifth Congress, the Federalists, still prepared for war with France, forthrightly rejected Republican-inspired petitions to reduce the army and navy and, in a formal report filed late in the session, also rejected petitions to repeal the Alien and Sedition Acts. Answering the charge that the statutes were unconstitutional, the report refined, embellished, and in some respects repeated the arguments of the prior session.

The report based the right to remove aliens on the war power, on the guarantee to protect the states from invasion under Article IV, Section 4, of the Constitution, and on the Necessary and Proper Clause. It rejected the applicability of Article I, Section 9, Clause 1, primarily on the ground that the restriction on congressional power regarding the "migration or importation" of persons was confined to slaves. If it were otherwise, it reasoned, it made no sense to limit congressional power for a period of only twenty years, nor to extend the power to permit such migration or importation only to states that were in existence at the time the Constitution was established.[23]

In any event, the power to remove dangerous aliens was distinct from the power to restrict immigration. Moreover, the report declared, since the former power must exist somewhere—an argument based on the principle of self-preservation—and since the Constitution had not given the power to the states during the twenty-year period, Congress must have it.[24]

To the charge that the law was in violation of the aliens' right to trial by jury under the Fifth Amendment, the report responded that aliens were not protected by the Constitution, that in any case the provision applied with respect to trial for the commission of crimes and not to the revocation of asylum, and that removal was not a punishment but a device to advance public safety.[25]

The report also defended the constitutionality of that part of the Sedition Act pertaining to the proscription of libelous and seditious writings. The defense rested primarily on the Necessary and Proper Clause, "because the direct tendency of such writings is to obstruct the acts of the Government by exciting opposition to them, to endanger its existence by rendering it odious and contemptible in the eyes of the people, and to produce seditious combinations against the laws, the power to punish which has never been questioned."[26]

The provision in the First Amendment respecting freedom of the press, the report continued, pertained to prior restraint. As had always been understood in the several states under their various state constitutions, it did not justify libel of individuals, nor did it justify, either in the states or in England, the publication of false, scandalous, and malicious writings against the government. Moreover, the statute was merely declaratory of, although somewhat in mitigation of, the common law. Such libels were punishable under the common law and therefore, by reason of Article III, Section 2, Clause 1, were punishable under the judicial power of the United States, which included the power to declare the common law.[27]

Finally, the report justified the Alien and Sedition Acts because of the dangers arising from the crisis in Europe following the French Revolution, dangers that the report regarded as still pressing. Under the circumstances, the report concluded, repeal of the laws would not be expedient. In effect, the Federalists, while not formally invoking the war powers, envisioned a clear and present danger.[28] A motion was then made to implement the report through the adoption of a resolution declaring the repeal of the Alien Act inappropriate.[29]

In response, Gallatin repeated his argument against the Alien Act from the previous session: The power to exclude non-enemy aliens had not been specifically granted to the United States, and recourse to the Necessary and Proper Clause might be made only in cases incidental to the exercise of the enumerated powers. In a new argument, applying the doctrine of strict construction to the facts at large, he said that the statute as written was too broad to rely on the Invasion Clause. An individual might be removed on mere suspicion, without proof that he schemed to promote an invasion; and the law continued in operation after the alarm of an invasion ended. In effect, Gallatin said, the committee was arguing that Congress might pass laws as necessary to carry into execution certain powers, even though the laws might not in fact be necessary for that purpose. Such a construction would allow Congress a broad discretion, governed by public clamor and private ambition, to justify any measure.[30]

Gallatin then took up the alternate, but inconsistent, argument he had advanced the year before, that under the immigration provision in Article I, Section 9, Clause 1, the states had the power, at least until the year 1808, to admit free aliens as well as slaves. The statements of members of the Constitutional Convention, he declared, had sometimes been offered to prove that when the convention used the word "persons" in that section, it meant slaves. But dismissing those statements, he said they proved only the intention of the particular individuals or of their belief of what might have been the intention of some of the other members of the convention.

Then, in rather cavalier disregard of his reliance the previous year on supposed inside knowledge of the convention's intention regarding the meaning of the general welfare clause, and of Baldwin's resort to his own recollections during the debate on the Immigration and Importation Clause, Gallatin now repeated the assessment he had made of members' recollections during the debate over Jay's Treaty in the Fourth Congress: These members were not the legislators who passed and ratified the Constitution, but only the framers who drew the instrument and offered it for the consideration of the ratifying conventions. He labeled as preposterous the use of parol evidence in supposed elucidation of the text.[31] When he finished, no reply was made. The resolution calling for the effective continuation of the Alien Act was adopted by a margin of four votes.[32]

John Nicholas spoke in opposition to the next proposed resolution, which declared repeal of the Sedition Act inexpedient. The Necessary and Proper Clause, he said, could not be used as support for the statute. Repeating an earlier argument that the clause meant little or nothing, he relied on the construction that friends of the Constitution had given it at the time of its adoption. In disregard of the Republican rule of construction utilized in the previous Congress during the House debate over its power to refuse implementation of Jay's Treaty—that the proceedings of the state ratifying conventions were unreliable—Nicholas referred to statements made in the Virginia convention to the effect that the Constitution would mean the same with or without the clause.[33]

Nicholas next attempted to meet the Federalist argument on the facts. While it was true, he contended, that Congress under the Constitution had an implied power to prohibit acts likely to hinder the execution of its laws, the power extended only to such acts as would interfere with their execution, "because the power can only be necessary as well as proper, when the acts really would hinder the execution." The report's construction, he added, extended the power of Congress "to all acts which have a relation, ever so many degrees removed, to the enumerated powers, or rather to the acts which would hinder their execution." By that construction, he concluded, all limitation was lost.[34]

If Congress could prohibit any act that had a tendency to produce opposition to the government, Nicholas said further, it could assume a general guardianship over the minds of the entire people and enter the field of education. For, he asked rhetorically, what had a greater tendency to fit men for insurrection than dissolute, immoral habits, which destroy love of order and dissipate the property that gives them an interest in society?[35]

The Sedition Act should be repealed, he further argued, because it had been applied to statements of opinion and not fact, thus rendering the defense of truth ineffective. Moreover, because it was in the interest of certain members of Congress to suppress opinions they did not like in order to be reelected, he continued, it was improper for them to pass legislation on the subject. Finally, he rejected resort to the common law because of its lack of uniformity throughout the states.[36]

After he finished, the question was called. The resolution declaring repeal of the Sedition Act inexpedient was carried, again by a margin of four votes.[37] The repeal of both the Alien and Sedition Acts continued to be a major source of controversy in the Sixth Congress, commencing in December 1799.

Adams vs. the Federalist Party: Clear and Present Danger?

Although neither Jefferson and the Republicans nor the Federalists realized it, the final session of the Fifth Congress, culminating in the reaffirmation of the Alien and Sedition Acts and their constitutionality, represented the zenith of Federalist power and the canon of broad constitutional construction. The central thesis of both statutes, the existence of a clear and present danger to the country, was based on the premises of a threat of war with France and an imminent French invasion. In fact, neither premise was sound. As all responsible persons in the government knew before the end of the Fifth Congress, the French were offering the United States not war but peace.[38] And both Adams and Washington had always considered it unlikely that, even in case of war, the French would invade.[39]

The reason for the now apparent French cordiality lay partly in the reversal of the fortunes of war. On August 1, 1798, the British navy under Nelson had all but destroyed the French fleet in the critical battle of the Nile, making it impossible for the French to invade the United States in the near future. With the destruction of the French fleet and the buildup of the American navy, Adams knew that American shipping could be protected from French privateers.

Adams was also aware that the land tax that the Fifth Congress had imposed to finance the buildup of the navy and army was unpopular. It would become an albatross around the Federalists' neck if it were employed to maintain an army that everyone of discernment understood was no longer needed for a war of defense. This would be particularly true since the South, which was the prime target of a supposed French invasion, wanted neither the army nor the tax. His assessment, then, led him to the early conclusion that for sound reasons he should not support the army and, when he discovered the French wanted peace, to the second conclusion that he should resume diplomatic relations with France.[40]

Adams's assessment, however, did not lead him to immediate action. The Federalists in Congress, disregarding the unlikeliness of a French invasion, persisted in preparing for war. Hamilton, the country's most influential Federalist after Washington, sided with Congress. He had good reasons for doing so. When the Fifth Congress in its second session had authorized the creation of the new army, as it was called, Adams had appointed Washington its commanding general, and with great reluctance and under great pressure had accepted Washington's designation of Hamilton as his second in command. In fact, since Washington had made it clear that he would not actually enter service until there was imminent danger of an invasion, Hamilton was in effect first in command.[41]

The new general had plans for his future army beyond the problematic realm of defending the South. He saw in the army an instrument for both the repression of rebellious southern sentiment and the waging of an offensive war of conquest. In the first case, alarmed by the sentiments of the Kentucky and Virginia Resolutions and reports of Virginia armament, Hamilton advocated the entry of the army, when ready, into Virginia, on some "obvious pretext." Measures would be taken, he wrote to Theodore Sedgwick, his ally in Congress, "to act upon the laws & put Virginia to the Test of resistance."[42]

In the second case, he contemplated a scheme whereby, with the help of the British navy, the United States could invade and wrest from Spain its possessions in Louisiana and the Floridas, and then plunge into Mexico and beyond in a colossal war of colonial liberation. Since Spain was France's chief ally in Europe, Hamilton believed that a preemptive war against Spain, striking at the heart of its wealth, would hurt the French, thwart them from seizing Spain's colonies for themselves, and serve the immediate purposes of both Britain and the United States. And since the liberation of the Spanish colonies would open them to trade with Great Britain and the United States, it would serve the long-range interests of both countries as well. Needless to say, the successful conduct of such an enterprise would make Hamilton's career.[43]

When Adams was apprised of Hamilton's plans, he became doubly convinced of the lack of wisdom of an army buildup and the urgent need to resume diplomatic relations with France. Early in February 1799, in the middle of the final session of the Fifth Congress, when he received the assurance from William Vans Murray, the United States minister at The Hague, that Talleyrand would cordially receive a United States minister, and the intelligence from George Washington that the French indeed were genuine in their desire to resume negotiations, Adams acted.[44]

He informed the cabinet and the Senate of his intention to reopen negotiations with France and to name Murray as his envoy for the mission. The cabinet, the Federalists in Congress, and later Hamilton were horrified and alarmed. Sedgwick called Adams mad; Hamilton later agreed, quoting Benjamin Franklin's assessment of Adams: "always honest, *sometimes* great, but *often mad*." But for all their protests, the only change the Federalists were able to make was to expand the delegation to three persons. On this basis, the mission was confirmed, and the Fifth Congress adjourned.[45]

Enforcement of the Sedition Act: Clear and Present Danger

As it turned out, Adams's mission did not please the Republicans. They were suspicious that in his new diplomatic maneuver Adams was playing peacemaker only to win votes. Their suspicions were heightened when the apparent change in foreign policy did not alter the course of prosecutions under the Sedition Act. During the congressional recess, prosecutions continued under the direction of Timothy Pickering, the secretary of state, as though the president had not made his judgment that the French did not present an imminent danger and were serious in their desire for peaceful negotiations. Similarly, the federal judiciary continued to support administration policies, irrespective of the president's judgment, and steadfastly upheld the law's constitutionality. Seemingly, nothing had changed. The Sedition Act, as the prevailing policy judgment of Congress, was the law of the land. Under the Constitution the administration was duty bound to execute the law as given by Congress, and the federal judiciary was bound to apply it.

Accordingly, in Pennsylvania, under a broad construction of the statute, John Fries was charged with treason for obstructing enforcement of the new federal tax law and, when convicted, was sentenced to death. (The Federalists by and large continued to ignore the extreme unpopularity of the tax.) Eventually, Adams, who in this matter showed more judgment than his cabinet and Hamilton, pardoned him.[46] In Trenton, Justice Iredell, following Justice Paterson's determination in the Lyon case, advised a grand jury that the Sedition Act was constitutional. And Oliver Ellsworth, now chief justice in place of Jay, was on record that federal courts had a common-law jurisdiction in seditious libel.[47]

Ellsworth's position as to a federal common law of crime was not unprecedented. Chief Justice Jay, and Justices Wilson, Iredell, Bushrod Washington, Paterson, and Cushing had already taken this position in charges to federal grand and petit juries.[48] In accordance with this view, Ellsworth in June 1799 charged a federal grand jury in South Carolina that under common law, and thus in the absence of a specific statute, it might indict for all acts manifestly "subversive of the National Government, or of some of the powers specified in the Constitution." In the fall of that year, declaring the principles of English common law binding on the federal courts, he held that a United States citizen who had renounced his citizenship in favor of France did not have the right of expatriation. Based on this holding, he sustained an indictment charging a violation of the neutrality law, which prohibited a United States citizen from accepting a commission to serve a foreign power.[49]

Ellsworth's actions were the final irritant for Republicans and served to reinforce their opinion that the federal judiciary was infected with the Federalist canon of broad constitutional construction. A systematic judicial inference of a general competency in the federal government, irrespective of any provision in the enumerated powers, they thought, was a foregone conclusion.

Republican newspapers and politicians protested. In private letters to Edmund Randolph and Charles Pinckney, Jefferson said that the assertion of a federal common-law jurisdiction, besides being novel, was the most formidable of all the powers the federal government had assumed. It was, he stated, "audacious, barefaced and sweeping," a wholesale encroachment on the Constitution, compared to which those that went before—such as the establishment of the Bank and the adoption of the Alien and Sedition Acts—were mere retail operations. If followed, he went on, it would allow anyone to sue in federal court, lead to the elimination of the state courts, and effect a complete consolidation. The assertion, he said, was alarming and wholly inconsistent with the delegation of enumerated powers and the reserved powers of the states.[50] And in the Sixth Congress, Charles Pinckney would raise the issue of Ellsworth's appointment as one member of the three-man mission to France.[51] Thus the federal judiciary, by its conduct, its close support of administration policies, its construction of the Constitution, and its invocation of the common law, became a political issue in the forthcoming presidential election campaign.

In 1800, to look ahead for a moment, the administration would continue prosecutions under the Sedition Act, and the federal courts would continue to uphold its constitutionality. Justices Washington and Chase of the Supreme Court invariably ruled in its favor during trials at which they presided. A trial at which Chase presided—that of James Callender, a pamphleteer, in federal court in Virginia—was especially significant because that state was understood to be the refuge of aliens and Republican pamphleteers. Callender's conviction demonstrated to the country in a presidential election year that even in a Republican stronghold the Federalist administration was in control. Chase attracted the special ire of Republican polemicists, and in 1801, after the Jefferson revolution was accomplished, his name appeared at the head of their impeachment list.[52]

Adding to Republican discomfort in 1799 were the unfavorable, even censorious, replies of seven state legislatures to the invitation for support of the sentiments expressed by the Kentucky and Virginia legislatures in their resolutions declaring the unconstitutionality of the Alien and Sedition Acts. The New York senate, under Federalist control, charged that the Kentucky and Virginia Resolutions contained "inflammatory and pernicious sentiments and doctrines . . . repugnant to the Constitution of the United States, and the principles of their union . . . [and] destructive to the federal government."[53]

The Massachusetts legislature, under Federalist control like the legislatures of the other New England states, propounded a detailed defense of the statutes' validity along the lines taken by the Federalists in Congress. More fundamentally, it questioned "the right of the state legislatures to denounce the administration of that government to which the people themselves, by a solemn compact, have exclusively committed their national concerns." Such power, it held, had been "exclusively vested by the people in the judicial courts of the United States." Finally, in a rebuke to the intimation of secession implicit in the Kentucky and Virginia Resolutions, the Massachusetts legislature concluded with a statement of "strong conviction, that the several United States are connected by a common interest, which ought to render their union indissoluble."[54]

While the Connecticut legislature simply disavowed the principles set forth in the resolutions,[55] the Vermont legislature repeated the criticism of Massachusetts, terming the Virginia Resolutions "unconstitutional in their nature, and dangerous in their tendency."[56] In a statement of support for the power of judicial review, the Vermont body announced its judgment that the power to pass on the constitutionality of federal law devolved not upon the individual state legislatures but upon the federal courts.[57] The legislatures of Delaware, New Hampshire, and Rhode Island similarly disclaimed the idea of a power in the Virginia legislature to determine the constitutionality of a federal statute; those of New Hampshire and Rhode Island affirmed the power of federal judicial review.[58]

All in all, the adoption of the Kentucky and Virginia Resolutions was not a great success. They had provoked a cascade of counterdeclarations upholding the doctrine of judicial review and inviting those dissatisfied with federal legislation to seek the protection of the federal courts. They had threatened disunity and laid the groundwork for a jurisprudence of confederacy and secession. And their implications of disunion had so alarmed the public as to lead voters even in the southern states to shift their support to the Federalists for the elections to the Sixth Congress. Reassured by Washington's acceptance of Adams's appointment to command the army, with its implicit approval of the conduct of his administration, and influenced by the candidacies on the Federalist ticket in Virginia of Henry Lee and John Marshall, two of Washington's closest friends, the southern electorate in the spring of 1799 helped return Federalists to the Sixth Congress with a substantially increased majority. In Virginia eight Federalists, including Lee and Marshall, were elected, as were five others in North Carolina. In fact, opinion had so turned against the Republicans that John Nicholas, co-leader in the House fight to prevent the adoption of the Alien and Sedition Acts, had a hard time getting reelected. Washington's influence had again proved decisive, although for the last time.[59]

Kentucky and Virginia Resolutions: Part Two

In the meantime, the federal judiciary's steady support of Federalist policies confirmed Jefferson and Madison in their belief that the courts would give no support to their contention that the measures of the Fifth Congress were unconstitutional. Therefore, they decided to put the best face on the poor showing in the elections and advise the Kentucky and Virginia legislatures to reaffirm their resolutions impugning the validity of the Alien and Sedition Acts. To deflect the criticism expressed in the resolutions of the other state legislatures, Madison, who had entered the state legislature that year, undertook a defense of the Virginia Resolutions of 1798 in a special report to the Virginia House of Delegates. In substance, it was his valedictory statement in defense of his own, now the Republican Party's, ideology, that of constitutional construction.[60]

Madison supported the position the resolutions had taken: The Constitution was a compact among the states, and consequently a state had the right to "interpose" between its people and the government of the United States.[61] But first he labored to meet the criticism of the Massachusetts and Vermont legislatures that the Virginia legislature in adopting the resolutions had arrogated to itself a power reserved to the people.[62]

At the Constitutional Convention Madison, as mentioned, had drawn a distinction between a league or treaty, established by the legislatures, and a constitution, established by the consent of the people.[63] As a member of the Virginia legislature who would be held responsible for its words and actions, he strove to render the action of the prior Virginia legislature consistent with the views he had expressed in the convention and with those of the New England legislatures. It was not an easy task.

Madison first set out to explain that in using the term "states," the Virginia legislature had really meant "the people of the states." In doing so, he had to take refuge in fine—perhaps overly fine—distinctions and run the risk of losing his readers, perhaps intentionally, in order to come to the desired conclusion. Madison wrote:

I T IS INDEED TRUE THAT THE TERM "states" is sometimes used in a vague sense, and sometimes in different senses, according to the subject to which it is applied. Thus it sometimes means the separate sections of territory occupied by the political societies within each; sometimes the particular governments, established by those societies; sometimes those societies as organized into those particular governments; and lastly, it means the people composing those political societies, in their highest sovereign capacity. Although it might be wished that the perfection of language admitted less diversity in the signification of the same words, yet little inconveniency is produced by it, where the true sense can be collected with certainty from the different applications. In the present instance, whatever different construction of the term "states," in the resolution, may have been entertained, all will at least concur in that last mentioned; because in that sense, the Constitution was committed to the "states"; in that sense the "states" ratified it; and in that sense of the term "states," they are consequently parties to the compact from which the powers of the federal government result.[64]

Having explained away the apparently improper use of the word "states" in the original resolutions, Madison set himself to controlling the damage arising from the resolutions' use of the word "interpose." To dampen the charges of disunion implicit in the term, he qualified the wording of the resolutions: "But in the case of an intimate and constitutional union, like that of the United States, it is evident that the interposition of the parties, in their sovereign capacity, can be called for by occasions only deeply and essentially affecting the vital principles of their political system."[65]

Nevertheless, in opposition to the northern state legislatures, he continued to insist upon the ultimate authority of the state—that is, the people thereof acting in their highest sovereign capacity—over that of the federal judiciary. While the authority of the courts might be final with respect to the other departments of the federal government, he asserted, it could not be final with respect to the parties to the constitutional compact: "The judicial department, also, may exercise or sanction dangerous powers beyond the grant of the Constitution; and, consequently, . . . the ultimate right of the parties to the Constitution, to judge whether the compact has been dangerously violated, must extend to violations by one delegated authority as well as by another—by the judiciary as well as by the executive, or the legislature."[66]

From 1828 on, John C. Calhoun and his states' rights colleagues in South Carolina would find support in Madison's insistence on the right of states, when acting in their sovereign capacities, to judge for themselves violations of the Constitution by the federal government. In defending their state's threat to secede from the Union during the controversy over federal tariff laws, South Carolinians declared that a state's secession was licit as long as the people of the state—and not merely the state legislature—so decided in a duly assembled convention.[67] But in 1798 Madison did not go that far. Indeed, the purpose of his report to the House of Delegates was not to stand by the belligerent language of the resolutions—the Republicans after all had lost the last election—but to soften the roughness of the earlier statements.

So far, Madison had attempted to explain away the use of the words "states" and "interpose" in the Virginia Resolutions while defending the resolutions' affirmation of a state's right to pass judgment on the constitutionality of a federal statute. He had yet to explain how it was that the Virginia legislature in adopting the resolutions had not meant to commit "the people" but was instead merely giving its own opinion. He did so by downplaying the significance of the resolutions, claiming that their sentiments were not novelties but declarations of the legislature's opinion, which, unlike those of the judiciary, had no immediate effect and were unaccompanied by force.

After all, Madison added, state legislatures had the right to propose constitutional amendments. The course Virginia followed, he wrote, had been suggested by a supporter of the Constitution at the time it was under consideration. Presumably he was referring to the essays in the *Federalist,* probably by way of advising Hamilton, the author of one of the essays, that he was an accomplice before the fact to the actions of the Kentucky and Virginia legislatures.[68]

Following his explanation of the action of the Virginia legislature, Madison proceeded to a discussion of the statutes whose adoption had given rise to the Virginia Resolutions. He first considered the constitutionality of the Alien Act. Giving full support to the now standard Republican line of a strict construction of the enumerated powers of the federal government, which he himself had established in the First Congress, he repeated Gallatin's argument that the statute was invalid. In disregard of the baleful consequences flowing from this position, he maintained that the Federalist argument—that it was impractical to leave to the states the admission or exclusion of aliens—was contrary to the constitutional plan. The federal government could act only if it was specifically authorized to do so.[69]

In the main, however, Madison concentrated his attack on the Alien Act's infringement of individual liberties, a point that Gallatin had only briefly touched upon in the Fifth Congress. The statute was invalid, Madison asserted, because it violated the principles of preventive justice basic to American jurisprudence: a showing of probable cause, based on evidence, given under oath or affirmation, before some judicial authority; a recourse by the accused to bail and the writ of habeas corpus; and the right to a discharge from confinement by order of a court on a showing of sufficient grounds. Under the statute, he continued, the president, instead of a judge, passed on the grounds of suspicion. In consequence, the alien, without recourse to judicial review, could be deprived of an asylum in the country and of his home, liberty, and property.[70]

The Alien Act was also invalid, Madison contended, because Congress had delegated to the president the power to make the rules under which an alien could be excluded. Congress had further empowered him to execute his own rules and to judge whether his execution was correct. In practice, therefore, the president would perform the functions of all three branches of the government. Such a concentration of power, he wrote, could only lead to the tyranny against which it was the constitutional design to protect. Even an alien, Madison concluded, so long as he was friendly, was entitled to this protection, in the same manner as a United States citizen.[71]

In arguing against the constitutionality of the Sedition Act, Madison first attacked the basis for Otis's justification of the statute in the Fifth Congress: that it was supplementary to the common-law power of crimes, which the federal government possessed under Article III of the Constitution. Madison's contention was that since the colonies had all modified the substantive rules of the English common law to suit their own circumstances, there were no uniform substantive common-law rules from which the federal courts could, without exercising a discretionary, quasi-legislative power, effectively posit a federal common law.[72]

Pushing on, Madison repeated the arguments of Macon and John Nicholas in the Fifth Congress: Congress did not have an enumerated power to adopt the Sedition Act, and only by conceding to Congress a largely unsupervised and discretionary power could the statute be considered necessary to the prevention of an insurrection.

Like Nicholas, he dwelled on the legislative history of the First Amendment. The amendment was proposed, he said, to assure those in the state ratifying conventions concerned about the extent of congressional power that Congress would have no power to affect the freedom of the press.[73] Madison, however, went beyond Macon and Nicholas in his analysis of the requirements of the First Amendment, and in doing so advanced a convincing case for the statute's unconstitutionality.

In passing, Madison discussed the impropriety of applying British precedents to America: The First Amendment by its express terms was directed against Congress, whereas the British prohibition against the infringement of free speech was directed only against the crown, a hereditary monarchy, and not against Parliament. Yet he emphasized that in practice both Great Britain and the states went beyond a simple guarantee against a prior restraint. A fair amount of criticism of government officials was tolerated, even though it might lead to a loss of public confidence.

Such practice should be the more accepted in America where all officials are elected, Madison continued, because it was necessary for the electorate to be able to judge the candidates' performance. (Gallatin had made this point in the Fifth Congress.) The First Amendment and the terms of the Sedition Act, Madison concluded, should therefore be construed to reflect practice. Instead, he charged, the statute was not only construed literally but applied unfairly: Incumbents were rendered immune from criticism, while their opponents were not. This argument could not be rebutted.[74]

The Virginia House of Delegates, following Madison's recommendations, reaffirmed in more moderate terms the sense of its resolutions: The federal statutes violated the terms of the compact. Typically, however, the Kentucky legislature adopted its own resolution framed in more pugnacious language:

> [T HAT WHILE KENTUCKY] WILL BE among the last to seek its [the compact's] dissolution . . . the several states who formed that instrument, being sovereign and independent, have the unquestionable right to judge of the infraction; and, *That a nullification, by those sovereignties, of all unauthorized acts done under color of that instrument, is the rightful remedy* . . . [And although the] commonwealth, as a party to the federal compact, will bow to the laws of the Union, yet it does, at the same time, declare, that it will not now, or ever hereafter, cease to oppose in a constitutional manner, every attempt, at what quarter soever offered, to violate that compact.[75]

Jefferson, in authoring the first drafts of the second set of Kentucky Resolutions, had gone further. Only at Madison's insistence did he eliminate a provision whereby the legislature would resolve "to sever ourselves from . . . [the] union," should the federal government not return to the true principles of the compact. Jefferson's original impulse reflected the sentiment of many among the Virginia Republican leadership at the time, a sentiment reported to the Federalists.[76] In 1828 and after, "nullification" became a key word in South Carolina. Calhoun and his colleagues were able to figure out for themselves the logical connection between nullification and secession.[77]

In this context, following the adoption of the second set of the Kentucky Resolutions, Hamilton wrote to Jonathan Dayton, the Federalist speaker of the House, calling for measures further strengthening the United States military forces and the consideration of the adoption of a constitutional amendment breaking the large states, such as Virginia, into smaller, more manageable ones. Wistfully, he admitted the impracticality of the constitutional amendment.[78] He did not know that Adams had no intention of ever allowing him to get his army ready, and that for him there would be no glorious military career.

The Fall of the Federalists

In a desire to stir up partisan interest in anticipation of the presidential election of 1800, the Republicans early that year raised a variety of constitutional issues in both branches of the Sixth Congress. None of the issues was major. In the House, after first trying unsuccessfully to repeal the provision in the Sedition Act for the prosecution of seditious libel,[1] the Republicans took up the cause of a supposedly impressed American seaman. They moved a resolution to censure the president and a federal judge for the allegedly wrongful delivery of the seaman to a British consul.

The proposed censure of the president was occasioned by an executive order, directed to the judge, to hand over to the British a person who was alleged to have been an American citizen. Such an order, it was further alleged, constituted an unlawful executive encroachment upon the province of the judicial department. The censure of the judge was based on his compliance with the presidential directive, allegedly in violation of the prisoner's right to trial by jury under Article III of the Constitution.[2]

The prisoner, Thomas Nash, had been held in Charleston on suspicion of involvement in acts of mutiny and piracy aboard a British frigate, and of desertion from the ship. At the direction of a federal judge, the British minister, pursuant to a provision in Jay's Treaty, applied to the president for Nash's delivery. Relying on the opinion of Timothy Pickering, the secretary of state, that Nash was a British subject, Adams advised the judge to deliver him to the British admiralty, provided there was evidence of his criminal conduct.

But before the British took custody, the prisoner filed an application for habeas corpus, in which he stated that his name was Jonathan Robbins and that he was an American citizen from Danbury, Connecticut. He stated further that he had been wrongfully impressed into the ship's service by its captain and that he had not taken part in the mutiny. After a summary hearing, the judge rejected his application and had him handed over to the British, who promptly tried, convicted, and executed him. The man, the admiralty later said, admitted he was Irish. The Republican press made the affair a cause célèbre. If Nash-Robbins was an American, the issue would heighten sentiment against the British for their impressment of American seamen. If he was Irish, the agitation would appeal to the party's Irish constituency.[3]

As he had in the Fourth and Fifth Congresses, Gallatin took the lead for the Republicans in the House and presented the principal constitutional argument on their behalf, declaring that the president had lacked the constitutional authority to direct the delivery of Nash-Robbins to the British. His case, Gallatin contended, involved questions of treaty interpretation, the resolution of which more properly pertained to the judiciary: whether, for instance, piracy and murder committed on a British naval vessel on the high seas constituted an offense within the exclusive jurisdiction of Great Britain. Under Article III, he maintained, such a question would be resolved by reference to the law of nations and the construction of the terms of Jay's Treaty. A similar case, involving a sailor charged with piracy and murder on the same vessel, he added, had been tried in federal court before a jury.[4]

In a masterful address,[5] John Marshall came to the defense of the administration. As a matter of constitutional law, Marshall said, it was not improper for the president, relying on the statement of the case as it came before him, to direct the federal court to deliver Nash to the British,[6] because the matter was one for the executive, and not the judicial, department. Characterizing the case as in effect a "political question," Marshall argued that the provisions of Article III of the Constitution, the judicial article, did not apply because the phrase "a case in law or equity," as there used, was "a term well understood, and of limited signification. It was a controversy between parties which had taken a shape for judicial decision." If the judicial power were to extend to every question under the Constitution, he continued, it would involve matters properly reserved for the legislature and the executive. As a result, those "departments would be swallowed up by the Judiciary."[7]

On the contrary, Marshall said, the power under discussion was executive. Affirming what Jefferson and Hamilton had earlier written on the subject, he declared:

T HE PRESIDENT IS THE SOLE ORGAN of the nation in its external relations, and its sole representative with foreign nations. Of consequence, the demand of a foreign nation can only be made on him.

He possesses the whole Executive power. He holds and directs the force of the nation. Of consequence, any act to be performed by the force of the nation is to be performed through him.

He is charged to execute the laws. A treaty is declared to be a law. He must then execute a treaty, where he, and he alone, possesses the means of executing it.[8]

Marshall conceded that Congress could, if it so desired, place the execution of treaty provisions in someone other than the president. But, he maintained, until this was done, it was the president's duty to execute the treaty. Not only was the executive branch, rather than the judicial branch, the proper constitutional department to supervise the operations of the extradition provision, it was "the proper department to which the power in question may most wisely and most safely be confided." He elaborated:

> THE DEPARTMENT WHICH IS ENTRUSTED with the whole foreign inter-course of the nation, with the negotiation of all its treaties, with the power of demanding a reciprocal performance of the article, which is accountable to the nation for the violation of its engagements with foreign nations, and for the consequences resulting from such violation, seems the proper depart-ment to be entrusted with the execution of a national contract like that under consideration.
>
> If, at any time, policy may temper the strict execution of the contract, where may that political discretion be placed so safely as in the department whose duty it is to understand precisely the state of the political intercourse and con-nexion between the United States and foreign nations, to understand the man-ner in which the particular stipulation is explained and performed by foreign nations, and to understand completely the state of the Union?[9]

On the basis of Marshall's speech, the Republican motion for censure lost decisively.[10]

More Constitutional Disputation

In the Senate as well as in the House, political and constitutional issues were raised against the administration. Advancing the Republican cause in the Senate, Charles Pinckney, an articulate delegate at the Constitutional Convention and the newly ap-pointed senator from South Carolina, set forth his party's standard claims that the executive branch was usurping congressional powers and that the federal govern-ment was engaged in an unwarranted extension of power at the states' expense—to the detriment of the people's rights and liberties. In a remarkable outburst of con-stitutional disputation, Pinckney advanced constitutional arguments on four sepa-rate questions in the session.

Although Pinckney was returning to national service after an absence of twelve years, he had not been wanting in ambition. During Washington's administration, he had sought, through Madison, a ministerial appointment in Europe.[11] Now, during the first session of the Sixth Congress, he worked hard for the Republican thesis of strict constitutional construction and, both before and after that session, worked equally hard for the election of the party's presidential candidates in South Carolina. In fact, his intervention on behalf of Jefferson and Burr ultimately proved decisive in their election, with the result that after the election Jefferson rewarded him with the ministerial appointment to Spain he had so long coveted.[12]

The first constitutional issue Pinckney raised concerned the continuation of the embargo on commercial relations between the United States and France and her colonies. Following standard Republican doctrine preached many times in the

House, Pinckney objected to a provision in a bill authorizing the president to discontinue the embargo "whenever he shall deem it expedient, and for the interest of the United States . . . [as to] which in his opinion a commercial intercourse may be safely renewed." This, he averred, constituted a delegation of legislative power to the executive branch not specifically authorized by the Constitution. It was therefore unconstitutional, having the tendency to increase executive and administrative influence in the government, already made too great by past delegations. Such excessive power, he proclaimed, tended to corrupt legislators who in hope of appointment to executive office were influenced to vote for administration measures. Such honors and riches, and the pleasures that attend them, said Pinckney (who coveted all of them), would ruin the country. Besides, he added, as if this were an afterthought and not the heart of the matter, the embargo worked to the disadvantage of South Carolina and the rest of the South. The bill passed easily despite his objections.[13]

Pinckney's abiding interest in an appointment to a foreign ministry was also evident during the discussion of his bill to amend the Judiciary Act.[14] Taking up a familiar Republican theme, he argued that the presidential practice of appointing federal judges, particularly the chief justice, to foreign ministries was fundamentally inconsistent with the principle of the separation of powers. The Constitutional Convention, he recalled as a former member, had considered it unwise to associate judges with the president in the exercise of his veto or revising power. Similarly, one who drafted a treaty as an envoy should not thereafter be called upon to pass on its merits as a judge. In effect, the remarks were a rebuke to Ellsworth, who was at that time in Paris assisting in the negotiation of a treaty with France, as well as to former Chief Justice Jay, who had negotiated the treaty with Great Britain. Pinckney went on to say that a judge who sought the office of foreign envoy might be tempted to lend his support to a presidential policy in his judicial actions.[15] Although Pinckney did not suggest it, the same might have been said of a United States senator who similarly sought such an office—that he was lending his support to the policies of a candidate whom he hoped would be president the following year.

A judge should not leave his office and duties unattended, Pinckney continued, particularly a chief justice who might be called upon to preside in the Senate over an impeachment. For all these reasons, he said, the practice of holding dual offices was unseemly and the Constitution should have provided against it. He did not argue, however, that since the practice was inconsistent with the spirit of the Constitution and the principle of separation of powers, it was unconstitutional. Instead, he urged Congress to apply the remedy. Inasmuch as Congress had the power to create the inferior federal courts and judgeships and to appropriate money for the judges' salaries, it could provide that a judge, upon acceptance of a second office, should not be paid his judicial salary so long as he cannot perform his judicial duties.[16]

Pinckney then introduced a more fundamental constitutional question: the power of the courts to exercise judicial review. It was, he said, the particular duty of Congress to guard against judicial bias in favor of the president "when we recollect that our Judges claim the dangerous right to question the constitutionality of the laws; and either to execute them or not, as they think proper; a right in my judgment as unfounded and as dangerous as any that was ever attempted in a free government; they however do exercise it, and while they are suffered to do so, it is impossible to say to what extent it might be carried."[17]

A president, Pinckney added, might try to rid himself of laws he found obnoxious by persuading the judges that they were unconstitutional and should not be executed.[18] There is no report that this argument was either pursued further or rebutted. It was one that Republicans would raise again in the Seventh Congress.[19]

Questioning the power of judicial review was a new development. Earlier, in mounting attacks against the constitutionality of the carriage tax and the Sedition Act, the Republicans had been pleased to invite the federal judiciary to set those laws aside.[20] Apparently having seen that their attacks did not bear fruit, they were now willing to doubt the power's existence. Just as Republican dissatisfaction with the exercise of executive power had led in the Second Congress to a constitutional challenge to the existence of the power itself,[21] so their dissatisfaction with the performance of the Federalist-appointed federal judiciary led in the Sixth and Seventh Congresses to a denial of the power of judicial review. For the moment, however, Pinckney's initiative lost. The Senate as a body refused to vote its rebuke.[22]

Pinckney lent his talents for constitutional disputation to a third issue. In an attempt to influence the election of 1800, the Federalists had proposed a bill creating a joint Senate-House committee of twelve to pass in secret session upon the validity of challenges to the votes of electors for president and vice-president. The bill had been intended to control the electoral votes from the state of Pennsylvania, whose legislature was so split between Federalist and Republican factions as to make it doubtful that any electoral vote would be cast from that state. But, as Pinckney urged, the committee that the bill contemplated could easily manipulate a close election in favor of its own political preferences.[23]

Pinckney's main contention, however, was that the proposal was unconstitutional because the Constitution did not specifically provide for it. And the reason the Constitution did not so provide—as Pinckney, one of its framers, remembered—was that the Constitutional Convention wished to make the election of the president independent of Congress. Pinckney here ignored the frequently repeated dicta of Gallatin, his fellow Republican in the House, that a framer's recollection of the convention's intent was improper. Instead, he maintained that the convention meant to have the president elected by the people through the electors in the several states, and not by Congress, around whom foreign ministries with their foreign gold would congregate.

The Constitution therefore presupposed that state electors would perform their functions properly. Asserting that it was a federal principle to trust the states, Pinckney deemed it better to tolerate a few errors committed at the local level than to resort to a dangerous and unconstitutional measure. This, he added, was the principle embodied in the act of 1792 on the subject, a law passed when Washington was president and when both houses of Congress contained a number of members who had participated in the Constitutional Convention. Despite Pinckney's objection, the Senate approved the bill. When the two houses disagreed over its provisions, however, it was carried to the second session where, too late to affect the 1800 election, it died.[24]

Pinckney also played a large role in a fourth constitutional issue, which arose out of the proceedings connected with the election bill. The *Aurora,* the Philadelphia Republican newspaper, had come into possession of a copy of the bill, which the committee was considering in closed session, and published it. The paper, protesting the bill's adoption, charged that it was the scheme of a Federalist-dominated caucus to deprive Jefferson, the protector of the people's rights, of the presidency. It protested further that Pinckney, a member of the committee, had not been consulted. The Senate, following British parliamentary practice, considered both the publication and commentary to be a breach of its privileges and to constitute "false, defamatory, scandalous, and malicious" statements.[25] Uriah Tracy of Connecticut moved referral of the matter to the Committee on Privileges.[26]

The Senate's move seemed a continuation of Federalist policy under the Sedition Act whereby the political reporting and criticism of the Republican press would be subject to prosecution. On behalf of the Republican cause Pinckney objected, employing against the Federalist Senate the same line of argument that Gallatin and John Nicholas had earlier used in the House against the adoption of the Sedition Act.

Senatorial privileges, Pinckney said, taking up the Republican canon of strict constitutional construction, were limited to those set forth in Article I, Section 6, Clause 1, of the Constitution, namely the privilege "from Arrest during their Attendance at the Session of their respective Houses, and in going to and in returning from the same; and [against being questioned] for any Speech or Debate in either House." In opposition to Tracy's typically Federalist assertion of an inherent Senate right to self-protection and self-preservation, a right reflected in British parliamentary practice and precedent, Pinckney, taking the usual Republican line, maintained that since the matter was not within the enumerated privileges and therefore within the powers of Congress, it had been reserved to the states and to the people under the Tenth Amendment. However, Pinckney did not push strict construction too far. He did concede that the Senate had the authority to keep order and decorum within its own chamber, to clear the galleries of an unruly audience, and to punish its own members.[27]

Nevertheless, he insisted, the Senate had no authority over private attacks on the public conduct or opinions of a senator. Although his construction might lead to public abuse, such abuse was the price members of Congress must pay. The Constitution, Pinckney declared in a reference to the First Amendment, left them answerable to their constituencies and public opinion. Individual members might have recourse in libel against their attackers, he said, but the question of libel would be for the courts and juries to determine.[28] He could not have anticipated the construction the United States Supreme Court would place upon the First Amendment in *New York Times v. Sullivan,* whereby that recourse would largely be denied an individual senator.[29] Pinckney concluded with a rhetorical question: Why, if the *Aurora* was properly in contempt of the Senate for its publication, had the Constitution left the president unprotected, and why had Congress passed the Sedition Act?[30]

Pinckney's arguments were difficult to answer and went unheeded. Instead, the Federalist majority referred the matter to the Committee of Privileges and required the paper's editor, William Duane, to appear before it and answer the charges directed against his publication. When the Senate refused to permit him to challenge the constitutionality of the proceedings, Duane declined to appear. The Senate then voted to hold him in contempt, finally requesting the president to institute proceedings against him for false, defamatory, scandalous, and malicious publication. On that note, the Sixth Congress adjourned its first session.[31]

Adams did eventually oblige the Senate, but instead of proceeding against Duane for breach of its privilege, had him indicted under the Sedition Act. The indictment was still pending at Jefferson's inauguration. He ordered it dismissed, but to preserve the theory of the Senate's privilege, he directed the United States Attorney to present the Senate's case to a new grand jury. That body, under Republican auspices, refused to indict, ending the matter.[32]

In the first session of the Sixth Congress, Senator Pinckney, by his ready arguments on various issues, had shown that he was a reliable spokesman for the Republican cause. In the line of Madison and Gallatin, he proved himself able to invoke suitable provisions of the Constitution in the light of the Republican doctrine of strict construction, against federal power generally and that of the president and the Senate in particular.

At the conclusion of the session, the country was poised for the pivotal election of 1800–1801, in which for the first time a Republican president and a Republican-dominated Congress would be elected. With this turn of events, strict rather than broad construction would become the official canon of constitutional interpretation and governmental policy.

The Election of 1800: Adams vs. Hamilton and Jefferson

Despite all the disputation of the previous decade, no constitutional issue played a crucial part in the presidential election of 1800. This is not to minimize the constitutional differences between the parties or the role that constitutional issues had played in the formation of the parties and the presentation of their policies. Nevertheless, party strength in this election turned more on practical considerations: political and economic regional interests, the extension of the franchise—the Re-

publicans escorted large numbers of Irish and German aliens to the polls—the unpopularity of the 1798 property tax, and the public perception of the parties as
champions of either the British or French in the causes of law and order or republicanism. The formulation and popular appeal of those issues had rendered the parties almost equal in strength.

The most crucial action in the weakening of the Federalists' position was Adams's
decision to send a peace mission to France. This signal to the country that there was
no clear and present danger from France had widespread results. Zeal for the new
army flagged, and recruitment fell off. The public chafed at the burden and inconvenience of the new taxes and were repelled by the harshness of the sedition prosecutions. In December 1799 George Washington, who had given life and sustenance
to the national ideals and measures of the Federalists, died. Within the following
year Federalist party fortunes faltered.

In a remarkable letter to Madison written in early March 1800, Jefferson reviewed
his political chances. With unusual perception, he calculated that except for New
Jersey and New York, the country's remaining electoral votes were equally divided.
Since New York's votes would outweigh New Jersey's, he believed that everything depended on New York, whose presidential electors would be chosen by the legislature
elected that May. And since control of the legislature depended largely on the vote
in New York City, the election of 1800, Jefferson predicted, would turn on the results there.[33]

When Burr was able to carry the Republican ticket for New York City in New
York's May election, Adams's reelection was in serious trouble.[34] The Federalists in
Congress realized that their cause was lost unless they could entice southern electors to vote for Adams. With Hamilton's approval, they settled on a geographically
balanced ticket coupling Charles Cotesworth Pinckney from South Carolina with
Adams. Jefferson, desirous of Burr's support in New York and mindful of his prediction that that state was the key to his election, agreed to take Burr as his running mate.[35]

But Jefferson's prediction had been premised on the supposition that South Carolina, as a southern state, would support him. With the introduction by the Federalists of Charles Cotesworth Pinckney as a candidate for the presidency, however,
South Carolina's support of Jefferson was in jeopardy. To insure that the state's electoral vote would not be split, its legislature organized a convention and empowered
its delegates to instruct the state's eight electors how to vote. When the convention
met, it was generally known that electors from the country's remaining states were
committed to casting their votes so that Jefferson, Adams, and Burr would each receive sixty-five votes. Charles Cotesworth Pinckney, South Carolina's favorite son, it
was also known, would be fourth, with sixty-four electoral votes.

During the convention an overture was made to Charles Cotesworth Pinckney,
seeking his approval of an arrangement whereby the convention would direct the
electors to cast their votes so as to choose him president and Jefferson vice-president.

Pinckney, realizing that such an offer would be impractical and his acceptance of it ignoble, rejected it. Senator Pinckney, working against his cousin's interest, then persuaded the convention to direct the electors to cast their votes for Jefferson and Burr. As a result, the election was decided: Jefferson and Burr each had seventy-three votes, Adams sixty-five, and cousin Pinckney sixty-four. The senator deserved his foreign ministry.[36]

Sixth Congress, Second Session: Jefferson vs. Burr (1800–1801)

A constitutional crisis ensued. Since Jefferson and Burr had tied, the election—pursuant to the then provisions of Article II, Section 1, Clause 3, of the Constitution—had to be decided in the House of Representatives in the second session of the Sixth Congress, in which Federalist influence was strong. In those circumstances, questions naturally arose. Would the Federalists arrange their votes to create a deadlock so that on the morning of March 4, 1801, with Adams's term as president and Jefferson's as vice-president expiring, their offices would be vacant? Jefferson thought that in such an eventuality legislation would be enacted conferring the presidency on the chief justice or the secretary of state.

Lending credence to the report was the fact that in December Adams had nominated Jay chief justice to succeed Ellsworth, who had recently resigned because of poor health. Earlier, Adams had appointed Marshall to succeed Pickering as secretary of state. According to this plan, the next president of the United States would be either Jay or Marshall.[37]

Hearing these rumors, Jefferson let it be known that the middle states would regard such a case as a usurpation and would rise up against it. He also let it be known that the next Congress, under Republican control, would call for a second constitutional convention to provide for the question of presidential succession and to cure the recent Federalist "perversions" of the Constitution. The first threat, Jefferson wrote, merely shook the Federalists; the second horrified them.[38] Ultimately, Jay declined his nomination, and Adams nominated Marshall chief justice in his stead. Marshall accepted and was confirmed.[39]

In the end, the Federalists abandoned any schemes they might have had to deprive the Republicans of the presidency, and concentrated on the matter at hand: the election of either Jefferson or Burr in the House of Representatives. Pursuant to Article II, Section 1, Clause 3, of the Constitution, as it then provided, the House vote was to be "taken by States, the Representation from each State being one Vote." Since there were at that time sixteen states—Kentucky, Vermont, and Tennessee had been added to the original thirteen—the winner needed nine. In caucus, the Federalists decided to support Burr, partly out of hope that his victory would split the Republican Party, and partly out of disdain for Virginia, whose ambition, James A. Bayard wrote, was "the source of [the] present [growth of] Party [spirit]" and the aim of whose ruling faction was "to govern the UStates."[40]

Sedgwick placed his opposition to Jefferson and Virginia on a more constitutional basis. Writing to Hamilton, who favored Jefferson over Burr, he stated his reason for opposing Jefferson: "Because he is known to be devoted to the views of those men, in his state whose unceasing efforts it has been & is to reduce, in *practice,* the administration of this government to the *principles* of the old confederation, in which that state by her numerous representation, & the influence which she has on surrounding states, will be the dictatrix."[41]

Although Marshall as secretary of state would not participate in the voting, he also feared Jefferson's presidency on constitutional grounds. Jefferson's triumph, Marshall wrote Hamilton, would result in the official subordination of executive power to the will of the prevailing House majority: "Mr. Jefferson appears to me to be a man who will embody himself with the house of representatives. By weakening the office of President he will increase his personal power. He will diminish his responsibility, sap the fundamental principles of the government & become the leader of that party which is about to constitute the majority of the legislature."[42]

Because of Federalist prejudice against Jefferson, he received the vote of only eight states on the first ballot, one short of the required majority.[43] This pattern prevailed during the next five days when the impasse was broken. On the thirty-sixth ballot Jefferson was chosen the third president of the United States.[44]

Epilogue: Text, Intent, and Practicality

In the beginning was the text of the Constitution, but sometimes the text was wrapped in ambiguity. When, for instance, the text of Article I, Section 8, Clause 18, says: "Congress shall have power . . . to make all Laws which shall be necessary and proper for carrying into Execution the foregoing Powers," what do these words mean? Do they mean that Congress has the power "to legislate in all cases for the general interests of the Union, and also in those to which the States are separately incompetent, or in which the harmony of the United States may be interrupted by the exercise of individual legislation?"[1] Or, more narrowly, do they mean that Congress has merely the incidental power to pass laws carrying into effect the powers already enumerated in Section 8?

When, following the Constitutional Convention, opponents of ratification charged that the sweeping provisions of the Necessary and Proper Clause would give Congress broad and indefinite powers,[2] and supporters of ratification denied it,[3] both sides created a major problem for those who, after ratification, would run the new government. If the new government were organized on the basis of the assurances given during ratification—that the powers of Congress were limited to those enumerated in Section 8—it would not work. If, however, to make it work, members of the new government went beyond those powers, they would lay themselves open to the accusation that they were repudiating the position they had taken to secure ratification.

In the face of this dilemma, the new government might have faltered and the Constitution might soon have been revealed to be a deeply flawed document. But both in Congress and in the executive branch, there were those who, convinced of their responsibility to show the world that Americans could govern themselves, would not allow this to happen. For them, the cause of republicanism was at stake. As Hamilton so eloquently stated in the opening essay of the *Federalist*:

I T HAS BEEN FREQUENTLY REMARKED, that it seems to have been reserved to the people of this country, by their conduct and example, to decide the important question, whether societies of men are really capable or not, of establishing good government from reflection and choice, or whether they are forever destined to depend, for their political constitutions, on accident and force. If there be any truth in the remark, the crisis, at which we are arrived, may with propriety be regarded as the æra in which that decision is to be made; and a wrong election of the part we shall act, may, in this view, deserve to be considered as the general misfortune of mankind.[4]

Animated, therefore, by a desire to make the Constitution and the new government organized pursuant to it operate successfully, members of the First Congress, in the opening days of the very first session, passed a law imposing a uniform oath of allegiance to the Constitution on state officers, despite the absence of a specific power authorizing them either to provide for the form of such an oath or to adopt uniform laws. Some, relying on the Necessary and Proper Clause, ignored Madison's doubts and Gerry's skepticism concerning congressional power.[5]

Later in the same session, Congress enacted a law recognizing the president's power to remove an incompetent department head, again in the absence of a specific constitutional provision authorizing such an enactment. Approximately three-fifths of those in the House who voted for the measure again relied on the Necessary and Proper Clause, although Madison, for the others, relied on what he termed the implied powers of the presidency under Article II.[6]

The desire for an effective government also led Hamilton to propose the establishment of a national bank. The framers' decision, limiting Congress to the adoption of a metallic currency, seemed to him a highly unrealistic provision for an underdeveloped country such as the United States of that time.[7] In recommending a national bank, Hamilton cited its several advantages. The paper it would issue would serve as a currency, enabling the government more easily to pay the principal of its foreign debt and the interest on its foreign and domestic debt to its creditors, and make it easier to borrow in times of emergency. In addition, a paper currency would enhance trade.[8]

When Madison challenged the bill establishing the Bank of the United States as beyond the powers of Congress even under the Necessary and Proper Clause,[9] Ames in support of Hamilton argued that the clause should be construed so as to promote "the good of the society, and the ends for which the government was adopted."[10] In his opinion to President Washington defending the bill's constitutionality, Hamilton ingeniously agreed with Madison that the Necessary and Proper Clause merely authorized the enactment of laws carrying into execution one of the specified powers. However, in his application of the clause, as though reasons of practicality carried their own weight, he repeated the positions set forth in his initial report: The bill would ensure an adequate money supply, help the government with its debt, enhance trade, etc.[11]

The wisdom of Hamilton's plan became evident during the War of 1812. The Bank's charter expired, a credible national paper currency disappeared, and the

United States defaulted on its debt.[12] The painful lessons learned from that experience forced the Republican majority in Congress to repent and pass a bill chartering the Second Bank of the United States—and forced Madison as president to sign it, in silent acknowledgement that the presence of such an institution was, after all, necessary and proper.[13] After Chief Justice Marshall justified the constitutionality of the law in *McCulloch v. Maryland*,[14] Justice Johnson, in his concurring opinion in *Osborn v. The Bank of the United States,* confirmed that the Bank's ultimate usefulness lay in its ability to float a national paper currency as an effective supplement to the constitutionally mandated but inadequate metallic currency.[15]

Practicality—the desire to make the government operate efficiently—was also the basis for Hamilton's construction of the provision for spending for the general welfare in his report to the House in the Second Congress: There are certain needs for the alleviation or advancement of which local resources are inadequate; resort must be had to the larger revenues of the national government. Even Madison in opposition had to bend to the necessity of spending federal money in particular cases, for instance, in his concession to the New England fisheries and his support of the Santo Domingo refugees.[16] Eventually, the Supreme Court sanctioned the Hamiltonian thesis in *United States v. Butler*[17] and *Helvering v. Davis.*[18]

Again, on the basis of practicality, the Federalists in the Fifth Congress contended for the constitutionality of the Alien Act. Disregarding the historical evidence to the contrary that Gallatin cited, and the evidence from the Constitutional Convention he might have cited, they spoke against the argument that for want of a specific power the governance of immigration was reserved to the several states.[19] They took the position that the power was implied in the grant of national sovereignty to the United States and, as well, in the principle of good government: Where no one state could effectively legislate on a subject, Congress must have, and, indeed, did have the power. In *The Chinese Exclusion Case,* the Supreme Court—ignoring counsel's references to Madison's report of 1799 to the Virginia House of Delegates, in which he affirmed the Gallatin argument, and the various positions taken in the Kentucky and Virginia Resolutions—sanctioned the Federalist interpretation.[20]

The Federalist defense of the constitutionality of the Sedition Act in the Fifth Congress was also based on practical need: that of the national government to protect itself against forceful overthrow and against written or spoken incitement to that end. As a general proposition, the Supreme Court has upheld that position rather than the highly unrealistic Republican argument that the national government lacked the power because it had not been enumerated.[21]

In the circumstances of 1798, however, as we know, the controversial provisions of the Sedition Act—those proscribing writing or speech that brought the federal government, Congress, or the president into disrepute or contempt or excited hatred against them—were administered to suppress political criticism of the administration. As Gallatin in Congress and Madison in his report to the Virginia House of

Delegates correctly argued, such legislation tends to immunize incompetent, corrupt, or despotic public officials from criticism and maintain them in office. In effect, it perpetuates bad, not good, government. For that reason, although recognizing the power of the federal government to defend itself, the Supreme Court has held this type of legislation to be contrary to the provisions of the First Amendment.[22]

None of the measures that the Federalists adopted, however, could have been enacted into law without the concurrence of George Washington. The military leader in the successful revolt from British rule, Washington had accepted the presidency to consolidate that victory. As a man of action and an outstanding administrator with a deep commitment to the success of the new government during his presidency, he naturally favored such legislative and executive measures as would ensure his administration's success. Thus, in the first Congress, he signed both Madison's bill to recognize the president's power to remove a department head and Hamilton's bill to establish a national bank.

In the conduct of foreign affairs, Washington's commanding presence and the widespread public respect for his person and his achievements won him a practical latitude of operation, despite the lack of a specific constitutional provision to that effect. In advocating such a prerogative, Hamilton, acting as Washington's principal adviser, disregarded both his own prior position in the *Federalist* and the argument raised by Madison in his Helvidius essays.[23]

Indeed, during the period under discussion, when he had influence in the government, even Madison labored under the necessity to be practical and, like Hamilton, disregarded the authority of the *Federalist*. Thus, while acting as the Federalist leader in the House in the first session of the First Congress, he worked for the exclusive presidential power to remove a department head in the executive branch, on the ground that otherwise the country might be saddled with an officer who intrigued with members of the Senate against presidential policies. (This subsequently happened to Madison in his own administration, despite the removal power.)[24]

And when Washington asked for his advice or when he was in pursuit of his own legislative agenda, Madison, like Hamilton, followed the dictates of practicality and ignored the authority of the framers. For example, his notes of the proceedings of the Constitutional Convention reveal that the framers intended to exclude the president from participating in fixing the place to which Congress shall return following an adjournment. Yet in the very first session of the First Congress, when he supported a bill to fix the permanent seat of government and remove the temporary seat from New York, Madison assigned the president such a role.[25] He later confirmed that position in the advice he gave to Washington regarding a contemplated change in the location of the first session of the Third Congress from Philadelphia following an outbreak of yellow fever.[26]

During the same period Jefferson, while serving as Washington's secretary of state, also gave practical advice. Thus, regardless of what the *Federalist* said and what the framers intended respecting the power of Congress to declare war and the power of the Senate to participate in the ratification of a peace treaty, Jefferson admitted that in the circumstances of 1793 the president should not call Congress into special session but should decide himself against honoring the provision in the treaty with France that required the United States to go to war against Great Britain.[27]

The Federalist dependence on Washington in carrying on the business of government in an efficient manner—albeit in disregard of the many assurances given in the *Federalist* and in the state ratifying conventions regarding the limited powers of Congress—became evident on his death. Thereafter, Federalist power quickly waned. Jefferson's election to the presidency in 1800, coinciding with Republican control of the Seventh Congress, established a new order of constitutional interpretation. With Jefferson's approval, the Virginia delegation, the largest in the House and the leader of southern interest, limited the powers of the federal government through the routine application of strict construction: Congress was to be confined within the strict limits of its specified powers under Article I. Sedgwick's assessment—that Jefferson's election would reinstate the principles of the old Confederation—was vindicated.[28]

There were even then, to be sure, limits to the doctrine of strict construction. In certain cases, Republicans, Jefferson and Madison included, had to set aside ideology and be practical. Thus Jefferson, having decided that the Louisiana Purchase was necessary to secure the nation's southern and western borders, disregarded his scruples and the absence of a specific constitutional provision authorizing the acquisition of territory. Later, to carry into effect his policy of a trade embargo upon British shipping, he countenanced a scandalously broad construction of the Commerce Clause. Similarly, Madison signed the bill chartering the Second Bank of the United States despite his own earlier argument against the constitutionality of the Bank under its first charter.[29] And in his conduct of foreign policy, President Jefferson frequently acted without consulting Congress.[30]

On the whole, however, Jefferson, Madison, and their party followers regarded these deviations from the strict limits of Articles I and II as momentary concessions to necessity, tolerable specific exceptions to their general principles, but not repudiations of the principles themselves. After all, their political success was based on strict construction. This party line was maintained until the Civil War. Indeed, Marshall's 1819 opinion in *McCulloch v. Maryland* caused a fury in Virginia, not because it upheld the statute establishing the Bank—Virginians were willing to concede this on practical grounds—but because he dared to invoke the Necessary and Proper Clause and use the Hamiltonian rationale of implied governmental powers.[31]

In private correspondence, Madison aided the purists' cause with his advocacy of an alternate theory of constitutional justification of the Second Bank's charter, amounting to a constitutional validation by *stare decisis:* However questionable in the beginning, he wrote, congressional establishment of the First Bank had been constitutionally legitimated by the public's general acceptance of its operations during the twenty years of its charter. He did not add that the reason for its acceptance was that despite his and Jefferson's constant political rhetoric as to its invalidity, its practicality was widely perceived and appreciated from the beginning, even by such strict constructionists as Gallatin and Senator Maclay.[32]

In writing his opinion in *McCulloch,* Marshall was well aware of his fellow Virginians' fiercely held convictions regarding the limits of federal power in general and of the Necessary and Proper Clause in particular. This awareness led him to include in his opinion the statement that the federal government was "one of enumerated powers,"[33] which reinforces the basic premise, still invoked today, that indeed the authority of the federal government is limited in scope.

But, ultimately, the Madisonian-Jeffersonian thesis—that the powers of Congress and the presidency must be strictly construed, that their powers are confined to those specifically enumerated, that the Necessary and Proper Clause is limited in its application to the execution of the enumerated powers, and that federal spending must be limited to the purposes set forth in Article I—has been substantially eroded, although not completely set aside. The process by which Congress and the Supreme Court effected the erosion has been gradual and, to say the least, convoluted.

Thus, in *Juilliard v. Greenman* in the nineteenth century, the Court, despite the Coinage Clause in Article I, Section 8, Clause 3, ultimately upheld as necessary and proper the power of Congress to make its paper currency legal tender in time of peace as well as war.[34] And later, when persons distrusting the inherent value of government greenbacks insisted by contract that their creditors pay their obligations in gold, the Court early in this century, in *Norman v. B. & O. R. Co.,* also upheld legislation proscribing those arrangements under the Necessary and Proper Clause.[35]

Indeed, so tenacious has been adherence to the strict construction thesis that resort to a substantive interpretation of the Necessary and Proper Clause has been almost a matter of desperation. Instead, in order to create a government of energy and efficiency, Congress and the Court have preferred to work within what has appeared to be the specific provisions of the Commerce Clause. Thus, in a series of decisions the Court accommodated a broad reading of the Commerce Clause to enable Congress to legislate in matters it considers in the general interests of the country, and in so doing rendered almost irrelevant the requirement that for the federal government to act the commerce must be interstate.

A historical summary of these decisions is set forth in *United States v. Lopez.*[36] Under the Commerce Clause, Congress has the power to regulate matters generally reserved to the states, such as gambling and prostitution, by prohibiting the movement across state lines of certain things, such as lotteries,[37] or of certain persons, such as prostitutes.[38] Congress may also protect the channels of interstate commerce, and regulate the carriage of things and persons in such commerce, even though the harm against which it provides protection or regulation may come only from intrastate activities.[39] Finally, Congress may regulate wholly intrastate economic activity, such as manufacturing,[40] mining,[41] or agriculture,[42] where it substantially affects interstate commerce. Indeed, the economic activity may itself in a given case be insubstantial.[43]

Furthermore, beginning in *Helvering v. Davis,* the Court has approved, as falling within the spending power of Congress, appropriations having the effect of legislation in cases where no one state is competent to act.[44] It thereby confirmed Madison's fears that a Hamiltonian reading of the spending power would enable Congress, in effect, to adopt laws beyond the specified powers.

Today, therefore, in most instances, despite Madison and Jefferson, Congress does have the power to legislate, either under the Commerce Clause or the spending power, in cases in which—to use the language of Gunning Bedford's resolution in the Constitutional Convention—the general interests of the United States are concerned, the several states are incompetent to act, or the harmony of the United States may be interrupted by the exercise of individual legislation.[45] Congress has also been held to possess wide legislative powers under the enforcement provisions of the Thirteenth, Fourteenth, and Fifteenth Amendments to the Constitution to address problems involving racial discrimination. Those powers, the Court has held, are as broad as those under the Necessary and Proper Clause, the clause of ultimate resort.[46]

Nevertheless, the basic thesis that Madison propounded in the *Federalist* persists: "The powers delegated by the proposed Constitution to the Federal Government, are few and defined. Those which are to remain in the State Governments are numerous and indefinite."[47] Indeed, as was mentioned in the Introduction, this thesis served as the cornerstone of the Supreme Court's 1995 decision in *Lopez,* where it held that the mere act of possessing a firearm in a local school zone was not subject to federal regulation under the Commerce Clause.[48] Furthermore, the Court said, "areas, such as criminal law enforcement or education, [are subjects] where States historically have been sovereign."[49]

Later, in *Printz v. United States,* the Court invalidated a federal statute that, as part of a detailed national scheme governing the distribution of firearms, imposed upon state and local enforcement officers the duty to conduct background checks on prospective handgun purchasers. Such an imposition, the Court held, was a constitutionally impermissible intrusion upon state sovereignty.[50]

Despite these decisions, however, the road to effective federal regulation in these and other areas has been only partially blocked. As Justice O'Connor, in a concurring opinion in *Printz* pointed out, Congress, once again acting pursuant to its spending power, can circumvent the roadblock by providing for the continuation of its program on a contractual basis with the states.[51] Thus, federal grants to states in aid of their criminal law enforcement capabilities can be conditioned on their agreement to make background checks.[52] Presumably, Congress could also circumvent the force of the decision in *Lopez* by conditioning grants to states in aid of education on their agreement to enact statutes prohibiting the possession of firearms in a school zone.

Of course, as Madison realized, such a Hamiltonian construction of the spending power undercuts his premise that the federal government is one of enumerated powers. Presumably, Madison would take little comfort in the fact that in recent years the congressional penchant for spending has been curbed as a result of its past predilection for increasing the national debt. Nor would he find solace in the circumstance that a federal regulatory scheme may be frustrated, in whole or in part, by the decision of one or more states to forego the offer of federal money.

Despite Justice O'Connor's suggestion, the spending power is not the exact equivalent of a direct power to pass a uniform law where one is needed. In addition, the obstacles to enacting such legislation, in the absence of a federal power to do so, are considerable: A model uniform act must be proposed; state legislators in each of the fifty states must be importuned to adopt it. Yet the sessions of many state legislatures are short and sometimes infrequent. Different bodies may adopt their own variations of the proposed model act. Finally, different courts in different states will inevitably construe the same or similar provisions differently.

However, there are certain situations where a quick recourse to the adoption of a uniform act is desirable, such as that proposed in the June 1997 report of the National Bioethics Advisory Commission to President Clinton. Prompted by the cloning of the sheep called Dolly in Scotland a few months before, the commission recommended that Congress enact a law "to prohibit anyone [for a period of up to three or five years] from attempting, whether in a research or clinical setting, to create a child through somatic cell nuclear transfer cloning."[53] As matters then stood, the commission pointed out, there was a serious potential for severe physiological and psychological abnormalities in a child emanating from this process.[54]

The commission recognized the advantage resulting from the enactment of federal legislation, as opposed to the adoption of laws state by state:

[S]UCH] ADVANTAGE . . . LIES PRIMARILY IN its comprehensive coverage and clarity, as it would cover both private and public work in both research and clinical settings. Besides ensuring interstate uniformity, a federal law would relieve the need to rely on the cooperation of diverse medical and scientific societies, or the action of diverse IRBs [Institutional Review Boards], to achieve the policy objective. As an additional benefit, federal legislation could displace the varied state legislative efforts now ongoing, some of which suffer from ambiguous drafting that could inadvertently prohibit the important cellular and molecular cloning research [described earlier in] this report. Further, by unifying law at the national level, federal legislation could prevent "forum shopping," in which researchers or clinicians are enticed to relocate to states where protections against dangerous uses of cloning are fewer.[55]

In response to the commission's report, President Clinton sent Congress his draft of proposed legislation entitled the "Cloning Prohibition Act of 1997."[56] No action was taken, however, until after public outrage erupted over an announcement by a Chicago scientist in January 1998 of his intention to open a clinic for the purpose of cloning a human being. In reaction, Senate leadership sought quick action on a bill that would go beyond the recommendations of the National Bioethics Advisory Commission and ban "the creation of cloned human embryos that would never have the opportunity for implantation and that would therefore be created solely for research."

Influenced, however, by the biotechnology and pharmaceutical industries' objection that the bill would hinder medical research beneficial to the public health and safety, and by these industries' assurance that they had no intention to clone human beings, the Senate voted against quick adoption of the bill and instead sent the bill to committee.[57]

At the same time, in a move calculated to counter the Senate leadership, Senators Dianne Feinstein of California and Edward M. Kennedy of Massachusetts filed a bill that did follow the recommendations of the National Bioethics Advisory Commission. Setting forth the commission's recommendations as the purported "findings" of Congress, the bill also would "find" that since biomedical research facilities operate in interstate commerce, the prohibited conduct—using "the product of somatic cell nuclear transfer to create a human being genetically identical to an existing or deceased human being"—would affect interstate commerce.[58]

Perhaps, when and if such legislation is enacted and challenged, the courts will accept those findings.[59] The facts underlying *Lopez* were very different from those giving rise to the adoption of a federal statute prohibiting the cloning of human beings. In that case, the defendant could have been prosecuted under the laws of Texas, which like approximately forty other states at the time, had a statute specifically prohibiting the possession of firearms in a school zone.[60] Not only were the states competent to regulate such possession, in fact, they had already done so. But only Congress can prohibit the cloning of human beings throughout the United States.

If such a statute is passed and challenged, the courts may accept congressional findings supporting the conclusion that a biomedical research facility engaged or wishing to engage in the prohibited conduct of cloning humans beings substantially affects interstate commerce, even though in the case before the court the facility may not be involved in the biotechnology or pharmaceutical business or any other kind of business, and even though these industries have assured Congress that they do not intend to engage in the cloning of human beings.[61]

This convoluted reliance on the Commerce Clause, of course, would be unnecessary if Madison's original proposal to the Constitutional Convention, set forth in his Virginia Plan, had been adopted. Congress could thereby legislate "in all cases to which states are incompetent or in which the harmony of the United States may be interrupted by the exercise of individual Legislation."[62] A federal statute prohibiting human cloning falls within that language. But Madison abandoned his proposal and fought against the adoption of a substitute resolution whereby Congress could enact legislation in the general interests of the country as well as in the cases he had set forth in his own plan.[63]

To return to the question posed at the outset of this epilogue: When the Committee of Detail replaced the Bedford resolution with the Necessary and Proper Clause and the delegates to the Constitutional Convention approved it, did they intend to deprive Congress of the power to pass uniform laws? After the convention, Madison said that they did.[64] During and after the convention, two of the delegates—George Mason and Elbridge Gerry—said that they did not.[65] Edmund Randolph equivocated.[66]

During ratification, Hamilton agreed with Madison and said in the *Federalist* that they did. But in his opinion to Washington on the bank bill, he said they did not: "Necessary and proper" should be interpreted so as to further the general interests of the country. His construction of the spending power confirmed his reading of the Necessary and Proper Clause and gutted the heart of Madison's construction of that clause. Others, including Washington, agreed with Hamilton's later opinion.[67]

Elsewhere in the *Federalist,* Hamilton openly set forth his views concerning the manner in which constitutions should be written and construed: "Nations pay little regard to rules and maxims calculated in their very nature to run counter to the necessities of society. Wise politicians will be cautious about fettering the government with restrictions that cannot be observed."[68]

In our system, it is the Supreme Court that ultimately construes the Constitution. In the twentieth century, in cases where the general interests of the country have been involved and matters of great importance at stake, it has construed the Commerce Clause so as to permit Congress to attend to the necessities of the country.

Where no federal power enumerated in the Constitution has appeared pertinent, where the general interests of the country or matters of great importance are at stake, and where all else has failed—as in the legal tender and gold clause cases—the Court has sometimes taken refuge in the wonderfully ambiguous language of the Necessary and Proper Clause and held the legislation at issue to be valid.[69]

In all these cases, whether under the Commerce Clause or the Necessary and Proper Clause, the Supreme Court, custodian of Constitutional Law, deciding for the nation, has paid little regard to the rules and maxims of strict construction.

Madison, diligent advocate of strict construction, has been called Father of the Constitution. After constitutions are written, however, they must be interpreted and made to work. It is Hamilton who deserves the title of Father of Constitutional Law.[70]

Cases Cited

Abbreviations

ANNALS — DEBATES AND PROCEEDINGS OF THE CONGRESS OF THE UNITED STATES, 1789–1824 (Joseph Gales comp., 42 vols., 1834–56).

DHFFC — DOCUMENTARY HISTORY OF THE FIRST FEDERAL CONGRESS, MARCH 4, 1789–MARCH 3, 1791 (Linda Grant Depauw et al. eds., 14 vols. to date, 1972–).

DHRC — THE DOCUMENTARY HISTORY OF THE RATIFICATION OF THE CONSTITUTION (Merrill Jensen et al. eds., 18 vols. to date, 1976–).

ED — THE DEBATES IN THE SEVERAL STATE CONVENTIONS ON THE ADOPTION OF THE FEDERAL CONSTITUTION, AS RECOMMENDED BY THE GENERAL CONVENTION AT PHILADELPHIA, IN 1787, COLLECTED AND REVISED FROM CONTEMPORARY PUBLICATIONS BY JONATHAN ELLIOT (2d ed., 5 vols., 1941).

ELKINS & MCKITRICK — STANLEY ELKINS & ERIC MCKITRICK, THE AGE OF FEDERALISM (1993).

FEDERALIST — THE FEDERALIST (Jacob E. Cooke ed.) (1961).

FR — RECORDS OF THE FEDERAL CONVENTION OF 1787 (Max Farrand ed., rev. ed., 3 vols., 1996).

HP — THE PAPERS OF ALEXANDER HAMILTON (Harold C. Syrett ed., 27 vols., 1961–87).

JP — THE PAPERS OF THOMAS JEFFERSON (Julian P. Boyd et al. eds., 27 vols. to date, 1950–).

MP — THE PAPERS OF JAMES MADISON (William T. Hutchinson and William M. E. Rachal eds., 17 vols. to date, 1962–).

WJ — THE WORKS OF THOMAS JEFFERSON (Paul L. Ford ed., 12 vols., 1904–5).

WJA — THE WORKS OF JOHN ADAMS (Charles F. Adams ed., 10 vols., 1850–56).

WW — THE WRITINGS OF GEORGE WASHINGTON (John C. Fitzpatrick ed., 39 vols., 1931–41).

Notes

Introduction

1. FEDERALIST No. 45, at 308, 313 (James Madison).
2. 514 U.S. 549, 561 (1995).
3. *Id.* at 564.
4. *Id.* at 602 (Stevens, J., dissenting), 603 (Souter, J., dissenting), and 615 (Breyer, J., dissenting).
5. — U.S. —, 117 S. Ct. 2365, 2376 (1997). The Court also held that by reducing the law-enforcement powers of the president, the statute violated the principle of the separation and equilibrium of powers among the branches of the federal government. *Id.* at 2376–78.
6. *Id.* at 2386–87.
7. *Id.* at 2378–79; FEDERALIST No. 33 at 207 (Alexander Hamilton).
8. The best argument for this position is to be found in ROBERT H. BORK, TEMPTING OF AMERICA (1990). *See also* William H. Rehnquist, *The Notion of a Living Constitution*, 54 TEX. L. REV. 693 (1976).

Justice Scalia has added his own refinement to this discussion. While disclaiming an interest in searching for what he terms the framers' subjective intent, he proclaims his fidelity to what he calls textualism, a construction of the constitutional text according to its original meaning, irrespective of whether or not that meaning accords with the framers' intent. Thus, he would have recourse to the writings of John Jay in the *Federalist* or of Thomas Jefferson for their views of the meaning of the constitutional text, even though they were not framers, as well as to the writings of Madison and Hamilton, who were. Antonin Scalia, *Common-Law Courts in a Civil-Law System: The Role of United States Federal Courts in Interpreting the Constitution and Laws,* in A MATTER OF INTERPRETATION: FEDERAL COURTS AND THE LAW 3–47 (Amy Gutmann ed., 1997).

9. For an overall view of the inquiry, *see* the statements and essays in INTERPRETING THE CONSTITUTION (Jack N. Rakove ed., 1990); in Laurance H. Tribe & Michael C. Dorf, ON READING THE CONSTITUTION (1991); and in *Symposium: Fidelity in Constitutional Theory,* 64 FORD. L. REV. 1247–1818 (1997).
10. The most influential statement of this position is to be found in H. Jefferson Powell, *The Original Understanding of Original Intent, reprinted in* INTERPRETING THE CONSTITUTION, *supra* note 9, at 53–115.
11. Leonard W. Levy recognizes that Washington and others, against Madison and Gallatin, did rely on the proceedings of the Constitutional Convention and the sense of the state ratifying conventions when they construed the Constitution in the Fourth Congress debates. Levy, nevertheless, agrees with H. Jefferson Powell that original intent is not a valid standard for constitutional interpretation. Unlike Powell, who, relying on the debates in the Fourth

Congress, maintains that the original understanding of those construing the Constitution in and out of Congress was that such a reference was improper (*see supra* note 10), Levy holds that there was no such original understanding: Since the sources used to discover original intent are unreliable and since there was widespread disagreement as to the propriety of their use, he says, the intent is unknowable. LEONARD W. LEVY, ORIGINAL INTENT AND THE FRAMERS' CONSTITUTION 1–29 (1988).

12. My study differs substantially from that of David P. Currie. Although Currie is not unaware of the various arguments members of Congress and the Washington administration employed during the course of the debates to further their interpretations of the Constitution, the canons of construction they used, and the interests they served in advancing those arguments, his aim is to recount the legal and constitutional precedents established during that period. Those precedents, he notes, have been almost as hallowed as the Constitution itself. DAVID P. CURRIE, THE CONSTITUTION IN CONGRESS, 1789–1801 (1997).

Although Levy (*supra* note 10) mentions some of the material covered in this book, his work does not purport to be a history, systematic or otherwise, of the early years of the United States. He pays little attention to the main controversies of the period: the extent of federal power and, within the federal government, the extent of executive power. Instead, desirous of defending the Supreme Court against charges of judicial activism in the area of civil liberties, Levy focuses on aspects of the country's early history pertaining to the origins of judicial review and the adoption and interpretation of the Bill of Rights.

1. The Constitutional Convention: Virginians and Power

1. For Madison's nationalism at that time, *see* his notes, *Vices of the Political System of the United States,* compiled early in 1787, and the excellent accompanying editorial note in 9 MP 345–58. *See also* JACK N. RAKOVE, THE BEGINNINGS OF NATIONAL POLITICS 392–94 (1979), and WILLIAM L. MILLER, THE BUSINESS OF MAY NEXT 22–25 (1992). For a discussion of Washington's nationalism, based on his wartime army experiences, *see* GLENN A. PHELPS, GEORGE WASHINGTON AND AMERICAN CONSTITUTIONALISM 47–79 (1993).

2. 1 FR 20–22. The Articles of Confederation did not provide for, but assumed, a unicameral Congress to which, pursuant to art. 5, delegates from the separate states would be annually appointed to manage the general interests of the United States. In the Continental Congress, Madison and Samuel Adams distinguished themselves by their untiring fidelity to political activity. For them, politics was a career. RAKOVE, *supra* note 1, at 225. Madison maintained that fidelity to politics until his retirement from the presidency in 1817.

3. According to the census of 1790, certified by Thomas Jefferson, as secretary of state, Oct. 24, 1791, the combined populations of Virginia (747,610) and Kentucky (73,677) were almost twice that of the combined populations of Massachusetts (378,787) and Maine (96,540), or of Pennsylvania (434,373), the next largest states. RETURN OF THE WHOLE NUMBER OF PERSONS WITHIN THE SEVERAL DISTRICTS OF THE UNITED STATES 3 (1976). At the convention, William Paterson and David Brearley of New Jersey and Charles Cotesworth Pinckney prepared their own estimates of the population among the states, 1 FR 572–74, and SUPPLEMENT TO MAX FARRAND'S THE RECORDS OF THE FEDERAL CONVENTION OF 1787 160–62 (James H. Hutson ed., 1987) (hereinafter Hutson).

4. 1 FR 21. Washington to Francis Lewis, July 6, 1780, 19 WW 132; PHELPS, *supra* note 1, at 56–57.

5. 1 FR 21.

6. 1 *id.* at 21–22.

7. Madison to Washington, Apr. 16, 1787, 9 MP 382–83. To the same effect, *see* Madison to Jefferson, Mar. 19, 1787, 9 *id.* at 317–19, and Madison to Randolph, Apr. 8, 1787, 9 *id.* at

368–71. For a discussion of the then recent greater increases in population in the southern states on which Madison and others based their expectations for a future increase in southern "populousness," *see* Drew R. McCoy, *James Madison and Visions of American Nationality in the Confederation Period: A Regional Perspective,* in BEYOND CONFEDERATION 226–58 (Richard A. Beeman et al. eds., 1987).

8. *See infra* ch. 3 notes 18–64.

9. 1 FR 18. Did Randolph furnish Madison with a sanitized version of his speech, cleansed of the remarks McHenry reported and which Yates found objectionable? *See infra* notes 10–11.

10. 1 FR 24 (statement of Randolph) (emphasis in original). The integrity of the Yates notes has been challenged. *See* Hutson, *supra* note 3 at xxv–xxvi. Edmond C. Genêt, who published the Yates notes in 1821, changed them at least in part in preparing them for publication. It is Hutson's judgment, however, that Genêt "may have exercised a lighter editorial hand on . . . the notes for the first week of the Convention." *Id.* at xxv. This would include those for May 29, the day Randolph presented the Virginia Plan.

11. 1 FR 26 (statement of Randolph). For Washington's interest in an interstate canal system, *see* PHELPS, *supra* note 1, at 75–79.

12. 1 FR 33–34 (statements of Charles Pinckney and Randolph).

13. 1 *id.* at 53 (statements of Charles Pinckney, Rutledge and Butler) (emphasis in original).

14. *See* RAKOVE, *supra* note 1, at 144. Madison was familiar with the Franklin draft, having alluded to it in the introduction to his NOTES OF DEBATES IN THE FEDERAL CONVENTION OF 1787, 5 (1969). Franklin, Madison observed, had submitted it to Congress on July 21, 1775, and although "not copied into their Journals [it remains] on their files in his handwriting." *Id.*

15. RAKOVE, *supra* note 1, at 170. *See* ARTICLES OF CONFEDERATION art. II. Congress did not act on the Franklin draft. Indeed it was not even inserted in the journals because at the time some members were afraid that its publication might forestall reconciliation with Great Britain. Soon after, Silas Deane of Connecticut prepared another draft in which he proposed a broad grant of powers for Congress and reserved to the states matters of internal legislation and police. The state modified his proposal, however, by limiting the powers of Congress to foreign affairs, war and peace, and the regulation of the army. RICHARD B. MORRIS, THE FORGING OF THE UNION 80–83 (1987).

16. RAKOVE, *supra* note 1, at 327–28, 364–68.

17. *Id.* at 368–72.

18. 1 FR 53 (statement of Randolph).

19. *Id.* (statement of Madison).

20. For the reference to the word "grave" in Madison's original manuscript, *see* IRVING BRANT, FATHER OF THE CONSTITUTION 35 (1950); *see also* 1 FR 59–60 (statements of Sherman, Wythe, King, Madison, and Wilson according to the report by William Pierce of Georgia). As Pierce had it, Madison was the first to take the line that "it was necessary to adopt some general principles on which we should act"; but then, later in the debate, he stated his conviction that "the defining of the limits and powers of the federal Legislature . . . could not be done." *Id.* at 60. Pierce also reported Randolph as coming close to the Wythe-King position: "It would be impossible to define the powers and the length to which the federal Legislature ought to extend just at this time." *Id.*

21. Madison to Robert S. Garnett, Feb. 11, 1824, Hutson *supra* note 3, at 313. Nine years later, in 1833, Madison repeated his explanation in an undelivered letter. For the undelivered letter from Madison to John Tyler, written sometime in 1833, repeating the statements of his letter to Garnett, 3 FR 524, 526–27.

But by 1824—following southern alarm over the admission of Missouri as a slave state and the adoption of the Missouri Compromise—it had become an enormous political sin in many quarters in Virginia to have ever espoused anything other than a grant of specifically enumerated powers for the Congress of the United States and a strict construction of those powers. This was the line which Madison himself had set down during the controversy over the establishment of the Bank of the United States in 1791 and publicly maintained thereafter. By 1833, following the bitter nullification dispute precipitated by South Carolina over the protective tariff, the sin had become even more grievous. For the pressures placed on Madison in Virginia and in the South to construe the Constitution in such a way as to advance slave-owning interests during the Missouri crisis, and for southern plantation interests during the nullification crisis precipitated by South Carolina over the constitutionality of the protective tariff, *see* DREW R. MCCOY, THE LAST OF THE FATHERS 113–18, 119–31 (1989).

Lance Banning, however, has taken Madison's statements in his undelivered letter to Tyler as true. On this basis, and in opposition to the views in BRANT, *supra* note 20, RALPH KETCHAM, JAMES MADISON (1990), and CLINTON ROSSITER, THE CONSTITUTIONAL CONVENTION (1956), Banning has constructed a revisionist theory of Madison's intentions with regard to the scope of congressional power at the start of the convention. LANCE BANNING, THE SACRED FIRE OF LIBERTY 157–64 (1995).

If we wish to assess Madison's position in the Constitutional Convention in the light of his letter to Garnett and Tyler, we should remember the circumstances in which they were written. Madison was in his declining years. He would have wished to avoid the extreme unpleasantness that a more forthright statement on his part would have elicited. We should also remember that Madison had spent the best part of his life as a practicing politician, so successful as to have become president of the United States. The letters therefore were not the declarations of a prophet or self-abnegating philosopher in retreat from the world. They were explanations that, in the language of today's politicians, enabled him to get off the hook.

From our vantage point in history, we may disregard his latter-day versions of the Constitutional Convention and conclude—on the basis of his own extended posthumous report of the convention and of the other notes and documents from the convention—that Madison had indeed meant to include in the Virginia Plan a power in Congress to legislate "in all cases to which the separate States are incompetent, or in which the harmony of the United States may be interrupted by the exercise of individual Legislation."

The Banning thesis must also ignore the internal evidence from Madison's own notes of the convention and from other documents. From these, it appears that (1) Sherman and Wilson shared with Madison his initial doubts concerning the practicability of enumerating congressional powers, *supra* note 20; (2) it was the judgment of Rutledge, Charles Pinckney, and Butler of South Carolina that the Virginia proposal had intended conferring a general power on Congress, *supra* notes 12–13; (3) Madison himself, as reported in his own notes, gave the South Carolinians no assurance to the contrary, *supra* note 19; (4) Dickinson subsequently shared the South Carolina fears, *infra* note 22; (5) Randolph, as well as Madison, explicitly linked the grant to Congress of a power to achieve harmony among the states to a Congress entirely based on population, *infra* notes 40, 53; (6) before the repudiation of his scheme for a Congress entirely based on population, Madison advocated a national government in which the thirteen states, like so many counties, would be incorporated within and constitute "one entire republic, subject to one common law," *infra* note 44; and (7), most important of all, after the vote to extend equal representation to all states in the Senate, Virginia supported South Carolina's renewed objection to its own original proposal to confer a general power on Congress, and opposed the general language of the subsequent Bedford resolution on the same subject, *infra* notes 59–64.

For a restatement of the general view of Madison's nationalist position at the beginning of the Constitutional Convention, against an earlier version of Banning's revisionist theory, *see*

George W. Carey, *James Madison on Federalism: The Search for Abiding Principles*, 3 BENCHMARK, No. 1 & 2, 27–57 (1987).

22. 1 FR 47; Hutson, *supra* note 3, at 96 (emphasis in original).

23. 1 FR 53–54.

24. 1 *id.* at 162.

25. 1 *id.* at 164 (statement of Madison).

26. 1 *id.* at 168 (statement of Madison).

27. 1 *id.* at 166–67 (statement of Wilson).

28. 1 *id.* at 167 (statement of Bedford).

29. 1 *id.* at 163.

30. 1 *id.* at 176–77 (statement of Brearley). For a commentary on the large and small state controversy, *see* MILLER, *supra* note 1, at 67–76. The struggle has been characterized as one between states having claims to western lands and those without them. FORREST MCDONALD, E PLURIBUS UNUM, 164–65, 174–75 (1965).

31. 1 FR 177–78 (statement of Paterson).

32. 1 *id.* at 178 (statement of Paterson).

33. 1 *id.* at 180 (statement of Wilson).

34. For the vote on broad powers in Congress, *see* 1 *id.* at 47; on fixing the representation in both houses of Congress, *see* 1 *id.* at 192–95. For the debate and vote on the manner of electing the Senate, *see* 1 *id.* at 149–55.

35. 1 *id.* at 51–52.

36. 1 *id.* at 242–45.

37. 1 *id.* at 250–22 (statement of Paterson). On the disputes in the Continental Congress concerning the settlement of the western land claims and the ratification of the Articles of Confederation, *see* MERRILL JENSEN, THE ARTICLES OF CONFEDERATION 150–60, 188, 190–93 (1940); RAKOVE, *supra* note 1, at 155–60, 176–79, 190; and Jack N. Rakove, *Ambiguous Achievement: The Northwest Ordinance, in* THE NORTHWEST ORDINANCE 1–20 (Frederick D. Williams ed., 1989). *See also* Peter S. Onuf, *Maryland, The Small Republic in the Nation, in* RATIFYING THE CONSTITUTION 171–200 (Michael A. Gillespie & Michael Lienesch eds., 1989).

38. 1 FR 255 (statement of Randolph).

39. 1 *id.* at 256 (statement of Randolph).

40. *Id.*

41. 1 *id.* at 314, 321 (statement of Madison).

42. 1 *id.* at 313.

43. 1 *id.* at 445.

44. 1 *id.* at 446, 449 (statement of Madison) (the words "States" and "may" bracketed in original).

45. 1 *id.* at 468–69 (statement of Ellsworth).

46. 1 *id.* at 469 (statement of Ellsworth) (words bracketed in original).

47. 1 *id.* at 485, 486 (statement of Madison). But his position did not explain why the Pennsylvania delegation, which, reflecting its Quaker constituency, was generally opposed to slavery, did not join Connecticut in favoring the Ellsworth motion. (Instead, Wilson spoke out vigorously against it. 1 *id.* at 482–84.) Nor did it explain why King, speaking for the large-state Massachusetts delegation, also opposed Ellsworth. 1 *id.* at 489–90. Nor why Maryland, a slave but small state, supported him, or why Georgia, a slave state, divided. 1 *id.* at 510.

48. *Id.*

49. *Id.*

50. 1 *id.* at 509–10, 515.

51. 1 *id.* at 524.

52. 2 FR 13–14.

53. 1 FR 551 (statement of Madison).

54. 2 FR 1–2.

55. 2 *id.* at 9 (statement of Madison). In his letter to Washington of April 16, 1787, Madison had connected his proposal for granting Congress broad legislative powers with his other proposal for basing representation in both houses of Congress on population, saying that without approval of the second, the large states would object to the first: "But the consideration which particularly urges a change in the representation is that it will obviate the principal objections of the larger States to the necessary concessions of power." 9 MP 383. But he had not expected the disapproval of the first proposal. *See supra* note 7.

56. 2 FR 9.

57. 2 *id.* at 9–10 (statement of Madison) (brackets in original).

58. 2 *id.* at 1–2.

59. 2 *id.* at 17. *See supra* note 4.

60. 2 FR 17. *See also supra* note 13.

61. 2 FR 17 (statements of Butler and Gorham).

62. 2 *id.* at 21, 26 (brackets in original). For the earlier Bedford eruption, *see supra* note 28.

63. 2 FR 26 (statement of Randolph) (brackets in original).

64. 2 *id.* at 27 (statement of Bedford) (emphasis in original).

65. 2 *id.* at 106. For the differences between the needs of the upper and lower South, *see* McDONALD, *supra* note 30, at 64–66. For a different view of the mandate and the work of the Committee of Detail, *see* John C. Hueston, *Altering the Course,* 100 YALE L. J. 765–83 (1990). Hueston believes the mandate of the committee was merely to draft a constitution implementing the resolutions the convention had already approved. Thus, in his view the committee, by specifically enumerating the powers of Congress, including the incidental powers implicit in the Necessary and Proper Clause, and by scrapping the general terms of the Bedford resolution, subverted the will of the convention. *Id.* at 768–69.

66. The committee's proposed art. VII, § 4 and 6, 2 FR at 183; and art. XV, 2 *id.* at 187–88; BANNING, *supra* note 21, at 174; McDONALD, *supra* note 30, at 64–66, 177.

67. Art. IX, § 2 and 3, 2 FR 183–85; McDONALD, *supra* note 30, at 178.

68. The statement of George Bancroft, who wrote that he heard it from Madison, Hutson, *supra* note 3, at 322.

69. For a confirmation of this compromise, *see* Madison's statement, dated March 1836, 3 FR 538: "It is well known that the equality of the States in the Federal Senate was a compromise between the larger and the smaller States. . . . But it is equally true . . . that, as soon as the smaller States had secured more than a proportional share in the proposed Government, they became favourable to augmentations of its powers, and that, under the administration of the Government, they have generally, in contests between it and the State governments, leaned to the former."

70. 2 FR 137, 142–44.

71. The amendment appears in the handwriting of Rutledge, the committee chairman. 2 *id.* at 137, 144.

72. 2 *id.* at 163, 167–68 (emphasis added).

73. Art. VII, § 1, 2 *id.* at 177, 181–82. The final version of the committee's proposal included the words bracketed in the Wilson version. *See supra* note 70 and accompanying text.

74. Hutson, *supra* note 3, at 231.

75. *See infra* notes 93–96.

76. *See infra* note 86.

77. Both Mason and Randolph were also deeply interested in a further recommendation of

the Committee of Detail in art. IV, § 5, which they considered as essential to a republican form of government. That recommendation would have prohibited the Senate from originating or amending money bills, 2 FR 163–64.

78. 2 *id.* at 451–52 (statement of Madison).

79. 2 *id.* at 324–25. Charles Pinckney, joining Madison, also offered an additional list of powers for the Committee of Detail's consideration. *See infra* note 80. Many years later, Madison, in defending the spending power against a broad construction, posed the question: "Why, on that supposition, so much critical labor was employed in enumerating the particular powers; and in defining and limiting their extent?" Madison to Andrew Stevenson, Nov. 27, 1830, 3 FR 483, 486. The answer lies in the fact that it was southerners, Madison and Pinckney, not northerners, who employed the "critical labor." It was in southern interest to lay the groundwork for a post-convention argument that the Necessary and Proper Clause was not intended to confer broad powers of legislation on Congress. For a more complete discussion of Madison's views on the spending power as expressed in his letter to Stevenson, *see infra* ch. 5 at notes 30, 32–34.

80. 2 *id.* at 325–26, 447. The convention also referred to committee Gerry's motion for the addition of provisions regarding the grant of letters of marque and reprisal, and for "public Securities." The first part of his motion repeated a part of Pinckney's. 2 *id.* at 326, 328.

On the same day, the convention unanimously approved Ghorum's motion to amend the report of the Committee of Detail by adding the phrase, "and support," to its proposal for a congressional power "[t]o raise armies." 2 *id.* at 329. RAOUL BERGER, *in* FEDERALISM: THE FOUNDERS' DESIGN 92 (1987) relies on Ghorum's motion to prove his Madisonian thesis: that the inclusion of the many specifically enumerated powers revealed the founders' design that the Necessary and Proper Clause contemplated only the use of means appropriate to the achievement of an enumerated end.

The more likely explanation of the motion is that after making their report, Ghorum and the other members of the Committee of Detail had agreed among themselves upon a rewording of the "Army" Clause. Randolph, the most anxious of that committee regarding the scope of the Necessary and Proper Clause, would probably have been the most willing to agree to the change—to preserve the appearance of a Congress constitutionally limited to specifically enumerated powers. If the convention had approved the "Army" Clause as originally reported, it would have been impossible in practice, once Congress had raised an army, to deny the power to support it. Yet Berger seems to suggest that, if the convention had not made the amendment and thereafter Randolph had been in Congress, he would have denied that it had the power to support the army it had raised.

81. 2 FR 344–45.

82. 2 *id.* at 366, 367.

83. 2 *id.* at 374–75, 473.

84. 2 *id.* at 396, 414–17, 445–46, 449–53.

85. 2 *id.* at 453–54.

86. For the opposition to the provision for the continuation of the slave trade, *see* 2 *id.* at 370 (statement of Mason), and at 374 (statement of Randolph); for the objection to the elimination of the two-thirds requirement for commercial legislation, *see* 2 *id.* at 452–53 (statement of Randolph), and 451, 479 (statements of Mason); for the discussion concerning the importance to Virginia of the retention of the two-thirds requirement, *see also supra* notes 77–78. McDonald points out that the humanitarian position of Mason and Randolph coincided with the fact that Virginia and the upper South already had too many slaves. *See* MCDONALD, *supra* note 30, at 64–66.

87. 2 FR 483, 486, 505–6.

88. 2 *id.* at 493. Art. 8, § 1 of the Articles of Confederation provided in part: "All charges

of war and all other expences, that shall be incurred for the common defence or general welfare, and allowed by the United States, in Congress assembled, shall be defrayed out of a common treasury." For the resolution of the Committee of Detail, *see supra* note 82.

89. 2 FR 615.

90. *Id.*

91. 2 *id.* at 616.

92. *Id.* For Washington's interest in the construction of interstate canals, *see supra* note 11; for his interest in the establishment of a national university, *see* PHELPS, *supra* note 1, at 140, 192.

93. Madison to Van Buren, May 13, 1828, 3 FR 477.

94. Hutson, *supra* note 3, at 249.

95. 2 FR 563–64 (statement of Randolph).

96. 2 *id.* at 631 (statement of Randolph).

97. 2 *id.* at 632 (statement of Mason). *See infra* ch. 2 at notes 2–6. For a discussion of the other objections of both Randolph and Mason to the Constitution, *see* BANNING, *supra* note 21, at 175–76.

98. 2 FR 632, 633 (statement of Gerry).

99. 2 *id.* at 631–33 (statements of Randolph, Mason, and Gerry).

100. For the use of this sense of Madison's nationalism, *see generally* BANNING, *supra* note 21.

101. IRVING BRANT, JAMES MADISON: THE NATIONALIST, 358–59, 361–62 (1948).

102. U.S. CONST. art. III, § 2, cl. 1: "The judicial Power shall extend to . . . Controversies . . . between Citizens of different States . . . and between a State, or the Citizens thereof, and foreign States, Citizens or Subjects."

103. U.S. CONST. art. I, § 10, cl. 1: "No State shall . . . coin Money; emit Bills of Credit; . . . pass any . . . Law impairing the Obligation of Contracts."

104. Madison expressed both these fears in the *Federalist.* The Union and the Constitution, he first wrote, were essential to the security of the American people against foreign dangers, against the internal contentions and war among the states, and the build-up of military establishments within the states so dangerous to the liberties of the people. FEDERALIST No. 45, 308–09 (James Madison).

The danger in frequent constitutional conventions, and by implication in a second constitutional convention, he wrote, lay in that the same influence over the people which had led certain persons to gain an ascendancy in the state legislatures would lead to their gaining a predominance in the conventions. "The *passions* not *the reason,* of the public, would sit in judgment." FEDERALIST No. 49, 338, 342–43 (James Madison) (emphasis in original).

On the dangers of war to Virginia and the South, *see also* BANNING, *supra* note 21, at 179–80. On Washington's positive view of the Constitution as adopted, *see* PHELPS, *supra* note 1, at 116–20.

105. Madison to Washington, Apr. 16, 1787, 9 MP 382, 385.

106. 1 FR 21, 77.

107. On Madison's decision, following the Great Compromise, to counter the power of the small-state dominated Senate by increasing the powers of the presidency, *see* KETCHAM, *supra* note 21, at 214–17.

108. 2 FR 23, 33–36. To counter charges of monarchist tendencies for his support of McClurg's motion, Madison appended to his report a series of notes. The first explained: "The probable object of this motion was merely to enforce the argument against the re-eligibility of the Executive Magistrate, by holding out a tenure during good behaviour as the alternative for keeping him independent of the Legislature." 2 *id.* at 33.

The second note explained that his speech supporting the motion "was meant to aid in parrying the animadversions likely to fall on the motion of Dr. McClurg, for whom J. M. had a particular regard." 2 *id.* at 34. The third note, commenting on the vote of four states, including that of Virginia, in favor of the motion, against that of six states opposing, stated: "This vote is not to be considered as any certain index of opinion, as a number in the affirmative probably had it chiefly in view to alarm those attached to a dependence of the Executive on the Legislature, & thereby facilitate some final arrangement of a contrary tendency. [The avowed friends of an Executive, 'during good behaviour' were not more than three or four nor is it certain they would finally have adhered to such a tenure.]" 2 *id.* at 36 (brackets in original). If all that Madison said were true, it is hard to see why Mason, his fellow delegate from Virginia, became so exercised in his opposition to the motion. 2 *id.* at 35.

109. 2 *id.* at 80–83.

110. 2 *id.* at 31.

111. 2 *id.* at 587.

112. 2 *id.* at 43, 81, 121. For Wythe's departure from the convention on June 5, *see* Madison to Jefferson, June 6, 1787, 10 MP 28–29. For McClurg's departure some time after July 20th, *see* 10 *id.* at 135, n.1. For Randolph's absence on the key vote on July 26, *see* 2 FR 121. Six years later, exasperated at Randolph's habitual shifts of position during Cabinet discussions in the Washington administration, Jefferson said of Randolph: "He is the poorest Chameleon I ever saw having no colour of his own, and reflecting that nearest him. When he is with me he is a whig, when with H. he is a tory, when with the P. he is what he thinks will please him." Jefferson to Madison, Aug. 11, 1793, 26 JP 651, 652.

113. 2 FR 35 (statements of Mason and Madison).

114. 2 *id.* at 80–81 (statement of Madison).

115. Art. X, § 1, 2 *id.* at 185; art. IX, § 1, 2 *id.* at 183.

116. 2 *id.* at 392 (statement of Madison), and 394.

117. 2 *id.* at 401–4.

118. 2 *id.* at 493–95. During the North Carolina ratifying convention, William Davie explained the reason for the ultimate resolution of the appointments clause: "In other countries, the executive or chief magistrate, alone, nominates and appoints officers. The small states would not agree that the House of Representatives should have a voice in the appointment to offices; and the extreme jealousy of all the states would not give it to the President alone." 4 ED 122 (speech of July 28, 1788).

119. 2 FR 540.

120. 2 *id.* at 540–41, 547–49. For the significance of Gerry's remarks concerning the fisheries and the disposition of territory, *see* Jack N. Rakove, *Solving a Constitutional Puzzle: The Treatymaking Clause as a Case Study,* in Perspectives in Am. Hist., New Series, I 233, 270–80 (1984).

121. Madison supported a motion for a presidential veto of legislation, subject to an overriding three-fourths vote of both branches of Congress. 2 FR 298. He was successful at first, 2 *id.* at 301; but he lost in one of the convention's last sessions when, to satisfy an objection by Randolph, and perhaps to secure his and Mason's support for the Constitution, the delegates decided in favor of a two-thirds override. Significantly, Washington joined with Madison against Randolph and Mason on the motion. 2 *id.* at 587.

2. The Politics and Promises of Ratification

1. Federalist No. 33, at 203, 204 (Alexander Hamilton).

2. George Washington to James Madison, Oct. 10, 1797, 8 DHRC 49.

3. Mason to Washington, Oct. 7, 1787, 8 *id.* at 43–46.

4. *See* editorial note, 8 *id.* at 40–41.

5. *See* editorial note, 14 DHRC 147–48.

6. *See supra* note 3, at 45.

7. 13 DHRC 402 (emphasis in original).

8. 13 *id.* at 416–17.

9. Gerry to the Massachusetts General Court, published Nov. 3, 1788, 13 *id.* at 548.

10. 14 DHRC 18–54. The attribution of *Letters* to Lee has recently been effectively challenged. *See* editorial note, 14 *id.* at 14–18. Instead, it has been suggested, Gerry was the author. 4 *id.* at 94, 95.

11. 14 *id.* at 44–45.

12. 2 DHRC 395 (Robert Whitewill's speech in the Pennsylvania ratifying convention, Nov. 28, 1787) and 410 (John Smilie's speech in the Pennsylvania ratifying convention, Nov. 28, 1787).

13. 2 *id.* at 482 (Wilson's speech in the Pennsylvania ratifying convention, Dec. 4, 1787).

14. 2 *id.* at 496 (Wilson's speech in the Pennsylvania ratifying convention, Dec. 4, 1787). To the same effect, *see also* Wilson's speech of Dec. 1, 1787 in the Pennsylvania ratifying convention, 2 *id.* at 454.

15. 2 *id.* at 599. For the provision in the Articles of Confederation, *see infra* at n. 62. For a similar proposal which Henry and Mason offered in the Virginia ratifying convention, based on the Articles, *see infra* at note 88.

16. 2 DHRC 618–39.

17. *See supra* notes l, 13–14.

18. FEDERALIST No. 33, at 203, 204 (Alexander Hamilton).

19. *Id.* at 205.

20. 15 DHRC 123, 133, 134.

21. FEDERALIST No. 44, at 299, 303–4 (James Madison) (emphasis in original).

22. *Id.* at 304–5. Garry Wills reads Madison's explication as a broad construction of the Necessary and Proper Clause, one essentially at odds with that of Hamilton in FEDERALIST No. 33, which he correctly reads as a strict construction. *See* GARRY WILLS, *in* EXPLAINING AMERICA 46–50, 76 (1981).

But, as I have attempted to show, Madison and Hamilton as Publius were in agreement. In fact, if they had not agreed on the very important question of the true construction to be given the Necessary and Proper Clause, opponents of ratification, especially in the Virginia convention, would have made a great point of it, and an even greater point of the supposed advocacy by Publius in FEDERALIST, No. 44, of a broad reading of the clause.

See also FEDERALIST No. 52, at 353, 355–59, where Madison assured his readers that the powers of Congress were to be only a part of those entrusted to the British Parliament, and that in consequence the duration of the term in the House of Representatives might be safely limited to two years instead of, as in the case of the representatives in many state legislatures, one year. On the same basis, he later argued that the membership of the House of Representatives need not be as numerous as would have been the case had their powers been unlimited. FEDERALIST No. 55, at 372, 374–75 (James Madison).

23. FEDERALIST No. 39, at 250, 256 (James Madison).

24. FEDERALIST No. 52, at 353, 358 (James Madison).

25. FEDERALIST No. 55, at 372, 374 (James Madison).

26. FEDERALIST No. 25, at 158, 163 (Alexander Hamilton). The reference to Pennsylvania concerned the resistance of Connecticut settlers in the Wyoming Valley, Pennsylvania to the jurisdiction of the state of Pennsylvania. The settlers claimed allegiance to the state of Connecticut. The reference to Massachusetts concerned Shays' Rebellion. *Id.* at 162.

27. *Id.* at 163.

28. FEDERALIST No. 38, at 239, 248 (James Madison). The reference was to the adoption of the Northwest Ordinance in July 1787 and its implementation the following October, CONSTITUTIONAL DOCUMENTS AND RECORDS 1776–1787, 60–63, 168–74; and 33 JOURNALS OF THE CONTINENTAL CONGRESS, 1774–1789, 610 (Worthington C. Ford ed. 1904–1937). *See also* 15 DHRC 360 n. 7.

29. FEDERALIST No. 38, at 239, 248–49 (James Madison).

30. FEDERALIST No. 43, at 288, 290 (James Madison).

31. John M. Murrin, *The Great Inversion, or Court versus Country: A Comparison of the Revolution Settlements in England (1688) and America (1776–1816), in* THREE BRITISH REVOLUTIONS: 1641, 1688, 1776, 371–404 (J. G. A. Pocock ed., 1980).

32. J. G. A. Pocock, THE MACHIAVELLIAN MOMENT 423–88 (1975).

33. 1 FR 66 (Randolph).

34. 2 FR 35 (Mason).

35. 2 *id.* at 224 (Mason), 278 (Randolph).

36. 2 *id.* at 616 (Mason), 632–33 (Gerry).

37. 2 *id.* at 412–13 (Mason).

38. 1 FR 214–15, 569 (Gerry).

39. 1 *id.* at 284 (Mason), 285–86 (Gerry), 290 (Randolph).

40. 2 FR 297 (Mason), 319, 548 (Gerry).

41. 2 *id.* at 271–72 (Mason).

42. 8 DHRC 43–46 (Mason).

43. 15 DHRC 123, 133–34 (Randolph).

44. 13 DHRC 548 (Gerry).

45. FEDERALIST No. 69, at 462, 465, 468 (Alexander Hamilton).

46. U.S. CONST. art. VII, cl. 1. The delegates to the Constitutional Convention had also resolved that the proposed Constitution would be sent to the Continental Congress, with a request that it be referred to the state legislatures which in each state would submit it to a convention of delegates expressly chosen by the people for their approval. 2 FR 189, 478–79, 559–63.

47. ROBERT A. RUTLAND, THE ORDEAL OF THE CONSTITUTION 31–32 (1983).

48. *Id.* at 55–62, 84–88.

49. *Id.* at 51–58, 62, 82, 87. *See also* essays on ratification in Delaware, Pennsylvania, New Jersey, Georgia, and Connecticut by Gaspare J. Saladino, George G. Graham, Jr., Sara M. Shumer, Edward J. Cashin, and Donald S. Lutz, respectively, *in* RATIFYING THE CONSTITUTION 29–137 (Michael A. Gillespie & Michael Lienesch eds., 1988); and essays on ratification in Delaware, Pennsylvania, New Jersey, Georgia, and Connecticut by Harold Hancock, Paul Doutrich, Mary R. Murrin, Albert B. Saye, and Christopher Collier, respectively, *in* THE CONSTITUTION AND THE STATES 21–112 (Patrick T. Conley & John P. Kaminski eds., 1988); and MERRILL JENSEN, THE NEW NATION 274–81 (1950).

On Connecticut's part in the compromise over congressional representation, *see also* ch. 1 *supra* notes 45–51. For a good summary of that state's role in securing agreement in the convention for approval of a power to regulate commerce by a simple majority rather than by a two-thirds requirement in exchange for an agreement to forbid federal and state taxation of exports, and to permit the importation of slaves without restrictions until 1808, *see* CHARLES WARREN, THE MAKING OF THE CONSTITUTION 567–88 (1928).

50. RUTLAND, *supra* note 47, at 66–82, 89–114, 150–59, 162–69. *See also* essays on ratification in Massachusetts, Maryland, and South Carolina by Michael A. Gillespie, Peter S. Onuf, and Robert M. Weir, respectively, *in* Gillespie & Lienesch, *supra* note 49, at 138–234; and essays on ratification in Massachusetts, Maryland, and South Carolina by John J. Fox,

Gregory Stiverson, and Jerome J. Nadelhaft, respectively, *in* Conley & Kaminski, *supra* note 49, at 113–79. For the reason for the opposition of Maine settlers to ratification, *see* Madison to Washington, Jan. 20, 1788, 10 MP 399.

51. RUTLAND, *supra* note 47, at 212–13. *See also* essays on ratification in New Hampshire by Jean Yarbrough, *in* Gillespie & Lienesch, *supra* note 49, at 235–58; and by Jere Daniell, *in* Conley & Kaminski, *supra* note 49, at 181–200.

52. RUTLAND, *supra* note 47, at 124–25, 171–80, 200–203, 269–70; *see also* essays on ratification in Virginia, New York, North Carolina, and Rhode Island by Lance Banning, Cecil L. Eubanks, Michael Lienesch, and John P. Kaminski, respectively, *in* Gillespie & Lienesch, *supra* note 49, at 261–390; and essays on ratification in Virginia, New York, North Carolina, and Rhode Island by Alan V. Briceland, John P. Kaminski, Alan D. Watson, and Patrick T. Conley, respectively, *in* Conley & Kaminski, *supra* note 49, at 201–94.

53. RUTLAND, *supra* note 47, at 171–80.

54. *Id.* at 171–80, 226–27, 233.

55. U.S. CONST. art. I, § 8, cl. 1. For the opposition of state officeholders to the Constitution generally, *see* FEDERALIST Nos. 1, 3, 4 (Alexander Hamilton).

56. U.S. CONST. art. I, § 10, cl. 2 provides: "No State shall, without the Consent of the Congress, lay any Imposts or Duties on Imports or Exports, except what may be absolutely necessary for executing it's inspection Laws: and the net Produce of all Duties and Imposts, laid by any State on Imports or Exports, shall be for the Use of the Treasury of the United States; and all such Laws shall be subject to the Revision and Controul of the Congress."

57. U.S. CONST. art. I, § 8, cl. 3.

58. Congress's control of the currency emanates from the Coinage Clause. U.S. CONST. art.I, § 8, cl. 5, which provides: "To coin Money, regulate the Value thereof, and of foreign Coin, and fix the Standard of Weights and Measures."

59. U.S. CONST. art. I, § 10, cl. 1 forbids the states to "coin Money; emit Bills of Credit; [or] make any Thing but gold and silver Coin a Tender in Payment of Debts."

60. "No state shall . . . pass any . . . Law impairing the Obligation of Contracts." *Id.*

61. ARTICLES OF CONFEDERATION art. 5, para. 1, 2.

62. *Id.,* art. 2.

63. *Id.,* art. 9, para. 5.

64. U.S. CONST. art. I, § 2, cl. 1, 4.

65. U.S. CONST. art. I, § 3, cl. 1.

66. Under the terms of U.S. CONST. art. II, § 1, cl. 2, the president would be chosen by electors who shall be appointed "in such Manner as the [state] Legislature . . . may direct."

67. For the presidential appointment, "by and with the Advice and Consent of the Senate," of judges of the Supreme Court and of all other "Officers of the United States, whose Appointments are not herein otherwise provided for, and which shall be established by Law," *see* U.S. CONST. art. II, § 2, cl. 2. For the life tenure of the judges of the Supreme Court and of the inferior courts, *see id.,* art. III, § 1.

68. 9 DHRC 1035, 1046–47 (Henry's speech in the Virginia ratifying convention, June 7, 1788).

69. 9 *id.* at 1102 (Randolph's speech in the Virginia ratifying convention, June 10, 1788).

70. 9 *id.* at 1112 (Monroe's speech in the Virginia ratifying convention, June 10, 1788).

71. 9 *id.* at 1135 (Nicholas's speech in the Virginia ratifying convention, June 10, 1788) (emphasis in original).

72. U.S. CONST. art. I, § 8, cl. 17.

73. 10 DHRC 1321–22 (Henry's speech in the Virginia ratifying convention, June 14, 1788).

74. 10 *id.* at 1323 (Madison's speech in the Virginia ratifying convention, June 14, 1788).

75. *Id.*

76. 10 *id.* at 1326 (Mason's speech in the Virginia ratifying convention, June 14, 1788).

77. *See* his public letter of objections to the proposed constitution, *supra* note 5.

78. *See infra* ch. 9 notes 135–38, and ch. 10 note 26.

79. 10 DHRC 1326 (Mason's speech in the Virginia ratifying convention, June 14, 1788).

80. 10 *id.* at 1326, 1327 (Nicholas's speech in the Virginia ratifying convention, June 14, 1788).

81. *See supra* note 69.

82. 10 DHRC 1347–53 (Randolph's speech in the Virginia ratifying convention, June 15, 1788).

83. 10 *id.* at 1353 (Randolph's speech in the Virginia ratifying convention, June 15, 1788).

84. 10 *id.* at 1354 (Randolph's speech in the Virginia ratifying convention, June 15, 1788).

85. 10 *id.* at 1402 (Mason-Madison colloquy in the Virginia ratifying convention, June 18, 1788).

86. Earlier in the convention, as part of a general criticism of the Constitution, Mason had made the statement that the Constitution would have adverse effects on slavery. By permitting, under art. I, § 9, cl. 1, the importation of more slaves until the year 1808, he had said, it countenanced the growth of the slave population, which had already reached dangerous proportions. At the same time, he had pointed out, the Constitution had failed to include a provision protecting the slave owner's interest in his property. 9 DHRC 1161 (Mason's speech in the Virginia ratifying convention, June 11, 1788).

87. 10 DHRC 1338, 1341, 1342 (Mason's and Henry's speeches in the Virginia ratifying convention, June 17, 1788). Nicholas at first attempted to dismiss these charges by pointing to the requirements of the U.S. Const. art. I, § 2, cl. 3, whereunder direct taxes had to be apportioned among the states, according to their respective numbers. Such a tax would constitute a direct poll tax, he said, and would never be passed because the tax would lie just as hard on the northern states, and two-fifths of the slaves would be exempt. 10 DHRC 1342 (Nicholas's speech in the Virginia ratifying convention, June 17, 1788). But when Mason pointed out that Congress could achieve its object by laying its tax on one kind of property, namely slaves, 10 *id.* at 1343–44 (Mason's speech in the Virginia ratifying convention, June 17, 1788), Madison relied on the consideration that the imposition of such a tax was unlikely. 10 *id.* at 1343 (Madison's speech in the Virginia ratifying convention, June 17, 1788). The census of 1790 revealed that New York had 21,324 slaves, New Jersey, 11,423, and Connecticut, 2,764. 10 *id.* at 1369 n.3.

88. 9 DHRC 819, 821 (text of Henry's proposed amendments, offered in the Virginia ratifying convention, June 24, 1788), and 10 DHRC 1476–79 (Henry's speech in the Virginia ratifying convention, June 24, 1788). *See also supra* notes 15, 62.

89. 10 DHRC 1481, 1484 (Randolph's speech in the Virginia ratifying convention, June 24, 1788), and 10 *id.* at 1498, 1503 (Madison's speech in the Virginia ratifying convention, June 24, 1788).

90. 10 *id.* at 1481, 1485 (Randolph's speech in the Virginia ratifying convention, June 24, 1788).

91. 10 *id.* at 1498, 1502 (Madison's speech in the Virginia ratifying convention, June 24, 1788).

92. 10 *id.* at 1504–6 (Henry's speech in the Virginia ratifying convention, June 24, 1788). For the emotional impact of Henry's speech, *see* the comments of William Wirt and Spencer Roane, 10 *id.* at 1511–12.

93. 10 *id.* at 1537–42.

94. James Monroe to Thomas Jefferson, July 12, 1788: "[B]e assured his [Washington's] influence carried this government." 10 *id.* at 1704, 1705.

95. *See supra* ch. 1 notes 74–75.
96. 10 DHRC 1541, 1553.
97. *See infra* ch. 3 notes 67–68.
98. RUTLAND, *supra* note 47, at 257–65; 271–78, 303–4.
99. *Id.* at 302–3.
100. 1 ANNALS 981.

3. Virginia Interests: Madison's Shifting Canons

1. ROBERT A. RUTLAND, THE ORDEAL OF THE CONSTITUTION 293–94 (1983); and ROBERT D. MEADE, PATRICK HENRY: PRACTICAL REVOLUTIONARY 380–86 (1969); Kenneth R. Bowling, *"A Tub to the Whale": The Founding Fathers and Adoption of the Federal Bill of Rights,* 8 JER 223, 231 (1988).

2. *See* editorial note on Madison's election to the First Congress, 11 MP 301–4.

3. Federalists Henry Lee and John Marshall opposed Monroe's candidacy in the Virginia legislature, but with the enthusiastic endorsement of that inveterate opponent of the Constitution, George Mason, and of Thomas Jefferson, whose protégé he was, he was elected. Presumably, Jefferson, then serving as secretary of state in Washington's administration, was at that time a federalist. Interestingly, Monroe did not receive Henry's endorsement, perhaps because Henry did not like Monroe's close relationship with Jefferson. *See* HARRY AMMON, JAMES MONROE: THE QUEST FOR NATIONAL IDENTITY 81–82 (1971).

4. RUTLAND, *supra* note 1, at 262–66, 283–88.

5. *Id.* at 294, 298.

6. Madison's motion, offered on May 4, was readily adopted over Bland's objection. The following day, Madison with the support of Elias Boudinot of New Jersey foiled Bland's attempt to have the House consider Virginia's petition for the call of a second constitutional convention. The petition contemplated that such a convention rather than Congress would be the appropriate body to consider constitutional amendments. *See supra* note 4. Boudinot and Madison opposed Bland's motion, arguing that until a total of two-thirds of the states had applied for the call, the House could only accept the petition for filing. Their view prevailed. 10 DHFFC 429–32; *see also* Bowling, *supra* note 1, at 234.

7. 6 DHFFC 1610–16. For a different view of the debates in the first session of the First Congress, *see* Kent Greenfield, *Original Penumbras: Constitutional Interpretation in the First Year of Congress,* 26 CONN. L. REV. 79 (1993). His work discusses the different interpretive methodologies the members of the House employed in construing the Constitution. *Id.* at 40–41.

8. 10 DHFFC 270–71 (statement of Rep. Madison).

9. 9 *id.* at 271–75.

10. 6 DHFFC 1610–13.

11. 9 DHFFC 22–23. Proceedings in the Senate were not conducted in public until the second session of the Third Congress. 1 ANNALS 22–23. Through the diary of William Maclay, which makes up a substantial part of 9 DHFFC, we are able to have some idea of what transpired in the Senate in the First Congress. Unfortunately, from our point of view, Maclay did not serve in the Senate after that. When, pursuant to the mandate in art. I, § 3, cl. 2 of the Constitution, the senators drew lots to determine their initial term of service, it fell out that Maclay was among those whose term expired at the end of the First Congress. 1 ANNALS 37. He was not reelected.

12. 6 DHFFC 1611.

13. 10 DHFFC 481–82 (statement of Rep. Gerry). For Gerry's stated opposition to ratification of the Constitution on the ground, inter alia, of the indefinite nature of the Necessary and Proper Clause, *see supra* ch. 2 note 9.

14. 10 DHFFC 482 (statement of Rep. Bland).

15. *See supra* ch. 1 notes 62–63.

16. *See supra* notes 4–5, and ch. 2 note 93.

17. 10 DHFFC 484–88 (statements of Reps. Laurance, Sherman, and Boudinot). For the provisions of controversial § 3, *see* Act of June 1, 1789, 1 Stat. 23–24.

18. 10 DHFFC 727, 729–30, 734–36; 11 DHFFC 845–47, 895–904.

19. For the many services Madison performed for Washington during the first session of the First Congress, *see* editorial note on Madison's relation to Washington during the first session of the First Congress, in 12 MP 120–21. Since during that period the executive and judicial branches had not yet been organized, Congress for all practical purposes constituted the government. Most of the legislation originated in the House, where Madison was considered the leader. *See* editorial note on Madison's role in the first session of the First Congress. 12 *id.* at 52–53. Madison's action on behalf of the president was also consistent with his advocacy in the *Federalist* of an energetic executive: "Energy in Government is essential to that security against external and internal danger, and to that prompt and salutary execution of the laws, which enter into the very definition of good Government." Federalist No. 37, at 231, 233 (James Madison). *Cf.* these remarks with those of Hamilton in Federalist No. 70, at 471: "Energy in the executive is a leading character in the definition of good government."

That Washington himself wanted the removal power is evident from his concern for centralization of administrative responsibility, his insistence on control of his administrators' actions, and his requirement that his subordinates carry out the policies of his administration and retain a personal loyalty to him. Glenn A. Phelps, George Washington and American Constitutionalism 145–49 (1993).

20. 11 DHFFC 911–15 (statement of Rep. Jackson).

21. 11 *id.* at 915–16 (statement of Rep. Page).

22. 9 DHFFC 109–15. Suspicions of an attempt to establish a monarchy and an aristocracy had been aroused earlier in the session when Vice-President Adams led a movement in the Senate to confer a title of address upon the president. At one point, over Senator Maclay's strenuous objection, a Senate committee reported in favor of the title "His Highness the President of the United States of America and Protector of their Liberties." But when the House refused to agree, the matter was dropped. For a summary of the controversy, *see* Elkins & McKitrick 46–48.

23. 10 DHFFC 727, 732 (statements of Rep. Smith), and 729 (statement of Rep. Jackson). There were two representatives named William Smith in the First Congress. All references to William Smith in this book are to the South Carolina congressman.

24. 10 *id.* at 727, 729–30, 734–35 (statements of Rep. Madison); 728 (statement of Rep. Vining); 730–31 (statement of Rep. Boudinot); 11 DHFFC at 844–45 (statement of Rep. Sedgwick).

25. 11 *id.* at 860 (statement of Rep. White). Roger Sherman later agreed with White, contending that the president could only remove the secretary of foreign affairs without the consent of the Senate on the supposition that the president himself was the departmental head and the secretary an "inferior officer." He quickly added, "This reasoning however was not to be admitted." 11 *id.* at 892.

26. 11 *id.* at 860, 861 (statement of Rep. Smith); Federalist No. 77, at 515–16 (Alexander Hamilton).

27. 11 DHFFC 845–47 (statement of Rep. Madison). *See also* other versions of this speech, 11 *id.* at 854–55; 867–69.

28. *Id.*

29. 11 *id.* at 878 (statement of Rep. Gerry).

30. 11 *id.* at 884–85 (statement of Rep. Livermore).

31. *See infra* ch. 6 notes 18–19.

32. 11 DHFFC at 850–51 (statement of Rep. Ames). There had been an alternate suggestion. In response to Madison's argument that senatorial participation in the removal decision would undermine executive responsibility, Sherman, who supported White's position, said Congress could empower the president to suspend executive officers for incompetence without senatorial approval. 11 *id.* at 916, 917–18.

Michael Stone of Maryland, who also supported White, suggested as well that the president might have the power to suspend an executive officer for incompetence, but only while the Senate was not in session. 11 *id.* at 893, 895. The majority of the House, however, did not regard either suggestion as realistically addressing the question of official incompetence.

33. 11 *id.* at 850, 851 (statement of Rep. Ames).

34. 10 DHFFC 729–30 (statements of Rep. Madison).

35. 11 DHFFC 845 (statement of Rep. Madison); see also the versions of this speech, 11 *id.* at 854, 866.

36. 11 *id.* at 847 (statement of Rep. Madison); *see also* other versions of this speech, 11 *id.* at 855, 866; 11 *id.* at 849 (statement of Rep. Smith).

37. 11 *id.* at 879, 882 (statement of Rep. Ames).

38. 11 *id.* at 886 (statement of Rep. Hartley). For the earlier use of the Necessary and Proper Clause during the debate over the power of Congress to impose a requirement on state officials to take the oath Congress prescribed for federal officials, *see supra* note 17.

39. 11 DHFFC 886, 888 (statement of Rep. Laurance).

40. 11 *id.* at 895–900 (statement of Rep. Madison).

41. 11 *id.* at 900 (statement of Rep. Madison). *See also* 11 *id.* at 927.

42. *Id.*

43. *See supra* note 8.

44. 11 DHFFC 927, 929–30 (statement of Rep. Gerry); *see also* 11 *id.* at 900, 901–2.

45. 11 *id.* at 934, 937 (statement of Rep. Smith).

46. 11 *id.* at 937, 939 (statement of Rep. Vining).

47. 11 *id.* at 939–45 (statement of Rep. White); *see also* 11 *id.* at 951–54. For Virginia's preparation of an amendment to limit indefinite federal powers, *see supra* ch. 2 note 96. In response to Madison, White also denied that the removal power could be considered within or incidental to the general nature of executive power, because, as Gerry had stated earlier, *see supra* note 29, such a power was contrary to American precedent.

48. 11 DHFFC 978, 979 (statement of Rep. Ames).

49. 11 *id.* at 982–83 (statement of Rep. Ames).

50. 11 *id.* at 986–87 (statement of Rep. Madison).

51. FEDERALIST No. 25, at 158, 163 (Alexander Hamilton). *See supra* ch. 2 notes 26–27.

52. FEDERALIST No. 38, at 239, 248–49 (James Madison). *See supra* ch. 2 notes 28–29.

53. 11 DHFFC 1024.

54. 11 *id.* at 985, 986 (statement of Rep. Smith).

55. 11 *id.* at 1028.

56. 11 *id.* at 1028 (statement of Rep. Benson); 1029 (statement of Rep. Madison).

57. 11 *id.* at 1029, 1030 (statements of Rep. Sedgwick); 3 DHFFC 92.

58. 11 DHFFC 1030, 1031–32 (statements of Reps. Benson and Madison).

59. 11 *id.* at 1033–36; 3 DHFFC 93.

60. 1 DHFFC 86; 9 DHFFC 109–19.

61. For the provisions of controversial § 2, *see* Act of July 27, 1789, 1 STAT. 28, 29. From this account, it is evident that Chief Justice Taft accepted the Madisonian version of the House voting when in his opinion for the Court in *Myers v. United States,* 272 U.S. 52, 114 (1926),

he wrote "that the exact question which the House voted upon [during its consideration of a bill to establish the Department of Foreign Affairs] was whether it should recognize and declare the power of the President under the Constitution to remove the Secretary of Foreign Affairs without the advice and consent of the Senate."

Chief Justice Taft also wrote "that the vote was, and was intended to be, a legislative declaration that the power to remove officers appointed by the President and Senate vested in the President alone." *Id.*

But both statements concealed the fact that by their votes the Sedgwick-Hartley-Laurance bloc intended to confer the sole power of removal on the president by legislation, because they did not think he had the power under the Constitution; and that they thought that the end result of the Benson-Madison maneuvers would be that Congress had not conferred the power.

The holding in *Myers* was that a statute providing that postmasters of the first three classes, whom the president had appointed for a term of four years with the advice and consent of the Senate, might be removed by him only with the advice and consent of the Senate, was unconstitutional. *Id.* at 176.

The majority opinion cited with approval the statements of Madison and his associates, *id.* at 115–32; but in doing so, it included those of Hartley, Laurance, and Sedgwick, *id.* at 123, 132. This confusion enabled a majority on the Court to ascribe to a majority in the First Congress positions, in statements as well as in vote, that it did not possess. This mistake was especially crucial because of the respect the Court paid to the judgment of the First Congress insofar as its members "numbered among its leaders those who had been members of the Convention." *Id.* at 136.

But if the Taft opinion did not truly follow the actions or intentions of the First Congress, in holding that under the Constitution the president alone has the power to remove an officer whom he appoints, regardless of a contrary congressional provision, it did follow to a substantial extent the thesis Madison set forth: That the president should have the sole power of removing all levels of executive officers: high, middle, and low. 11 DHFFC 921, 925.

Because of a suggestion in the Taft opinion that the Court would extend its reasoning even to uphold a presidential removal of an inferior officer performing quasi-legislative or quasi-judicial duties in an administrative agency (*Myers,* 272 U.S. at 135), Edward S. Corwin subjected the opinion to a lengthy criticism in an essay, *The President's Removal Power under the Constitution, reprinted in* CORWIN ON THE CONSTITUTION 317–71 (Richard Loss ed., 1981).

In passing, Corwin pointed out that in 1789 Madison himself had drawn a distinction between an officer who performed a purely executive function and one who did not. *Id.* at 336–37. Speaking to a bill to organize the Treasury Department, Madison considered that because the comptroller would perform duties of a judicial character in passing on the validity of claims brought by citizens against the United States, he should not hold office at the mere pleasure of the executive branch. He suggested instead a scheme whereby the officer would hold his office for a term of years unless sooner removed by the president. But when Benson objected that his suggestion was an undesirable intrusion on the executive branch, Madison withdrew his suggestion. 11 DHFFC 1082–83.

Later, in *Humphrey's Executor v. United States,* 295 U.S. 602, 629 (1935), the Court, adopting the Madison distinction, retreated from the broad language of the Taft opinion, and held that the president could not remove an inferior officer performing quasi-legislative and quasi-judicial duties in an administrative agency except for the reasons specified in the statute pursuant to which the officer was appointed. For a summary of the removal cases, *see* LOUIS FISHER, CONSTITUTIONAL CONFLICTS BETWEEN CONGRESS AND THE PRESIDENT, 64 *et seq.* (rev. ed. 1991).

62. *See* the pseudonymous writing of Brutus in the NEW YORK JOURNAL, Jan. 31, 1788, 15 DHRC 513–14. Without saying so, Brutus was following WILLIAM BLACKSTONE, COMMENTARIES, 61–62 (1765).

63. *See supra* notes 26, 29.

64. Madison to Washington, Mar. 19, 1789, 12 MP 22–23; Madison to Jefferson, Mar. 29, 1789, 12 *id.* at 37.

65. 1 ED 322 (Massachusetts), 325 (South Carolina), 325–26 (New Hampshire), and 327 (New York). The conventions of Massachusetts, New Hampshire, and South Carolina had requested a reservation of powers not "expressly" delegated, and New York a reservation of powers not "clearly" delegated.

66. 11 DHFFC 1300. The further reservation on federal power, embodied in the Tenth Amendment in the words "or to the people," was added later for reasons of draftsmanship. Since Madison had originally proposed that the amendments be incorporated in the text of the Constitution, some thought that the words "We the People" in the preamble made any reference to a reservation in the people redundant. When, however, the House voted to place the amendments in a section following the Constitution, the phrase "or to the people" was added. *See* CHARLES A. LOFGREN, GOVERNMENT FROM REFLECTION AND CHOICE 108–9 (1986).

For support of the Lofgren analysis, *see* Thomas B. McAffee, *Federalism and the Protection of Rights: The Modern Ninth Amendment's Spreading Confusion*, 1996 B.Y.U. L. REV. 351, 356. For the view that the Tenth Amendment refers to fundamental rights that limit the powers of the federal government and, after the adoption of the Fourteenth Amendment, those of the states, *see* David N. Mayer, *The National Rights Basis of the Ninth Amendment: A Reply to Professor McAffee*, 16 S. ILL. U. L. J. 313, 318–19 (1992); Norman G. Redlich, *Are There "Certain Rights . . . Retained by the People"?*, 37 N.Y.U. L. REV. 787, 806–7 (1962).

67. 11 DHFFC 1300, 1301 (statement of Rep. Madison). *Cf.* this statement of Madison with one he made earlier in defense of the Necessary and Proper Clause in the *Federalist*: "It would be easy to shew if it were necessary, that no important power, delegated by the articles of confederation, has been or can be executed by Congress, without recurring more or less to the doctrine of *construction* or *implication*. As the powers delegated under the new system are more extensive, the government which is to administer it would find itself still more distressed with the alternative of betraying the public trust by doing nothing; or of violating the Constitution by exercising powers, indispensably necessary and proper; but at the same time, not *expressly* granted." FEDERALIST No. 44, at 299, 303–4 (James Madison) (emphasis in original).

Lofgren correctly states that Madison viewed the proposed amendment as adding nothing to the Constitution. LOFGREN, *supra* note 66, at 107–8. From this he incorrectly concludes, however, that people then must have understood that the Tenth Amendment was not restrictive. He adds: "Indeed, in its historical context, it [i.e., the Tenth Amendment] probably reaffirmed the centralizing tendencies of the new system." *Id.* at 111. If this were so, it is impossible to explain why Madison and Jefferson relied on the Tenth Amendment in arguing that the bank bill was beyond the powers of Congress.

But contrary to Lofgren, Madison intended the Tenth Amendment to reaffirm *his* views of the Constitution: that the Constitution permitted the assertion of implied, incidental powers; and that the Necessary and Proper Clause merely authorized Congress to adopt such incidental measures as would execute the enumerated powers.

68. 11 DHFFC at 1301 (statement of Rep. Madison).

69. For the Henry-Mason motion and the ensuing debate, *see supra* ch. 2 notes 88–93.

70. *See supra* notes 38–39, 46, 57.

71. Compare the votes on the successive motions in the text accompanying notes 57, 59 *supra*.

72. 11 DHFFC 1300–301.

73. Edmund Pendleton to Madison, Oct. 6, 1788, 11 MP 275; Madison to Edmund Randolph, Aug. 2, 11 and 22, 1788, 11 *id.* at 215, 227–28, and 237–38; and Madison to Washington, Aug. 24, 1788, 11 *id.* at 240–42.

74. For Madison's summary of southern difficulties with the New York City site, *see* 11 DHFFC 1435–36.

75. 11 *id.* at 1437–38 (statement of Rep. Madison).

76. 11 *id.* at 1400–1401.

77. 11 *id.* at 1421, 1432 (statement of Rep. Madison).

78. 11 *id.* at 1400, 1405–14, and 1433–47.

79. 11 *id.* at 1492.

80. 11 *id.* at 1492–93 (statement of Rep. Madison).

81. *Id.*

82. *Id.*

83. 2 FR 261–62.

84. 2 *id.* at 301.

85. 2 *id.* at 304–5.

86. 11 DHFFC 1494–97.

87. 11 *id.* at 1494–96 (statement of Rep. Laurance); 1496–97 (statement of Rep. Ames).

88. 11 *id.* at 1496 (statement of Rep. Ames).

89. 11 *id.* at 1498–99.

90. For the vote, *see* 1 DHFFC 190–95. On the split in the Pennsylvania delegation, Maclay preferring a site on the Susquehanna, and Robert Morris Philadelphia, *see* 9 DHFFC 161–64.

91. 3 DHFFC 238–39.

92. 3 *id.* at 238; 11 DHFFC 1513.

93. 1 DHFFC 203.

94. 1 *id.* at 207; 3 DHFFC 246.

95. *See infra* ch. 4 note 24.

4. Madison and Strict Construction

1. 6 HP 65–81. E. James Ferguson, *The Nationalists of 1781–1783 and the Economic Interpretation of the Constitution, in* AFTER THE CONSTITUTION 113–14, 123 (Lance Banning ed., 1989).

2. 12 DHFFC 19; E. JAMES FERGUSON, THE POWER OF THE PURSE 251–69 (1961); ELKINS & McKITRICK 138–39.

3. 2 FR 392 (statement of Butler).

4. 2 *id.* at 413 (statement of Mason).

5. FERGUSON, *supra* note 2, at 271–86; ELKINS & McKITRICK 115–18; RICHARD A. BEEMAN, THE OLD DOMINION AND THE NEW NATION, 1788–1801 69–70 (1972).

6. There were problems with Virginia's claims: Some of its debt had been incurred without authorization of the Continental Congress; much of it could not be supported with adequate documentation. FERGUSON, *supra* note 2, at 203–19, 309–33; BEEMAN, *supra* note 5, at 72–73; Madison to John Randolph, Mar. 14, 1790, 13 MP 106.

7. Monroe to Madison, July 26, 1790, *id.* at 283–84. This argument had also been raised during ratification. *See* FEDERALIST No. 31, at 193, 196–97 (Alexander Hamilton). In reply to this argument, Hamilton had written that the maintenance of a proper equilibrium between the state and federal governments was for the people to decide. *Id.* at 197–98.

8. 6 HP 78–83.

9. For Madison's support of assumption in the Continental Congress, *see* his report to the Congress, 24 JOURNALS OF THE CONTINENTAL CONGRESS 277–83 (Apr. 26, 1783) (Gaillard Hunt ed., 1912). For his support of non-discrimination in the Congress, *see* 24 *id.* at 283.

10. 12 DHFFC 294.

11. 12 *id.* at 479.

12. 12 *id.* at 606–7, 609–10 (statements of Rep. Madison).

13. 12 *id.* at 655 (statement of Rep. Madison).

14. Hamilton to Edward Carrington, May 26, 1792, 11 HP 428.

15. 12 DHFFC 510 (statement of Rep. Stone), 514 (statement of Rep. Sherman), 521 (statement of Rep. Gerry).

16. For Gerry's prior statements regarding his fears of the scope of the Necessary and Proper Clause, *see supra* ch. 1 note 98, ch. 2 note 9, ch. 3 note 44. Gerry's holdings of Massachusetts debt, in excess of $16,000, had been purchased from individuals after the Constitutional Convention. He also held almost $33,000 in federal debt, most of which he had purchased before the convention, for a total of over $49,000. GEORGE A. BILLIAS, ELBRIDGE GERRY 132 (1976).

17. 12 DHFFC 575–76 (statement of Rep. Gerry). Earlier, Andrew Moore of Virginia had said that while he would not argue that assumption was unconstitutional, it was contrary to the light in which the Constitution was contemplated when it was adopted. 12 *id.* at 555–56.

18. 13 DHFFC 1175–76 (statement of Rep. Madison). The newspaper noted that the gentleman to whom Madison referred was Gerry.

19. 13 *id.* at 1420–21 (statement of Rep. Sherman) (emphasis added).

20. 2 FR 356 (statement of Gerry).

21. 13 DHFFC 1712 (statement of Rep. Jackson).

22. 13 *id.* at 1719 (statement of Rep. Gerry).

23. 11 DHFFC 1003–4 (statement of Rep. Baldwin), 1021–22 (statement of Rep. Gerry).

24. Act of July 16, 1790, 1 STAT. 130. The four who switched their votes were Reps. White and Bland of Virginia and Carroll and Gale of Maryland, all of whose districts bordered the Potomac. On the compromise, *see* editorial note, 13 MP 243–46, and ELKINS & MCKITRICK 156–61.

25. GLENN A. PHELPS, GEORGE WASHINGTON AND AMERICAN CONSTITUTIONALISM 28–32, 74–79, 151–52 (1993). Washington's idea coincided with that of Robert Morris and, of course, Hamilton, who believed that gaining the support of persons with money would greatly contribute to the success of the Union. Ferguson, *supra* note 1, at 112–13.

26. The states which benefited from this arrangement were Maryland, Virginia, North Carolina, and Georgia. The debts of South Carolina, like those of Massachusetts, had been unpaid. FERGUSON, *supra* note 2, at 307–9, 312–13.

27. Henry Lee to Madison, Apr. 3, 1790, 13 MP 136–37; Edward Carrington to Madison, Apr. 7, 1790 and Apr. 30, 1790, 13 *id.* 142, 181–83; John Dawson to Madison, Apr. 13, 1790, 13 *id.* at 149–50. *See also* BEEMAN, *supra* note 5, at 77.

There were practical reasons for the underparticipation of southerners in the ownership of the public debt: The South's limited commercial development led to the devotion of its capital to the acquisition and cultivation of land and of slaves; the southern states had taken on a proportionately large share of the war debt; and after the war, southerners had tended to transfer their ownership of public securities to northerners. FERGUSON, *supra* note 2, at 335.

28. Carrington to Madison, Dec. 24, 1790, 13 MP 331–32. *See also* editorial note, 13 *id.* at 332; and BEEMAN, *supra* note 5, at 78–82.

29. Madison to Randolph, May 19 and May 25, 1790, 13 MP 222, 227; James Madison to Ambrose Madison, May 27, 1790, 13 *id.* at 230–31.

30. 14 DHFFC 271–74, 319–22, 323–25. Rep. Aedanus Burke of South Carolina set the chances against the death or impeachment of the president and vice-president during the same administration as one in 840 years. 14 *id.* at 324. In fact, it happened sooner, when in

the second Nixon administration, with the threat of impeachment hovering over them, both President Richard M. Nixon and Vice-President Spiro Agnew resigned.

31. 4 DHFFC 174–78.

32. 4 *id.* at 184–85.

33. 4 *id.* at 187–88.

34. For the Morris recommendation to create a bank for the purposes of insuring an adequate money supply through the issuance of private bank notes that would serve as a paper currency, *see* Ferguson, *supra* note 1, at 114–15. Hamilton also followed the advice of the wealthy Philadelphia merchant William Bingham, who, like Hamilton, was a Morris disciple. ROBERT C. ALBERTS, THE GOLDEN VOYAGE: THE LIFE AND TIMES OF WILLIAM BINGHAM, 1752–1805 200–205 (1969).

35. Benjamin B. Klubes, *The First Federal Congress and the National Bank: A Case Study in Constitutional Interpretation,* 10 JER 19, 23–25 (1990). The senators opposed to all or parts of the bill were Monroe of Virginia, Benjamin Hawkins of North Carolina, Pierce Butler and Ralph Izard of South Carolina, and William Few and James Gunn of Georgia.

36. 1 DHFFC 535–36.

37. Act of July 16, 1790, 1 STAT. 130.

38. *See supra* note 35, at 26; and 1 DHFFC 535–36.

39. *See supra* note 35, at 26; Maclay did not approve of some aspects of the bill, such as the subscription of its stock, 9 DHFFC 361–64.

40. Carrington to Madison, Feb. 21, 1791, 13 MP 398–99: The subject of the bank bill was too remote to excite much inquiry among the people, except among merchants who favored it.

41. 14 DHFFC 325 (statement of Rep. Sedgwick).

42. Hamilton to Carrington, May 26, 1792, 11 HP 441.

43. 4 DHFFC 196–97.

44. 14 DHFFC 423, 424 (statement of Rep. Stone).

45. 4 DHFFC 173; 14 DHFFC 362–63 (statement of Rep. Smith).

46. For the interrelation of the bank bill and the bill amending the Residence Act, Act of July 16, 1790, 1 STAT. 130, *see* editorial note, 19 JP 36. For Smith's report, *see* KENNETH R. BOWLING, POLITICS IN THE FIRST CONGRESS, 1789–1791 235 (1990). For southern suspicions regarding northern motives in blocking the amendment to the Residence Act, *see* 14 DHFFC 424 (statement of Rep. Stone).

47. For rejection of the Smith and Williamson motions, *see* 3 DHFFC 693–94, 696–97.

48. 14 DHFFC 367–75 (statement of Rep. Madison).

49. On Jan. 11, 1791, before the vote on the succession bill, Jefferson, writing to Thomas M. Randolph, his son-in-law, was unconcerned about the bank, 18 JP 488–89. But by Feb. 4, after the vote and Madison's attack on the bank bill, Jefferson was complaining to George Mason about the improper influence of the Treasury, the corruption of government, and the interest of stock-jobbers at the expense of agriculture, 19 JP 241–42. On the same day, writing to Robert E. Livingston of New York, and inquiring of him regarding the possibility of discontent "in your quarter . . . with the proceedings of our government," he told him of the "vast amount of discontent gathered in the South." 19 *id.* at 240, 241. For the Livingston-Clinton alliance against Schuyler, *see* ELKINS & MCKITRICK 242.

50. 14 DHFFC 367, 368–74 (statement of Rep. Madison). For the Federalist complaint regarding Madison's last-minute constitutional argument, *see* 14 *id.* at 385, 386 (statement of Rep. Ames).

51. 14 DHFFC 367, 368 (statement of Rep. Madison). For his motions in the Constitutional Convention, *see* 2 FR 325, 615–16.

52. 14 DHFFC 369–71 (statement of Rep. Madison) (emphasis in original).

53. 14 *id.* at 370–71 (statement of Rep. Madison). Madison's reference to the borrowing power was made in response to an argument for the bill's constitutionality based on that power, which Laurance had advanced the previous day. 14 *id.* at 364.

54. *See supra* ch. 1 note 4.

55. *Id.* at notes 53, 55.

56. *Id.* at notes 59–63, 82–90.

57. *See supra* ch. 2 notes 21–25, 75.

58. *See supra* ch. 3 notes 8, 27–28, 35–36, 40–42, 50.

59. *See supra* notes 32, 33.

60. 14 DHFFC 372–74 (statement of Rep. Madison).

61. GERARD C. HENDERSON, THE POSITION OF FOREIGN CORPORATIONS IN AMERICAN CONSTITUTIONAL LAW 3, 10–11 (1918); Note, *Incorporating the Republic: The Corporation in Antebellum Political Culture,* 102 HARV. L. REV. 1883, 1890–92 (1989); 14 DHFFC 373–74 (statement of Rep. Madison). The states proposing constitutional amendments were Massachusetts, 1 ED 322–23; New Hampshire, 1 *id.* at 325–26; New York, 1 *id.* at 329–30; and Rhode Island, 1 *id.* at 336–37.

62. 14 DHFFC 374 (statement of Rep. Madison). For Jefferson's embellishment, *see* his opinion to Washington, 19 JP 278–79.

63. 14 DHFFC 374–75 (statement of Rep. Madison).

64. *See supra* ch. 2 note 13. *See also* his statement, *id.* note 14.

65. FEDERALIST No. 33, at 203, 205 (Alexander Hamilton) (emphasis in original). *See also supra* ch. 2 notes 17–18.

66. *Id.* at notes 21–22.

67. *Id.* at note 75.

68. 14 DHFFC 394 (statement of Rep. Ames). Madison seemed to assume that the operations of the bank would be confined to a single location, albeit § 15 of the bill authorized the bank's directors to establish branches wherever they sought fit within the United States. 1 STAT. 191. Furthermore, in reply to Madison's argument that the United States could rely on the agency of state banks (*see supra* note 62), Ames pointed out that at the time ten of the states had no banks. 14 DHFFC 394.

69. *Id.* at 390, 393 (statement of Rep. Ames). Later Ames also reasoned that since the power to govern the Western Territory was not expressed in the Constitution, it was "derived from the nature of the case, or by implication from the power to regulate the property of the United States [pursuant to art. IV, § 3, cl. 2]. If the power flows from the nature and necessity of the case, it may be demanded, Is there not equal authority for the Bank?" 14 DHFFC 395.

70. 14 DHFFC 397 (statement of Rep. Ames).

71. *See supra* ch. 1 notes 95–98; ch. 2 notes 6–11.

72. 14 DHFFC 398–403 (statement of Rep. Sedgwick). For Madison's position on the presidential removal power, *see supra* ch. 3 notes 27–28, 35–36, 40–42.

73. *Id.* at notes 38–39, 46, 57.

74. 14 DHFFC 400 (statement of Rep. Sedgwick). His argument echoed remarks of Madison in FEDERALIST No. 44, at 299, 304, set forth *infra* note 84.

75. 14 DHFFC 421–22 (statement of Rep. William Smith).

76. 14 *id.* at 452–53 (statement of Rep. Gerry).

77. *See supra* notes 17, 22.

78. 14 DHFFC 453–57 (statement of Rep. Gerry); WILLIAM BLACKSTONE, COMMENTARIES 59–60 (1765).

79. 14 DHFFC 457–58 (statement of Rep. Gerry); BLACKSTONE, *supra* note 78, at 61.

80. For Gerry's position in the Constitutional Convention, *see supra* ch. 1 note 97–98; for his position during the ratification campaign, *see supra* ch. 2 note 9.

81. 14 DHFFC 459–60 (statement of Rep. Gerry).

82. 14 *id.* at 460 (statement of Rep. Gerry).

83. On Dec. 31, 1781, the Continental Congress passed an ordinance establishing a corporate bank under the name of "The President, Directors and Company of the Bank of North America." 21 JOURNALS OF THE CONTINENTAL CONGRESS, *supra* note 9, at 1187–89. For referral to the states by Robert Morris, superintendent of finance under the Continental Congress, *see* BRAY HAMMOND, BANKS AND POLITICS IN AMERICA 46–51 (1957). For Gerry's statement in the third session of the First Congress, 14 DHFFC 460–61. For the state recommendations of constitutional amendments, *see supra* note 61. For Gerry's purchase of the stock of the Bank of the United States, *see* BILLIAS, *supra* note 16, at 242.

84. 14 DHFFC 363–64 (statement of Rep. Jackson), 439 (statement of Rep. Boudinot). According to Boudinot, Jackson had relied on the *Federalist* No. 44 in his argument and had identified Hamilton as the author of that paper. *Id.* In fact, although Boudinot did not know, Jackson was mistaken: Madison was the author. Boudinot went on to quote the following passage from the same paper: "Had the Convention attempted a positive enumeration of the powers necessary and proper for carrying their other powers into effect; the attempt would have involved a complete digest of laws on every subject to which the Constitution relates; accommodated too not only to the existing state of things, but to all the possible changes which futurity may produce: For in every new application of a general power, the *particular powers* which are the means of attaining the *object* of the general power, must always necessarily vary with that object; and be often properly varied whilst the object remains the same." FEDERALIST No. 44, at 299, 304 (James Madison) (emphasis in original). Boudinot was also mistaken. In this paper, Madison, like Hamilton before him in the *Federalist* and like James Wilson in the Pennsylvania convention (*see supra* notes 64–65), had been defending the Necessary and Proper Clause against the charge raised by Mason, Gerry, and others that it was a "sweeping clause" whereunder all kinds of unexpressed general powers would be read into the Constitution. What Madison had insisted was that the clause included provision for only incidental powers, that is, powers that would enable Congress to provide for such measures as would enable it to carry the enumerated powers into operation.

In *McCulloch v. Maryland,* 17 U.S. (4 Wheat.) 316 (1819), Luther Martin on behalf of Maryland relied on the *Federalist* and on the debates in the state conventions as authority for his contention that Congress did not have power under the Necessary and Proper Clause to establish a national bank. *Id.* at 372. Chief Justice Marshall in his opinion, in which he upheld the constitutionality of the statute rechartering the bank in 1816, disregarded the authority of the *Federalist,* something which he would not have done if it agreed with his position. *Id.* at 401 *et seq.*

Among others, DOUGLASS ADAIR, FAME AND THE FOUNDING FATHERS 44 (Trevor Colbourn ed., 1974), and GARRY WILLS, EXPLAINING AMERICA 48 (1981) follow Boudinot in his error.

85. Madison to Edmund Pendleton, Feb.13, 1791, 13 MP 390–91; Madison to Edward Carrington, Feb. 27, 1791, 13 *id.* at 40; and Carrington to Madison, Apr. 20, 1791, 14 MP 10–11. For a defense of the sincerity of Madison's denunciation of the bank on policy and constitutional grounds, *see* LANCE BANNING, THE SACRED FIRE OF LIBERTY 328–31 (1995). Clearly, Madison opposed the bank on policy grounds. Like most southerners, he was convinced that it would operate for the benefit of the merchant capitalist class, situated largely in the North, at the expense of their region's agricultural economy. At the same time, he opposed the bill establishing the bank on constitutional grounds, because he considered it important to counter the argument that Congress somehow had the power to pass such legislation.

Nevertheless, since he himself at the Constitutional Convention had favored a constitutional clause specifically conferring such a power on Congress, it is hard to see how in good faith he could have argued that as a matter of policy such an establishment should be beyond the powers of the national government.

86. 4 DHFFC 173.

87. For Jefferson's opinion, 19 JP 275–80 (emphasis in original). The reference to the convention proceedings is at 277–78.

88. *See supra* ch. 2 note 83.

89. For Randolph's opinion, *see* LEGISLATIVE AND DOCUMENTARY HISTORY OF THE BANK OF THE UNITED STATES 89 (Matthew St. Clair Clarke & D. A. Hall eds., 1832). A recent commentary on the Necessary and Proper Clause follows the Randolph opinion. On this basis, the commentary distinguishes *McCulloch v. Maryland,* 17 U.S. (4 Wheat.) 316 (1819), on the ground that it decided only the question of the necessity of the Bank's establishment, not its propriety. That question supposedly remains open. For this neo-Randolphian view, *see* Gary Lawson & Patricia B. Granger, *The "Proper" Scope of Federal Power: A Jurisdictional Interpretation of the Sweeping Clause,* 43 DUKE L. J. 267, 327 n. 244 (1993).

90. 17 U.S. (4 Wheat.) 316, 404–10 (1819).

91. 8 HP 97–99.

92. 8 *id.* at 101.

93. 8 *id.* at 106 (emphasis in original).

94. 8 *id.* at 121–28; *see also supra* notes 31–32, 70.

95. 8 HENRY ADAMS, HISTORY OF THE UNITED STATES DURING THE ADMINISTRATIONS OF THOMAS JEFFERSON AND JAMES MADISON 212–15, 244–45 (1931); HAMMOND, *supra* note 83, at 227–30.

96. U.S. CONST. art. I, § 8, cl. 5, authorizes Congress "to coin Money, regulate the Value thereof, and of foreign Coin, and fix the Standard of Weights and Measures." At the Constitutional Convention a motion to strike "and emit bills on the credit of the U. States" carried by a vote of 9 to 2. 2 FR 303, 308–10. For a discussion of Hamilton's views on the necessity of creating an adequate money supply through the agency of a national bank in the light of the failure of the Constitution to permit Congress to emit bills of credit, *see* Joseph M. Lynch, *McCulloch v. Maryland: A Matter of Money Supply,* 18 SETON HALL L. REV. 223 (1988).

97. 4 DHFFC 187.

98. 8 HP 110.

99. 8 *id.* at 111 (emphasis in original).

100. *See infra* ch. 8.

101. 4 DHFFC 183–85.

102. 4 *id.* at 188–91.

103. Act of Feb. 25, 1791, 1 STAT. 191.

104. For Madison's efforts, *see* IRVING BRANT, MADISON: THE NATIONALIST 204–5 (1948). For Jefferson's efforts, *see* editorial note, 18 JP 516–21.

105. *See* DREW R. MCCOY, THE ELUSIVE REPUBLIC 120–32 (1980).

106. *See* the excellent summary of the legislative history of the Tonnage Act of 1789 in WINIFRED E. A. BERNHARD, FISHER AMES 88–91 (1965); *see also* editorial note, 18 JP 521–25. Interestingly, during ratification Hamilton had taken note that the southern states would naturally prefer a system which would allow the ships of all nations to be the carriers as well as the purchasers of southern commodities. FEDERALIST No. 13, at 80, 82 (Alexander Hamilton).

107. Madison's revived proposal is printed in 13 MP 219–20. William Smith of South Carolina and Jackson of Georgia opposed it, 13 DHFFC 1324–25, 1626. For the reasons for southern opposition, *see supra* note 106.

108. 19 JP 206–20; 2 ANNALS 1909.

109. For the progress and disposition of the bill, *see* SAMUEL F. BEMIS, JAY'S TREATY 112–13 (rev. ed. 1962).

110. FEDERALIST No. 11, at 66–68 (Alexander Hamilton).

111. BEMIS, *supra* note 109, at 49–50. In fact, it was the people's antipathy to state taxation that led state governments during the Confederation period to resort to paper money and laws for debtor relief. As Gouverneur Morris and Stephen Higginson, a Boston merchant, both understood, the enactment of direct federal taxes would endanger the stability of the government. Apparently, Madison did not understand that, because when Hamilton initially asked him for his advice as to how raise federal revenues, Madison advocated the enactment of various kinds of direct taxes, including a tax on land. *See* ROGER H. BROWN, REDEEMING THE REPUBLIC 234–40 (1993).

112. For a discussion of Hamilton's crucial role in opposing Jefferson's and Madison's policies on foreign trade—and more specifically in connection with the formulation of a legislative response to Jefferson's report on the New England fisheries and to Jefferson's reply concerning French remonstrances against the provisions of prior tonnage acts—*see* the editorial note, 18 JP 516–58.

113. The use of the title "prime minister" is anachronistic. *See* ELKINS & MCKITRICK 227. Elkins and McKitrick surmise that William Pitt, then chancellor of the exchequer in Great Britain and the country's functioning prime minister (the title had not yet been applied), served as Hamilton's model.

5. *The Emergence of Opposition*

1. JAMES R. SHARP, AMERICAN POLITICS IN THE EARLY REPUBLIC 39–41 (1993); GORDON S. WOOD, THE RADICALISM OF THE AMERICAN REVOLUTION 255–61 (1993); Alfred E. Young, *The Democratic Republicans of New York,* and Joyce Appleby, *Commercial Farming and the "Agrarian Myth" in the Early Republic, in* AFTER THE CONSTITUTION, 215–29, 268–88 (Lance Banning ed., 1989); *generally,* JOYCE APPLEBY, CAPITALISM AND A NEW SOCIAL ORDER (1984).

2. *See* LANCE BANNING, THE JEFFERSONIAN PERSUASION (1978).

3. ELKINS & MCKITRICK 46–48, 227–29; editorial note, 7 HP 236–56.

4. 23 JP 186–87.

5. BANNING, *supra* note 2.

6. *See supra* ch. 4 notes 16, 83; *see also* WOOD, *supra* note 1, at 261–63.

7. For the details of the transactions between Jefferson and Madison on the one hand and Frenau on the other, *see* DUMAS MALONE, JEFFERSON AND THE RIGHTS OF MAN 423–28 (1951). Typically, Malone's interpretation of these transactions is benign: Neither Jefferson nor Madison was politically motivated. For a more penetrating interpretation, *see* LEONARD WHITE, THE FEDERALISTS 229 (1948).

8. 14 MP 137–39, 217–18.

9. 14 *id.* at 233–34.

10. 14 *id.* at 274.

11. 14 *id.* at 370–72. *See* ELKINS & MCKITRICK 263–70, for Madison's development of a theory justifying the emergence of an opposition political party.

12. MALONE, *supra* note 7, at 354–59; Jefferson to Jonathan B. Smith, Apr. 26, 1791, 20 JP 290; Jefferson to Washington, May 8, 1791, 20 *id.* at 291–92. Washington did not reply. The editors of the Jefferson Papers make the following comment on Washington's "icy silence": "It is difficult to escape the conclusion that the deterioration of the bonds of friendship, trust, and affection that once existed between [Washington and Jefferson] had its origin in the authorized publication of Jefferson's letter to Jonathan Bayard Smith." 20 *id.* at 289.

For an appraisal of the Adams work, the controversy surrounding the publication of Paine's book, and the effect of Jefferson's endorsement of Paine's book upon the formation of public opinion against Federalist policy and Adams, *see* BANNING, *supra* note 2, at 155–60.

13. MALONE, *supra* note 7, at 359–61; Robert Troup to Hamilton, June 15, 1791, 8 HP 478–79. *See also* editorial note, 20 JP 434–53; DAVID LUDLUM, SOCIAL FERMENT IN VERMONT, 1791–1850 28–29 (1939). Lienesch points to the Livingston letter as one of Jefferson's early attempts to create regional alliances as the basis for forming an opposition political party. *See* Michael Lienesch, *Thomas Jefferson and the Democratic Experience, in* JEFFERSONIAN LEGACIES 324–25 (Peter S. Onuf ed., 1993). Reports of the Jefferson-Madison effort to stir up support for their policy of retaliatory discrimination against Great Britain are consistent with their dismay at the defeat of their efforts to establish that policy in the First Congress just ended. *See supra* ch. 4 note 105 *et seq.*

14. Madison to Jefferson, May 12, June 23, June 27, July 10, and July 13, 1791, 14 MP 22–23, 35–37, 42–43, 46–47.

15. Monroe to Madison, Oct. 9, 1792, and Beckley to Madison, Oct. 17, 1792, 14 *id.* at 377–79, 383–85.

16. *See generally* 10 HP 230–340. For a close analysis of Hamilton's report, as a response to the Jefferson-Madison view of domestic needs, and reaction against his scheme for the subsidization of an American factory system, *see* DREW R. McCOY, THE ELUSIVE REPUBLIC 146–52 (1980).

17. U.S. CONST. art. I, § 8, cl. 1. For Pinckney's proposal in the Constitutional Convention, *see* 2 FR 325.

18. 10 HP 302–4.

19. 3 DHFFC 252, 253 (President Washington's message to Congress). In recommending aid to higher education, Washington left it to Congress to decide the means of its accomplishment: whether by grants to existing institutions or by the establishment of a national university. Merely to follow the latter course would not involve the spending power, but inasmuch as the founding of a university was not within the enumerated powers, his recommendation seems to presuppose the existence of a legislative power to act in the general interests of the country. Apparently, Washington was a secret believer in the sweeping powers of the Necessary and Proper Clause.

For the statements of Reps. Stone and Sherman, *see* 13 DHFFC 1221. In fact, it would appear that the proposal to establish a national university at the Constitutional Convention had been rejected after Gouverneur Morris had termed it unnecessary on the ground that "the exclusive power at the Seat of Government will reach the subject." 2 FR 616.

Despite the indifferent response from members of the House in the First Congress, Washington, in his State of the Union address to the second session of the Fourth Congress, again called for legislation to establish a national university and to promote agriculture. 6 ANNALS 1592, 1594–95.

20. 2 FR 615–16.

21. Hamilton wrote: "There can certainly be no object, more worthy of the cares of the local administrations; and it were to be wished, that there was no doubt of the power of the national Government to lend its direct aid, on a comprehensive plan. This is one of those improvements, which could be prosecuted with more efficacy by the whole, than by any part or parts of the Union." 10 HP 310.

22. 3 ANNALS 362–74.

23. 3 *id.* at 384–85 (statement of Rep. Laurance); *id.* at 385–86 (statement of Rep. Madison). Madison's approval of "drawbacks" to the fisheries, it has been observed, permits Congress to do indirectly what it supposedly cannot do directly, that is, give aid to a specific industry by allowance of a refund under its taxing power, rather than by subsidy under its spending power. DAVID P. CURRIE, THE CONSTITUTION IN CONGRESS, 1789–1801 169 (1997).

Of course, at that time, the budget of the federal government was small. The bulk of its receipts came from tariffs on imports. Madison did not anticipate the huge increase in federal revenue made possible by the imposition of taxes on income following the adoption of the Sixteenth Amendment.

24. 3 *id.* at 386–89 (statement of Rep. Madison).

25. Madison had defended the spending power against the argument that, like a broadly conceived Necessary and Proper Clause, it would enable Congress to pass any legislation it deemed in the advancement of the common defense and general welfare of the nation. This argument, he had reasoned, was refuted by the structure of the section in which it appeared. He wrote: "But what colour can the objection have, when a specification of the objects alluded to by these general terms, immediately follows. . . . For what purpose could the enumeration of particular powers be inserted, if these and all others were meant to be included in the preceding general power? Nothing is more natural or common than first to use a general phrase, and then to explain and qualify it by a recital of particulars." FEDERALIST No. 41, at 268, 277–78 (James Madison). Almost everyone has agreed that by this language Madison intended to say that the enumeration of the particular powers exhausted the meaning of the phrase "general welfare."

Leonard Sorenson, however, disagrees. Madison's true position was, he writes, as follows: "The most important dual purposes of the subsequent enumeration of powers are definition and limitation: to define more precisely the ends alluded to by the phrase 'general welfare' and to stand as examples, exemplars, or models to indicate the powers granted by the clause as a whole, over and above those enumerated." LEONARD SORENSON, MADISON ON THE "GENERAL WELFARE CLAUSE" OF AMERICA 146 (1995).

That reading is incorrect. The effect of such a construction of the spending power would be the magnification of the powers of Congress, a result against which Madison had most persistently labored since the decision in the Constitutional Convention to grant equality of representation to the states in the Senate. After that date, Madison was a committed states' rights advocate. For that reason, the statement of William Crosskey that Madison's position with regard to the spending power as set forth in the *Federalist* did not reflect his honest beliefs concerning its meaning is also incorrect. *See generally* 3 WILLIAM W. CROSSKEY & WILLIAM JEFFREY, JR., POLITICS AND THE CONSTITUTION IN THE HISTORY OF THE UNITED STATES (1980).

26. Following the Supreme Court's vindication of Hamilton's construction of the spending clause in *United States v. Butler,* 297 U.S. 1, 66 (1936), and its more liberal reading of the general welfare phrase in *Helvering v. Davis,* 301 U.S. 619, 640–41 (1937), not only have the number and scope of federal programs greatly increased, but their utility as a substitute for federal regulatory legislation has been recognized. *See South Dakota v. Dole,* 483 U.S. 203, 207–9 (1987). In that case, the withholding of a portion of a federal appropriation in aid of state highway construction for the state's failure to abide by a qualifying condition for entitlement was sustained, even though, because of the Twenty-first Amendment, Congress may not have been able to achieve the same result by legislation.

27. 10 DHRC 1325–26. (Mason's speech in the Virginia ratifying convention, June 16, 1788). Mason coupled his concession to a provision for the general welfare of the Union with the requirement that it be accompanied by a clause that all powers not granted to the United States were retained by the states. 10 *id.* at 1326.

28. 10 *id.* at 1326–27 (Nicholas's speech in the Virginia ratifying convention, June 16, 1788); 10 *id.* at 1350 (Randolph's speech in the Virginia ratifying convention, June 17, 1788).

29. Thus one committee had recommended that Congress have the power to pay the debts of the United States and of the several states incurred during the war "for the common defence and general welfare." 2 FR 352. The Convention initially approved authorizing Congress to pay the debt of the United States, 2 *id.* at 382, but did not expressly provide for the

payment of state war debt. During further consideration of the subject, Sherman moved, again unsuccessfully, for a provision expressly authorizing the payment of debts and for "defraying the expences that shall be incurred for the common defence and general welfare." 2 *id.* at 414. Finally, the convention adopted the provision which later became art. I, § 8, cl. 1 of the Constitution. 2 *id.* at 493, 495. For the references authorizing Congress to legislate or provide for the general welfare of the country, *see infra* notes 35–36.

30. Madison to Andrew Stevenson, Nov. 27, 1830, 3 FR 483, 485.

31. Art. 8, cl. 1.

32. Madison to Stevenson, Nov. 27, 1830, 3 FR 483, 486.

33. IRVING BRANT, JAMES MADISON: THE NATIONALIST, 1780–1787 129 (1948). In his letter to Stevenson, Madison attempted to explain away his admission by saying that the Articles of Confederation had not been ratified until 1781; therefore what the Continental Congress did before that date was not in point, and what it did after that date, while unauthorized, was for a variety of reasons accepted: "Prior to that event the power of Congress was measured by the exigencies of the war, and derived its sanction from the acquiescence of the States. After that event, habit and a continued expediency, amounting often to a real or apparent necessity, prolonged the exercise of an undefined authority; which was the more readily overlooked; as the members of the Body held their seats during pleasure, as its Acts . . . depended for their efficacy on the will of the States; and as its general incompetency became manifest." 3 FR 484, 487. Brant charges Madison with a personal inconsistency in his construction of the general welfare provision, in that in the opening days of the first session of the First Congress he advanced a report to fund support for a scientific expedition to determine the causes of deviation of the magnetic needle, an object he could not have justified under his later analysis. 10 DHFFC 218–19; BRANT, *supra,* at 331. *See also* George W. Carey, *James Madison on Federalism: The Search for Abiding Principles,* 3 BENCHMARK, Nos. 1 & 2, 27, 39 (1987).

If there was culpability on Madison's part, however, it seems minor. He had been asked by a friend to do it. Samuel Stanhope Smith to Madison, Mar. 26, 1789, 12 MP 26. While it is true that in introducing the matter to Congress, he said that he saw no reason against funding the expedition, he did not object when Representative Thomas Tucker of South Carolina expressed a doubt as to the constitutional power of Congress to provide such funding. 12 *id.* at 119, 120. As a result of Tucker's intervention, the matter was sent to a committee. *See* reference to such action in a speech of Madison the following year, 12 DHFFC 312, n. 42.

Finally, on Jan. 6, 1991, Madison, in presenting a committee report on the petition for funding the scientific expedition, noted without comment that the question of funding involved an inquiry into the constitutional powers of Congress. 13 DHFFC 348. The House rejected the petition without debate. 3 DHFFC 689.

In the light of this legislative history, it would seem that Madison did his political duty in advancing the petition submitted by a friend, and did nothing in public to hinder its progress. At the same time, he did not come to its aid against the charge that it was unconstitutional.

34. John C. Calhoun posed this question during the debate in the Fourteenth Congress over the Bonus Bill, a measure providing for the segregation of the so-called bonus, accruing from the subscription for the recently rechartered Bank of the United States and the moneys annually accruing from the government's share in its dividends, in a fund to be used for the construction of internal improvements in the states, 30 ANNALS 855–57. Calhoun, who at the time was in his nationalist phase, then favored a literal construction of the general welfare phrase. *See* CHARLES WILTSE, JOHN C. CALHOUN, NATIONALIST, 1782–1828 132–36 (1944).

Interestingly, in opposition to Calhoun, Representative Timothy Pickering of Massachusetts adopted the Madisonian argument. As postmaster general, secretary of war and of state under Washington, and secretary of state under Adams, Pickering had always supported a strong, centralized national government. 30 ANNALS 858–59.

Calhoun's efforts were at first successful. The bill was passed, but President Madison, who was then about to leave office, vetoed it. 30 *id.* at 1059–61. *See also* EDWARD S. CORWIN, COR-WIN ON THE CONSTITUTION 253–55 (Richard Loss ed., 1981).

In his letter of Nov. 27, 1830, to Andrew Stevenson, Madison answered Calhoun's question, saying that the unqualified general welfare phrase had been inserted by the Committee of Eleven not with a specific intention, but rather out of inattention. Qualification had not been considered important. 3 FR 483, 486.

35. 2 FR 21.

36. 2 *id.* at 367.

37. 3 ANNALS 401. Act of Feb. 16, 1792, 1 STAT. 229.

38. 13 DHFFC 1686.

39. On Mar. 23, 1793, the following year, Jefferson listed the names of nineteen congress-men and seven senators reported to be, or suspected of being, stockholders in the Bank of the United States, 25 JP 432, 433.

40. 13 DHFFC 1686; 3 DHFFC 524–25.

41. 3 ANNALS 232–33. The reference was to the Act of Mar. 3, 1791, § 4, 1 STAT. 199, 200.

42. 3 ANNALS 238–39, 241. The argument regarding the improper delegation of legislative authority to the president, which has its origin in JOHN LOCKE, SECOND TREATISE ON CIVIL GOVERNMENT, § 141, became a staple of constitutional advocacy for over a century and a half. But in the second half of this century, the Court, with only an occasional murmur to the con-trary, has not found the argument a substantial one. *See Touby v. United States,* 500 U.S. 160, 165 (1991), and editorial note, GERALD GUNTHER & KATHLEEN M. SULLIVAN, CONSTITUTIONAL LAW 399–400 (13th ed. 1997).

43. 3 ANNALS 303–11.

44. The Act of Feb. 20, 1792, § 28, 1 STAT. 232, 239.

45. For Jefferson's account of his conversation with Washington, *see* 23 JP 184.

46. 23 *id.* at 186–87. 6 ANNALS 1592–97. *See also supra* notes 4, 19; MALONE, *supra* note 7, at 432–33; WHITE, *supra* note 7, at 226–27.

47. 3 ANNALS 437.

48. 3 *id.* at 441–44 (statement of Rep. Page).

49. 11 DHFFC 1045–46 (statement of Rep. Page), 1072 (statement of Rep. Madison).

50. 11 *id.* at 1073 (statement of Rep. Madison); U. S. CONST. art. II, § 3; the Act of Sept. 2, 1789, § 2, 1 STAT. 65. Thus, unlike the other executive departments created at the time, Trea-sury was told to report directly to Congress. *See* Gerhard Casper, *The American Constitutional Tradition of Shared and Separated Powers,* 30 WM. & MARY L. REV. 211, 239–42 (1989).

51. Madison's position was not reported, *but see* the characterization of his position by Rep-resentative Theodore Sedgwick, 3 ANNALS 437–40.

52. 3 *id.* at 452. Hamilton to Edward Carrington, May 26, 1792, 11 HP 426, 432–33; 23 JP 246, 247. On the subsequent history of this question, *see* WHITE, *supra* note 7, at 68–74.

53. 3 ANNALS 484 (statement of Rep. Page), 488–89.

54. U.S. CONST. art. I, § 2, cl. 3.

55. *Id.*

56. *See* the analysis in Hamilton's opinion to President Washington on the constitutional-ity of the bill, 11 HP 228–30.

57. For an analysis of the Senate's method of reapportionment, *see* 11 *id.* at 228; for the practical effect of the Senate and House methods of reapportionment on regional representa-tion, *see* Jefferson's opinion to President Washington on the constitutionality of the final ver-sion of the bill, 23 JP 370–76.

58. 3 ANNALS 482–83.

59. 11 HP 229–30.

60. 23 JP 371–72. The necessity of disregarding fractions, he continued, was to be inferred from the employment in the Constitution of a common ratio: "The Number of Representatives shall not exceed one for every thirty Thousand." Art. I, § 2, cl. 3. The necessity was reinforced by the subsequent sole provision for fractional representation: "but each State shall have at Least one Representative." The inclusion of that exception, he declared, proved that without it "the smaller number would . . . be involved on the general principle." 23 JP 370, 372.

61. 23 *id.* at 372–73; 3 ANNALS 407–8 (statement of Rep. Madison). Jefferson also presented an alternate argument: Even if the Constitution intended that the total representation of the House should be determined by reference to the total population of the United States, and that in consequence there should be 120 members in the House, this did not help the bill. The constitutional provision, that "Representatives . . . shall be apportioned among the several States . . . according to their respective Numbers," required the utilization of that "ratio of distribution . . . which, applied to every state, gives to them [sic] such numbers, as, added together, come nearest to 120." Since that ratio would be 1 : 28,050, it would distribute 119 of the 120 members, leaving only one undistributed. That procedure would not offend the constitutional prescription, that "the number of Representatives shall not exceed one for every thirty Thousand," because, he ingeniously argued, according to the premise followed, the prescription applies only to the initial determination as to the total membership of the House. 23 JP 373–74. Jefferson's alternate argument was, as Hamilton conceded in his opinion to the president, plausible.

62. 23 *id.* at 264.

63. See the statement of Nathaniel Gorham, chairman of the committee reporting on the apportionment of representatives in the House during the Constitutional Convention: "Fractions could not be observed." 1 FR 559. *See also* the later colloquy between Oliver Ellsworth and Elbridge Gerry, in which, opposing the latter's motion that previous to a census direct taxation should be proportioned among the states according to the number of representatives, Ellsworth observed that it would result in "a very inaccurate rule—A State might have one representative only, that had enough inhabitants for $1\frac{1}{2}$ or more, if fractions could be applied." 2 FR 357–58.

64. 1 FR 595 (statement of Wilson).

65. 1 *id.* at 590. *See* U.S. CONST. art. I, §2, cl. 3.

66. For Madison's complete defense of the inclusion of blacks in the reapportionment formula, *see* FEDERALIST No. 54, at 366–72. For his suggestion that thereby the South would pay more taxes, *see id.* at 368. For a commentary on the reapportionment formula, the convention's disposition of the slavery issue, Madison's essay in the *Federalist,* and his troubled conscience concerning his personal implication in the evils of slavery, *see* WILLIAM L. MILLER, THE BUSINESS OF MAY NEXT 117–41 (1992).

67. 23 JP 264. The editors of the *Jefferson Papers* state that Washington yielded to Jefferson and Randolph after learning that Wilson, then associate justice of the United Supreme Court, had grave reservations about the constitutionality of the bill. 23 *id.* at 377. If so, this would indeed have been ironic, because the idea of connecting representation with direct taxation in order to fool the public had been Wilson's. *See supra* note 64. As a result of Wilson, then, the South would have it both ways. Slaves would count in representation, but fractions would not.

68. 3 ANNALS 539; the Act of Apr. 14, 1792, 1 STAT. 253. The subsequent history of congressional reapportionment is set forth in *United States Dept. of Commerce v. Montana,* 503 U.S. 442 (1992): Beginning in 1842, and following the census of 1840, Congress awarded an additional representative to each state having a fraction greater than one half. From 1850 until 1911, however, it used the method Hamilton described to Washington. In 1911 Congress fixed the size of the House at 435, and after using alternate methods of apportionment for the

census of 1910 and 1920 rejected the method Hamilton described in favor of "the method of equal representation," more particularly described in the opinion.

When, following the census of 1990, the U.S. Department of Commerce applied this method and determined that the state of Montana was entitled to only one congressman, Montana challenged the determination. On appeal, the United States Supreme Court upheld the Department. In allocating representation among the states, the Court concluded, some method was required.

Reflecting what Hamilton had written in his opinion to Washington, the Court concluded that Congress must have a measure of discretion in choosing the means to achieve the end. Then, saying what Hamilton had not dared, the Court held that Congress in choosing the means had acted pursuant to the Necessary and Proper Clause. *Id.* at 464.

69. For the version that passed the House originally, *see* 3 ANNALS 406; for the Senate version, 3 *id.* at 37–38; for the House's belated accession to the Senate version, 3 *id.* at 417. The Act of Mar. 1, 1792, § 9, 1 STAT. 239, 240.

70. Monroe to Madison, Oct. 9, 1792, enclosing letters from Melancton Smith and Marinus Willett, New York Republican leaders, 14 MP 377–81; John Beckley to Madison, Oct. 17, 1792, 14 *id.* at 383–85; and Madison and Monroe to Smith and Willett, Oct. 19, 1792, 14 *id.* at 387.

71. Jefferson to Madison, Oct. 1, 1792, 14 *id.* at 375.

72. Washington to Hamilton, July 29, 1792, 12 HP 129–34.

73. Jefferson to Washington, May 23, 1792, 23 JP 535–41.

74. 23 *id.* at 537–38. On the effect of the panic of 1792 on Madison's and Jefferson's attitude toward Hamilton's fiscal policies, *see* ELKINS & McKITRICK 270–82. The panic, in which William Duer, Hamilton's assistant in the Treasury Department, played a crucial role, was caused by excessive speculation in the stock of the Bank of the United States.

75. 23 JP 538.

76. 23 *id.* at 538–39.

77. Hamilton to Washington, Aug. 18, 1792, 12 HP 228, 250.

78. 12 *id.* at 251.

79. *Id.*

80. 12 *id.* at 258.

81. For a discussion of the part that Hamilton's personal rivalries with Jefferson and Madison played in the formation and development of party structures and constitutional theorizing, *see* ELKINS & McKITRICK 77–79.

82. 3 ANNALS 646.

83. SHARP, *supra* note 1, at 53–68. On the fully constituted status of the Republican Party, *see* Madison's pseudonymous article of Sept. 22, 1792, *A Candid State of Parties,* NATIONAL GAZETTE, in which he refers to his party as the "Republican Party," *reprinted in* 14 MP 370–72. Characteristically, he refers to the other side in negative terms, as the "anti-republican" party.

84. 3 ANNALS 679, 680 (statement of Rep. Madison). For further details on the House investigation of the St. Clair military expedition, *see* Casper, *supra* note 50, at 228–31.

85. 3 ANNALS 684.

86. 3 *id.* at 696 (statement of Rep. Madison), 704 (statement of Rep. Baldwin), 706–8 (statements of Reps. Giles and Mercer), and 715–22 (statement of Rep. Ames). For the vote, *see* 3 *id.* at 722.

87. 3 *id.* at 895, 934–46, 955–63. A draft of the Giles Resolutions in Jefferson's own writing is *reprinted in* 7 WJ 220–23. For a discussion of the authenticity of Jefferson's authorship, *see* JOSEPH J. ELLIS, AMERICAN SPHINX: THE CHARACTER OF THOMAS JEFFERSON 130 (1997).

6. Opposition and Foreign Policy

1. For an account of the French Revolution as it affected American foreign and domestic policies, *see* ELKINS & McKITRICK 303–73. For American dependence on revenues from British imports, *see* SAMUEL F. BEMIS, JAY'S TREATY 49–50 (rev. ed. 1962).

2. DUMAS MALONE, JEFFERSON AND THE ORDEAL OF LIBERTY 69–70 (1962). The idea of exacting a price for American neutrality with respect to a European war was not new. Hamilton, who now opposed the idea, had advanced it in the course of arguing for the establishment of a federal navy, FEDERALIST No. 11, at 65, 68 (Alexander Hamilton).

3. *Id.* at 69.

4. *Id.* at 69–71. Elkins and McKitrick, observing that the task of drafting the proclamation was really the job of the secretary of state, suggest that Jefferson deferred to Randolph to escape criticism from his friends and to leave him free to attack Randolph's work. *See* ELKINS & McKITRICK 338–39.

5. 4 ANNALS 1285.

6. In the beginning, most newspapers supported France and attacked the president for the proclamation. Madison to Jefferson, June 19, 1793, 15 MP 33.

7. ELKINS & McKITRICK 335–37, 341–43.

8. The Pacificus essays are collected in 15 HP 33–43, 55–63, 65–69, 82–86, 90–95, 100–106, 130–35. The first essay concerns itself with the constitutional justification of the power of the president to declare a state of neutrality and to interpret treaties. The remaining essays constitute a justification of the president's decision to declare a state of neutrality.

9. 15 *id.* at 34 (emphasis in original).

10. FEDERALIST No. 69, at 462, 468 (Alexander Hamilton).

11. Hamilton characterizes the opposition to the powers of the executive department in the following terms:

THE WRITERS AGAINST THE CONSTITUTION seem to have taken pains to signalize their talent of misrepresentation, calculating upon the aversion of the people to monarchy, they have endeavoured to enlist all their jealousies and apprehensions in opposition to the intended President of the United States; not merely as the embryo but as the full grown progeny of that detested parent. . . . He has been decorated with attributes superior in dignity and splendor to those of a king of Great-Britain. He has been shown to us with the diadem sparkling on his brow, and the imperial purple flowing in his train. He has been seated on a throne surrounded with minions and mistresses; giving audience to the envoys of foreign potentates, in all the supercilious pomp of majesty. (FEDERALIST No. 67, at 452)

For his similar defense of the Necessary and Proper Clause, *see supra* ch. 2 notes 45–47.

12. FEDERALIST No. 70, at 471, 472 (Alexander Hamilton).

13. *See supra* ch. 4 notes 94, 97.

14. 16 JP 378, 379 (emphasis in original). The question with which President Washington was concerned was whether the power of the Senate to advise and consent to diplomatic appointments extended to the question of their grade. Jefferson concluded it did not, nor did it extend to their destination or commission. *Id.* at 378–80. For a more complete discussion of this question, *see infra* ch. 9 notes 22–25.

Rakove makes the point that since Jefferson was not there concerned with executive functions under the treaty power, he might have meant, in referring to the "transaction of business with foreign nations," only the ordinary conduct of foreign affairs, such as the appointment of ambassadors and routine communication with foreign powers. He did not mean to include the framing of foreign policy, which would encompass the delineation of the objectives of a treaty negotiation. He would leave that to the Senate. *See* Jack N. Rakove, *Solving a Constitutional Puzzle: The Treatymaking Clause as a Case Study,* 1 PERSPECTIVES IN AMER. HIST. 233, 266 n. 49 (New Series 1984).

In practice, Jefferson, when president, made no such distinction. He developed his own foreign policy objectives. *See* ABRAHAM D. SOFAER, WAR, FOREIGN AFFAIRS AND CONSTITUTIONAL POWER 196–205 (1976).

15. *See supra* ch. 3 notes 27–28.

16. 15 HP 37–38. *See also* the summation of his argument, 15 *id.* at 42–43.

17. 15 *id.* at 38–39.

18. 15 *id.* at 39 (emphasis in original).

19. 15 *id.* at 39–40. For a view adopting the Hamiltonian construction of art. II, § 2, *see* Randall H. Nelson, *The Termination of Treaties and Executive Agreements by the United States: Theory and Practice,* 42 MINN. L. REV. 879, 887 (1958). For a contrary opinion, *see* Arthur Bestor, *Respective Roles of Senate and President in the Making and Abrogation of Treaties,* 55 WASH. L. REV. 1, 28 (1979).

20. 15 HP 39, 42 (emphasis in original).

21. *See infra* note 31. The circumstance which gave rise to Hamilton's statement, it will be noted, was Washington's decision, without reference to Congress, to proclaim that the United States was at peace. The controversy therefore did not involve the issue of the circumstances under which the president, acting as the chief executive officer of the country and as commander in chief of the armed forces under art. II, § 2, cl. 1, may, without the consent of Congress, commit the military to action in a foreign country. For a thorough historical review and critique of presidential pretensions in this regard, *see generally* LOUIS FISHER, PRESIDENTIAL WAR POWER (1995).

A series of such presidential claims gave rise in 1973 to the adoption of the War Powers Resolution, Pub. L. No. 93–148, 87 STAT. 555 (1973), 50 U.S.C. §§ 1541 *et seq.* (1988), the constitutionality and wisdom of which have been challenged, *see* ROBERT W. TURNER, THE WAR POWERS RESOLUTION (1983); and defended, *see* John H. Sullivan, *The Impact of the War Powers Resolution, in* CONGRESS AND UNITED STATES FOREIGN POLICY 59–74 (Michael Barnhart ed., 1987). For a balanced view, *see* MARC E. SMYRL, CONFLICT AND CODETERMINATION (1988). Smyrl contends that in practice the president has been able to achieve his foreign policy goals under the War Powers Resolution for short-term initiatives and, as long as he has the support of Congress, for longer-term initiatives. Given congressional power over appropriations, he has not been able to sustain long-term policies when he has not had that support.

See the series of questions raised by SOFAER, *supra* note 14, at 1–2. There is of course a justification, based on Madison's notes of the debates over the war power in the Constitutional Convention, for some presidentially directed military action in the absence of a congressional declaration of war, 2 FR 318–19. *See infra* note 47. But outside of members or former members of the executive branch, there is hardly any support for the proposition that, in the absence of a threat to American security or to the safety of American citizens, the president may command the invasion of another country without congressional approval. Despite this, members of the Clinton administration, in September 1994, advanced the claim that the president, acting as commander in chief of the military (statement of Secretary of State Warren Christopher), or in directing "a police action" (statement of Madeleine K. Albright, United States representative to the United Nations), could authorize the invasion of Haiti. Neil A. Lewis, *Clinton Has Authority He Needs to Invade Haiti,* N.Y. TIMES, Sept. 12, 1994, A1.

Demonstrating once again that for most politicians constitutional construction is an instrument of politics, Senator George Mitchell and Representative Thomas S. Foley—leaders of the Democrat-controlled Congress, who in 1990, when President Bush had contemplated the use of military force in the Persian Gulf, had declared that such action, constituting an act of war, required congressional approval—saw no need for President Clinton to refer the matter of a Haitian invasion to Congress. *Id.* at A12. For other instances of President Clinton's insistence on the sole presidential power to deploy American military forces in foreign countries, *see* FISHER, *supra* at xi.

For a proposed revision of the War Powers Resolution in the light of its ineffectiveness in achieving its goal of compelling the president to seek congressional authorization before involving the military in armed combat, *see* JOHN H. ELY, WAR AND RESPONSIBILITY 115–31 (1993).

Louis Fisher and David Gray Adler urge that Congress repeal the War Powers Resolution, which they regard as contrary to the framers' intention. In practice, they say, the resolution grants the president the unbridled discretion to go to war against anyone, anytime and anywhere for at least ninety days. Instead, they urge that Congress keep presidential forays into foreign policy under control through the constitutional system of checks and balances, including, if necessary, resort to the impeachment process. *See* Fisher and Adler, *The War Powers Resolution: Time to Say Goodbye,* 113 POL. SCI. Q. 1 (1998).

22. 15 HP 40–41.

23. 15 *id.* at 41–42. In accordance with Hamilton's analysis, Congress on Jan. 14, 1991, adopted H.J.Res. 77, Pub.L. 102–1, 105 STAT. 3, authorizing the president to send U.S. armed forces against Iraq in the Persian Gulf area, pursuant to United Nations Resolution No. 678. In fact, since World War II, Congress generally has ceded to the president not only the power to make foreign policy but to engage the military in missions designed to further that policy without first obtaining authorization from Congress. Thereby, if the military engagements go awry, Congress has absolved itself from accountability and reserved to itself the right to blame the president. *See* ELY, *supra* note 21.

See also the statement of Senator James Hillhouse of Connecticut in 1807, that the president in conducting foreign and military affairs had acquired "the power not of declaring war in form, but of adopting a course of measures which will necessarily and inevitably lead to war." 17 ANNALS 335, quoted in SOFAER, *supra* note 14, at 208.

24. 15 HP 55–63.

25. Jefferson to Edmond Charles Genet, Nov. 22, 1793, 27 JP 414. On the basis of this position, Jefferson refused to discuss whether it was proper for the president under the Constitution to admit or exclude foreign consuls. Rakove points out that Jefferson may not have intended, by affirming the sole competence of the executive branch in the routine communications of the nation's policy to a foreign nation, a presidential competency in the initiation of foreign policy. *See* Rakove, *supra* note 14, at 266–67 n. 49. *But see* the summary of Jefferson's actions when president which reveal him as engaged in the widespread initiation of foreign policy, SOFAER, *supra* note 14, at 196–205.

26. Jefferson to Madison, July 7, 1793, 26 JP 443, 444.

27. 2 FR 392 (statement of Madison). Later, Madison in supporting a motion for the election of the president by the joint ballot of the House of Representatives and the Senate, observed that "the President is to act for the *people* not for the *States.*" 2 *id.* at 403 (emphasis in original). And earlier, in moving for presidential rather than senatorial appointments of the judiciary, he noted: "The Executive Magistrate wd. be considered as a national officer, acting for and equally sympathising with every part of the U. States. If the 2d branch alone should have this power, the Judges might be appointed by a minority of the people, tho' by a majority, of the States, which could not be justified on any principle as their proceedings were to relate to the people, rather than to the States." 2 *id.* at 81.

Bestor argues that by the statement quoted in the text Madison merely intended a matter of housekeeping: The president perforce, and not the Senate, was the agent for the actual negotiation of the treaty with the representative of a foreign sovereign. But, Bestor insists, Madison did not mean to suggest that the president should carry on these negotiations without preliminarily receiving the Senate's advice. In sum, while the president was the agent in making treaties, the Senate was the principal. *See* Arthur Bestor, *Separation of Powers in the Domain of Foreign Affairs,* 5 SETON HALL L. REV. 527, 635–36 (1974).

This interpretation is at odds with Madison's attitude toward the Senate in the convention following the decision to afford each state an equality of representation in that body. From that time forward, Madison's intention was to limit the prerogatives of the Senate, the members of which were to be elected by the state legislatures, and to elevate those of the president, who was to be elected by the people through the medium of presidential electors.

Hamilton specifically rejected the interpretation favored by Bestor: "To have entrusted the power of making treaties to the senate alone, would have been to relinquish the benefits of the constitutional agency of the president, in the conduct of foreign negotiations. It is true, that the senate would in that case have the option of employing him in this capacity; but . . . the ministerial servant of the senate could not be expected to enjoy the confidence and respect of foreign powers in the same degree with *the constitutional representative of the nation;* and of course would not be able to act with an equal degree of weight or efficacy." FEDERALIST No. 75, at 503, 506 (emphasis added). Rakove is curiously unimpressed with Hamilton's characterization of the president as "the constitutional representative of the nation." *See* Rakove, *supra* note 14, at 155.

That interpretation of Madison's position at the Constitutional Convention is repeated in Bestor, *Respective Roles of Senate and President in the Making and Abrogation of Treaties, supra* note 19, at 108–9. In also arguing that the framers did contemplate a president who would consult with the Senate before commencing treaty negotiations, Bestor is correct. But in practice Washington soon found this to be impolitic. He discovered, first, that the Senate as a whole was institutionally incapable of discussing the intricate details of negotiation and, then, that individual senators could not be trusted to keep confidential the administration's negotiating positions. For that reason, early in 1793, on the advice of Jefferson and the remainder of his cabinet, he withheld important information from the Senate about impending negotiations with an Indian tribe, out of fear that it might be leaked to the British. Later, because of the rise of party politics, he failed to consult with the Senate concerning the terms of a treaty that Jay should secure with the British. Instead, he confined his consultations to a small and influential group of Federalist senators. RALSTON HAYDEN, THE SENATE AND TREATIES, 1789–1817 20–94 (1920).

In recent years, the president has consulted with the Senate before commencing negotiations to determine the terms of a treaty to which the Senate is likely to consent. But for many years previously, the failure of the president so to consult inevitably led to the Senate's refusal to give its consent. *See* LOUIS HENKIN, CONSTITUTIONALISM, DEMOCRACY AND FOREIGN AFFAIRS 50–51 (1990).

28. 2 FR 540 (statement of Madison). *See also supra* ch. 1 notes 119–20.

29. ELKINS & MCKITRICK 354–65.

30. The Helvidius essays are collected in 15 MP 66–73, 80–87, 95–103, 106–10, 113–20.

31. 15 *id.* at 66–68. In Great Britain the crown, acting on the advice of ministers, makes war and peace. The House of Commons may refuse supplies or disapprove by condemnatory resolutions, but Parliament has no direct means of starting or ending a war. 2 WILLIAM R. ANSON & A. B. KEITH, THE LAW AND CUSTOM OF THE CONSTITUTION 136 (4th ed. 1935).

32. 15 MP 68–69. *See* the statement of James Wilson in the Constitutional Convention, in accord with Madison, that the power to declare war is legislative in nature. 1 FR 65–66; *but see* the statement of Chief Justice Marshall, that the declaration of war is not the equivalent of legislation, because it is not a law, in *Brown v. United States,* 12 U.S. (8 Cranch) 110, 125–26 (1814).

33. 15 MP 69–70.

34. 15 *id.* at 70–71.

35. 15 *id.* at 71.

36. 15 *id.* at 108.

37. *Id.*

38. 15 *id.* at 107. Wormuth and Firmage regard this statement of Madison's as "captious," inasmuch as he had argued that if the president, in interpreting a treaty, were to decide against peace, he would have to refer to Congress the question of declaring war. FRANCIS D. WORMUTH & EDWIN B. FIRMAGE, TO CHAIN THE DOG OF WAR 30 (1986).

39. 15 MP 96–97. For Hamilton's statement, *see supra* at note 10. In practice, the president has used the power to receive ambassadors, to recognize foreign governments, or to withhold recognition, as in the case of an ambassador from a rebellious colony when such reception might perhaps lead to war with the colonizing country. *See* WORMUTH & FIRMAGE, *supra* note 38, at 34.

40. 15 MP 98. Later, Madison said that on the subject of the declaration of war, the legislature was the organ of the national will. 15 *id.* at 106.

41. 15 *id.* at 110.

42. *See supra* ch. 3 note 28.

43. *See infra* ch. 8 note 40.

44. *Missouri v. Holland,* 252 U.S. 416, 432 (1920). *See* 1 RESTATEMENT (THIRD) OF THE FOREIGN RELATIONS LAW OF THE UNITED STATES § 302, cmt. d (1987).

45. FEDERALIST No. 75, at 503, 504–5 (Alexander Hamilton) (emphasis in original).

46. *See supra* note 27.

47. 2 FR 318, 319. Lofgren states that the delegates to the Constitutional Convention "*probably* understood [the Madison amendment] as a means to clarify that the executive could act against surprise attacks and would direct war once Congress had authorized it." *See* Charles A. Lofgren, *War Powers, Treaties, and the Constitution, in* THE FRAMING AND RATIFICATION OF THE CONSTITUTION 242, 251 (Leonard W. Levy and Dennis J. Mahoney eds., 1987) (emphasis in original). *Accord, see* WORMUTH & FIRMAGE, *supra* note 38, at 18; William Van Alstyne, *Congress, the President, and the Power to Declare War: A Requiem for Vietnam,* 121 U. PA. L. REV. 1, 7–9; Alexander M. Bickel, *Congress, the President and the Power to Wage War,* 48 CHI.-KENT L. REV. 131, 132 (1971).

In an earlier discussion of the subject, Lofgren concluded that Madison's notes, when read in connection with the official Journals of the Convention, and other contemporaneous sources, conferred upon Congress the nearly complete authority over the commencement of war; albeit, he conceded, it "remains possible that the President as Commander in Chief was *tacitly* accorded the initiative to meet sudden attacks on the United States." CHARLES A. LOFGREN, GOVERNMENT FROM REFLECTION AND CHOICE 3, 36 (1986) (emphasis in original). Bestor in his study of presidential power follows Lofgren's reading. *See* Bestor, *supra* note 27, at 527, 609.

48. FEDERALIST No. 64, at 432, 435–36 (John Jay). Marshall's statement was made during a debate in the Sixth Congress on a Republican motion to censure President John Adams for his order directed to a federal judge to deliver one Jonathan Robbins to the British navy, 10 ANNALS 613. The Marshall statement has been frequently cited by the Supreme Court, most notably in *United States v. Curtiss-Wright Export Corp.,* 299 U.S. 304, 319 (1936). In consequence, it can be stated that as "sole organ," the president is a separate source of law in foreign affairs. 1 RESTATEMENT (THIRD) OF THE LAW OF FOREIGN RELATIONS OF THE UNITED STATES, *supra* note 44, at § 1, Reporters' Note 2. *See also infra* ch. 11 note 8.

For a critical analysis of *Curtiss-Wright* and the reliance in the opinion of Justice George Sutherland therein on Marshall's "sole organ" speech, *see* LOFGREN, *supra* note 47, at 167–205. As Lofgren correctly states, whatever *Curtiss-Wright* means, it cannot support the proposition that presidential authority is independent of Congress in the formulation of foreign policy, as contrasted with its conduct. To similar effect, *see* WORMUTH & FIRMAGE, *supra* note 38, at 182; and HAROLD H. KOH, THE NATIONAL SECURITY CONSTITUTION 93–95 (1990).

49. FEDERALIST No. 72, at 486, 487 (Alexander Hamilton).

50. FEDERALIST No. 64, at 432, 434–35 (John Jay).

51. FEDERALIST No. 75, at 503, 505 (Alexander Hamilton). Lofgren is correct in his reading of No. 64 (Jay) and No. 75 (Hamilton) as not proposing an independent role in presidential treaty making. *See* LOFGREN, *supra* note 47, at 242–58. The president cannot act independently of the Senate, as Woodrow Wilson tragically discovered when, following World War I, in disregard of senatorial objections, he attempted to push through a treaty assuring the participation of the United States in the League of Nations.

According to Rakove, Jay's view of treaty making, as expressed in the *Federalist* No. 64, was that the Senate would define the objects of negotiation and leave it to the president to manage the details. *See* Rakove, *supra* note 14, at 254–55. A close reading of Jay's paper suggests a more complicated process. While he does not say who under the Constitution would initially determine foreign policy—the president, the Senate, or the president in consultation with the Senate—he is clear that because the tide of foreign affairs changes so rapidly, the president (working through the State Department) must be free to reformulate policy. If necessary, Jay concluded, he may convene and consult with the Senate for their advice and consent. *See* FEDERALIST No. 64, at 432, 435–36 (John Jay).

Rakove is of the opinion that by placing the provisions for treaty making in art. II, the framers intended to confer on the president a role in the making of treaties at least equal to that of the Senate, and perhaps one that in practice would become predominant. He bases his opinion, however, not on any express provision in the Constitution or any statement in the *Federalist* or the state ratifying conventions, but rather on the framers' experience of the inadequacies of government under the Articles of Confederation. Rakove, *supra*, at 267–81. On the effect of the Senate's inability to cope with the contingent complexities of negotiation and to maintain strict confidentiality, and the effect of partisan politics on the president's and the Senate's roles in treaty making, *see supra* note 27.

52. When Citizen Genet, the new French minister to the United States, publicly attacked Washington on his arrival in the country, and attempted to stir up the public against him, opinion, which initially had been disposed in favor of Genet and France, turned in favor of the president and the proclamation. *See supra* note 6. Observing this, Jefferson counseled Madison that he should not stress the substance of the proclamation in his essays, lest Republicans lose popular support. Jefferson to Madison, Aug. 11, 1793, 26 JP 651, 652.

53. *See supra* note 1.

54. Thus in his attack on the proclamation Madison charged that the reservation to the president of the unilateral power to terminate treaties was destined to impose on the country a monarchical form of government. 15 MP 110. For the ideological commitment of Madison, Jefferson, and Monroe to France as the European power that would advance the cause of republicanism in Europe and hence the world, as opposed to prevailing monarchical systems, *see* the resolutions of August 23, 1793 on Franco-American relations, prepared by Madison and Monroe for adoption by Republican rallies in Virginia. In these, they expressed the fear that the military defeat of France by a combination of monarchical governments would crush the cause of republicanism and liberty in France, and in America lead to the adoption of the forms and practices of the British monarchy by the government of the United States. 15 *id.* at 79–80.

55. *Witness* the tenacious but unsuccessful effort of Arizona Senator Barry Goldwater and other senators in 1979 to secure an opinion from the Supreme Court regarding President Jimmy Carter's unilateral, allegedly unconstitutional termination of a defense treaty with Tai-

wan. *See Goldwater v. Carter*, 444 U.S. 996 (1979), in which the Court upheld a judgment of the federal district court dismissing the complaint. Plaintiffs had sought a judgment declaring the decision of President Carter to terminate a treaty with the Taiwan government unconstitutional on the ground that such a decision, as that to make a treaty, required the consent of two-thirds of the Senate.

Four justices regarded the matter as "a political question," that is, one for the so-called political branches of the government—Congress and the president—to decide, and therefore not one within the cognizance of the judiciary. *Id.* at 1002. (For an early use of this expression by John Marshall during the Nash-Robbins debate in the Sixth Congress, *see infra* ch. 11 note 7). The plurality emphasized the absence of any specific constitutional provision governing treaty termination, *id.* at 1003; and pointed out that the case before the Court did not involve a dispute between private litigants over the scope of presidential authority, but was rather one between coequal branches of the government, *id.* at 1004–5.

Although Justice Powell considered the question justiciable, he concurred in the Court's judgment because he judged the suit premature, in that it had been brought by only a few members of Congress in advance of a decision by the full Senate. *Id.* at 997–98.

Justice Brennan, considering the question justiciable, would have dismissed the case on the merits. Agreeing with the judgment of the court of appeals, he held that the president unilaterally had the power to terminate a treaty. *Id.* at 1006–7.

Justices Blackman and White would have had the preliminary questions of justiciability and ripeness—Justice Powell's concern—fully briefed and argued. *Id.* at 1006.

For the opinion that the president, as "sole organ," has the power unilaterally to terminate a treaty, *see* 1 RESTATEMENT (THIRD) OF THE LAW OF FOREIGN RELATIONS OF THE UNITED STATES, *supra* note 44, at § 339, Reporters' Note 2.

56. For recent examples of the Senate's denial of the presidential power to interpret treaties and a reaffirmation of its power to do so, *see* HENKIN, *supra* note 27, at 47.

57. Uniformally, since Washington's proclamation, Congress has taken upon itself the responsibility of declaring neutrality, and the incumbent president has generally acceded to this action. LOUIS HENKIN, FOREIGN AFFAIRS AND THE CONSTITUTION 43 (2d ed. 1997). For a president who perhaps did not accede to the existing congressional policy of neutrality, Henkin cites President Franklin D. Roosevelt, who sent troops to Greenland and Iceland in 1940 apparently in the face of legislation forbidding it. *Id.* at 342 n. 27. The authority to terminate a treaty has been claimed, at various times, by the president—acting alone or in conjunction with the Senate—or by the Congress acting by joint resolution. *Id.* at 211–14. For a full discussion of the issue in the light of *Goldwater v. Carter, supra* note 55, *see* DAVID G. ADLER, THE CONSTITUTION AND THE TERMINATION OF TREATIES (1986).

7. Strict Construction: Impracticalities and Trivialities

1. Washington to Jefferson, Oct. 11, 1793, 33 WW 116–18; Washington to Hamilton, Oct. 14, 1793, 33 *id.* at 121–22; Washington to Madison, Oct. 14, 1793, 33 *id.* at 122–25. *See also* J. H. POWELL, BRING OUT YOUR DEAD (1949).

2. U.S. CONST. art. II, § 3 provides in part: "[The president] may, on extraordinary Occasions, convene both Houses, or either of them, and in Case of Disagreement between them, with Respect to the Time of Adjournment, he may adjourn them to such Time as he shall think proper."

3. Madison to Washington, Oct. 24, 1793, 15 MP 129–30.

4. 15 *id.* at 130; U.S. CONST. art. I, § 6, cl. 1 provides in part: "and for any Speech or Debate in either House, they [Senators and Representatives] shall not be questioned in any other

Place." *See also* 1 WILLIAM R. ANSON & A. B. KEITH, THE LAWS AND CUSTOM OF THE CONSTITUTION 157–61 (4th ed. 1935).

5. *See supra* ch. 3 notes 79–82. *See also* U.S. CONST. art. I, § 7, cl. 3 which provides in part: "Every Order, Resolution, or Vote to which the Concurrence of the Senate and House of Representatives may be necessary (except on a question of Adjournment) shall be presented to the President of the United States; and before the Same shall take Effect, shall be approved by him, or being disapproved by him, shall be repassed by two thirds of the Senate and House of Representatives, according to the Rules and Limitations prescribed in the Case of a Bill."

6. *See supra* ch. 4 note 24.

7. 15 MP 130.

8. 15 *id.* at 131.

9. Jefferson to Washington, Oct. 17, 1793, 27 JP 253, 254. It's hard to know why Jefferson gave the president the advice he did. Washington, he must have known, was a cautious and practical man. Therefore, it was much more likely that he would prefer the course Madison had recommended to the one that Jefferson had set forth. Did the latter, nevertheless, wish to avoid establishing a precedent that might be used against him in some future constitutional disputation? Or was he giving vent to the feeling that if members of the executive branch, including the president and himself, had had that autumn to remain in Philadelphia to keep the government going, thereby exposing themselves to the dangers of malaria, members of Congress should do the same—at least for the limited purpose of entering the city so that they could decide to meet somewhere else?

10. Hamilton to Washington, Oct. 24, 1793, 15 HP 373–74.

11. 15 *id.* at 375. *See also* JOHN C. MILLER, ALEXANDER HAMILTON 379–80 (1959).

12. *See* POWELL, *supra* note 1.

13. 4 ANNALS 74, 530–31. The Act of Apr. 3, 1794, 1 STAT. 353.

14. Jefferson to Madison, Jan. 22, 1797, 16 MP 473, in which as vice-president-elect, he expressed his disinclination to participate in the coming administration of President-elect John Adams: "I cannot have a wish to see the scenes of 93. revived as to myself, & to descend daily into the arena like a gladiator to suffer martyrdom in every conflict."

15. *See supra* ch. 4 note 112.

16. SAMUEL F. BEMIS, JAY'S TREATY 122–46 (rev. ed. 1962).

17. 27 JP 567–78, 579–80.

18. 4 ANNALS 155–56.

19. BEMIS, *supra* note 16, at 1–9, 243–44.

20. *Id.* at 130–31, 138.

21. *Id.* at 132–39. The British also laid claim under the Treaty of Peace to the restoration of property of loyal British subjects confiscated by various states during the Revolution. But Jefferson was able to show that, since most of the property had been confiscated before the treaty's conclusion, the treaty had not required but only recommended its restoration. *Id.* at 134–35.

22. *Id.* at 28–50.

23. The seizures resulted from the execution of a British order-in-council of June 8, 1793. The order was issued as part of an overall British determination to control the seas during the renewal of war with the French, and to prevent any merchandise from reaching their enemy. *Id.* at 210–13.

24. 4 ANNALS 343 (statement of Rep. Ames), 185–90 (statement of Rep. Smith). For a thorough analysis of the defects in the Jefferson-Madison position and of the Ames and Smith speeches, *see* ELKINS & MCKITRICK 377–87.

25. 4 ANNALS 156.

26. *See,* moreover, what Madison wrote in the *Federalist,* where in justification of the congressional power in question he observed:

> A DEFINITION OF FELONIES ON THE HIGH SEAS is evidently requisite. Felony is a term of loose signification even in the common law of England; and of various import in the statute law of that kingdom. But neither the common, nor the statute law of that or of any other nation ought to be a standard for the proceedings of this, unless previously made its own by legislative adoption. The meaning of the term as defined in the codes of the several States, would be as impracticable as the former would be a dishonorable and illegitimate guide. It is not precisely the same in any two of the States; and varies in each with every revision of its criminal laws. For the sake of certainty and uniformity therefore, the power of defining felonies in this case, was in every respect necessary and proper. (FEDERALIST No. 42, at 279, 281)

The same considerations would seem to apply to a prosecution for "Offences under the Law of Nations." For the discussion regarding a constitutional basis for a federal nonstatutory law of crime, based on the common law, *see infra* ch. 9 notes 128–31, and ch. 10 notes 27, 36, 72.

27. 4 ANNALS 169–70 (statement of Rep. Smith).

28. *See supra* ch. 5 notes 23–24.

29. 4 ANNALS 170 (statement of Rep. Madison).

30. 4 *id.* at 171 (statement of Rep. Madison).

31. *Id.*

32. *Id.*

33. 4 *id.* at 171–72 (statement of Rep. Madison). Moreover, Madison had not suggested that by virtue of its power to define offenses against the law of nations, Congress should impose penalties for violations of such a designated offense. In that case, presumably, Great Britain would be the offender, and as such should be expected to pay the penalties. Instead, Madison had proposed that British producers and shippers should make payments for the losses, but as duties, rather than as penalties.

That was not the end of the constitutional muddle. Ordinarily, duties are government revenues, imposed under the taxing power and paid into the Treasury and expended for governmental purposes. Was Madison suggesting that, instead, the duties he recommended be segregated in the Treasury as a special fund to be used for the benefit of the affected American shipping interests? If so, he contemplated a substantial expansion of his version of congressional power under the Spending Clause. *See United States v. Butler,* 297 U.S. 1 (1936).

34. 4 ANNALS 422. The bill became law, the Act of Feb. 12, 1794, 6 STAT. 13.

35. ELKINS & McKITRICK 388–91; BEMIS, *supra* note 16, at 264–65.

36. 4 ANNALS 524, the Act of Mar. 27, 1792, 1 STAT. 35.

37. ELKINS & McKITRICK 392–93.

38. Madison to Jefferson, Mar. 14, 1794, 15 MP 284.

39. 15 *id.* at 735–38.

40. FEDERALIST No. 69, at 462, 465 (Alexander Hamilton) (emphasis in original). For Hamilton's reassurances in the *Federalist* as to the president's limited powers with respect to his duty to receive foreign ministers, *see supra* ch. 6 note 10. Hamilton had given these reassurances to quell charges that the constitutional powers conferred on the president would make him "the full grown progeny of that detested parent," the king of Great Britain. FEDERALIST No. 67, at 452 (Alexander Hamilton).

41. 4 ANNALS 738 (statement of Rep. Madison).

42. *See supra* ch. 6 notes 36–38.

43. *See supra* ch. 1 note 128. Almost at the last minute, Mason had moved for the insertion

of a clause in art. I, § 8, cl. 16, empowering Congress to "provide for organizing, arming and disciplining the Militia," which would alert the public to the danger of standing armies. While he was aware, he said, that their absolute prohibition might be unsafe, nevertheless he favored prefacing the above clause with the words "And that the liberties of the people may be better secured against the danger of standing armies in time of peace." Randolph seconded the motion. 2 FR 616–17. Madison spoke in support, saying it would be well "to discountenance them by the Constitution, as far as will consist with the essential power of the Govt. on that head." 2 *id.* at 617. The motion was overwhelmingly defeated, only Georgia voting with Virginia. *Id.*

Earlier, the convention had also overwhelmingly defeated a motion made by Gerry to restrict the number of soldiers in peacetime to two or three thousand. Gerry had argued that otherwise there would be no check against standing armies. Jonathan Dayton of New Jersey had replied that since preparation for war was generally made in time of peace some kind of standing army might be inevitable. 2 *id.* at 329–30.

44. FEDERALIST No. 8, at 44, 46 (Alexander Hamilton).

45. The states of New Hampshire, New York, and Virginia all proposed amendments to the Constitution with respect to the maintenance of a peacetime standing army. New Hampshire's proposal would have conditioned a standing army on the approval of three-fourths of Congress, 4 DHFFC at 15, New York's, on the approval of two-thirds of the senators and representatives present. 4 *id.* at 23. Virginia, regarding a standing army as dangerous to liberty, would have avoided one "as far as the circumstances and protection of the Community will admit." 4 *id.* at 17. For Jefferson's post-convention advocacy of the adoption of a bill of rights which would include a provision for the abolition of peacetime standing armies, *see* Jefferson to Madison, July 31, 1788, 13 JP 440–43.

46. 4 ANNALS 738. A prior version of the move to increase the army was also rejected. 4 *id.* at 709. For a summary of the Federalist efforts to expand the military in the Third Congress, *see* RICHARD H. KOHN, EAGLE AND SWORD 220–21 (1975). For Washington's recommendation to the Continental Congress of the need for a professional army, *see* GLENN A. PHELPS, GEORGE WASHINGTON AND AMERICAN CONSTITUTIONALISM 33–34, 60 (1993). Later, in deference to anti-army sentiments, Washington did not press his position. *Id.* at 72, 132.

47. *See infra* ch. 9 notes 54–56.

48. U.S. CONST. art. I, § 2, cl. 3, then provided in part: "Representatives and direct Taxes shall be apportioned among the several States which may be included within this Union, according to their respective Numbers."

49. Gouverneur Morris described indirect taxes as those on imports and consumption, 1 FR 591–92. But, interestingly, when later in the convention Rufus King asked for "the precise meaning of *direct* taxation," Madison noted that no one answered. 2 FR 350 (emphasis in the original).

50. FEDERALIST No. 36, at 222, 225–26 (Alexander Hamilton). To the same effect, *see* FEDERALIST No. 12, at 73, 75–76 (Alexander Hamilton); and FEDERALIST No. 21, at 134–35 (Alexander Hamilton).

51. *See* statement of Rep. Samuel Dexter of Massachusetts, 4 ANNALS 646 .

52. 4 *id.* at 652–53 (statement of Rep. Murray).

53. 4 *id.* at 644 (statement of Rep. Sedgwick).

54. 4 *id.* at 730 (statement of Rep. Madison).

55. Madison played an integral part in the presentation of this case. He arranged for the publication in *Aurora,* the Republican paper in Philadelphia, of the views of Virginia's chief justice, Edmund Pendleton, who opposed the tax on constitutional grounds. Thereafter Madison consulted with Jared Ingersoll, counsel for the taxpayer, in the preparation of his argument before the United States Supreme Court. 16 MP 149.

56. *Hylton v. United States,* 3 U.S. (Dall.) 171 (1796). There were, however, many jurisdictional and procedural problems connected with the disposition of the case. In the first place, it is questionable whether the Court had jurisdiction over the appeal, since under § 22 of the Judiciary Act of 1789 (1 STAT. 73, 84) the amount in controversy in the matter before the Court had to *exceed* the sum of two thousand dollars and the plaintiff-appellant's complaint had alleged the amount to be exactly two thousand dollars. Moreover, the plaintiff, who had further alleged that he owned 125 carriages, in fact owned only one, upon which he owed taxes and penalties of about sixteen dollars. Finally, when following judgment in the court below, the plaintiff's attorneys withdrew from the case, the government retained and paid two other attorneys to prepare and argue the appeal in their place. All in all, the matter hardly seemed to have presented a genuine case and controversy, as required under the provisions of art. III, § 2, cl. 1 of the Constitution. WILLIAM R. CASTO, THE SUPREME COURT IN THE EARLY REPUBLIC: THE CHIEF JUSTICESHIPS OF JOHN JAY AND OLIVER ELLSWORTH 101–5 (1995). For a different account of the political circumstances giving rise to the *Hylton* case, *cf.* Jack N. Rakove, *The Origins of Judicial Power: A Plea for New Contexts,* 49 STAN. L. REV. 1031, 1039–41 (1997).

57. 4 ANNALS 602–3.

58. RALSTON HAYDEN, THE SENATE AND TREATIES, 1789–1817 63–67 (1970).

59. *Id.* at 70–73.

60. *See* GEORGE PELLEW, JOHN JAY 263–68 (1898), and FRANK MONAGHAN, JOHN JAY 325–41, 364–68, 388–90, 405–6 (1935).

61. *Id.*

62. 4 ANNALS 89–90.

63. Madison was married on Sept. 15, 1794, during the recess between the first and second sessions of the Third Congress. IRVING BRANT, JAMES MADISON: FATHER OF THE CONSTITUTION, 1787–1800 410 (1950).

64. BROADUS MITCHELL, ALEXANDER HAMILTON 366–69 (1962).

65. MILLER, *supra* note 11, at 396–99, 404–14.

66. 4 ANNALS 788. In the same address, Washington gave an account of the rebellion and its suppression. *Id.* at 787–90. Congress commended him. *Id.* at 794 (Senate), 947–48 (House). Thus, as to Washington's actions, no constitutional issue was raised.

67. 4 *id.* at 794; Alfred F. Young, *The Democratic Republicans in New York, in* AFTER THE CONVENTION 226–27 (Lance Banning ed., 1989).

68. 4 ANNALS 934–35 (statement of Rep. Madison).

69. 4 *id.* at 943–44.

70. 4 *id.* at 1030–32 (statements of Rep. Giles and Rep. Madison).

71. 4 *id.* at 1072–80 (statements of Rep. Nicholas, Rep. Giles, and Rep. Madison).

72. 4 *id.* at 1165–66 (statements of Rep. Samuel Smith and Rep. Giles).

73. *See* Fisher Ames to Christopher Gore, May 2, 1794, in which he quoted the remarks of Senator John Taylor, Republican of Virginia, to Senator Rufus King, Federalist of New York: "You are strange fellows: Formerly, you did what you chose with a small majority; now, we have a great majority, and can do nothing. You have baffled every one of our plans." 1 WORKS OF FISHER AMES 142 (Seth Ames ed., 1854).

8. Jay's Treaty and the Withering of Madison's Authority

1. Provisions for withdrawal of the troops were set forth in art. II of the treaty, 8 STAT. 117. Arbitration of the boundary disputes, concerning the location of the northern extent of the Mississippi River and the northern borders of the present state of Maine, was provided for in art. IV and V respectively. 8 *id.* at 118–19.

2. *See* art. VII, 8 *id.* at 121–22.

3. Art. XII applied to the British West Indies, 8 *id.* at 122–23; art. XIII, to the British East Indies, 8 *id.* at 123–24.

4. *See* art. VI, 8 *id.* at 119–21. Jay regarded the admission of American shipping into the British West and East Indies as compensation for the detention of the posts and other claims of that nature, including for the loss of the Negroes. *See* SAMUEL F. BEMIS, JAY'S TREATY 357 n. 6 (rev. ed. 1962). For a detailed criticism of the provision referring the settlement of British debt to a mixed commission and of other treaty provisions, *see* JERALD A. COMBS, THE JAY TREATY 152–53 (1970).

5. *See* art. XIV and XV, 8 STAT. at 124–25.

6. *See* art. XVII and XVIII, 8 *id.* at 125–26.

7. *See* BEMIS, *supra* note 4, at 358.

8. 4 ANNALS 853–55. For Washington's views on the treaty, expressed after the Senate returned the treaty, *see* Washington to Randolph, July 22, 1795: "My opinion respecting the treaty, is the same now as it was: namely, not favorable to it, but that it is better to ratify it in the manner the Senate have advised (with the reservation already mentioned), than to suffer matters to remain as they are, unsettled." 34 WW 243, 244.

9. The vote was twenty to ten, the two-thirds of the senators present required for ratification pursuant to U.S. CONST. art. II, § 2, cl. 2. 4 ANNALS 862–63. The amendment disapproved art. XII affecting the revival of commerce with the British West Indies. The reason for the disapproval was the limitation of American vessels to those not exceeding seventy tons and the prohibition against the reexportation of tropical produce from the United States. BEMIS, *supra* note 4, at 467–69; ELKINS & MCKITRICK 418–19.

10. To the Republicans, Jay's Treaty appeared to be a confirmation of their fears that the Federalist foreign policy was moving the United States to a reunion with Great Britain, the model in Republican eyes of the Federalist financial system and resulting domestic corruption. RICHARD R. BEEMAN, THE OLD DOMINION AND THE NEW NATION 153 (1972); LANCE BANNING, THE JEFFERSONIAN PERSUASION 234 (1978). For an extended commentary on the circumstances of the publication in *Aurora* and on Senator Mason's role in the leak, *see* 18 HP 389–92 n. 2.

11. JOHN A. CARROLL & MARY W. ASHWORTH, GEORGE WASHINGTON: FIRST IN PEACE 257 (1957).

12. *See* the introductory note to the Camillus essays, 18 HP 475–79. For Jefferson's comments, *see* his letter to Madison, Sept. 21, 1795: "Hamilton is really a colossus to the antirepublican party. Without numbers, he is an host within himself. They have got themselves into a defile, where they might be finished; but too much security on the Republican part, will give time to his talents & indefatigableness to extricate them. We have had only midling [*sic*] performances to oppose to him. In truth, when he comes forward, there is nobody but yourself who can meet him." 16 MP 88–89.

13. CARROLL & ASHWORTH, *supra* note 11, at 277–98. For a detailed account of the Fauchet report, *see* ELKINS & MCKITRICK 426–31.

14. *Id.* at 441–42.

15. 16 MP 96, 102.

16. For a report of Marshall's position in the Virginia General Assembly, *see* the excerpt from a letter of Thomas Mann Randolph, Jr., to Thomas Jefferson, Nov. 22, 1795, which Jefferson enclosed in his letter to Madison, Nov. 26, 1795, 16 MP 134–36; for the actions of the General Assembly in proposing amendments to the United States Constitution, *see* Thomas J. Farnham, *The Virginia Amendments of 1795*, VA. MAG. OF HIST. AND BIOG. 75–85 (1967).

17. Jefferson to Madison, Nov. 26, 1795, 16 MP 134–36.

18. 23 JP 256–57.

19. 23 *id.* at 263.

20. 23 *id.* at 263–64 (emphasis in original). By his emphasis, Jefferson probably intended to indicate a dangerous tendency against republican principles on Washington's part. For a full discussion of American foreign policy with regard to the Barbary Powers, particularly Algiers, from 1784 through 1821, *see* GERHARD CASPER, SEPARATING POWER 45–65 (1997).

21. Gouverneur Morris had moved the first resolution, 2 FR 382–83, 392–94; James Wilson, the second, 2 *id.* at 532, 538. The reason for the Pennsylvanians' motions was their state's fear that the interests of the large commercial states might suffer from treaties to which the Senate, dominated by the smaller states, might consent. George Mason also worried that the Senate might consent to a treaty ceding territory to a foreign power. 2 *id.* at 297.

22. Since under the Supremacy Clause a treaty was a law, it was binding on Congress until repealed. 20 HP 4.

23. 20 *id.* at 22–23.

24. 5 ANNALS 11, 47, 394.

25. ELKINS & MCKITRICK 439–41. Combs concludes that antipathy to the treaty had died down even before Washington's ratification, but that his action gave greater impetus to public acceptance of the treaty. *See* COMBS, *supra* note 4, at 170.

26. HENRY ADAMS, THE LIFE OF ALBERT GALLATIN 76–86 (1880).

27. 5 ANNALS 419, 424. For Edward Livingston's assessment of Madison's character, *see* the pertinent excerpt from his letter to his brother, Robert R. Livingston, Dec. 24, 1795, *reprinted in* 16 MP 248. The Livingston Papers are deposited in the Haverford College Library, Haverford, Pennsylvania.

28. 5 ANNALS 427, 428 (statement of Rep. Livingston). For Livingston's later admission, *see infra* note 33.

29. 5 *id.* at 429–35 (statements of Rep. Murray and Rep. Buck).

30. 5 *id.* at 436–37 (statement of Rep. Gallatin).

31. 5 *id.* at 462 (statement of Rep. Harper).

32. 5 *id.* at 463–64 (statement of Rep. Harper).

33. 5 *id.* at 461 (statement of Rep. Harper). Actually, the papers were in the custody of the Senate clerk. Presumably, House members seeking access would apply to the clerk for an inspection. Samuel Smith, a Republican spokesman, admitted that what Harper said was true, but argued that the House membership needed freer access so that they could quote from the papers and, if challenged, readily verify the quotation. 5 *id.* at 625.

Livingston also admitted he had seen the papers but said that what he had seen had convinced him of the propriety of their being laid before the House. He remembered, he said, that positive directions to Jay as to what was necessary for a satisfactory treaty of commerce had not been realized in the concluded treaty. 5 *id.* at 629–30.

34. 5 *id.* at 464–65 (statement of Rep. Gallatin).

35. 5 *id.* at 465–68 (statement of Rep. Gallatin). For Marshall's thesis, *see supra* note 16.

36. 5 ANNALS 467 (statement of Rep. Gallatin). *See infra* notes 92–100.

37. 5 ANNALS 469–74 (statement of Rep. Gallatin). For British practice, *see* 2 WILLIAM R. ANSON & A. B. KEITH, THE LAW AND CUSTOM OF THE CONSTITUTION 142 (4th ed. 1935). Gallatin would have referred to two series of United States laws: (1) relating to the imposition of an additional ten percent in duties on goods carried in foreign ships or vessels, such as imposed successively in the First Congress in § 5 of the Act of July 4, 1789, 1 STAT. 24, 27, and in § 2, the Act of Aug. 10, 1790, 1 STAT. 180, 181; in the Second Congress in § 5, the Act of May 2, 1792, 1 STAT. 259, 260; and in the Third Congress in § 4, the Act of Jan. 7, 1794, 1 STAT. 390, 392 and in § 5, the Act of Jan. 29, 1795, 1 STAT. 411; and (2) relating to the prohibition of the importation of goods by land except by way of Louisville, as provided in the First Congress in § 40, the Act of July 31, 1789, 1 STAT. 29, 48, and in § 70, the Act of

Aug. 4, 1790, 1 STAT. 145, 177 and, following the admission of Vermont as a state, by way of Allburg, Vermont, in § 8, the Act of Mar. 2. 1791, 1 STAT. 197, 198.

38. FEDERALIST No. 69, at 462, 467 (Alexander Hamilton). After "jurist" in "Every jurist of that kingdom," Hamilton inserted the following note: "*Vide Blackstone's Commentaries, vol. I, par. 257*" (emphasis in original). Later Hamilton explained why the House had not been included in the treaty-making process:

> THE FLUCTUATING, AND TAKING ITS FUTURE INCREASE into the account, the multitudinous composition of that body, forbid us to expect in it those qualities which are essential to the proper execution of such a trust [the formation of treaties]. Accurate and comprehensive knowledge of foreign politics; a steady and systematic adherence to the same views; a nice and uniform sensibility to national character, decision, *secrecy* and dispatch; are incompatible with the genius of a body so variable and so numerous. The very complication of the business by introducing a necessity of the concurrence of so many different bodies, would of itself afford a solid objection. The greater frequency of the calls upon the house of representatives, and the greater length of time which it would often be necessary to keep them together when convened, to obtain their sanction in the progressive stages of a treaty, would be source of so great inconvenience and expence, as alone ought to condemn the project. (FEDERALIST No. 75, at 503, 507 [Alexander Hamilton] [emphasis in original])

Presumably, because of the dim views this essay had taken of the capacity of the House to participate in the treaty-making process, House Federalists in the Fourth Congress decided not to refer to either *Federalist* paper. Instead, as will be seen shortly, they opted to refer to the reports of the proceedings of the state ratifying conventions and the Journals of the Constitutional Convention, thereby to attack Madison personally.

39. 5 ANNALS 487 (statement of Rep. Madison).

40. 5 *id.* at 487–95 (statement of Rep. Madison).

41. FEDERALIST No. 53, at 359, 364 (James Madison).

42. FEDERALIST No. 58, at 391, 394 (James Madison).

43. *See supra* ch. 6 notes 34–35. It should be noted that Hamilton had made use of Madison's Helvidius arguments in his newspaper defense of Jay's Treaty. 20 HP 4.

44. 5 ANNALS 514–16 (statement of Rep. Sedgwick). *See* Hamilton in FEDERALIST No. 75, at 504–5, quoted *supra* ch. 6 note 45. In the same speech, Sedgwick touched on one of the many incidental constitutional issues raised in the course of the debate when he said that the treaty-making power was illimitable by the Constitution; indeed, by its nature the power was illimitable. Thus a treaty could make provision for matters affecting person and property not delegated to the national government. 5 ANNALS 517. For a comment on Sedgwick's speech and on other early historical sources in the light of the later decision in *Missouri v. Holland,* 252 U.S. 416 (1920), *see* CHARLES A. LOFGREN, GOVERNMENT FROM REFLECTION AND CHOICE, 116, 148–55 (1986). *See also* Charles A. Lofgren, *War Powers, Treaties, and the Constitution, reprinted in* THE FRAMING AND RATIFICATION OF THE CONSTITUTION 242, 256–57 (Leonard W. Levy & Dennis S. Mahoney eds., 1987).

45. 5 ANNALS 522–26 (statement of Rep. Sedgwick). For the remarks in the Virginia convention, *see* 10 DHRC 1381–82 (Henry's speech of June 18, 1788); *id.* at 1390–91 (Mason's speech of June 19, 1788); *id.* at 1391–92 (Francis Corbin's speech of June 19, 1788); *id.* at 1394–95 (Henry's speech of June 19, 1788); and *id.* at 1395 (Madison's speech of June 19, 1788). In advancing this argument, Sedgwick was also following the line of Hamilton's newspaper defense of the treaty published on Jan. 9, 1796, 20 HP 23–25. Hamilton had also relied on the reasons that Gerry had publicly given for his not approving the Constitution at the Constitutional Convention: The Constitution had, by placing the treaty-making power in the

president and Senate, conferred on them the exclusive power of legislation. *Id.* at 23; 8 DHRC 43–46.

46. 5 ANNALS 526 (statement of Rep. Sedgwick).

47. 5 *id.* at 495–97 (statement of Rep. William Smith). *See also* JOURNAL OF THE HOUSE OF DELEGATES 91–92 (1795). For a discussion of the proposed amendments of the Virginia legislature, *see* Farnham, *supra* note 16. Smith also followed Hamilton's newspaper line of defense, published Jan. 9, 1796, 20 HP 24–25.

48. 5 ANNALS 565–75 (statement of Rep. Bourne).

49. 5 *id.* at 701 (statement of Rep. Murray).

50. 5 *id.* at 702 (statement of Rep. Murray).

51. 5 *id.* at 726–33, 737–38 (statement of Rep. Gallatin).

52. 5 *id.* at 733–34 (statement of Rep. Gallatin).

53. 5 *id.* at 734 (statement of Rep. Gallatin). Earlier, Baldwin, one of the framer-clerks to whom Gallatin had referred, had been more deferential to his fellow members of the Constitutional Convention. Replying to Sedgwick's speech and before Murray's attack on Madison, Baldwin admitted that the framers' reasons, along with the proposed amendments of the several states, might have had due force if they had been the common view of the subject and one that naturally presented itself on reading the Constitution; but under the circumstances he thought the arguments had been allowed more weight than was their due. In fact, he added, never before had so much time been employed on searching and settling this one point. 5 *id.* at 538–39.

54. FEDERALIST No. 40, at 258, 263–64 (James Madison).

55. *Id.* at 267. The remarks of James Wilson in the Pennsylvania ratifying convention were to the same effect, made to defend the delegates of the Constitutional Convention against the same charge:

> THE LATE CONVENTION HAVE DONE NOTHING beyond their powers. The fact is, they have exercised no power at all. And in point of validity, this Constitution, proposed by them for the government of the United States, claims no more than a production of the same nature would claim, flowing from a private pen. It is laid before the citizens of the United States, unfettered by restraint; it is laid before them to be judged by the natural, civil, and political rights of men. By their FIAT, it will be become of value and authority; without it, it will never receive the character of authenticity and power. 2 DHRC 483–84 (Wilson's speech in the Pennsylvania ratifying convention, Dec. 4, 1787) (emphasis in original).

See also statements to the same effect by William R. Davie and Archibald Maclaine in the first North Carolina ratifying convention, 4 ED 23 (Davie), and 25 (Maclaine). *See generally* 4 *id.* at 16–26 (debate in the North Carolina ratifying convention, July 24, 1788).

On the basis of those statements, as well as for other reasons, Lofgren concludes that the original understanding of original intent does not rule out a resort to the understandings and expectations voiced in the state ratifying conventions. Charles A. Lofgren, *The Original Understanding of Original Intent?* 5 CONST. COMM. 77, 83–84 (1988). *See also* 5 *id.* at 112–13.

56. 5 ANNALS 734 (statement of Rep. Gallatin). Earlier, Livingston had similarly disparaged the competency of the state ratifying conventions: "They were called in haste, they were heated by party, and many adopted it from expediency, without having fully debated the different articles." 5 *id.* at 635.

57. 5 *id.* at 736–37 (statement of Rep. Gallatin). 4 ED 125–31 (Iredell's speech in the North Carolina ratifying convention, July 28, 1788); 2 DHRC at 562–653 (Wilson's speech at the Pennsylvania ratifying convention, Dec. 11, 1787). Perhaps Gallatin did not know it, but it was Wilson who at the Constitutional Convention had made one of the rejected motions

that the advice and consent of the House of Representatives also be required in the treaty-making process. *See supra* note 21.

58. 5 ANNALS 745–46 (statement of Rep. Gallatin).

59. 5 *id.* at 746–47 (statement of Rep. Cooper).

60. *See supra* ch. 4 notes 51, 63, 84.

61. *See supra* ch. 5 note 24.

62. *See supra* ch. 3 notes 79–82; ch. 7 notes 2–5.

63. *See supra* ch. 6 note 36; ch. 7 notes 39–41.

64. *See supra* ch. 4 note 94.

65. For Hamilton's broad construction of the spending power, *see supra* ch. 5 notes 18, 21; for his broad construction of the presidential control of foreign affairs, *see supra* ch. 6 notes 16–23.

66. 5 ANNALS 759–60.

67. 5 *id.* at 630 (statement of Rep. Livingston).

68. 5 *id.* at 760–62. *See also supra* at notes 18–20.

69. 5 *id.* at 760–61 (message of President Washington).

70. 5 *id.* at 761 (message of President Washington).

71. 5 *id.*

72. *Id.* For Bourne's argument, *see supra* note 48.

73. 5 ANNALS 761 (message of President Washington). For the relevant proceedings of the Constitutional Convention, *see supra* note 21. For Murray's remarks, *see supra* notes 49–50.

74. Ames to George Richards Minot, Apr. 2, 1796, 1 WORKS OF FISHER AMES 190, 191 (Seth Ames ed., 1854). For the letter of Jonathan Trumbull, Jr., to Jonathan Trumbull, Apr. 2, 1796, *see* RALPH KETCHAM, JAMES MADISON 362 (1971); for the letter of Madison to Monroe, Apr. 7, 1796, *see* 16 MP 301, 303; for Adams's letter to his wife, Abigail, *see* ELKINS & MCKITRICK 846 n. 241.

75. Madison to Jefferson, Apr. 4, 1796, in 16 MP 285–86; 20 HP 66.

76. 5 ANNALS 771–72. Although the authorship of these resolutions has been attributed to Madison, the editors of his papers, while admitting the likelihood of the attribution, state that no documentary evidence of such has been located. *See* 16 MP 287 n. 6.

77. 5 ANNALS 774 (statement of Rep. Madison).

78. *See supra* note 67.

79. 5 ANNALS 772 (statement of Rep. Madison).

80. 5 *id.* at 775 (statement of Rep. Madison).

81. 5 *id.* For the remarks of Justice Wilson in the Pennsylvania ratifying convention, *see supra* note 55. For the reference to the protest meetings held in Charleston and Wilmington, *see* 16 MP 301 n. 5. John Rutledge and Charles Pinckney, the most prominent of the Charleston participants, and John Dickinson, the most prominent of the Wilmington participants, had all been delegates to the Constitutional Convention. Furthermore, Washington had recently nominated Rutledge to serve as chief justice of the United States in place of Jay, who had resigned. The Senate, however, rejected his nomination, partly out of displeasure over his participation at the Charleston protest meetings but also, supposedly, out of concern over reports that he was going insane. 1 CHARLES WARREN, THE SUPREME COURT IN UNITED STATES HISTORY 127–39 (1937). William Casto discredits the latter reason for the rejection of his appointment. *See* WILLIAM R. CASTO, THE SUPREME COURT IN THE EARLY REPUBLIC: THE CHIEF JUSTICESHIPS OF JOHN JAY AND OLIVER ELLSWORTH 90–95 (1995). For Madison's reference to his recollections of the Constitutional Convention and to Gerry's chastisement, *see supra* ch. 4 notes 51, 78.

82. 5 ANNALS 776 (statement of Rep. Madison).

83. 5 *id.* at 776–77 (statement of Rep. Madison).

84. 5 *id.* at 779–81 (statement of Rep. Madison).

85. For a friend's report of Madison's statement that his work in preparing his notes of the Constitutional Convention "almost killed him," *see* editorial note, 10 MP 3, 7.

86. Indeed, it is because of Madison's notes of the proceedings of the Constitutional Convention that lawyers, judges, and constitutional scholars have striven to identify and make use of framers' intent. For the same reason once the relevance of framers' intent is minimized, the value of his notes is diminished. Lofgren, *supra* note 55, at 102.

Lofgren's article constitutes a critical commentary on an article by H. Jefferson Powell, *The Original Understanding of Original Intent*, 98 HARV. L. REV. 885 (1985). Powell concludes that the original understanding of those who considered the Constitution from 1789 onward was that its meaning should be ascertained not by an inquiry into the expectations of those framing or ratifying the Constitution, but into such evidence of the proceedings of the state ratifying conventions as would shed light on the extent to which sovereign polities could delegate their rights and powers without destroying their own essential sovereignty. *Id.* at 887–88, 948. Lofgren for the most part agrees with Powell, but thinks that the original understanding of the period did not exclude the use of an individual ratifier's subjective intent; in fact, the understanding encompassed it. Lofgren, *supra* note 55, at 78–79, 112–13.

Common to both their approaches, however, is the conclusion that — despite Madison's dethronement as a reliable interpreter of constitutional meaning on the basis of his participation in the Constitutional Convention and his preparation and preservation of his notes of the proceedings — his views, as expressed in the debate over the Jay treaty papers and thereafter, have special value in seeking the interpretive intent underlying the Constitution. Lofgren, *supra* note 55, at 102, in approval of Powell, *supra* at 935. Thus, having pushed the king out one door, they readmit him through another. In according such weight to Madison's positions, Powell and Lofgren in effect embrace the Republican canon of constitutional construction as developed in the 1796 debate.

Both Powell and Lofgren give no weight to George Washington's view, *supra* at note 73, in support of William Vans Murray, *supra* at notes 49–50. They both also omit any reference to Madison's own use of the framers' intent during the debate over the bank bill. *See supra* ch. 4 note 51. And they fail to mention Gallatin's and Baldwin's reliance on framers' intent during the debate in the Fifth Congress over the alien bill, *infra* ch. 9 notes 100, 110; and Pinckney's reliance on such intent during the debate in the Sixth Congress over the presidential elector bill, *infra* ch. 11 note 24. Curiously, Lofgren himself makes extensive use of Madison's notes of the Constitutional Convention to shed light on the constitutional extent of presidential power to engage military forces in foreign countries without congressional permission. *See supra* ch. 6 note 47.

Furthermore, both Powell and Lofgren seem unaware that prior to 1796 the Republicans generally, and Madison in particular, relying both on the *Federalist* and on the debates in the state ratifying conventions, had committed themselves to a narrow construction of federal powers under the Constitution, particularly the Necessary and Proper Clause. For this reason, they underestimate how deeply Madison was compromised by the Republican insistence in 1796 that the debates of the state ratifying conventions were not reliable reports of what had actually transpired there. Because Madison's response to Washington was made to save his own reputation, his views on that occasion cannot be accepted as canonical. Indeed, to borrow a phrase from contemporary judicial usage, Madison's 1796 version of constitutional construction should be subjected to strict scrutiny.

For a more perceptive understanding of the House debate over the implementation of Jay's Treaty, *see* JACK N. RAKOVE, ORIGINAL MEANINGS 355–65 (1996). Rakove perceives the embarrassment to which Madison was subjected during the debate. He also recognizes that it was the Federalists who in that debate, albeit for political motives, sought the original intent of the framers and ratifiers. *Id.* at 364–65.

87. 5 ANNALS 782–83.

88. 5 *id.* at 940. For a convenient summary of the maneuvering, *see* the editorial note in 16 MP 310–11, 313.

89. 5 ANNALS 1280, 1289–92. The appropriated sum amounted to just over $80,000. Act of May 6, 1796, 1 STAT. 459. Adams reported that well before the final votes, Muhlenberg's prospective father-in-law told him either to vote for the treaty or forget marrying his daughter, COMBS, *supra* note 4, at 184.

90. Madison to Jefferson, May 22, 1796, 16 MP 363, 364.

91. Nevertheless, despite the strain the debate placed on Madison, the positions taken by the House have had long-term effects. First, they led to Washington's invocation of a qualified executive privilege, a doctrine which has become firmly established in constitutional law. *United States v. Nixon,* 418 U.S. 683, 705 (1974). *See* LOUIS FISHER, CONSTITUTIONAL CONFLICTS BETWEEN CONGRESS AND THE PRESIDENT 171–78 (rev. ed. 1991).

In addition, the House has continued to maintain that it has the constitutional power to withhold appropriations for the implementation of a treaty, albeit it has never done so. LOUIS HENKIN, FOREIGN AFFAIRS AND THE CONSTITUTION 205, 482 (2d ed. 1997) [hereafter HENKIN, FOREIGN AFFAIRS]; FISHER, *supra* at 266–67. Indeed, the House may be said to have the obligation to implement treaties. LOUIS HENKIN, CONSTITUTIONALISM, DEMOCRACY AND FOREIGN AFFAIRS 63 (1990).

The House has also continued to protest the conclusion of commercial treaties that fix, without its approval, the rates of duties imposed on foreign goods. *See* HENKIN, FOREIGN AFFAIRS, *supra* at 162, 410. And from time to time, the House has invoked the provisions of the U.S. CONST. art. I, § 3, cl. 3, governing the disposition of territory or property of the United States. *See* FISHER, *supra* at 229–31. *But cf. Edwards v. Carter,* 580 F.2d 1055, 1057 (D.C. Cir. 1978), *cert. denied* 436 U.S. 907 (1978), where it was held that the use of treaties for the purpose of disposing of government property is valid.

And, in fact, because of House sensibilities as to its prerogatives under the U.S. CONST. art. I, § 7, cl. 1, to originate revenue bills, provisions involving foreign duties are no longer usually included in treaties. Finally, because of House power over appropriations, presidents now customarily consult with House leaders during the course of treaty negotiations. *See* HENKIN, FOREIGN AFFAIRS, *supra* at 194–95. *See also* 1 RESTATEMENT (THIRD) OF THE FOREIGN RELATIONS LAW OF THE UNITED STATES, § 111, Reporters' Note 7; § 803 (2) and cmt. c (1987).

For the view that certain treaties are inherently not self-executing because of the congressional commerce and appropriations powers, *see* Jordan J. Paust, *Self-Executing Treaties,* 82 AM. J. INT'L. L. 760, 775–78 (1988). Paust notes that the distinction between treaties that were self-executing and those that were not originated with Chief Justice Marshall in *Foster and Elam v. Neilson,* 27 U.S. (2 Pet.) 253, 314–15 (1829). There it was held that when by the terms of a treaty either party engages to perform a particular act, Congress must by appropriate legislation implement the treaty and direct the performance of the act. But the precedential value of *Foster* was eroded four years later in *United States v. Percheman,* 32 U.S. (7 Pet.) 51, 88–89 (1833), wherein Marshall declared that the terms of the treaty, which the Court had construed in *Foster* as importing an executory contract, were actually self-executing, and thus did not require legislative implementation.

The law of subsequent cases, Paust concludes, is that whether a treaty is to be self-executory depends upon its terms and the context of its conclusion, with a strong presumption in favor of self-execution. Paust, *supra* at 775.

92. The bill provided for the marking of the boundaries of Indian lands both south and

north of the Ohio as previously fixed and described in the treaties of Nov. 28, 1785, 7 STAT. 18, of July 2, 1791, 7 STAT. 39, and of June 26, 1794, 7 STAT. 43, all with the Cherokees, affecting lands south of the Ohio; and in the treaty of Aug. 3, 1795, 7 STAT. 49, with a group of Indian tribes, affecting lands north of the Ohio. *See* the Act of May 19, 1796, § 1, 1 STAT. 469.

93. 5 ANNALS 894–95, 899–900.

94. 5 *id.* at 893. For the attribution to Rep. Thomas Blount of North Carolina as the maker of the motion, *see id.* at 905. For the text of the controversial section, *see* § 5 of the bill as finally adopted, Act of May 19, 1796, 1 STAT. 469, 470.

95. 5 ANNALS 893–96 (statement of Rep. Holland).

96. The relevant language in the Fifth Amendment provides: "nor shall private property be taken for public use, without just compensation."

97. 5 ANNALS 898 (statement of Rep. Hillhouse).

98. 5 *id.* at 899–900 (statement of Rep. Madison).

99. 5 *id.* at 902–3 (statement of Rep. Gallatin).

100. 5 *id.* at 904–5. Act of May 19, 1796, 1 STAT. 469.

101. Act of June 1, 1796, 1 STAT. 491–92; 6 ANNALS 1589.

102. For a comprehensive review of Jackson's Indian removal policies, *see* ROBERT V. REMINI, THE LEGACY OF ANDREW JACKSON 45–82 (1988). For a discussion of Jackson's veto of the bill to recharter the Second Bank of the United States and of the ultimately disastrous consequences of that decision on the economy of the country during the administration of Martin Van Buren, *see* BRAY HAMMOND, BANKS AND POLITICS IN AMERICA 405–545 (1957). It should be stated, however, that in the case of the Bank, Jackson followed Madison in his original thesis of 1791—that the creation of a national bank was beyond the powers of Congress—rather than following Gallatin. The latter believed in the Bank's constitutionality. *Id.* at 408.

103. 5 ANNALS 1349.

104. 5 *id.* at 1347–48, 1353 (statements of Rep. Heister and Rep. Gallatin).

105. 5 *id.* at 1348–50.

106. 5 *id.* at 1350, 1353 (statements of Rep. Swanwick and Rep. Gallatin).

107. 5 *id.* at 1350–53 (statement of Rep. Gallatin).

108. 5 *id.* at 1359.

109. Act of May 27, 1796, 1 STAT. 474.

110. *See supra* ch. 5 notes 38–42.

111. In 1835 Jackson as president asked Congress for legislation prohibiting the circulation in southern states, through the mails, of a so-called incendiary publication intended to instigate the slaves to insurrection. Actually, the proposal was intended to stop northern abolitionists from using the mail to distribute their literature to southern whites, particularly southern clergymen. Even without the authorization, Postmaster General Amos Kendall had already instructed southern postmasters to deliver such mail only to subscribers who specifically asked for it, and to obey state laws forbidding the circulation of incendiary materials. Presumably, although this was not stated, the question of what constituted incendiary material was a matter of state law.

This accommodation of federal to state law did not go far enough to suit Calhoun. Since it was up to each state, he said, to decide for its citizens what material was fit for them, he proposed that the postmasters be prohibited from delivering any mail the state judged unfit, and that they be held liable for any violation of pertinent state law. Neither Jackson's nor Calhoun's proposal was approved. Instead, Congress simply forbade the postmasters from delaying the delivery of the mails, but in practice southern postmasters did not deliver the offending material. Federal authority stopped at the local postoffice. ROBERT V. REMINI, ANDREW JACKSON

AND THE COURSE OF AMERICAN DEMOCRACY 258–62 (1984); CHARLES WILTSE, JOHN C. CAL-
HOUN, NULLIFIER 268–77 (1949); Act of July 2, 1836, 5 STAT. 80.

112. *See supra* ch. 11 note 41.

9. Turbulence, Aliens, and Sedition

1. Madison to Jefferson, Dec. 5, 10, 19, 25, 1796, and Jan. 8, 1797, 16 MP 422–23, 424–
25, 432–33, 435, 446–47.

2. MANNING DAUER, THE ADAMS FEDERALISTS 92–111 (1953).

3. ELKINS & MCKITRICK 515.

4. *Id.* at 519.

5. ALEXANDER DE CONDE, ENTANGLING ALLIANCE 427 (1958).

6. *Id.* at 378–90.

7. ELKINS & MCKITRICK 520–21, 537–39.

8. 7 ANNALS 49, 54–59. The president was also influenced by a letter from his son, John
Quincy, minister to the Netherlands. In that letter the son reported a French plot to invade
the South and, with the aid of Republicans in the South and the West, to separate those regions from the Union and establish a republic loyal to France. The president was alarmed. The
administration already had information that a French general, friendly with Gallatin and with
American General James Wilkinson, had been in the West on an intelligence mission to sound
out western sentiment and ascertain the state of American military defenses. When the president showed the letter to Federalist party leaders, they all suspected the worst of France and
the Republicans. RICHARD H. KOHN, EAGLE AND SWORD 205–8 (1975).

9. Jefferson to Madison, May 18, 1797, 17 MP 7–9.

10. ELKINS & MCKITRICK 549–79. Hamilton to Washington, Jan. 25–31, 1797, 20 HP
480–81.

11. Jefferson to Mazzei, Apr. 24, 1796, 8 WJ 235, 238–41; DUMAS MALONE, JEFFERSON
AND THE ORDEAL OF LIBERTY 302 (1962).

12. *Id.* at 308–11, albeit Malone attributes the suspension of their relations to other factors.

13. Jefferson to Edward Rutledge, June 24, 1797, 8 WJ 316–19.

14. MALONE, *supra* note 11, at 334–35.

15. *Id.* Jefferson to Peregrine Fitzhugh, June 4, 1797, 8 WJ 298, 302.

16. 1 CHARLES WARREN, THE SUPREME COURT IN UNITED STATES HISTORY 166 n. 2 (1937);
WILLIAM R. CASTO, THE SUPREME COURT IN THE EARLY REPUBLIC: THE CHIEF JUSTICESHIPS OF
JOHN JAY AND OLIVER ELLSWORTH 126–29 (1995).

17. 8 WJ 322, 328. For a review of Jefferson's commitment to natural rights, *see* DAVID N.
MAYER, THE CONSTITUTIONAL THOUGHT OF THOMAS JEFFERSON 74–83 (1994).

18. For Jefferson's view as to the proper allocation of power between the federal government and the states, *see* his letter to Madison of Dec. 16, 1786: "To make us one nation as to
foreign concerns, and keep us distinct in Domestic ones, gives the outline of the proper division of powers between the general and particular governments." 10 JP 602, 603. One year
later, in a letter to Madison, Dec. 20, 1787, Jefferson, commenting on the final draft of the
Constitution, approved the grant of a taxing power to the federal government. 12 JP 438, 439.
See also Jefferson to Gideon Granger, Aug. 13, 1800: "[The powers of the] general government
[should] be reduced to foreign concerns only." 9 WJ 138, 140.

19. Madison to Jefferson, Aug. 5, 1797, 17 MP 38–40.

20. Monroe to Jefferson, Sept. 5, 1797, 3 WRITINGS OF JAMES MONROE 85 (Stanislaus M.
Hamilton ed., 1892–1903); Jefferson to Monroe, Sept. 9, 1797, 8 WJ 339–41; HARRY AM-
MON, JAMES MONROE 170–71 (1971); and editorial note, 17 MP 34.

21. 7 ANNALS 848–52. For a discussion of "Country" complaints against the practice of "placemen," the executive appointment of legislators to fill executive offices, *see supra* ch. 2 note 39.

22. 16 JP 378 (emphasis in original).

23. 16 *id.* at 379 (emphasis in original). *See supra* ch. 6 note 8.

24. *Id.* (emphasis in original).

25. 16 *id.* at 379–80 (emphasis in original).

26. *See* editorial note to Plans and Estimates for the Diplomatic Establishment, 17 JP 216–22, including the plan presented to the conference committee during the second session of the First Congress. 17 *id.* at 223–24.

27. 23 JP 19–24. On the same day that he gave the Senate the information it wanted, Jefferson drafted a statement for the president to be issued to the Senate, in which he declared: "That the constitution has made the President the sole competent judge to what places circumstances render it expedient that Ambassadors or other public ministers should be sent, and of what grade they should be: and that it has ascribed to the Senate no executive act but the single one of giving or withholding their consent to the person nominated." 23 *id.* at 18.

In response to pending Senate resolutions that it was not in the interest of the United States to appoint ministers plenipotentiary to reside permanently at foreign courts, 23 *id.* at 11–15, the president was advised to protest "against the validity of any resolutions of the Senate asserting or implying any right in that house to exercise any executive authority but the single one before mentioned." 23 *id.* at 18. The protest was never sent. *See* editorial note, 23 *id.* at 19.

In practice, Jefferson's opinion notwithstanding, Congress has by law restricted the president's power of nomination by imposing requirements of citizenship, residence, professional attainments, occupational experience, age, gender, race, property, etc. For an early list of such statutory restrictions, *see* the dissenting opinion of Justice Brandeis in *Myers v. United States*, 272 U.S. 52, 265–74 (1926).

28. *See* entry of Apr. 27, 1790, 4 GEORGE WASHINGTON, DIARIES, 1784–1799 122 (1929).

29. *See supra* ch. 6 note 14–19.

30. 7 ANNALS 859–62 (statement of Rep. Sitgreaves); 867–69 (statement of Rep. Nathaniel Smith); 890–93 (statement of Rep. Griswold); and 893–97 (statement of Rep. Bayard).

31. ELKINS & MCKITRICK 498–513; 7 ANNALS 874–77 (statement of Rep. Harper).

32. 7 *id.* at 883–86 (statement of Rep. Dana).

33. 7 *id.* at 888–90 (statement of Rep. Gallatin).

34. *Id.*

35. Gallatin's version of the Constitution had been expressly included in the original Virginia Plan: Members of both branches of the national legislature were to be largely ineligible to hold national office during the term of their legislative office and for a number of years, to be determined thereafter, 1 FR 20–21. The period of ineligibility was initially fixed at one year. 1 *id.* at 235. It was later, during the debate on a motion to strike the proposal for ineligibility, that Butler made his remarks with reference to British practice and that George Mason referred to the practice of the Continental Congress. 1 *id.* at 376. The motion to strike failed on a tie vote. 1 *id.* at 377. A more moderate motion which Madison advanced, to render persons ineligible only for offices established or their emoluments augmented during their term of legislative office, was more decisively rejected. 1 *id.* at 386, 390. The Convention next agreed to limit the ineligibility of members of the House to their term of office, and of members of the Senate to their term plus one year. 1 *id.* at 390, 429. But in the last weeks of the convention, the delegates adopted the substance of Madison's motion. 2 FR 491–492.

36. For the support of the Connecticut delegation at the Constitutional Convention, especially that of Sherman for the more restrictive proposal, *see* 1 FR 387–88, 390, and 2 FR 490;

and for that of Ellsworth, 2 *id.* at 288. Nathaniel Smith, Griswold, and Dana, who all supported Adams's appointment policy, were from Connecticut. For Adams's appointment of Chief Justice Ellsworth as a special envoy to France, *see infra* ch. 11 notes 15–16.

37. For Madison's support of the less restrictive proposal, *see* 1 FR 386, 388–89; for Charles Pinckney's, 2 FR 283–84, 489–91.

38. *See supra* ch. 8 notes 52–53.

39. *See* report submitted by the Committee of Privileges to the House on Feb. 2, 1798, 7 ANNALS 961–62.

40. 7 *id.* at 962.

41. 7 *id.* at 1006 (statement of Rep. Gallatin).

42. 7 *id.* at 1008–9.

43. U.S. CONST. art. I, § 5, cl. 2, provides: "Each House may determine the Rules of its Proceedings, punish its Members for disorderly Behaviour, and, with the Concurrence of two thirds, expel a Member."

44. 7 ANNALS 1034.

45. 7 *id.* at 1036, 1043.

46. 7 *id.* at 1098–1101 (statement of Rep. Coit).

47. 7 *id.* at 1138–39 (statement of Rep. Gallatin).

48. 7 *id.* at 1175–78, 1181, 1192 (statement of Rep. Harper).

49. 8 ANNALS 1234.

50. 8 *id.* at 1271–72; PAGE SMITH, 2 JOHN ADAMS 952–57 (1962).

51. 8 ANNALS 1370–71, 1374–75.

52. SMITH, *supra* note 50, at 959–60.

53. On creating the Department of the Navy, *see* 7 ANNALS 541–42, 8 ANNALS 1553–54, and Act of Apr. 30, 1798, 1 STAT. 553; on raising a provisional army, *see* 7 ANNALS 584, 8 ANNALS 1772, and Act of May 28, 1798, 1 STAT. 558; on provision for an armed convoy, *see* 7 ANNALS 601, 8 ANNALS 2083, and Act of July 9, 1798, 1 STAT. 578; and on increasing the army, *see* 7 ANNALS 611, 8 ANNALS 2132, and Act of July 16, 1798, 1 STAT. 604.

54. 8 ANNALS 1631–34.

55. 8 *id.* at 1634–35 (statement of Rep. Sewall); the statute to which Sewall referred was the Act of June 22, 1798, 1 STAT. 569.

56. 8 ANNALS 1637 (statement of Rep. Dana).

57. 8 *id.* at 1725–29 (statement of Rep. Gallatin).

58. 8 *id.* at 1732 (statement of Rep. Otis).

59. 8 *id.* at 1761–62 (statement of Rep. Davis).

60. *See infra* ch. 10 note 42.

61. In response to Gallatin's remarks, however, the House did defer the president's authorization to raise a provisional army until the next session of Congress. *See supra* note 53. For an extended discussion of the debates over the many provisions for increasing the army, *see* KOHN, *supra* note 8, at 224–29.

62. In Philadelphia feelings between French sympathizers and their opponents became intense. Attacks were threatened on the mint and military armories. Substantial fires erupted; in two cases arson was suspected. Adams had the cavalry patrol the streets, and, fearing for his own safety and that of his household, he had guns brought into his house. In Virginia, an eminent lawyer said publicly that if a French army invaded the United States, 100,000 Americans—he among them—would join it. KOHN, *supra* note 8, at 213–18.

63. MICHAEL DUREY, TRANSATLANTIC RADICALS AND THE EARLY AMERICAN REPUBLIC 231–57 (1997). One Federalist paper reported a plan by the United Irishmen to help France in the overthrow of the United States government. KOHN, *supra* note 8, at 213.

64. 7 ANNALS 430–31; Act of July 6, 1797, 1 STAT. 527.

65. 7 ANNALS 429.

66. 7 *id.* at 429–30 (statement of Rep. Otis). It was well known at the time that many recent Irish immigrants had allied themselves with the cause of the Republican Party. In 1793 the Irish had joined the newly founded Democratic Societies to support revolutionary France against their mutual enemy, the British. In 1794, the Irish had helped defeat incumbent Federalist congressmen in New York and Pennsylvania. Later, they had been in the forefront in the opposition to Jay's Treaty. Even more worrisome to the Federalists was the knowledge that some of the Irish had been expelled from Ireland by the British for their involvement in a secret society known as the United Irishmen, which was dedicated to the forceful overthrow of British rule in Ireland. In 1797 they were joined in America by hundreds of other Irishmen whom the British had also expelled for insurrectionary activities. Most alarming to the Federalists was the fact that many of the new immigrants had formed in the United States new oath-bound secret societies, which they also called the United Irishmen. The ultimate Federalist fear was that just as the United Irishmen had plotted the forceful overthrow of British authority in Ireland, so they were plotting the forceful overthrow of the government of the United States to realize their version of democratic rule. DAVID A. WILSON, UNITED IRISHMEN, UNITED STATES: IMMIGRANT RADICALS IN THE EARLY REPUBLIC 40–47 (1998).

67. 8 ANNALS 1567. JAMES M. SMITH, FREEDOM'S FETTERS 23–26 (1956).

68. 8 ANNALS 1568. For the crucial impact of the Irish vote in New York and, along with the German vote, in Pennsylania on the presidential and congressional elections of 1800, *see* WILSON, *supra,* note 66, at 55.

69. 8 *id.* at 1571 (statement of Rep. Otis).

70. 2 FR 235–36, 12 DHFFC 149 (statements of Madison).

71. 8 ANNALS 1571.

72. 8 *id.* at 1569. As to the latter point, *see* statements of Rep. John Laurance in the First Congress, 12 DHFFC 148, 152.

73. 8 ANNALS at 1569.

74. 8 *id.* at 1573. This result led to a movement in Massachusetts and five other states to amend the Constitution so as to disqualify all naturalized citizens from holding office. JOHN C. MILLER, FEDERALIST ERA 230 (1960).

75. 7 ANNALS 576, 8 ANNALS 1776, 1783, Act of June 18, 1798, 1 STAT. 566.

76. *See* the observation of James A. Bayard of Delaware that in many of the states aliens were allowed to vote both in state and federal elections. Therefore, under the proposed law, as he pointed out, the only privilege that would be denied them was the "capacity of becoming members of the Federal Government." 8 ANNALS 1779. In consequence, many Republican politicians befriended aliens. In New York, for example, De Witt Clinton, of Irish descent, took up Irish causes. With the support of his uncle, Gov. George Clinton, he became a United States senator in 1802 and worked for the restoration of the five-year residence period for naturalization. He made himself popular with the Irish in other ways. GUSTAVUS MYERS, THE HISTORY OF TAMMANY HALL 38 (1917).

77. 7 ANNALS 598, 8 ANNALS 2049, Act of July 6, 1798, 1 STAT. 577. For a summary of the debates on the bill, which as passed raised no constitutional questions, *see* SMITH, *supra* note 50, at 35–49.

78. 9 ANNALS 3744–45. For a summary of the progress of the Senate bill, *see* SMITH, *supra* note 50, at 50–58.

79. 8 ANNALS 1956 (statement of Rep. Gallatin).

80. 8 *id.* at 2007–9 (statement of Rep. Livingston).

81. *See infra* ch. 10 note 71.

82. 8 ANNALS 1954–55 (statement of Rep. Gallatin).

83. 8 *id.* at 1956 (statement of Rep. Gallatin). Baldwin was probably the source for Gal-

latin's historical recollection, because it was Baldwin who on Sept. 16, 1778, introduced the resolution in the Continental Congress to which Gallatin referred, 34 JOURNALS OF THE CONTINENTAL CONGRESS 528 (Gaillard Hunt ed., 1912). *See also* PA. ACT of Mar. 27, 1789, ch. 463. New Jersey later followed Pennsylvania. *See* Act of Jan. 28, 1797, ch. 611, § 3, 1797 N.J. ACTS 131.

84. U.S. CONST. art. IV, § 2, cl. 1, provides: "The Citizens of each State shall be entitled to all Privileges and Immunities of Citizens in the several States." For Madison's exposition of this provision, *see* FEDERALIST No. 42, at 285–87 (James Madison).

85. *See supra* ch. 4 note 52.

86. *See infra* ch. 10 note 69.

87. 48 U.S. (7 How.) 283 (1849). Wherein the unconstitutionality lay, the judges in majority were not in agreement—whether the taxes constituted an impermissible regulation of or had placed an impermissible burden on foreign and interstate commerce, or whether they conflicted with a valid national policy implicit in federal treaties. Any of these rationales constituted a broader construction of federal power than the justices in the minority were willing to countenance. However, the majority did agree on the result: For the good of all the states, the federal government must control the flow of immigration. In dissent, Chief Justice Taney adopted the Gallatin position—the position generally taken by the slave-holding states in the nineteenth century before the Civil War—that the states were completely free to admit and exclude from their territory any person not a citizen of the United States. *Id.* at 464, 466–67.

88. *See supra* ch. 8 notes 103–9.

89. 8 ANNALS 1957–59 (statement of Rep. Sewall).

90. *Id.*

91. The convention approved the Bedford motion, but the Committee of Detail, deleting an explicit statement of the principle from its version of the Constitution, had instead conferred on Congress power under the enigmatic Necessary and Proper Clause. Later, the committee had proffered language incorporating the essence of the Bedford resolution in the general welfare provision, but that effort had failed to bear fruit. *See supra* ch. 1 notes 62, 82, 88.

92. *See supra* ch. 1 notes 95–98.

93. 8 ANNALS 1957 (statement of Rep. Sewall).

94. 8 *id.* at 1965–66 (statement of Rep. Bayard). For the opposition to a broad construction of those clauses in the Virginia convention, *see supra* ch. 2 notes 68, 70, 73, 76.

95. 8 ANNALS 1983–84 (statement of Rep. Gordon).

96. 8 *id.* at 1962–63 (statement of Rep. Williams).

97. 8 *id.* at 1967–69 (statement of Rep. Baldwin); 1975 (statement of Rep. Gallatin).

98. 8 *id.* at 1975 (statement of Rep. Gallatin); FEDERALIST No. 41, at 268, 277–78 (James Madison).

99. *See supra* ch. 8 notes 52–53.

100. 8 ANNALS 1976 (statement of Rep. Gallatin).

101. For a detailed summary of the history of the general welfare provision in the Constitutional Convention, *see* CHARLES WARREN, THE MAKING OF THE CONSTITUTION 464–79 (1928). For the progress of the provision in the convention, *see* 2 FR 181–82, 304–8, 326–28, 355–56, 376–77, 392, 412–14, 481, 496–99, 553, 569. For Madison's letter to Stevenson with accompanying notes on the progress of the general welfare clause through the convention, *see* 9 WM 411–24. James M. Smith, following a reference in Farrand, incorrectly gives as Gallatin's source remarks that Jefferson attributed to George Mason. *See* SMITH, *supra* note 50, at 74 n. 24; 3 FR 367–68. An examination of these remarks reveals, however, that what Mason had reported to Jefferson had nothing to do with the formulation of the general welfare provision. Rather, Mason had recalled that at the Constitutional Convention Gouverneur Morris, a delegate from Pennsylvania, had so worded a committee report as to place

the power of proposing constitutional amendments solely in Congress; and that he, Mason, not Sherman, had caught Morris out and raised an objection.

102. 8 ANNALS 1956–57, 1978–79 (statement of Rep. Gallatin).

103. FEDERALIST No. 42, at 279, 281–82 (James Madison). Of course, despite Madison's reading of art. I, § 9, cl. 1, Gallatin could still argue that Congress had no power to exclude European immigrants either before or after 1808 because it had not been granted a specific power to do so.

104. 2 FR 415–16.

105. 48 U.S. (7 How.) 464, 474–75 (1849).

106. For Madison's use of the principle in the first session of the First Congress, *see supra* ch. 3 notes 27–28; for Hamilton's use of the principle in his Pacificus essays, *see supra* ch. 6 notes 18–19.

107. 8 ANNALS 1958 (statement of Rep. Sewall). Chief Justice Marshall adopted Sewall's construction of art. I, § 9, cl. 1, in his wide-ranging discussion of the power of Congress over commerce in *Gibbons v. Ogden,* 22 U.S. (9 Wheat.) 1, 206 (1824).

108. 8 ANNALS 1961–62 (statement of Rep. Otis).

109. 8 *id.* at 1962–63 (statement of Rep. Williams).

110. 8 *id.* at 1968–69 (statement of Rep. Baldwin). Berns, citing this speech, ascribed the principal motivation for the Republican opposition to the Alien Act to a desire to protect southern slave-holding interests. *See* Walter Berns, *Freedom of the Press and the Alien and Sedition Laws,* 1970 SUP. CT. RVW. 109, 115–19. Undoubtedly, Virginia's opposition to a broad grant of congressional powers in the Constitutional Convention, following the decision to grant equal representation in the Senate, was based in large part on its desire to protect its plantation owners. The same might be said of that state's determination, after the organization of the new government, to confine the construction of the Necessary and Proper Clause and the general welfare provision within narrow limits. But neither publicly nor in their private correspondence did Jefferson and Madison acknowledge this. Nor could they, if they wanted to build a national party and secure control of the government. Moreover, the Berns thesis suggests that Gallatin, who was the leader in the opposition to both the alien and sedition bills, was either a dupe or a front for southern interests. This overlooks the fact that Gallatin was himself an immigrant and therefore especially sensitive to the plight of the resident aliens, and that the Republican Party had been and would be the beneficiary of their votes.

111. 8 ANNALS 1992–93 (statement of Rep. Dayton).

112. 2 FR 415 (statements of Morris and Dickinson). Actually, the remarks of Morris supported Gallatin's first argument, that the power to admit aliens had been reserved to the states. *See supra* note 82.

113. As Chief Justice Taney later conjectured in *Passenger Cases,* the word "migration" was probably used:

TO PREVENT DOUBTS OR CAVILS upon [the clause's] meaning; for as the words imports and importation in the English laws had always been applied to property and things, as contradistinguished from persons, it seems to have been apprehended that disputes might arise whether these words covered the introduction of men into the country, although these men were the property of the persons who brought them in. The framers of the constitution were unwilling to use the word slaves in the instrument, and described them as persons; and so describing them, they employed a word that would describe them as persons, and which had uniformly been used when persons were spoken of, and also the word which was always applied to matters of property. (48 U.S. [7 How.] 464, 476 [1849])

114. The bill passed by a majority of six votes. 8 ANNALS 2028–29. For the Senate vote, *see* 7 ANNALS 586, Act of June 25, 1798, 1 STAT. 570.

115. 8 ANNALS 2093. For the proceedings in the Senate prior to its adoption of the bill, *see* 7 ANNALS 599, and for the proceedings in the House prior to its consideration of the Senate bill, *see* SMITH, *supra* note 50, at 109–11.

116. *United States v. Worrall,* 2 Dall. 384 (Cir. Ct. Pa. 1798); FRANCIS WHARTON, STATE TRIALS OF THE UNITED STATES 189 (1849).

117. RICHARD ROSENFELD, AMERICAN AURORA 169–70 (1997).

118. WHARTON, *supra* note 116, at 45–59; *United States v. Henfield,* 11 F. Cas. 1099 (C.C.D. Pa. 1793) (No. 6360). For a discussion of *Henfield* and *Worrall, see* JULIUS GOEBEL, JR., ANTECEDENTS AND BEGINNINGS TO 1801, *in* 1 HISTORY OF THE SUPREME COURT OF THE UNITED STATES 623–32; CASTO, *supra* 16, at 130–147; Stewart Jay, *Origins of Federal Common Law: Part One,* 133 PA. L. REV. 1003, 1039–75 (1985); Kathryn Preyer, *Jurisdiction to Punish,* 4 LAW & HIST. REV. 223, 227–35 (1986); and STEPHEN B. PRESSER, THE ORIGINAL MISUNDERSTANDING 67–92 (1991).

119. 8 ANNALS 2093–2101 (statement of Rep. Allen). For the report of Livingston's speech, in which he recommended merely that the government of the United States instruct Gerry, who was still in France, to commence negotiations for a treaty with that country, *see* 8 *id.* at 2083. For the controversy regarding Rep. Cabell's letter to his constituency, *see supra* note 14–20. For a summary of Federalist harangues in the House against the Republicans, *see* SMITH, *supra* note 50, at 112–28.

120. 8 ANNALS 2104–6 (statements of Rep. Livingston and Rep. Macon).

121. 8 *id.* at 2107–8 (statement of Rep. Gallatin).

122. 8 *id.* at 2110–11 (statement of Rep. Gallatin). Gallatin was not the first to make this connection. In 1789 John Adams, responding to an inquiry from Chief Justice William Cushing of Massachusetts, stated that because of the need for an informed electorate, the English common law rule of seditious libel should be modified. Therefore, to safeguard a free press as secured by the state constitution, Adams remarked, a court presiding at a trial for seditious libel should permit the introduction of evidence as to the truth of the accusation, and should instruct the jury that if it found the accusation to be true and published for the public good, it should acquit. *See* LEONARD W. LEVY, EMERGENCE OF A FREE PRESS 198–200 (1985).

123. 8 ANNALS 2111–13 (statement of Rep. Dana), 2148–49 (statement of Rep. Otis). *See* the survey of the statutes of Virginia, Pennsylvania, and Massachusetts in support of the Otis statements, *in* LEVY, *supra* note 122, at 195–96, 206–13, 213–18.

See also President Jefferson to Governor Thomas McKean of Pennsylvania, Feb. 19, 1803, complaining about the lies of the Federalist press against his administration: "The restraints provided by the laws of the states are sufficient for this if applied. And I have therefore long thought that a few prosecutions of the most prominent offenders would have a wholesome effect in restoring the integrity of the presses." 9 WJ 449, 451–52, quoted in LEONARD W. LEVY, JEFFERSON AND CIVIL LIBERTIES 59 (1963).

124. 8 ANNALS 2113 (statement of Rep. Kittera). *See supra* notes 116, 117.

125. 8 *id.* at 2134–38. Levy agrees that the Federalist amendments did ameliorate the English common law rule of seditious libel and were superior to the reforms enacted by Parliament in 1792, which merely empowered the jury to return a general verdict. The amendments were also superior to the reforms enacted in New York in 1805 and widely adopted afterwards by many states. The New York rule, which was the prevailing state standard before the Civil War, also empowered the jury to return a general verdict in trials for seditious libel. And going beyond the English reform, the New York statute allowed truth as a defense, but, unlike the Federal amendment, required that a defendant show that the truth was published

for a good motive and for justifiable ends. LEVY, *supra* note 122, at 283–85, 339. *See also* Mark DeWolfe Howe, review of JAMES M. SMITH, FREEDOM'S FETTERS, 13 WM. & MARY Q., Third Series, 573–76 (1956).

126. 8 ANNALS 2141–45 (statement of Rep. Nicholas). In making this argument, Nicholas followed the contention made a few months earlier in the *Worrall* case: that in the absence of an expressed constitutional or statutory prohibition of such an offense, the prosecution was not cognizable in a federal court. In short, there was no such thing as a federal common law crime. *See supra* note 116.

127. 8 ANNALS 2145–46 (statement of Rep. Otis).

128. 8 *id.* at 2146–47 (statement of Rep. Otis).

129. Madison to Washington, Oct. 18, 1787, 10 MP 196, 197 (emphasis in original); for Mason's objections to the Constitution, *see* 8 DHRC 43.

130. 10 ANNALS 413 (statement of Rep. Gallatin).

131. For a discussion of this problem, *see* Stewart Jay, *Origins of Federal Common Law: Part Two*, 133 PA. L. REV. 1231, 1282–83 (1985). *See also infra* ch. 10 note 72.

132. 8 ANNALS 2152–53 (statement of Rep. Macon). For Justice Iredell's comment, *see* 4 ED 219 (Iredell's speech in the North Carolina convention, July 30, 1788). Justice Wilson said: "What is meant by the liberty of the press is, that there should be no antecedent restraint upon it; but that every author is responsible when he attacks the security or welfare of the government or the safety, character, and property of the individual." 2 DHRC 455 (Wilson's speech in the Pennsylvania ratifying convention, Dec. 1, 1787).

As to the opinion expressed in the First Congress regarding the need for a constitutional amendment protecting the rights of a free press and of free speech in light of the Necessary and Proper Clause, *see* statement of James Madison, 11 DHFFC 823–24.

133. 8 ANNALS 2156–58 (statement of Rep. Gallatin).

134. 8 *id.* at 2158–60 (statement of Rep. Gallatin). The statutes to which Gallatin referred are the Act of Apr. 30, 1790, 1 STAT. 112, and the Act of June 5, 1794, 1 STAT. 381.

135. 8 ANNALS 2159 (statement of Rep. Gallatin).

136. *See supra* ch. 2 note 76. *Cf.* FEDERALIST No. 84, at 575, 579, wherein Hamilton defended the failure to include a bill of rights in the Constitution on the ground that it would have been idle to declare that things could not be done which the federal government had not the power to do: "Why for instance, should it be said, that the liberty of the press shall not be restrained, when no power is given by which restrictions may be imposed?"

137. 8 ANNALS 2161 (statement of Rep. Gallatin).

138. 8 *id.* at 2164–65 (statement of Rep. Harper).

139. 8 *id.* at 2171. The Senate concurred in the House amendments, 7 ANNALS 609. Act of July 14, 1798, 1 STAT. 596.

140. 7 ANNALS 624; 8 ANNALS 2186.

10. Sedition and the Kentucky and Virginia Resolutions

1. Act of July 14, 1798, 1 STAT. 597.

2. Jefferson to John Taylor, Nov. 26, 1798, 8 WJ 479–83.

3. Jefferson to Madison, May 3 and May 31, 1798, 17 MP 123–24, 138–40. In July, Secretary of State Pickering reported this development to Adams, MANNING DAUER, THE ADAMS FEDERALISTS 206 (1968).

4. JAMES M. SMITH, FREEDOM'S FETTERS 188–204 (1956); JOHN C. MILLER, CRISIS IN FREEDOM 93–94 (1951).

5. SMITH, *supra* note 4, at 221, 226; MILLER, *supra* note 4, at 106–8, 110.

6. 7 ANNALS 591; Jefferson to Taylor, Nov. 26, 1798, 8 WJ 479–83; Jefferson to Monroe, Jan. 23, 1799, 9 WJ 9, 12.

7. On Republican speculation that Hamilton would likely have the actual command, *see* Henry Tazewell, United States Senator from Virginia, to Madison, July 12, 1798, 17 MP 163. For an assessment of Jefferson's political motives in drafting the resolutions, *see* MERRILL PETERSON, THE JEFFERSON IMAGE IN THE AMERICAN MIND 299–300, 313 (1960), and JAMES R. SHARP, AMERICAN POLITICS IN THE EARLY REPUBLIC 193–94 (1993).

8. *See supra* ch. 9 note 17.

9. FEDERALIST No. 28, at 176, 179 (Alexander Hamilton).

10. *Id.* at 179–80.

11. FEDERALIST No. 46, at 315, 320 (James Madison).

12. 4 ED 540 (emphasis in original).

13. 4 *id.* at 540–41.

14. 4 *id.* at 542–43.

15. 8 WJ 458, 471, 476–77; Adrienne Koch & Harry Ammon, *The Virginia and Kentucky Resolutions,* 5 WM. & MARY Q. 145, 157 (1948).

16. 4 ED 528. Some of Jefferson's more drastic language—as for example, that endorsing the state's power to nullify federal law—was deleted. RICHARD A. BEEMAN, THE OLD DOMINION AND THE NEW NATION 194 (1972).

17. JOHN C. MILLER, THE FEDERALIST ERA 241 (1960). There is considerable disagreement among historians as to the authenticity of this report. Many argue that the measures taken by the Virginia legislature had been discussed for many years and that their adoption during the same session as the passage of the resolution condemning the Alien and Sedition Acts was purely coincidental. ELKINS & MCKITRICK 715. For an opinion denying the coincidence, *see* SHARP, *supra* note 7, at 203–6.

18. The Kentucky Resolution had stated expressly that for the states to ignore the usurpation of federal authority resident in the Alien and Sedition Acts "would be to surrender the form of government we have chosen, and live under one deriving its powers from its own will, and not from our authority." 4 ED 544. The Virginia Resolutions had merely stated that the states were parties to the Constitution. *See supra* note 16.

19. 2 FR 93 (statement of Madison). In the same speech, Madison also spoke in favor of invalidation by judicial review (as opposed to invalidation by a state legislature), as the appropriate method for setting aside a law in conflict with the terms of a constitution: "A law violating a constitution established by the people themselves, would be considered by the Judges as null & void." *Id.*

20. The convention first rejected a motion that the Constitution be referred to the state legislatures for ratification. 2 *id.* at 88–93. It then approved a motion to refer the Constitution, after approval by the Continental Congress, to assemblies chosen by the people. 2 *id.* at 93–94. Later, Gouverneur Morris and Charles Pinckney moved to strike the necessity for approval by the Continental Congress; instead, it was agreed that the Constitution be merely referred to Congress and thereafter submitted to the states for their ratification. 2 *id.* at 478. It was during the course of the debate on the procedure according to which the states would ratify that Madison made his statement. 2 *id.* at 476. Ten days later, the convention reaffirmed its decision not to require congressional approval. 2 *id.* at 559–663. It then determined the method to be followed for state ratification. 2 *id.* at 608–9. *See also* FEDERALIST No. 43, at 288, 297, wherein Madison, justifying the supersession of the Articles of Confederation, noted: "A compact between independent sovereigns, founded on ordinary acts of legislative authority, can pretend to no higher validity than a league or treaty between the parties."

21. MILLER, *supra* note 17, at 241. Privately, however, Madison was well aware of this distinction. As he wrote to Jefferson on Dec. 29, 1798:

I HAVE NOT SEEN THE RESULT of the discussions [of the Virginia state legislature] at Richmond on the Alien & Sedition laws. It is to be feared their zeal may forget some considerations which ought to temper their proceedings. Have you ever considered thoroughly the distinction between the power of the *State* & that of *the Legislature,* on questions relating to the federal pact. On the supposition that the former is clearly the ultimate Judge of infractions, it does not follow that the latter is the legitimate organ especially as a Convention was the organ by which the Compact was made. (17 MP 191 [emphasis in original])

22. Jefferson to Madison, Jan. 3, 1799, 17 *id.* at 193–94.

23. 9 ANNALS 2986–87.

24. 9 *id.* at 2987.

25. *Id.*

26. 9 *id.* at 2988.

27. 9 *id.* at 2988–89.

28. 9 *id.* at 2990–91.

29. 9 *id.* at 2992.

30. 9 *id.* at 2993–96 (statement of Rep. Gallatin).

31. 9 *id.* at 2996–3002 (statement of Rep. Gallatin). For Gallatin's resort to supposed inside knowledge of what transpired at the Constitutional Convention during the second session of the Fifth Congress, *see supra* ch. 9 note 100; for Baldwin's use of his recollections of the convention in the same session, *see supra* ch. 9 note 110. For Gallatin's repudiation of the use of a framer's recollections during the Fourth Congress, *see supra* ch. 8 notes 52–53.

32. 9 ANNALS 3002 (statement of Rep. Nicholas).

33. 9 *id.* at 3002–4 (statement of Rep. Nicholas). For the debates in the Virginia convention, concerning the meaning of the Necessary and Proper Clause, *see supra* ch. 2 notes 68–75, in which Henry, Mason, and Monroe all contended for a sweeping meaning of the clause, and Randolph, Madison, and George Nicholas, John's brother, contended for a strict meaning.

34. 9 ANNALS 3004 (statement of Rep. Nicholas).

35. 9 *id.* at 3005 (statement of Rep. Nicholas).

36. 9 *id.* at 3005–14 (statement of Rep. Nicholas).

37. 9 *id.* at 3016–17.

38. King to Secretary of State Timothy Pickering, Sept. 21, 1798, 2 THE LIFE AND CORRESPONDENCE OF RUFUS KING 422–24 (Charles R. King ed., 1895); King to Hamilton, Sept. 23, 1798: "You will have no war!" *Id.* at 424–25; RALPH BROWN, THE PRESIDENCY OF JOHN ADAMS 84–85 (1975).

39. Adams to McHenry, Oct. 22, 1798, 8 WJA 612–13; Washington to Hamilton, May 27, 1798, 36 WW 271–74.

40. *See* correspondence from William Vans Murray, the United States envoy to The Hague, to Adams, from July 1 through Oct. 7, 1798, concerning French interest in reopening negotiations with the United States, 8 WJA 677–691. Adams to McHenry, Oct. 22, 1798, *id.* at 612–13. The land tax was imposed pursuant to the Act of July 14, 1798, 1 STAT. 597. For the general unpopularity of land taxes at that time, *see* ROGER BROWN, REDEEMING THE REPUBLIC 32–40 (1993). In an early essay, Hamilton had warned against the imposition of such an unpopular tax. FEDERALIST No. 12, at 73, 79.

41. RALPH BROWN, *supra* note 38, at 66–71.

42. Hamilton to Sedgwick, Feb. 2, 1799, 22 HP 452–53. Kohn concludes that Federalist fears of a Republican armed rebellion were genuine. Kohn holds that, despite the sentiments

Hamilton expressed in his letter to Sedgwick, he and his Federalist allies did not plan on using the army as an instrument of political suppression since they knew that neither Adams nor the general public would stand for such a move. Rather, the Federalists saw the army as a means of discouraging a Republican armed rebellion and inhibiting partisan attacks on the administration. RICHARD H. KOHN, EAGLE AND SWORD 249–52 (1975).

43. For details of a budding plan involving Hamilton at the head of the U.S. army, the British Foreign Office and the British navy, and Francisco de Miranda, a Venezuelan patriot, to organize a joint military enterprise for the liberation of the Spanish colonies, *see* RALPH BROWN, *supra* note 38, at 138–46. *See also* Hamilton to Harrison Gray Otis, Jan. 26, 1798, 22 HP 440–41. Stourzh judges that Hamilton's scheme should be viewed in the light of his long-standing belief in the necessity of securing for the United States the city of New Orleans, the area surrounding it and all territory east of the Mississippi so as to maintain American control of navigation on the river. In that view, Hamilton would have no interest in American sovereignty over Mexico and lands south of it. *See* GERALD STOURZH, ALEXANDER HAMILTON AND THE IDEA OF REPUBLICAN GOVERNMENT 192–97 (1970).

44. Murray to Adams, *see supra* note 40; Washington to Adams, Feb. 1, 1799, 37 WW 119–20. In his reply to Washington, Adams as much as told Washington he should have saved himself the trouble. He first informed him that he had determined to nominate Murray as minister plenipotentiary to France, because he had received many other and more reliable assurances than the one he had received from Washington. To Washington's source of information, Joel Barlow, an American living in Paris, Adams said he gave little weight. He characterized Barlow as a "wretch," a "worthless fellow" who had given "many and so unequivocal symptoms of blackness of heart." 8 WJA 624, 625.

Despite this disclaimer, it is most probable that the receipt of Washington's letter gave Adams the assurance he needed that Washington would not side with Hamilton and the others against him in his decision to reopen negotiations with the French, RALPH BROWN, *supra* note 38, at 97.

45. *Id.* at 95–101. Sedgwick to Hamilton, Feb. 22, 1799, 22 HP 494–95; and later, Hamilton to Charles Carroll, July 1, 1800, 25 HP 1–2. Franklin actually wrote about Adams: "He means well for his Country, is always an honest Man, often a wise one, but sometimes, and in some things, absolutely out of his senses." See Franklin to Robert R. Livingston, July 22, 1783, 9 THE WRITINGS OF BENJAMIN FRANKLIN 62 (Albert E. Smythe ed., 1906). *See also* Jefferson's assessment of Adams to Madison, Jan. 30, 1787: "He is vain, irritable and a bad calculator of the force and probable effect of the motives which govern men. This is all the ill which can possibly be said of him. He is as disinterested as the being which made him: he is profound in his views: and accurate in his judgment except where knowledge of the world is necessary to form a judgment. . . . He would be, as he was, a great man in Congress." 11 JP 92, 94–95.

46. DAUER, *supra* note 3, at 207.

47. JULIUS GOEBEL, JR., ANTECEDENTS AND BEGINNINGS TO 1801, *in* 1 HISTORY OF THE SUPREME COURT OF THE UNITED STATES 630–31 (1971).

48. STEPHEN B. PRESSER, THE ORIGINAL MISUNDERSTANDING 80–82 (1991). For an opinion excluding Cushing from the list of justices agreeing to this position, and listing Bushrod Washington as uncertain, *see* Kathryn Preyer, *Jurisdiction to Punish,* 4 LAW & HIST. REV. 223, 228–31 (1986). For an opinion supporting the thesis that Jay affirmed the existence of a federal common law in crime, *see* John D. Gordon, *United States v. Ravara, in* ORIGINS OF THE FEDERAL JUDICIARY 106–72 (Maeva Marcus ed., 1992).

49. WILLIAM R. CASTO, THE SUPREME COURT IN THE EARLY REPUBLIC: THE CHIEF JUSTICESHIPS OF JOHN JAY AND OLIVER ELLSWORTH 150–54 (1995). The statute in question was an amendment to the crimes law, Act of June 5, 1794, 1 STAT. 381.

50. Jefferson to Edmund Randolph, Aug. 18, 1799, 9 WJ 73–77; Jefferson to Charles Pinckney, Oct. 29, 1799, 9 *id.* at 86–88.

51. For Pinckney's criticism of the Ellsworth appointment, *see infra* ch. 11 notes 15–16.

52. MILLER, *supra* note 4, at 129–30, 219; and SMITH, *supra* note 4, at 334–58.

53. 4 ED 537–38.

54. 4 *id.* at 533, 534, 537.

55. 4 *id.* at 538.

56. 4 *id.* at 539.

57. *Id.*

58. 4 *id.* at 532–33, 538–39.

59. DAUER, *supra* note 3, at 233–37; Jefferson to Archibald Stuart, May 14, 1799, 9 WJ 66–67.

60. Jefferson to Madison, Aug. 23, 1799, 17 MP 257–258.

61. 17 *id.* at 308–310; 4 ED 546–48.

62. *See supra* notes 54, 56–57.

63. *See supra* notes 19–20.

64. 4 ED 546, 547.

65. 4 *id.* at 548.

66. 4 *id.* at 549.

67. For a discussion of Calhoun's use of Madison's report to the Virginia legislature, *see* SAMUEL H. BEER, TO MAKE A NATION 316 (1993). Beer regards Calhoun as making effective use of Madison's discussion of the ratification of the Constitution in the *Federalist,* where Madison maintained that the people in ratifying the Constitution did so in conventions in their respective states. In consequence, he wrote, ratification was a federal, not a national act. FEDERALIST No. 39, at 250, 253–54. In response to Calhoun, Madison later denied that any one state, or any number of states fewer than all, could by this tactic dissolve the Union. *See* BEER, *supra* 318. For a detailed analysis of Madison's last thoughts on this subject, *see* DREW R. MCCOY, THE LAST OF THE FATHERS 119–70 (1989).

68. 4 ED 579. For the Jefferson-Madison use of Hamilton's essay in the *Federalist, see supra* notes 8–21.

69. 4 ED 554, 558–59. For Gallatin's argument, *see supra* ch. 9 notes 80–81.

70. 4 ED 555. For Gallatin's civil liberties argument in the Fifth Congress, *see supra* ch. 9 notes 77–78.

71. 4 ED 559–60. For Livingston's attack on the Alien Act, which was based on the principle of separation of powers, *see supra* ch. 9 note 80. *See also* FEDERALIST No. 47, at 323, 324, wherein Madison had stated: "The accumulation of all powers legislative, executive and judiciary in the same hands, whether of one, a few or many, and whether hereditary, self appointed or elective, may justly be pronounced the very definition of tyranny."

72. 4 ED 561–67. For Otis's justification of the statute based on a federal common-law power in crimes, *see supra* ch. 9 note 128. Probably influenced by Madison's letter to George Washington of Oct. 18, 1787, in which Madison reminded the general that the question of adopting the common law had not been discussed at the recently concluded Constitutional Convention, *supra* ch. 9 note 129, Julius Goebel is of the opinion that the framers had not intended a federal common law, civil or criminal. Thus he thinks that the explicit references to the common law in the Constitution and in the Fifth, Sixth, and Seventh Amendments were premised on the view that the federal courts would have recourse to the rules and practices, the institutions, and procedures of the common law. These references did not reflect the exercise of a substantive jurisdiction beyond what was prescribed by statute. *See* GOEBEL, *supra* note 47, at 295–97, 654–55.

In diversity cases involving commercial disputes, Goebel goes on, the federal courts necessarily had to develop their own common-law rules, because state law in this area was either not settled or not to be found, thus precluding resort to state authority as directed in § 34 of the Judiciary Act of 1789. He also concedes that the Act of Punishment of Crimes, 1 STAT. 112, specified as crimes offenses such as murder and manslaughter, without definition, thus compelling the judiciary to define these offenses in the light of their common-law meaning. GOEBEL, *supra* note 47, at 655–56. Similarly, at trial the federal judiciary referred to common-law practices. *Id.* at 656–58. Nevertheless, Goebel earlier admits that commencing in 1799 Chief Justice Ellsworth asserted a federal common law of crime. *Id.* at 630–31.

Goebel's analysis is essentially based on a Madisonian interpretation of the Constitution. It fails in one key respect: If the federal courts lacked constitutional authority for the exercise of a federal common-law jurisdiction, they could not exercise it in diversity cases even in the absence of state precedent. Strict construction of the Constitution would require that before the federal courts applied a federal common-law rule in these circumstances the Constitution be amended to enable them to do so.

In keeping with his position of a basic federal disability in this matter, Goebel also disagrees with Charles Warren's construction of the Judiciary Act of 1789: that § 9 of the statute conferred on the federal courts a jurisdiction in the common law of crime. *See* Charles Warren, *New Light on the History of the Federal Judiciary Act of 1789,* 37 HARV. L. REV. 49, 73 (1923). Warren apparently assumes that Congress had the constitutional authority to confer such jurisdiction. For a more recent opinion that Congress conferred such jurisdiction on the federal courts, but under § 34 of the Judiciary Act, rather than § 9, *see* WILFRED J. RITZ, REWRITING THE HISTORY OF THE JUDICIARY ACT OF 1789 126–48 (Wythe Holt & L. H. La Rue eds., 1990). Neither the Warren nor the Ritz position seems persuasive: Chief Justice Ellsworth, who was one of the draftsmen of the Judiciary Act, did not advert to the statute in asserting a federal common law of crime. And if the Judiciary Act did indeed confer such jurisdiction, the Federalists would not have had to adopt the Sedition Act. At the very least, they would have argued that they were merely making manifest the implications of the provisions of the Judiciary Act.

Presser states that while it is impossible to tell whether either Goebel or Warren is correct about the intention of the First Congress in adopting § 9, or whether Goebel is correct in ascribing to the framers of the Constitution an intention not to confer a common-law jurisdiction on the federal courts, federal judges asserting such a jurisdiction prior to 1801 based their decision not on the constitutional text but on supraconstitutional principles inherent in the law of nations and the law of nature. PRESSER, *supra* note 48, at 82–99. Casto agrees with this assessment. He considers Madison's analysis of the question of a federal common-law jurisdiction of crimes fundamentally at odds with the then prevailing natural-law jurisprudence. CASTO, *supra* note 49, at 156–63. In this connection, *see* the colloquy between Robert Goodloe Harper and John Nicholas in the Sixth Congress, in which Harper, arguing against repeal of the Sedition Act, defended the provision for the punishment of seditious libel as "an affirmance of this common or universal law" and Nicholas protested against the term "universal law" as something more uncertain than the common law of England by itself. 10 ANNALS 414, 416. Following Presser and Casto is Andrew Lenner, *A Tale of Two Constitutions: Nationalism in the Federal Era,* 40 AM. J. LEG. HIST. 72 (1996).

In *United States v. Hudson and Goodwin,* 11 U.S. (7 Cranch) 32 (1812), the Supreme Court, undoubtedly influenced by the fact that both the Congress and the presidency were under the control of the Republicans—Madison was president—adopted the Republican thesis that there was no federal common law of crime. For a full discussion of the subject, *see* GEORGE L. HASKIN & HERBERT A. JOHNSON, FOUNDATIONS OF POWER: JOHN MARSHALL, 1801–15, *in*

2 HISTORY OF THE SUPREME COURT OF THE UNITED STATES 633–46 (1981); *see also* Gary D. Rowe, *The Sound of Silence:* United States v. Hudson & Goodwin, *The Jeffersonian Ascendancy, and the Abolition of Federal Common Law Crimes,* 101 YALE L. J. 919 (1992).

Madison in his argument did not address the inconvenient consideration that this argument might have been used against the language of the Seventh Amendment, which he himself had drafted. The amendment states that "in Suits at common law [in federal courts], . . . the right of trial by jury shall be preserved." What constitutes such a suit at common law is a matter over which the Supreme Court has struggled for years. For a discussion of the full complexity of the entitlement to trial by jury under the Seventh Amendment, *see* 9 CHARLES A. WRIGHT & ARTHUR R. MILLER, FEDERAL PRACTICE AND PROCEDURE §§ 2301–16 (1971).

73. 4 ED 571–73. For the Macon argument, *see supra* ch. 9 note 132; for the Nicholas argument, *see supra* note 33. Madison repeated their arguments even to the point of seeming to concede the lack of wisdom in their construction of the First Amendment, while insisting, nevertheless, on its validity. In conclusion, Madison posed the question whether the federal government was destitute of authority to restrain the licentiousness of the press and to shield its ministers against libelous attacks. The Constitution alone, he wrote, could answer the question. If the power was not expressly delegated, if it was not both necessary and proper to carry into execution an enumerated power, and, above all, if it was expressly forbidden by a declaratory amendment to the Constitution, the federal government must be destitute of such authority. The answer, he added, "does not turn either on the wisdom of the Constitution or on the policy which gave rise to its particular organization . . . but on the actual meaning of the instrument." 4 ED 572–73.

Leonard Levy incorrectly interprets this statement as an endorsement of what he terms the libertarian right of speech and press subject only to a subsequent civil suit for libel. LEONARD W. LEVY, EMERGENCE OF A FREE PRESS 319–20 (1985). But this interpretation overlooks the context in which Madison's statement was made. As is evident from what has just been set forth, it was written in support of his second argument—a states' rights argument—against the constitutionality of the Sedition Act: the power to regulate the press does not lie within the expressed powers of the federal government.

Of course, Madison did proffer an alternate argument, which might be called a more libertarian view of free speech and press: Free elections and political practice in Great Britain and in the United States required a modification of the common-law rule of seditious libel. *See infra* note 74. But Madison was arguing in broad terms. It was sufficient for his purpose that the Federalists were prosecuting a variety of opposition publications that, in his view of the Constitution, should be permitted to function. But it is difficult to infer from what he wrote in the Virginia report and from what Gallatin had said in the Fifth Congress that they favored a complete abandonment of the doctrine of seditious libel.

74. 4 ED 569–71, 575–76. *Cf.* Gallatin's argument in the Fifth Congress, *supra* ch. 9 note 122, concerning the practical effect of the Sedition Act as inhibiting the right of an informed electorate to pass on the measures and officers of government.

Levy, in the face of much criticism, insists on the thesis he put forth in an earlier edition: In 1789 the framers of the First Amendment did not contemplate the abolition of the crime of seditious libel. Instead, he writes, the seeds of that position were sown in Madison's report to the Virginia legislature. LEVY, *supra* note 73, at xii–xiv.

For a later argument, joining the earlier critics in arguing that a framers' and state ratifiers' intention to abolish the crime of seditious libel in adopting the First Amendment can be adduced from a study of the political climate of the period, *see* David M. Rabban, *The Ahistorical Historian,* 37 STAN. L. REV. 795 (1985).

On the other hand, Rabban has documented how for the most part, in the late nineteenth century and in the early twentieth century before the First World War, state and federal courts interpreted the First Amendment in markedly less libertarian ways. For instance, Justice Holmes, writing for the United States Supreme Court in *Patterson v. Colorado,* 205 U.S. 454, 462 (1907), announced a Blackstonian view of freedom of the press. The First Amendment, he wrote, was intended to eliminate all prior restraints on publication, leaving the publisher open to subsequent punishment for matter deemed contrary to the public welfare, including prosecution for seditious libel even for true statements. Rabban also set forth the history of how and why Holmes came to change his position, and how this change led to the present view of the Supreme Court that the First Amendment intended the abolition of seditious libel. DAVID M. RABBAN, FREE SPEECH IN ITS FORGOTTEN YEARS (1997).

75. 4 ED 544, 545 (emphasis in original).

76. Jefferson to Madison, Aug. 23, 1799, 17 MP 257–59; Koch & Ammon, *supra* note 15, at 164. Indeed, the previous year, inspired by a letter from Jefferson, the Virginia House of Delegates, in their original series of resolutions on the subject, had included a statement that the Alien and Sedition Acts "were *ab initio,* null, void, and of no force, or effect." *Id.* at 160; Jefferson to Wilson Cary Nicholas, Nov. 29, 1798, 8 WJ 483.

77. *See* PETERSON, *supra* note 7, at 52–66.

78. Hamilton to Jonathan Dayton, Oct.–Nov., 1799, 23 HP 599–604. The problem of the states as competitors to the federal government was not a new concern for Hamilton. During the Constitutional Convention he had conceded the utility of retaining the states for local governmental purposes, but he had then advocated their abolition for all other purposes so that they would be completely subordinate to the federal government. 1 FR 328.

11. The Fall of the Federalists

1. Following a motion by Macon to repeal the Sedition Act, 10 ANNALS 404, Bayard moved an amendment providing that "the offences . . . specified [in the statute] shall remain punishable as at common law," but that truth would be a defense. 10 *id.* at 410. The House first approved both motions. 10 *id.* at 419–20, 423–24. Confronted with the dilemma that thereby they had affirmed a common-law jurisdiction in seditious libel in the federal courts, the Republicans moved for and carried the repeal of the original Macon motion. 10 *id.* at 424–25.

2. 10 *id.* at 532–33.

3. Ruth Wedgwood, *The Revolutionary Martyrdom of Jonathan Robbins,* 100 YALE L. J. 229, 235–37, 286–90, 323–28 (1990).

4. Gallatin's speech was not reported, but Wedgwood provides a summary based on an examination of the unpublished Gallatin papers. *Id.* at 337–38. In fact, the sailor to whom Gallatin referred, William Brigstock, was an American, who had most probably been impressed. For these reasons, he had been acquitted. *Id.* at 277.

Gallatin also raised a nonconstitutional issue, that of the proper interpretation of the provision in Jay's Treaty concerning the delivery of prisoners to the British. Gallatin argued that since the treaty neither had designated the means and manner of the execution nor had named the officer by whom the execution was to be made, the president lacked the authority to direct the delivery of the prisoner. *Id.* at 336–38.

5. Jefferson, reporting to Madison on the Nash-Robbins debate in the House, observed that "Livingston, Nicholas & Gallatin distinguished themselves on one side & J. Marshall greatly on the other." Jefferson to Madison, Mar. 8, 1800, 17 MP 368.

6. 10 ANNALS 597 (statement of Rep. Marshall). Marshall assumed that, as the federal judge had initially reported to the secretary of state, the prisoner was a British subject. He conceded that had in fact the prisoner been an American citizen, it would have presented a case to which the jurisdiction of the federal courts extended. 10 *id.* at 598–99.

7. 10 *id.* at 606 (statement of Rep. Marshall). Marshall concluded as follows: "To come

within this description [i.e., within the judicial power], a question must assume a legal form for forensic litigation and judicial decision. There must be parties to come into court, who can be reached by its process, and bound by its power; whose rights admit of ultimate decision by a tribunal to which they are bound to submit." *Id.*

For the continued vitality of the "political question" doctrine in the area of foreign relations, *see* 1 Restatement (Third) of Foreign Relations Law of the United States § 1, Reporters' Note 4 (1987).

8. 10 Annals 613 (statement of Rep. Marshall). *See supra* ch. 6 notes 14, 25. Marshall's reference to the president as the nation's "sole organ" of communication has been cited as a separate source of executive power in the conduct of foreign affairs. *Id.* at note 48. Some historians attempt to read Marshall's position in the Sixth Congress narrowly. In their view, all that Marshall meant was that the president was the instrument of communication with other governments. *See* Edward S. Corwin, The President, Office and Powers, 1787–1957 178 (4th rev. ed. 1957); Leonard W. Levy, Original Intent and the Framers' Constitution 52 (1988); and Harold H. Koh, The National Security Constitution 81 (1990). This view overlooks the fact that Marshall, like Hamilton in the Pacificus papers, tied the role of the president as sole organ of communication to his power to execute and interpret the laws—including treaties with foreign countries. Nevertheless, it is true that one cannot make a case for presidential preeminence in foreign affairs from the context of the Nash-Robbins controversy. Credit for that claim, or discredit if you prefer, should be given to Hamilton, who advanced that position in defending Washington's proclamation of neutrality. *See supra* ch. 6 note 23. Indeed, the verdict of history has been that although the power to determine the substantive content of foreign policy is a divided one, the lion's share usually falls to the president. Corwin, *supra* 171.

9. 10 *id.* 614–15 (statement of Rep. Marshall). Marshall also addressed the questions of whether the United States might have made a mistake in the case of Nash-Robbins, and of whether the president was to blame, by delivering someone to the British who was in fact not a British subject but an American citizen, and who was at the time of the mutiny an impressed seaman. Marshall reaffirmed that on the evidence presented to the president, he had properly decided that Nash was a British subject accused of murder on a British naval vessel on the high seas. He conceded that if the seaman had in fact been an impressed American citizen on board the frigate, the homicide would not have been murder and, Marshall asserted, the president would not have directed his delivery to the British. In any case, if in fact the president were mistaken, the court, Marshall assured the House, ought not to have ordered the prisoner's delivery. 10 *id.* at 615–17.

10. 10 *id.* 619.

11. Pinckney to Madison, Aug. 6, 1791, 14 MP 66–68. In fact, Pinckney did not receive an appointment. Instead, the claims of South Carolina were satisfied when Thomas Pinckney, his cousin, was named minister to London. 14 *id.* at 187–88.

12. *See infra* note 36. It is not unlikely that before and during the first session of the Sixth Congress, Pinckney and Jefferson discussed the contributions that Pinckney, as a framer of the Constitution, could make to the Republican cause in Senate debates involving constitutional issues. *See* Jefferson to Pinckney, Oct. 29, 1799, 9 WJ 86–88, in which the vice-president, acknowledging receipt of a letter from Pinckney, wrote that he was flattered to learn that the senator planned to travel to Philadelphia by land instead of by sea and to visit with him, Madison, and Monroe en route.

13. *See* § 6 of an act "further to suspend the commercial intercourse between the United States and France, and the dependencies thereof," approved Feb. 27, 1800, 2 Stat. 7, 9–10; 10 Annals 55–62 (statement of Sen. Pinckney).

14. Pinckney proposed a bill that would establish a uniform method of selecting jurors by lot in federal courts. 10 *id.* at 35–41.

15. 10 *id.* at 98–99 (statement of Sen. Pinckney). Pinckney's position was contrary to that taken by Madison during the Constitutional Convention. Madison had been one of the principal advocates for the inclusion of federal judges in a Council of Revision to assist the president in reviewing federal legislation. Indeed, he had included such a proposition in the Virginia Plan, 1 FR 21, but his proposal was rejected. 1 *id.* at 104.

When Wilson moved for a reconsideration of the question, Madison seconded the motion. 1 *id.* at 138. He noted the objections against the practice: "The Judges ought not to be subject to the bias which a participation in the making of laws might give in the exposition of them"; and the judicial department should be kept separate and distinct from the other departments. But he considered that the good of having judges preliminarily pass on both the form and substance of the legislation outweighed the supposed hazards implicit in the objections. 1 *id.* at 138–39. Wilson's motion was also defeated. 1 *id.* at 140.

When Wilson again moved for reconsideration, arguing that the judges would help protect against unwise, unjust, and dangerous laws, Madison again agreed, speaking against "a powerful tendency in the Legislature to absorb all power into its vortex." 2 FR 73–74. But it was objected that the power of making the laws should be kept distinct from the power of expounding them. 2 *id.* at 75. Luther Martin observed that inasmuch as the judiciary would pass on the constitutionality of the laws, they would, under the Wilson proposal, have a double negative on the laws. 2 *id.* at 76. The motion was again defeated. 2 *id.* at 80.

Finally, a subsequent motion by Madison, seconded by Wilson, that before all acts became law they should be submitted both "to the Executive and Supreme Judiciary Departments" for their approval, was defeated. 2 *id.* at 298.

16. 10 ANNALS 99–101 (statement of Sen. Pinckney). The Constitution would have provided against holding dual offices had the convention taken Pinckney's advice. He had submitted to the Committee of Detail the proposal, inter alia, that the Constitution specifically prohibit a person holding the office of judge of the Supreme Court or the president or one of his cabinet from "holding at the same time any other office of Trust or Emolument under the U. S. or an individual State." 2 FR 341–42. The proposal was not adopted.

17. 10 ANNALS 101 (statement of Sen. Pinckney).

18. *Id.*

19. *See* the speech of Senator John Breckenridge of Feb. 3, 1802, in the Seventh Congress, attacking judicial review as an unspecified power, 11 ANNALS 178–80.

20. For Republican-inspired litigation attacking the constitutionality of the carriage tax, *see supra* ch. 7 notes 55–56. For litigation attacking the constitutionality of the Sedition Act, *see supra* ch. 10 notes 47, 52.

21. For Republican attacks on the limits of executive power and their challenge to legislation delegating authority to the president, *see supra* ch. 5 note 38; to the power of the executive to advise the House on revenue, *see id.* at notes 48, 86; and to personal appearances in the House by members of the president's cabinet, *see id.* at note 84.

22. In addition, Pinckney's proposed amendment to the Judiciary Act was not approved. *See supra* note 16. Eventually, the Sixth Congress did modify the method of jury selection in federal courts, but it did not adopt the uniform method of selection by lot that Pinckney had proposed. Previously, § 29 of the statute had provided for the selection of juries by lot or otherwise "according to the mode of forming juries therein now practised" in the several states. Act of Sept. 24, 1789, 1 STAT. 73, 88. The new amendment provided for selection of juries by lot according to the mode practiced in the highest courts of law in the respective states. Act of May 17, 1800, 2 STAT. 82. For a discussion of the political context in which the bill was

offered and for the bill's progress through Congress, *see* JULIUS GOEBEL, JR., ANTECEDENTS AND BEGINNINGS TO 1801, *in* 1 HISTORY OF THE SUPREME COURT OF THE UNITED STATES 659–61 (1971).

23. 10 ANNALS 129–31 (statement of Sen. Pinckney). On the political background to the bill, *see* DUMAS MALONE, JEFFERSON AND THE ORDEAL OF LIBERTY 463–64 (1962).

24. 10 ANNALS 130–41 (statement of Sen. Pinckney). For Pinckney's resort to his own recollections of the convention, *see* 10 *id.* at 130. For Gallatin's usual position on use of a framer's personal recollections of the convention, *see supra* ch. 8 notes 52–53 and ch. 10 note 31.

During the convention, Madison spoke in favor of placing the election of the president in electors or in the people themselves instead of in Congress because in the latter case, inter alia, foreign ministers would "mix their intrigues & influence with the Election." 2 FR 109. To avoid the twin dangers of cabal and corruption, Gouverneur Morris preferred that all states cast their votes in a presidential election at the same time, either in the United States Senate or in Congress. 2 *id.* at 500.

Earlier, Morris spoke against entrusting the election of the president to the Senate for the same reasons. But at that time he placed the source of corruption in domestic not foreign influence, in "tax-gatherers & other officers, by fleets armies &c." 2 *id.* at 403–04.

James Wilson, opposing a proposal to give the Senate the power to supplement a failure in the electoral college and choose a president (2 *id.* at 497–98), stated that there would be already too much danger arising from foreign influence with the Senate in its participation in the making of treaties. 2 *id.* at 527. Eventually, Roger Sherman's motion, that the House of Representatives be substituted for the Senate, was unanimously approved. *Id.*

For the progress of the 1800 presidential electors bill, *see* 10 ANNALS 146, 182, 697, 710, 713; for support of Pinckney's position, *see* FEDERALIST No. 68, at 457, 458–59 (Alexander Hamilton).

25. MALONE, *supra* note 23, at 464–65; RICHARD ROSENFELD, AMERICAN AURORA 741–42 (1997). The characterization of the newspaper accounts appears at 10 ANNALS 113. In theory, British parliamentary practice was very strict. By resolution of Mar. 3, 1762, the House of Commons, to secure the privacy of its debates, had made any publication of speeches a breach of its privileges, punishable by commitment for contempt. E.C.S. WADE & A.W. BRADLEY, CONSTITUTIONAL LAW 152, 160 (7th ed. 1965).

But in practice, after 1775, due to the efforts of John Wilkes and others, reporters had access to the debates with only minor harassment. It was not until 1909, however, that full and official publication of the debates began. Introduction, 10 DHFFC xi–xv.

26. 10 ANNALS 63.

27. 10 *id.* at 69–72 (statement of Sen. Pinckney). Pinckney had a special interest in the constitutional law of privileges. During the Constitutional Convention he had submitted to the Committee of Detail an extensive proposal on the subject of congressional privileges. He had proposed: "Each House shall be the Judge of its own privileges, and shall have authority to punish by imprisonment every person violating the same; or who, in the place where the Legislature may be sitting and during the time of its Session, shall threaten any of its members for any thing said or done in the House, or who shall assault any of them therefor—or who shall assault or arrest any witness or other person ordered to attend either of the Houses in his way going or returning; or who shall rescue any person arrested by their order." 2 FR 340–341. When Pinckney's proposal was not accepted, he later renewed it, moving "that each house should be judge of the privilege of its own members." 2 *id.* at 502. But Wilson opposed the proposal because the power was implied; Madison opposed it because it would allow each house the discretion to determine its own privileges. He thought that the convention should authorize Congress to define by law the privileges of each house. No action was taken and the convention adjourned for the day. The matter was apparently dropped. 2 *id.* at 503.

28. 10 ANNALS 72–74 (statement of Sen. Pinckney).

29. 376 U.S. 254, 276 (1964).

30. 10 ANNALS 73–74 (statement of Sen. Pinckney). Pinckney may have remembered that when Madison had opposed his motion that the Constitution should authorize each house to be the judge of the privileges of its members, he had suggested that the convention consider the privileges to be allowed the president. 2 FR 503. Neither Pinckney's nor Madison's suggestion was acted on, probably in part because the convention was running out of time.

31. 10 ANNALS 105, 113, 118–19, 121, 183–84, 720.

32. JOHN C. MILLER, CRISIS IN FREEDOM 201–2 (1951); JAMES M. SMITH, FREEDOM'S FETTERS 300–306 (1956).

33. Jefferson to Madison, Mar. 4–8, 1800, 17 MP 369. Jefferson also foresaw that the Pennsylvania vote would be almost equally divided. *Id.*

34. For a colorful report of the New York city campaign, *see* NATHAN SCHACHNER, AARON BURR 170–77 (1937).

35. ELKINS & MCKITRICK 734–40.

36. *Id.* at 741–43. Senator Pinckney also used the bait of liberal promises of patronage, which Jefferson later fulfilled. *See* Jefferson to Pinckney, Mar. 6, 1801, 9 WJ 200–201; 10 ANNALS 1024.

37. Jefferson to Madison, Dec. 26, 1800, 9 WJ 161–62; Jefferson to Tench Coxe, Dec. 31, 1800, 9 *id.* at 162–63.

38. Jefferson to Monroe, Feb. 15, 1801, 9 *id.* at 178–80. Jefferson's was not an idle threat. There were reports of Republican readiness in Pennsylvania and Virginia to take up arms should the Federalist majority in the House of Representatives conspire to keep the offices of president and vice-president vacant after the conclusion of Adams's term. In that event, Monroe alerted the Virginia legislature, he would summon them to a special session. HARRY AMMON, JAMES MONROE 191–93 (1971).

39. Many thought that Adams passed over Justice Paterson and Charles Cotesworth Pinckney because they were too close to Hamilton, whereas Marshall was not. 1 CHARLES WARREN, THE SUPREME COURT IN UNITED STATES HISTORY 174–78 (1937).

40. Bayard to Hamilton, Jan. 7, 1801, 25 HP 301.

41. Sedgwick to Hamilton, Jan. 11, 1801, 25 *id.* at 311 (emphasis in original).

42. Marshall to Hamilton, Jan. 1, 1801, 25 *id.* at 290–92.

43. Bayard to Hamilton, Mar. 8, 1801, 25 *id.* at 344–45; 10 ANNALS 1025.

44. 10 *id.* at 1025–29.

Epilogue: Text, Intent, and Practicality

1. This was the language of the resolution which Gunning Bedford proposed and the delegates of the Constitutional Convention approved and sent to the Committee of Detail. *See supra* ch. 1 notes 62–65.

2. *See supra* ch. 2 notes 2–12, 68, 70, 73.

3. *Id.* at notes 13–14, 17–19, 21–22, 71, 75.

4. FEDERALIST No. 1, at 3 (Alexander Hamilton).

5. *See supra* ch. 3 notes 7–17.

6. *See supra* ch. 3 notes 18–61. For the Benson-Madison strategy by which the bill passed the House, *see id.* at notes 56–59.

7. As early as 1781, Hamilton had regarded the plan to abolish paper credit and force the country to depend completely on gold and silver for commerce, revenues, and government finance as "altogether visionary and in the attempt . . . fatal." He added: "We have not a competent stock of specie in this country, either to answer the purposes of circulation in Trade,

or to serve as a basis for revenue." Alexander Hamilton to Robert Morris, Apr. 30, 1781, 2 HP 604, 619. For details on how Hamilton implemented this view from the earliest days of his tenure as secretary of the Treasury, *see* Joseph M. Lynch, *McCulloch v. Maryland: A Matter of Money Supply,* 18 SETON HALL L. REV. 223, 225–29 (1988).

8. *See supra* ch. 4 notes 31–33.

9. *Id.* at notes 52–53, 60, 62.

10. *Id.* at notes 69–70.

11. *Id.* at notes 90–94.

12. 8 HENRY ADAMS, HISTORY OF THE UNITED STATES OF AMERICA DURING THE ADMINISTRATIONS OF THOMAS JEFFERSON AND JAMES MADISON 212–15 (1931) [hereafter ADAMS, HISTORY].

13. 9 ADAMS, HISTORY, *supra* note 12, at 118. Act of Apr. 10, 1816, 3 STAT. 266.

14. 17 U.S. (4 Wheat.) 316, 404–23 (1819).

15. 22 U.S. (9 Wheat.) 738, 869–73 (1824). *See also* Chief Justice Marshall's more guarded statement to this effect. *Id.* at 863–64.

16. For Hamilton's position, *see supra* ch. 5 notes 16–21; for Madison's position, *id.* at note 24; and for his concession to the New England fisheries, *id.* at note 23. For his support of the Santo Domingo refugees, *see supra* ch. 7 notes 27–34. Madison's approval of refunds to the fisheries, it has been observed, permits Congress to do indirectly what it supposedly can't do directly: give aid to a specific industry by allowance of a refund under its taxing power, rather than by subsidy under its spending power. DAVID P. CURRIE, THE CONSTITUTION IN CONGRESS, 1789–1801 169 (1997).

17. 297 U.S. 1, 66 (1936).

18. 301 U.S. 619, 640–41 (1937).

19. For Gallatin's position and the historical support in his favor, *see supra* ch. 9 notes 83–84. For the Federalist position, *see id.* at notes 89–90, 94, and *supra* ch. 10 notes 23–24.

20. 130 U.S. 581, 603–6 (1889). For Madison's report to the Virginia House of Delegates, *see supra* ch. 10 note 69; for the Kentucky and Virginia Resolutions, *id.* at notes 12–20. For the reference of counsel to these documents, *see* 130 U.S. 581, 583. *See also Fong Yue Ting v. United States,* 149 U.S. 698, 705–14 (1893).

21. For the Republican position, *see supra* ch. 9 note 126; for the Federalist position, *id.* at note 127; for the vindication of the Federalist position, *see Schenck v. United States,* 249 U.S. 47, 52 (1919), and *Dennis v. United States,* 341 U.S. 494, 501 (1951).

22. For Gallatin's argument, *see supra* ch. 9 note 122; for Madison's report to the Virginia House of Delegates, *see supra* ch. 10 note 74. Under the First Amendment, Congress may legislate against seditious writings or speech which constitute a clear and present danger. *See* cases summarized in *Brandenburg v. Ohio,* 395 U.S. 444, 447–48 (1969). Adopting the Gallatin-Madison rationale, the Supreme Court has held, however, that Congress may not, under the First Amendment, proscribe writings or speech because they bring the federal government, Congress or the president into disrepute, contempt, etc. *New York Times v. Sullivan,* 376 U.S. 254, 276 (1964).

23. *See supra* ch. 6 notes 10, 16–23, 31–41.

24. *See supra* ch. 3 notes 27–28. *See* 5 ADAMS, HISTORY, *supra* note 8, at 185–89, for a discussion of the intrigue between a faction of the Senate led by William Smith of Maryland and his brother Robert, Madison's secretary of state from 1809. Finally, in 1811 Madison removed Robert Smith from the State Department in order to appoint in his place James Monroe, Madison's rival for the presidency in 1808 and his potential rival in 1812. *Id.* at 366–79.

25. *See supra* ch. 3 notes 73–87.

26. *See supra* ch. 7 notes 1–8.

27. *See supra* ch. 6 note 3.

28. *See supra* ch. 11 note 41.

29. For Jefferson's scruples concerning the constitutionality of the Louisiana Purchase, *see* 2 ADAMS, HISTORY, *supra* note 8, at 8–92; for a discussion of the constitutionality of Jefferson's shipping embargo, in which the Republicans led by Jefferson contended for a broad construction of the Constitution, and the Federalists, contrary to Hamiltonian principles, for a strict construction, *see* 4 *id.* at 264–71. Once again, the parties were led by interest rather than principle in their constitutional lawmaking: Jefferson and the Republicans hoped to render effective his policy of strict neutrality in the war between Britain and France; the Federalists, whose mercantile and shipping interests were badly damaged by Jefferson's policy, hoped to obtain a judicial order invalidating the embargo law. A Federalist-appointed federal district court in Massachusetts disappointed them by upholding the statute in *United States v. Brigantine William,* 28 F. Cas. 614, 623 (1808). The Federalists, recognizing that a Marshall-led Supreme Court would sustain the ruling, did not appeal. *See* 1 CHARLES WARREN, THE SUPREME COURT IN UNITED STATES HISTORY 341–51 (1937). For Madison's approval of the bill chartering the Second Bank of the United States, *see supra* note 9.

30. *See supra* ch. 6 note 14.

31. *See* Gerald Gunther, *John Marshall,* "'A Friend of the Constitution': In Defense and Elaboration of McCulloch v. Maryland," 21 STAN. L. REV. 449 (1968).

32. Madison to C. E. Haynes, Feb. 25, 1831, 9 WM 442–43; 9 DHFFC 347 (statement of Sen. Maclay); HENRY ADAMS, THE LIFE OF ALBERT GALLATIN 156–57, 308–9 (1880).

33. 17 U.S. (4 Wheat.) 316, 405 (1819).

34. 110 U.S. 421, 447–50 (1884). *Juilliard* involved the peacetime power of Congress. The right of Congress to issue legal tender notes as an incident to its war power had already been sustained in *Knox v. Lee [The Legal Tender Cases],* 79 U.S. (12 Wall.) 457, 533–47 (1870). A recent commentary on the latter case states that "the Court's reasoning must be read to be disbelieved." Gary Lawson & Patricia B. Granger, *The "Proper" Scope of Federal Power: A Jurisdictional Interpretation of the Sweeping Clause,* 43 DUKE L. J. 267, 327 n. 244 (1993).

The authors take a neo-Madisonian view of the Necessary and Proper Clause, which leads them to conclude that *Wickard v. Filburn, infra* notes 42–43, was wrongly decided, and even to distinguish *McCulloch, supra* note 14, on the ground that it decided only the question of the necessity of the Bank's establishment. They add that the propriety of the establishment, however, perhaps remains an open question, because the Bank's opponents did not raise the issue. *Id.* at 288.

The Lawson & Granger interpretation of the Necessary and Proper Clause has been alternately rejected and defended. *See* Thomas B. McAffee, *Federalism and the Protection of Rights: The Modern Ninth Amendment's Spreading Confusion,* 1996 B.Y.U. L. REV. 351, 368; Randy E. Barnett, *Necessary and Proper,* 44 UCLA L. REV. 745, 777, 793 (1997). As the title of the first article suggests, the renewed interest in the Necessary and Proper Clause is in part related to a desire to expand the scope of rights retained by the people under the Ninth Amendment by, if need be, limiting the scope of federal power. *See* McAffee, *supra* at 354, 387–88; Barnett, *supra* at 747–48.

35. 294 U.S. 240, 311 (1935).

36. 514 U.S. 549 (1995).

37. *Champion v. Ames [The Lottery Case],* 188 U.S. 321, 354 (1903).

38. *Hoke v. United States,* 227 U.S. 308, 323 (1913).

39. *Shreveport Rate Cases,* 234 U.S. 342, 353–54 (1914); *Southern R. Co. v. United States,* 222 U.S. 20, 26–27 (1911).

40. *NLRB v. Jones & Laughlin Steel Corp.,* 301 U.S. 1, 43 (1937).

41. *Hodel v. Virginia Surface Mining & Reclamation Assn., Inc.,* 452 U.S. 264, 281–82 (1981).

42. *Wickard v. Filburn,* 317 U.S. 111, 118 (1942).

43. *Id.* at 124–29. Engdahl considers the Court's reliance on the Commerce Clause misconceived. Rather, he writes, the power of Congress to regulate intrastate conduct affecting interstate commerce is a function of the Necessary and Proper Clause. DAVID E. ENGDAHL, CONSTITUTIONAL FEDERALISM IN A NUTSHELL 16–63 (1987). This may be true, but the Court's disinclination to resort to the Necessary and Proper Clause may be explained by historical circumstances: Because of the frequent use of the clause by the Federalists in advancing their claims of broad federal power during the period of their ascendancy (1789 through 1801), "necessary and proper" was very unpopular with Jefferson and his followers, who for the most part controlled the political branches from 1801 until the Civil War and, following Marshall's death in 1835, the Supreme Court.

After the war, of course, Union-minded parties assumed control of the federal government. Clearly, the government had the power to regulate the conduct of railroads operating in interstate commerce. But when Congress enacted legislation regulating certain intrastate railroad activities, industry counsel argued that commercial conduct purely within a state, such as agriculture, was not subject to congressional control, and cited as authority statements of Hamilton (FEDERALIST No. 17, at 105–6); and Chief Justice Marshall, in *Gibbons v. Ogden,* 22 U.S. (7 Wheat.) 1, 203. It was in response to such arguments that the Court upheld the legislation as within the Commerce Clause.

44. 301 U.S. 619, 640–45 (1937). In that case, the Court upheld, as within the constitutional provision for spending for the "general welfare," the establishment under federal auspices, with the cooperation of the states, of a program for old age benefits for covered employees.

45. *See supra* note 1.

46. As to the Thirteenth Amendment, *see Jones v. Mayer Co.,* 392 U.S. 409, 443 (1968); as to the Fourteenth Amendment, *Katzenbach v. Morgan,* 384 U.S. 641, 650 (1966); and as to the Fifteenth Amendment, *South Carolina v. Katzenbach,* 383 U.S. 301, 326 (1966). In these cases, the Court construed the enabling section in each of the amendments as empowering Congress to do whatever was necessary and proper to effectuate the purposes of the respective amendments, and cited in reliance *McCulloch v. Maryland, supra* note 14.

47. FEDERALIST No. 45, at 308, 313 (James Madison).

48. 514 U.S. 549, 561 (1995).

49. *Id.* at 564. The Court rejected the argument that since gun possession may result in violent crime, which in turn may affect the national economy by increasing the cost of insurance or by discouraging people from traveling to areas perceived to be unsafe, such conduct substantially affects interstate commerce. The Court also rejected the alternate argument that since the possession of guns in schools disturbs the educational process, which in turn results in a less productive citizenry, which in turn adversely affects the national economy, Congress could rationally have concluded that gun possession substantially affects interstate commerce. *Id.* at 563–64.

Despite the Court's opinion that education has been an area where states have historically been sovereign, there is respectable historical authority to the contrary. In his State of the Union address to the second session of the First Congress in 1790, President George Washington spoke as follows:

KNOWLEDGE IS, IN EVERY COUNTRY, the surest basis of public happiness. In one, in which the measures of government receive their impression so immediately from the sense of the community, as in our's, it is proportionately essential. To the security of a free Constitution it contributes in various ways: By convincing those who are entrusted with the public administration, that every valuable end of government is best answered by the enlightened confidence of the people; and by teaching the people themselves to know and to value their own rights; to discern and provide against invasions of them; to distinguish between oppression and the necessary exercise of lawful authority; between burthens proceeding from a disregard to their convenience, and those resulting from the inevitable exigencies of society; to discriminate the spirit of liberty from that of licentiousness, cherishing the first, avoiding the last, and uniting a speedy, but temperate vigilance against encroachments, with an inviolable respect to the laws. (3 DHFFC 252, 253)

It was on this basis that Washington recommended to Congress the promotion of "science and literature," either by grants to "seminaries of learning already established—by the institution of a national university, or by any other expedients." *Id.* at 253–54. *See supra* ch. 5 note 19.

50. — U.S. —, 117 S. Ct. 2365 (1997). The statute, the Court held, violates the constitutional principle of dual federal and state sovereignty and, by reducing the law-enforcement powers of the president, that of the separation and equilibrium of powers among the branches of the federal government. *Id.* at 2376–78. The dissent upheld the statute as a valid exercise of the Commerce Clause, when coupled with the power accruing to Congress under the Necessary and Proper Clause. *Id.* at 2386 (Stevens, J., dissenting), *id.* at 2401 (Souter, J., dissenting), and *id.* at 2404 (Breyer, J., dissenting).

Justice Scalia for the Court, derisively characterizing the dissent's reliance on the Necessary and Proper Clause, as "the last, best hope of those who defend *ultra vires* congressional action," dismissed that clause's relevance: "When a 'la[w] . . . for carrying into execution' the Commerce Clause violates the principle of state sovereignty reflected in the various constitutional principles we mentioned earlier . . . it is not a 'la[w] . . . *proper* for carrying into execution the Commerce Clause,' and is thus, in the words of the *Federalist,* 'merely [an] ac[t] of usurpation' which 'deserve[s] to be treated as such.' THE FEDERALIST No. 33, at 207 (A. Hamilton)." *Id.* at 2378–79. The opinion also relied on the article by Lawson & Granger, *supra* note 34, at 297–326, 330–33. 117 S. Ct. 2365, 2379.

51. *Id.* at 2385.

52. There must, however, be some connection between the purpose of the grant and the conditions upon which it is made. *South Dakota v. Dole,* 483 U.S. 203, 207–8 (1987).

53. NATIONAL BIOETHICS ADVISORY COMMISSION, CLONING HUMAN BEINGS: REPORT AND RECOMMENDATIONS, recommendation II, iii–iv (1997) (hereafter ADVISORY COMMISSION). In early 1998, however, the credibility of the experiment involving the cloning of Dolly was sharply challenged in a scientific journal. Nicholas Wade, *With No Other 'Dollys,' Cloning Report Draws Critics,* N.Y. TIMES, Jan. 30, 1998, A8.

54. ADVISORY COMMISSION, *supra* note 53. at 65–70.

55. *Id.* at 100. The commission also recognized that federal or state action may be limited by an individual's civil liberties. *Id.* at 90–95.

56. Proposed "Cloning Prohibition Act of 1997," H. R. DOC. NO. 105-97, 105th Cong., 1st sess.

57. S. 1601, 105th CONG., §§ 2, 3 (1998); 144 CONG. REC. S. 566–601 (statement of Sen. Feinstein); *id.* at 608 (daily ed. Feb. 11, 1998), rollcall vote no. 10; Lizette Alvarez, *Senate, 54-42, Rejects Republican Bill to Ban Human Cloning,* N.Y. TIMES, Feb. 12, 1998, A20.

58. S. 1602, 105th CONG., §§ 2 (13), 3 (1) (1998). The bill would also "find" that patients travel regularly across state lines in order "to access reproductive services facilities." § 2 (13) (C).

59. The Supreme Court, however, did not accept legislative findings in *Lopez.* Strictly speaking, the statute at issue in that case had not been supported by findings. But after it had

been set aside in a lower court as beyond the reach of the Commerce Clause, and while the appeal was pending before the Supreme Court, Congress had amended the statute to include findings of fact purporting to buttress the conclusion that the possession of firearms in and around schools had adverse effects on interstate and foreign commerce. The Court, however, disregarded the amendment and upheld the judgment of the lower court that the statute was beyond the power of Congress. It was apparent from the opinion of the Court that it would have disregarded the findings had they been included in the statute originally. *United States v. Lopez,* 514 U.S. 549, 562–63 (1995).

60. Brief of defendant-respondent at 24, n. 20, *United States v. Lopez,* 514 U.S. 549 (1995) (No. 93-1260).

61. In the light of the Supreme Court's statement in *Lopez,* Congress would be well advised to find that biomedical research facilities *substantially* affect interstate commerce: "We conclude, consistent with the great weight of our case law, that the proper test requires an analysis of whether the regulated activity 'substantially affects' interstate commerce." 514 U.S. 549, 559 (1995). For the assurances of industry representatives, *see* statement of Sen. Feinstein, *supra* note 57.

Even so, such a congressional finding may not be sufficient. A later news article reports that a venture capitalist in Hawaii is setting up a consortium of companies and academic scientists to make the cloning of adult animals a commercial reality within a few years. The investor, however, is quoted as having no interest in cloning humans, because, he said, "we can't see any business in it." Gina Kolata, *In Big Advance in Cloning, Biologists Create 50 Mice,* N.Y. TIMES, July 23, 1998, A1, A20. If in fact there isn't "any business" in cloning humans, can a statute proscribing such activity be grounded in the commerce clause?

62. *See supra* ch. 1 note 4.

63. *Id.* at notes 53–64.

64. *See supra* note 1 and ch. 3 notes 7–8.

65. *See supra* ch. 1 notes 97–98, ch. 2 notes 2–6, 9, and ch. 3 note 13.

66. *See supra* ch.2 notes 69, 82–83.

67. *Id.* notes 18–19; *see also supra* ch. 5 note 19.

68. FEDERALIST No. 25, at 158, 163 (Alexander Hamilton).

69. Presumably, reliance on the Necessary and Proper Clause would not appeal to Justice Scalia who, in his opinion for the Court in *Printz v. United States,* characterized such a course as "the last, best hope of those who defend *ultra vires* congressional action." 117 S. Ct. 2365, 2378 (1997).

In *Printz,* however, a federal statute imposed duties on state and local officials, contravening constitutional principles of state sovereignty and of the separation of powers in the federal government. It was these principles that Justice Scalia was at pains to protect. *See supra* note 50.

A federal statute mandating throughout the country a uniform prohibition of the creation of a child through somatic cell nuclear cloning would not impose any duty on state or local officials. Therefore, it would not contravene the constitutional principles at stake in *Printz.* In view of this, resort to the protection of the Necessary and Proper Clause, if needed to sustain the cloning statute, may seem the better course to a new majority of the Court. Even in *Printz,* it should be pointed out, the four dissenting judges were willing to rely on the clause.

70. In making this statement, I have in mind the prevailing constitutional controversies over the scope of congressional and presidential powers during the administrations of Washington and Adams, and not the debates concerning the range of protection to be afforded civil liberties under the Constitution, particularly under the First Amendment. Hamilton did not contribute to these debates, and everyone today agrees that he and his party were on the wrong side.

Hamilton's claim to the title of Father of Constitutional Law with regard to matters of federalism goes beyond his construction of the Necessary and Proper Clause, which Chief Justice Marshall followed in *McCulloch v. Maryland,* and of the spending power, which the Supreme Court has followed this century in a number of cases.

His exposition in the *Federalist* (No. 82, at 553, 555–56) of the Supreme Court's appellate jurisdiction over judgments of state courts under Article III of the Constitution laid the groundwork for the Marshall rationale in *Cohens v. Virginia,* 19 U.S. (6 Wheat.) 264, 413 (1821), supporting such jurisdiction in criminal cases involving questions of federal law; and for Justice Story's opinion supporting such jurisdiction in civil cases involving questions of federal law, *Martin v. Hunter's Lessee,* 14 U.S. (1 Wheat.) 304, 337 (1816).

Similarly, Hamilton's insistence in the *Federalist* (No. 32, at 199, 200) on the principle of the subordination of state power to federal power when their operations were in conflict was the source of Chief Justice Marshall's dictum in *Gibbons v. Ogden,* 22 U.S. (9 Wheat.) 1, 209 (1824), mandating the subordination of state power to federal power in matters of interstate and foreign commerce, later modified in *Cooley v. Board of Wardens of the Port of Philadelphia,* 53 U.S. (12 How.) 299, 319 (1851).

Hamilton's letter opinion to a private client, applying the Contract Clause to state public contracts and to grants of real estate by a state legislature, was the source of Chief Justice Marshall's holding and reasoning in *Fletcher v. Peck,* 10 U.S. (6 Cranch) 87, 136 (1810), 4 THE LAW PRACTICE OF ALEXANDER HAMILTON 430–31 (Julius Goebel & Joseph H. Smith eds., 5 vols., 1964–81).

Hamilton's construction of the Constitution was also followed in areas affecting the distribution of powers within the federal government. This century's presidents routinely assume the prerogative in the conduct of foreign affairs for which, against Madison, he argued on behalf of George Washington. *See supra* ch. 6 notes 16–20, 22–23. His defense of the power of judicial review in the *Federalist* (No. 78, at 521, 524–28), which Jefferson's representatives in the Sixth Congress and the Seventh Congress threw into question, formed the basis for Chief Justice Marshall's justification of the power in *Marbury v. Madison,* 5 U.S. (1 Cranch) 137, 180 (1803).

And in this century, Hamilton's construction of the provision governing the decennial reapportionment of congressional districts, in opposition to Jefferson's, was followed in *U.S. Dept. of Commerce v. Montana,* 503 U.S. 442 (1992). *See supra* ch. 5 notes 54–68. Indeed, it was only after almost all the Hamiltonian principles had been incorporated into the Constitution that the Supreme Court turned to the systematic interpretation of the Bill of Rights.

Credit belongs also to Washington, under whose leadership Hamilton's influence flourished, to Marshall, and to Adams, who by his appointment of Marshall to the Court enabled him to display his genius for judicial craftsmanship in the act of construing a Constitution fit for the governance of a nation.

Index